# Management and Change in Africa

While there is a thirst for management knowledge and education throughout Africa, there are few truly relevant texts coming out of the West. Additionally, the unhelpful dichotomy of developing and developed world has hampered understanding of the cultural, historical and economic influences on management. This book is a welcome antidote to this, providing an invaluable empirical base for extending knowledge of management and change in Africa.

Arising from a research project funded primarily by the Danish International Development Assistance, *Management and Change in Africa* includes results of management surveys across fifteen sub-Saharan countries, and of organizational surveys taken across a range of sectors in South Africa, Kenya, Nigeria and Cameroon. It combines methodology, theory, and case examples to explore thoroughly the influences on management in Africa and attempts to push the boundaries of cross-cultural theory. In doing so, it explores how much can be learned from studying both the successes and failures of African management towards realizing the potential of an African renaissance, and to understanding what the global community may learn from Africa.

A website accompanies this book (www.africamanagement.org) where additional materials and updates of this ongoing project may be obtained.

*Management and Change in Africa* is a much-needed study of the cross-cultural dynamics of an emerging area that will be welcomed by managers working in Africa, as well as researchers and policy makers in both the international development and management communities.

**Terence Jackson** is Professor and Director of the Centre for Cross Cultural Management Research at ESCP-EAP European School of Management.

'Our lack of knowledge of Africa has given the world community cognitive and conceptual jetlag. Terence Jackson's impressive book invites us to increase our understanding of Africa and with it our ability to manage and to lead wisely in a world where no continent can or should remain isolated from the economic activity, political progress, and scholarly conceptualizations that structure the possibilities for humanity's success in the twenty-first century. Having read Jackson's book, all of our contributions to global society will be wiser.'

Dr Nancy J. Adler, *McGill University, Montreal Canada*

'Professor Jackson's analysis helps explain why the failure to appreciate the impact of cultural dynamics on the working of local institutions has thwarted attempts by the international community and aid donors to influence the development of effective governance structures or promote vibrant civil society. In conclusion, this study is essential reading for anyone concerned with understanding the issues facing African organisations and the development of a new generation of African managers.'

John Hailey, *International NGO Training and Research Centre (INTRAC), Oxford*

'Thanks to this book, Africa is now on its way to claiming a management theory and practice of its own. This book makes African Management come of age. Terence reminds us that effective and appropriate management in Africa can make a difference to the well-being of all humankind, and that hybridization in an important cross-cultural issue that has to be managed in Africa.'

Professor Moses N. Kiggundu, *Carleton University, Ottawa*

'Terry Jackson has written the major book of the decade on management in Africa. His fresh, challenging perspective aptly reflects and reinforces the ideals of the African Renaissance.'

Merrick Jones, *Consultant in Development Management*

'This book challenges conventional wisdom and undertakes a critical assessment of the diversity and complexity of African contexts. It is a timely, compelling and valuable addition to African management literature that promises to shape future management research and practice in Africa.'

Rabindra N. Kanungo, *Professor Emeritus, McGill University*

'We are all increasingly facing multi-ethnic challenges – as citizens and managers – and badly need to learn how best to release the many potentials which this holds. Here, Africa has much to teach us as this innovative and brilliant work is making it clear.'

Klaus Winkel, *Danida, Danish Ministry of Foreign Affairs*

'Terence Jackson's tour-de-force on African management is a groundbreaker on a long neglected topic. Jackson's descriptions and insights are excellent and take readers far beyond a superficial level of understanding. Jackson and his research team are to be commended for an outstanding piece of research. This is a must-read book for anyone working in Africa.'

Joyce Osland, *San José State University*

# Management and Change in Africa

## A cross-cultural perspective

Terence Jackson

Routledge
Taylor & Francis Group

LONDON AND NEW YORK

First published 2004
by Routledge
11 New Fetter Lane, London EC4P 4EE

Simultaneously published in the USA and Canada
by Routledge
29 West 35th Street, New York, NY 10001

*Routledge is an imprint of the Taylor & Francis Group*

© 2004 Terence Jackson

Typeset in Galliard by
Keystroke, Jacaranda Lodge, Wolverhampton
Printed and bound in Great Britain by
The Cromwell Press, Trowbridge, Wiltshire

*British Library Cataloguing in Publication Data*
A catalogue record for this book is available from the British Library

*Library of Congress Cataloging in Publication Data*
Jackson, Terence, 1952–
   Management and change in Africa : a cross-cultural perspective /
Terence Jackson.
      p.   cm.
Includes bibliographical references (p.   ).
1. Management–Africa, Sub-Saharan. 2. Management–Africa,
Sub-Saharan–Cross-cultural studies. I. Title.

HD70.A357J33 2004
658′.00967–dc22                                      2003018849

ISBN 0–415–31203–5 (hbk)
ISBN 0–415–31204–3 (pbk)

To Eleanor and Tamzin – our futures

# Contents

# Illustrations

## Figures

## Tables

# Preface

Good organizational management is essential for the well-being of humankind. This is not in the least the situation in sub-Saharan Africa, which has long suffered from varying degrees of mis-management (e.g. de Sarden, 1999), poor management (e.g. Kiggundu, 1989) and inappropriate management (Dia, 1996; Iguisi, 1997). Effectively managing resources (Africa has a wealth of resources: for example see Barratt-Brown, 1995) would seem a logical way of alleviating human hardship and poverty, and ensuring the welfare and dignity of all people within the sub-continent, and creating wealth. This can only be driven by a firm understanding of the multi-cultural context of African countries, based on empirical research and a cross-cultural methodology, and a development of cross-cultural competencies in conjunction with local and international stakeholders.

These stakeholders, for whom this book is intended, and who may have different purposes in mind, are as follows:

- the growing numbers of management teachers, researchers and students (including practising managers) with an interest in international and cross-cultural management around the world;
- development scholars and policy makers interested in the issues of governance, institutional development and management;
- students and managers in African countries who are studying in increasing numbers on MBA and other management courses, and require management texts that are relevant to the African context.

For the first group, sub-Saharan Africa is a neglected area. What possibly can we learn from a continent that is so bound up with its own problems? It has nothing to offer management theory and practice in the rest of the world! Yet this perception is changing. Interest in Africa has increased significantly over the last ten years, especially with events in South Africa. Scholars in the high-income countries are perhaps beginning to realize that there is much to learn from managers who are actually highly skilled in managing cultural diversity and multiple stakeholders. Mindsets are also changing to incorporate something of the humanism of Africa within management practices. Yet the hegemony of Western management ideas and practices is a heavy burden, not least under the influences of multilateral agencies. There is still a long way to go to realize the potential of an African renaissance in the area of management.

For the development community, there is a heightened interest in cultural and management issues. UNESCO's World Decade for Cultural Development led the way in highlighting the need for an awareness of the cultural appropriateness of development initiatives. Also driven by a move away from purely economic solutions, the World Bank published in 1996 Dia's *Africa's Management in the 1990s and Beyond*. This posited the disconnect thesis, that institutions were imposed inappropriately on African societies, and provided limited discussion of cultural issues that impact on management.

For the management community in sub-Saharan Africa there are few alternatives to Western textbooks. There is a thirst for management knowledge and management education in Africa, but this is being satisfied mainly through MBA and other Western driven programmes with varying degrees of appropriateness.

Despite the growing interest from the various stakeholder communities there is a paucity of literature in this area. This book is intended to fill this gap through generating theory that is related to the multicultural context of African countries; to thus develop cross-cultural theory generally; and, to provide an empirical base for extending our knowledge in this area.

It is based on extensive multi-method/multi-level empirical research in Botswana, Burkina Faso, Cameroon, Côte d'Ivoire, Democratic Republic of Congo, Ghana, Kenya, Malawi, Mozambique, Namibia, Nigeria, Rwanda, South Africa, Zambia and Zimbabwe. In each of these countries a management survey has been carried out across a sample of managers using local databases through local collaborators. In-depth organizational surveys have also been carried out with local partners across a range of sectors in four key countries: South Africa, Kenya, Cameroon and Nigeria. This research has demonstrated that:

- The perceptions of the efficacy of management methods and styles, the way these are changing, and the desirability of these changes may vary among different cultural groups within countries, among African countries, and according to the relative influences of Western, African and post-colonial principles and practices. There is therefore a need to be aware of and to manage these differences within a complex and rapidly changing multicultural context, if management in sub-Saharan Africa is going to be effective.

- Historical, cultural and power influences are leading to the development of different hybrid forms of management and organizations. Some are highly adaptive to the context in which they operate, some are mal-adaptive. Therefore, to develop effective management there is a need to understand the dynamics of hybridization and to learn from the successes of those adaptive organizations, and from the shortcomings of those that are mal-adaptive.

- For employees and managers there is often a split between the world of work and community/home life. Staff going into work in the morning step out of their own culture and enter a different one. This is not being managed well in many organizations, often leading to low levels of employee morale and alienation from the work place. To develop effective and appropriate organizations within which to work, people management principles and practices should understand and reconcile this split between work and community/home life.

- Organizations in sub-Saharan Africa have to operate within a complexity of different stakeholder interests. Often the interests of different stakeholder groups are not adequately recognized and incorporated within the wider decision processes of the organization. Often attempts at developing a more democratic organization (for example, from Western principles) do not include a wider stakeholder base. Similarly, attempts at corporate responsibility programmes are not inclusive of community stakeholder interests, and sometimes simply appear as cynical marketing ploys by foreign companies. In order to develop effective organizations in Africa, there is a need to understand this aspect of decision-making and incorporate a wider stakeholder base into a truly participative decision process.

- Within organizations, cultural differences are not adequately managed within the different power relationships that operate. Different cultural groups, and gender groups, may not have the same access to resources and decision processes. There is therefore a need to positively manage cross-cultural relationships within organizations in Africa, and to take account of power relations and unequal access to organizational resources.

The book therefore aims to provide:

1   a re-conceptualization of our understanding of management in Africa: the unhelpful dichotomy of 'developing–developed world' has hampered knowledge and understanding of the different cultural, historical and economic influences on management. This text explores these issues;

2   a cross-cultural methodology for research on management in Africa that is helpful for future research and management practice. Some of the pit-falls of doing research in Africa are also discussed;

3   an awareness of the main management systems and their influence on management in Africa: hybridization is seen as an important cross-cultural issue that has to be effectively managed. This has lessons for other emerging regions;

4   knowledge of cross-cultural differences and similarities within and among African countries: all sub-Saharan African countries are multi-ethnic; there is greater intra-regional cooperation and cross-border activity; and there has always been interaction between Western (or Northern) cultures and African cultures. It is essential to understand these influences, differences and similarities and to manage them effectively to develop synergies through, for example, working in multicultural teams;

5   an awareness, through example and discussion, of how management strengths may be enhanced, by developing effective hybrid management systems and synergistic multicultural teams;

6   an understanding of the wider implications of effective management in sub-Saharan Africa to future prosperity and cohesive civil society.

## The project and the project team

The nature of cross-cultural research dictates collaboration among a number of scholars and practitioners. Although the overall responsibility of authorship of this book rests with me, the book and its legitimacy would not have been possible without the willing help and inputs of others on the ground, so to speak, in the African countries that are included as examples of a very diverse and complex sub-continent.

In particular, I would like to thank here the main collaborators and co-authors of two of the chapters, on South Africa and Cameroon, who have given much to this project, namely Dr Lynette Louw of the University of Port Elizabeth, South Africa and Dr Olivier Nana Nzepa of Institut Superieur de Management Public and Advisory Network for African Information Society, Yaounde, Cameroon.

I would also like to thank the following:

### Nigeria

Prof. Bedford A. Fubara (Rivers State University of Science and Technology, Port Harcourt); Prof. G.O. Olusanya (Nigerian Institute of Management, Lagos); Dr Melvin D. Ayogu (University of Jos); Prof. S.O. Okafor (University of Maiduguri); Dr Nathaniel C. Ozigbo (University of Abuja).

### South Africa

Prof. Frank Horwitz (University of Cape Town); Susan Hill (University of Cape Town and Shell, now London Business School); David Coldwell (University of Natal); Martin Brand (University of Stellenbosch); Lukas Wentzel (University of Stellenbosch and Old Mutual).

### Kenya

Mwai wa Kihu (Kenya Institute of Management); Alfred Micheni Muchai (Kenya Institute of Management); Dan Kaseje, Retta Menberu, Judith Raburu (Tropical Institute of Community Health and Development); Ciru Getecha (United States International University).

### Botswana

Dr Merrick L. Jones (formerly University of Botswana); Mr Rebana Mmereki (University of Botswana).

### Burkina Faso

Dr Nathalie Prime (ESCP-EAP, Paris).

### Côte d'Ivoire

Pierre Djemis (ESCP-EAP, Paris).

### Democratic Republic of Congo

Leanard Kasereka (Tropical Institute of Community Health).

### Ghana

John Kuada (University of Aalborg, Denmark).

### Malawi

Rhoda Cynthia Bakuwa (Malawi Polytechnic).

### Mozambique

Charles Oyaya (Tropical Institute of Community Health).

### Namibia

Dr Esau Kaakunga (University of Namibia).

### Rwanda

Dr Rama Roa (University of Kigali); Ms Sophie Hitimana (Kigali Institute of Education).

### Zambia

Pascal Sztum (consultant).

### Zimbabwe

Dr Ziv Tamangani (University of Zimbabwe); Charity Ndlovu (Zimbabwe Institute of Management).

This project could not have been possible without the generous funding of Danida, and I would particularly like to thank Klaus Winkel for his unstinting support over a number of years. I would also like to thank Insitut Vital Roux, Paris, for generous initial funding for this project, as well as the many managers and staff who participated in the study.

Terence Jackson
Centre for Cross Cultural Management Research
ESCP-EAP European School of Management, Oxford

# Africa – why bother?

> Civilization is not a predetermined consequence of human progress, as the Victorians believed, with white Anglo-Saxons leading the way, the rest of the world following in their wake, and the Africans straggling several centuries behind. On the contrary, civilization is more like a protective skin of enlightened self-interest that all societies develop as they learn to regulate their interactions with the environment, and with other people, to the long-term benefit of all parties.
>
> (Reader, 1997: x)

The reason why effective management in Africa is important is a complex issue because of the various stakeholders concerned. Viewed simplistically, we could proffer a belief that good organizational management is essential for the well-being of humankind. The issue of effective management becomes complex because it can be viewed from the perceptions of different stakeholder communities, which may have an influence on the way management in Africa is understood, researched and practised. The diversity of perspectives must be built into an appreciation of the factors that contribute to a research agenda in this area, and ultimately to the way effective and appropriate management is developed.

Similarly an understanding of the context of management in Africa should be integrated into a research framework, as a means of understanding different stakeholder perspectives. This may primarily be understood through an appreciation of the cross-cultural dynamics operating on organizational and management factors south of the Sahara. Reframing of perspectives of management in Africa from the various communities should also be undertaken from a cross-cultural perspective, not least to overcome the pejorative and obstructive influences on research of the 'developing–developed' world paradigm (itself a cultural construct, and one defined by the 'developed' world and also adopted by intellectuals and elite in the 'developing' world) which still seems to persist (see, for example, in Jaeger and Kanungo, 1990; and to a lesser degree in Blunt and Jones, 1992). The 'developing–developed' world dichotomy is perhaps indicative of the power relations that exist among the various stakeholder communities. When considering the cross-cultural dynamics of effective management in Africa (most countries in sub-Saharan African countries are multicultural, all are subject to Western cultural influences, and many are operating across borders in regional grouping), these power relations must be taken into consideration (see, for example, Human's 1996b, view on this in the context of South Africa). The disparaging of African culture is but one example of such power relations, and the 'developing–developed' world dichotomy is an articulation of this.

Attention has been directed at the cultural aspects of development through initiatives such as the UNESCO World Decade of Cultural Development (UNESCO, 1997) but so far little systematic analysis of the different cross-cultural levels of interaction have been undertaken. These levels at the very least are as follows:

- inter-continental: at the level of interaction between Western (in its different varieties) and African cultural influences which can be pervasive in areas such as education and management practices;
- inter-country: at the level of interaction across borders, particularly as organizations are increasingly doing business in neighbouring countries encouraged through regional economic agreements (an interaction that was generally discouraged during colonial times); and
- inter-ethnic: at the level of intra-country, inter-cultural working within organizations where many African countries have a complexity of ethnic and language groupings, and where such cross-cultural working is commonplace.

These are the levels of analysis that affect daily lives, and affect the management of organizations, and we discuss these levels in detail in the ensuing chapters. Other levels (inter-organizational, inter-professional and between genders, the latter being affected by cultural considerations) may also be considered. Yet the dynamics of cross-cultural interaction in African organizations operating at these different levels and involving power relations has not yet been undertaken. Concepts and theories which are now commonplace in the global management community such as Hofstede's (1980a) dimensions of culture, seem inadequate in explaining cultural interaction in Africa, despite the fact that members of the development community are starting to employ such concepts (see, for example, Dia, 1996).

Similarly empirical research on management in Africa is inadequate, even at the descriptive level: little systematic empirical data exists on the characteristics of management and organization in African countries (Carlsson, 1998). Conceptual frameworks that make sense of data, either existing or still to be collected, are lacking. Again, a cross-cultural approach to model building, which incorporates a concept of a hierarchy of stakeholders in this area, can help to develop an understanding of management in organizations, and help to develop an analytical framework.

Africa's history, even before the slave trade, is one of cross-cultural interaction and often antagonistic dynamics (for example, Reader, 1998), normally within systems of power relations (based on military, political, social, technological and economic domination). Modern organizations in Africa still contain these diverse cultural elements: ideas and practices as well as people (Dia, 1996; Noorderhaven *et al.*, 1996; Merrill-Sands and Holvino, 2000). Not only is an understanding of these dynamics necessary, but also a reconciling, integrating and synergizing of disparities contained within these dynamics are essential to management and organization development efforts in Africa. Cross-cultural theory suggests that such cultural dynamics contain both disintegrating factors (ready to tear organizations and societies apart) and integrating factors (capable of drawing great strength from the wealth of different perspectives and approaches) (Jackson, 1992; Lau and Murnighan, 1998; Elron *et al.*, 1999; Jackson and Kotze, in press). An understanding of how these disintegrating/integrating dynamics are operating in organizations in Africa is essential to effective management. Again, this understanding can only be built up on a consideration of stakeholder perspective and stakeholder influence (see Chapters 3 and 4).

This introductory chapter, and indeed this book, is therefore premised on the following assumptions:

1    The recognition of the importance of effective management (why it is important and how it is important) in Africa is a product of the cultural and socio-economic perspectives of the different stakeholders' communities, and the power dynamics that regulate and influence the relationships among these stakeholders.
2    As a consequence, the way management has been, and will be studied is a product of those dynamics.
3    Cross-cultural theory is able to address these dynamics, and offers viable conceptual and methodological tools for understanding them.
4    These dynamics need to be addressed and understood in order to develop a research agenda that can produce knowledge, which can ultimately inform management and organizational development in sub-Saharan Africa, which is able to meet the often differing agendas of the stakeholder communities.

## A stakeholder perspective of effective management: differing agendas

### The issues

The first assumption focuses on why effective management is important, in what way is it important to the various stakeholder communities, and how this issue of effectiveness is framed by the power dynamics that regulate and influence relations among the stakeholders. This assumption involves a number of issues: Who are the stakeholders? What are the cultural (and other) perspectives that they bring to bear on the importance of effective management in Africa? What is the nature of the power dynamics that frame these issues?

### Stakeholder communities' perceptions

The importance of good management in Africa may be approached from several diverse perspectives that are not necessarily conflicting.

## Development community

The first is the more traditional route of the development community. Wohlegemuth *et al.* (1998) remind us that the relationship between institutional building and economic development has been established for some time (from North, 1990). Here the argument is that good management is important in order to develop the subcontinent. Work such as that of Dia (1996), sponsored by the World Bank, and that of Wohlegemuth *et al.* (1998), sponsored by the Swedish International Development Cooperation Agency (SIDA) and the African Development Bank, make a strong case for considering management of organizations in Africa a major component in development activities. Influential articles, discussing the importance and role of management in African development, were published in the late 1980s in *World Development* by Leonard (1987) and Montgomery (1987). Here the main question has been: what sort of management? Thus Leonard argued strongly against inappropriate management technologies being employed in Africa, which often lead to failure. He flags up the importance of considering the political influences on managing in Africa, which often stem from patronage through strong pressures from kinsmen for support and sometimes lead to corrupt practices. The importance of policy making, leadership, general internal administration and 'bureaucratic hygiene' are central to effective management, which is central to African development. Yet simply transferring Western managerial technologies, he argues, is not the answer: 'A great deal of thought and experiment is needed to help us find administrative reforms and managerial improvements that flow with, rather than against the logic of African social reality' (Leonard, 1987: 908).

Montgomery (1987), too, is critical of ready solutions from Western agencies believing that there are many misconceptions about administrative management in Africa not least the unrealistic perceptions of African governments. He argues from his empirical research results in southern Africa that private sector development cannot be seen as a main development route as in Southeast Asia, as there is more a dependency and expectation of government involvement and initiative. He concludes that:

> It is the superpowers that are, for the moment, living in a kind of political fantasyland, and their approach to Africa is so alien to the real concerns of government there that creative communication on the subject of development seems itself a form of political fantasy.
>
> (Montomery, 1987: 927)

The importance of considering indigenous management factors in Africa was also discussed within the development community in the early 1990s (Marsden, 1991; ODA, undated). In the late 1990s and into the new millennium, the role of good management both in effective governance within public sector reform (Wescott, 1999), and in the renewal of private enterprise and foreign investment in the commercial sector has become an issue (despite the concerns voiced by Montgomery). Hence the United Nations Industrial Development Organization states among its objectives 'to promote investment and private sector development' (UNIDO, 1999: 17), placing an emphasis on foreign direct investment.

This suggests a second perspective: the international business community that may look on Africa as a poor investment prospect.

### International business community

Commercial organizations in Western (as well as Southeast Asian) countries may not invest in business opportunities in Africa, for very good reasons. These include political instability, problems of personal security and difficult labour relations (Collier, 1997; Morais, 1997; UNIDO, 1999). This timidity towards investment may also be a result of lack of information and knowledge. However, despite this reticence Ibru (1997) concludes that there has been considerable growth and development in the involvement of foreign multinational companies in Africa between 1947 and 1997, while Mbaku (1998) argues that multinational companies can bring real benefits in terms of resources, expertise and opportunities to African countries. It may also be that through new organizational forms such as international joint ventures and other strategic alliances (see for example from the general literature: Doz *et al.*, 1990), Western (and Eastern) companies are more willing to share risk and develop joint expertise with local companies in Africa. For example, within our study in South Africa, one manufacturer, previously a South African family-owned business with minimum investment and involvement from its Japanese multinational sponsor, has progressively been invested in by the Japanese multinational including more management involvement to a point where the majority shareholding will be with the parent in Japan with a view to South Africa being a bridge to the rest of Africa for the multinational (see Chapter 12).

The issue here would therefore be to provide stability and effective management in order that Africa may be attractive as an investment opportunity. The perception of Africa as such a prospect for commercial exploitation goes back long before the European, 'scramble for Africa' (Pakenham, 1991) and to the slave trade. During the 'scramble' it is for example reflected in King Leopold of Belgium's belief that the Congo would eventually realize a huge profit if it could be correctly exploited (which of course it was at great human cost: Hochschild, 1998).

The number of multinational companies operating in sub-Saharan Africa may be indicative of this confidence in realizing a profit, not only in oil producing countries such as Nigeria and Cameroon, but also in the tertiary sector such as finance and banking. Here management approaches may well be Western, yet there is evidence, from companies such as Guinness in Cameroon (Chapter 10) that such policies and practices coming from headquarters are successfully being adapted and modified to meet local conditions. 'Crossvergence' or the hybridization of organizational forms and management systems through an admixture of different cultural influences, rather than convergence of cultural influences, is a main thesis of this book. The way that Western approaches are adapted to the African environment may well be a success factor in providing good and stable management that multinational organizations are looking for in their investment decisions. The way this is conceived and studied leads us on to a further perspective.

### Global management community

This third perspective is that of the global management community, if it is possible to identify such a grouping. It may comprise management academics, international management consultants, and managers who operate across borders, and may contain much of the research and development expertise needed to address issues of a lack of empirical research and a lack of conceptualization. The main interest here would be to develop management knowledge in order to better equip managers to manage internationally. Yet why should a scientific study of management in Africa be important to an understanding of global management generally? The growing literature in this area, even work that includes Africa (for example, Hickson and Pugh, 1995) says little or nothing about the contribution which African approaches to management and organization can make to global management generally. However, good practice in African organizations which skilfully manages the apparent contradictions between post-colonial institutions, the instrumentalism of Western traditions and the humanism of the African tradition in managing people (for example, Jackson, 1999), may have valuable lessons for management elsewhere, not least in other emerging regions.

Despite this assertion, there is still a lack of work published on management in Africa in what are regarded as 'first division' management journals. This may indicate either a lack of interest in Africa of the global management community, or work in this area is mediocre, or both. Certainly few academics in 'first division' international business schools show interest in Africa. It could be argued that this reflects a lack of interest in Africa by their clients, the multinational organizations. Yet this is a weak argument. Companies such as Shell, Citibank, Guinness, Toyota, and many others (who have in fact participated in our current study) have major interests in Africa. A stronger argument is that there is a belief among their clients, and the academics and consultants themselves, that there is no need to research and develop knowledge on management in Africa, because the key to effective management is already there: the use of Western management principles. It is a belief in the convergence thesis (proposed by Kerr *et al.*, 1960); a belief that the world's cultures are converging (or in terms of global power relations are moving more towards the Western Anglo-America model). It takes us back to the question 'What can African managers offer the global management community?' Yet despite the comparative success of multinational companies in Africa (perhaps through their global competitiveness and economic power compared with local companies), they appear often not to have transferred this success to the wider host community, and do not appear to have contributed to a stable environment, although they may satisfy the requirement of one set of stakeholders: the shareholders. It is easy to point to companies such as Shell in Nigeria (Chapter 3) who have appeared to be at odds with the context in which they operate, and with the local community. Yet also companies that are under pressure to operate competitively under a 'mean and lean' strategy by cutting the local workforce may in the end contribute very little to the wider stakeholder base. Such companies in South Africa (Chapter 12) are under increasing pressure of this sort, yet are trying to do their best to contribute at least money for local projects (an issue that we look at in Chapter 3).

Some of the more farsighted global managers operating in Africa are attempting to integrate indigenous approaches, and attempting to learn from local managers, but this still has a long way to go, and is not reflected in the interest of the academic global management community, and is certainly not reflected in, nor influenced by the level of research into management in sub-Saharan Africa (see, for example, Noorderhaven *et al.*, 1996).

### African management community

A fourth perspective, which in fact may be primary in the scheme of things, also suggests itself: that of the African manager. Events in South Africa have given major impetus to thoughts on the nature of an indigenous African management. This is most noticeable in the popular management literature (Mbigi and Maree, 1995; Boon, 1996; Mbigi, 1997), and around the *ubuntu* movement that has had its effect on management development initiatives in major corporations and management education in South Africa (Swartz and Davies, 1997). This may be a worthwhile endeavour, yet a rather naïve approach (see Human, 1996b), to try to tease out from the complex historical circumstances of colonization and imperialism, as well as apartheid, a purity of African tradition and thought manifest in management styles and practices. Yet it is the development of African management, among the development of management in Africa generally (which can be taken as including non-'African' elements and management by foreign expatriates), which is paramount to the current thesis. In particular, the building of a research paradigm should be based on the interaction effects (integrating and dis-integrating influences) of a cross-cultural dynamic within organizations in Africa. It should take into consideration the paradoxical context of the historical legacy and future requirements, and antithetical concepts of management which co-exist side by side, and which may give rise to conflicts within African organizations.

This has relevance from the four perspectives outlined above to an understanding of effective management in Africa. It also has implications for the study of management in other emerging regions, and for more effective global management generally. It may only be through considering all these elements that a modern African management can be developed.

### The study of management in Africa

Our next assumption, stemming from a consideration of stakeholder views of the importance of management in Africa, is that the study of management in Africa is a product of the dynamics of such views. For example, we noted above that the global academic management community appears to pay little attention to Africa. Indeed this also has also been the situation among the development community. Ayittey

(1999) notes the fact that despite some 600 billion US dollars being put into foreign assistance, loans and credit since independence, aid to Africa has not been effective. How little of this development aid has been put into issues of management? How little still has been put into the systematic study of management in Africa? And how little further has been put into cross-cultural study of management in Africa, despite the prima facie case discussed above? Dia's (1996) study *Africa's Management in the 1990s and Beyond* represented a breakthrough in the recognition (by the World Bank) of the case for developing effective and appropriate management, by first instigating an empirical study. The study had shortcomings: particularly the use of case studies alone, and the lack of cross-cultural insight and model building, relying mainly on Hofstede's (1980a) cultural dimensions.

Yet it would seem that little follow-up or application of this serious scholarly work has been made. The Nordic Africa Institute in Uppsala in Sweden, with the support of SIDA and the African Development Bank, as we noted above, attempted to open up the debate by publishing its book *Institution Building and Leadership in Africa* (Wohlgemuth *et al.*, 1998). Yet the contributions to this book were mainly 'appetizers' rather than the products of systematic research. Certainly this work provided a clarion call for such research. We believe that Danida (Danish International Development Assistance), whose officer Klaus Winkel in his capacity as Chairman of the Programme and Research Council of the Nordic Africa Institute provided impetus for this work's publication in English to attract a wider readership, has answered this clarion call through its steadfast support of the current work over some three years.

Yet, not wanting to belittle this support, in the scheme of things ($600 billion) the support for such endeavours has been miniscule. We discuss an argument in Chapter 3 that it is in the interests of development agencies to perpetuate the dependent nature of 'developing' countries on the benefice of such agencies, as this perpetuates such organizations and careers within them. It reflects and perpetuates the power relationship between developed and developing countries. This in its turn is manifest in the developing–developed world paradigm that is very much reflected in the nature of previous work undertaken on management in Africa and in 'developing' regions, and has largely militated against producing serious cross-cultural studies.

Once it is accepted that 'African' management has little to offer, and 'modern' management from the West presents a model for solving the issues of poor management in Africa, then the motivation for looking at the issues cross-culturally is gone. This is certainly reflected (either explicitly or implicitly) in much of the work on management in Africa that has emanated from the global management community (the authors of which often having one foot in the development community: for example Kiggundu, 1989; Blunt and Jones, 1992). More recent work, by African academics working in America, has unfortunately reflected this reliance on the convergence perspective and on Western management principles when looking at management in Africa (Waiguchu *et al.*, 1999; Ugwuegbu, 2001). This paradigm may seriously hamper informed research in Africa, within both the development and global management communities. This reflection in the research of the interests of these two 'academic' communities, may also be reflected in the interests of the global business community: representing more directly its economic interests. Yet the irony may be that this world view does not really lead to an understanding of the complexities of the issues in managing effectively in Africa, and probably does not further the interests of multinational companies in Africa. This is because, logically, if there is a lack of understanding of the issues, then it is difficult to manage effectively within the context of sub-Saharan Africa.

During our interviews undertaken as part of this study, we were sometimes asked by local managers, managing local firms if we were simply going to use the information they were giving us in order to make multinationals even more competitive. This may well be a valid point. Yet one of our major arguments is that to manage effectively, it is necessary to manage appropriately, and to take account of the different stake-holders within the African context (Chapter 4). This involves an understanding of, and a willingness to incorporate the interests of stakeholders, including the local community and local firms. However, local firms and local managers may themselves be better positioned and more able to take into consideration local contingencies, and to better adapt their management practices to the context. This may be dependent on shedding an over-reliance on Western management principles, and developing effective hybrid management systems that can incorporate different cultural elements, as well as being capable of managing cross-culturally and the different levels of analysis: inter-continental, inter-country, and inter-ethnic (Chapters 1, 2 and 8).

### Addressing dynamics through cross-cultural theory

We therefore propose that the dynamics of these different stakeholder interests may be addressed though cross-cultural theory: although extant cross-cultural theory is probably insufficient, and itself needs developing by considering the context of sub-Saharan Africa. Hence we have asserted that cross-cultural analysis must be undertaken on at least three levels: inter-continental, inter-country and inter-ethnic. Very few cross-cultural studies in the existing literature have simultaneously addressed these different levels. At these different levels there are power dynamics operating among the stakeholders involved. We have already discussed the effect of this (specifically at the intercontinental level) on the study of management in Africa. Existing cross-cultural theory rarely considers these issues of power. The power relations involved in the hegemony of Western approaches to management are critical to the way organizations are managed in Africa. The appropriateness of such approaches has been studied (noticeably, Hofstede, 1980b) in the general literature, yet the power dynamics are implied rather than directly addressed (Chapter 2).

The operation of power dynamics is particularly apparent in inter-ethnic inter-actions. Almost inevitably within an organization there is a dominant ethnic, racial or cultural group (see Chapter 10). In the private sector this may be Asian or Kikuyu in Kenya, Bamileke in Cameroon, or White in South Africa. It is difficult to know how prevailing Western principles of management, developed mostly within one particular society with a culture quite dissimilar to those found on the African continent, can successfully inform the management of such cross-cultural dynamics.

On the contrary, it is likely that Western observers (within the global management community) can learn a great deal by studying the successes of managers in Africa. However, there are still a number of pitfalls to studying these dynamics and in developing cross-cultural theory to accommodate them: not least the definition of what constitutes a cultural group in the ever-changing scenario of sub-Saharan Africa (see, for example, Chapter 9).

### Developing a research agenda

One of the major landmarks of the study of management in Africa has been Blunt and Jones' (1992) book *Managing Organizations in Africa*. The approach this took was to examine aspects of (Western) management theory, and see how they apply to Africa. This has much to commend it, as it went from the familiar, to the not so familiar context of Africa. Yet this work was still stuck within a Western framework, and arguably the developing–developed world paradigm. It was unfortunate that this contribution did not obtain much space within the numerous MBA and other management courses in Africa (not even in South Africa), which have proliferated in the last decade, within the Anglo-America mould.

The current study, of which the current book is a product, took a different approach (Chapter 2). It first developed out of a tradition of cross-cultural management (rather than being an 'add-on' as it was in Chapter 9 of Blunt and Jones' 1992 book). This meant that Western theory and its appropriateness to African cultures is treated critically. It also recognized an appalling lack of empirical information on management in Africa. The first job was to do something about this on two levels: a management survey in what turned out to be fifteen countries, and in-depth studies of organizations in four countries. Through this work, we set about identifying crucial areas for both the elaboration of what management looks like in Africa, identification of good (and poor) practice, and identifying competency areas for development. These areas are:

- the ability to manage complexity and uncertainty in the African environment (Chapter 3);
- the willingness and ability to manage multiple stakeholders in organizational decision-making and change (Chapter 4);
- the understanding and ability to use appropriate leadership and management styles (Chapter 5);
- the ability to motivate and reward managers in the context of Africa (Chapter 6);
- the ability to gain employee commitment through managing work attitudes and organizational climate. In this respect we saw as crucial the ability to manage the relationship between the world of work, and the world of home and community (Chapter 7);
- The ability to manage and develop cross-cultural working and multicultural teams (Chapter 9).

In order to develop these and other issues we place them in the context of Nigeria, Cameroon, Kenya and South Africa (Chapters 9–12).

Yet the quest, started in this book to find some of the answers, continues. It is not possible to include all our material within this text. This is why we have set up a website (www.africamanagement.org) in order to make this project ongoing, and to disseminate resources for scholars, managers and management developers. Whichever category you fall into, and whichever stakeholder community, we hope that you will learn from Africa from this book, and continue to do so from its accompanying website.

# Part I

# Rethinking management in Africa

# Chapter 1

# Management systems in Africa

## The cross-cultural imperative*

> The foreigner interested in designing, implementing and evaluating effective management development programmes must read widely in order to gain an appreciation of this diverse and complex continent, its peoples and social organizations, and the context within which organization and management takes place.
>
> (Kiggundu, 1991: 32–3)

> For many centuries, Africa remained a mystery. It attracted the curiosity of explorers while fascinating and captivating empire-builders by its vast wealth. The length and breadth of Africa were explored, discovered, conquered and colonized. Its people were denigrated as 'backward and inferior'.
>
> (Ayittey, 1991: xxiii)

The need to understand and appreciate the diversity and complexity of sub-Saharan Africa has been largely hampered by an apparent continuation of a pejorative view of Africa, Africans and the contributions that can be made not only to the development of their own continent, but especially to other continents: not least in the area of management. It is rare to find a chapter on African management and its contributions to global managing in textbooks on international management, as we discussed in the Introduction. Indeed, the current literature on management in 'developing' countries generally (e.g. Jaeger and Kanungo, 1990) and management in Africa specifically (e.g. Blunt and Jones, 1992) presents a picture which sees management in these countries as fatalistic, resistant to change, reactive, short-termist, authoritarian, risk reducing, context dependent, and basing decisions on relationship criteria, rather than universalistic criteria. Apart from the pejorative nature of this description and contrast with 'developed' countries, there is the danger that the objective of development is to make the 'developing' world more like the 'developed' world, and that this should be reflected in the direction of organizational change and the way people are managed.

It is unfortunate that this perspective paints a rather negative picture of management in Africa, and one within the 'developing–developed' world paradigm that is not just pejorative, but actually hampers constructive research into the nature of management of people and change in Africa. Yet it is likely that the perceived 'African' approach reflects a colonial legacy rather than an indigenous approach to organizing. Indeed, the dynamics of management of organizations in Africa arise fundamentally from the interaction of African countries with foreign powers and corporations, as well as through exposure to foreign management education. In addition, managers in Africa increasingly have to manage the cross-border dynamics as regional cooperation increases (Mulat, 1998), and have had to manage the internal dynamics of inter-ethnic cross-cultural difference and diversity since the 'scramble for Africa' ensured national boundaries which conformed to the claims of European powers rather than existing African ethnic divisions.

If anything, 'African Management' is cross-cultural management. One of our main objectives is trying to understand the complex cross-cultural dynamics in African countries. The aim of managers and management developers should be to ensure the more effective management of these dynamics, by first understanding them, and then addressing the need to develop effective cross-cultural management and management teams.

This chapter therefore attempts to reframe our understanding of the management of people, organizations and change in sub-Saharan African countries, by employing a paradigm that reflects the different perceptions of the value of human beings in organizations (Jackson, 1999), and by explore a model of cross-cultural dynamics in Africa which incorporates at least some of the complex elements which may be important to our understanding (Figure 1.1). We then look in more detail at the cross-cultural processes and dynamics in Chapter 2.

## The African context

The context can best be understood as an historical dynamic that has created a number of paradoxes in Africa. The paradoxes can only be really understood by first considering the *inter-continent* level of cultural analysis. The main paradox is between the nature of organizations, and the need to develop human capacity. Many African economies are going through a stage of transition from large and often overly staffed public corporations, to enterprises which are more publicly accountable and private enterprises which have to compete globally and be profitable (Barratt-Brown, 1995; Ibru, 1997) (this aspect is shown as 'Economic Reform' in Figure 1.1). At the same time there is an overriding need to develop people (Bazemore and Thai, 1995; Kamoche, 1997; Kifle, 1998), and to do this predominantly within work organizations (cf. Anyanwu, 1998). Yet organizations that can take this development role are divesting themselves of people.

A legacy of under-skilling largely through a concentration on export-led primary production and low development of consumer economies (Barratt-Brown, 1995; Adedeji, 1999) now hampers human capacity building particularly in the service sector. Also, the current need to develop relevance, flexibility, responsiveness and accountability in the public sector is hampered by a legacy of administration that was tacked onto African societies with a standardization of functions and low transferability of skills (Picard and Garrity, 1995; Carlsson, 1998) ('Legacy' in Figure 1.1). More recently an imposition of economic structural adjustment programmes which have reduced government spending, removed subsidies, deregulated goods,

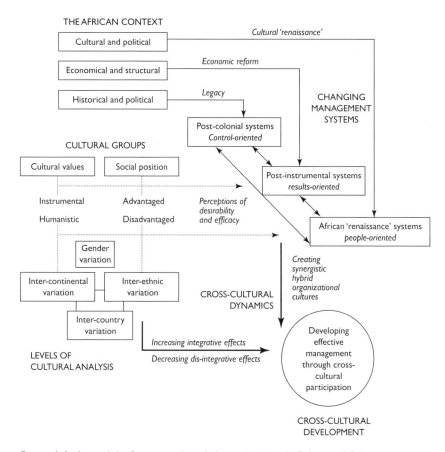

*Figure 1.1* A model of cross-cultural dynamics in sub-Saharan Africa.

money and labour markets, and decontrolled prices to respond to market forces and liberalization of trade (Mbaku, 1998; Wohlgemuth *et al.*, 1998) has militated against protecting and developing indigenous organizations through long-term government and private investment in organizations to develop human capacity ('Economic Reform' in Figure 1.1). The accompanying trend to downsize organizations has also militated against training and developing people in these organizations.

The paradox (and conflicts in policies and practices) between historical legacy and future requirements; between the need to downsize organizations through economic reform, to make them 'meaner and leaner' and globally competitive on the one hand and the future requirement to skill, re-skill and develop people in work organizations up to managerial levels, may be understood through a conceptualization of an antithesis between the cultural need in Africa to recognize people as having a value in their own right and as part of a social community, which may be in direct contradiction to a predominant Western view in organization and management theory which sees people as a means to an end within the organization (Jackson, 1999). This perception of the direction and nature of the value that is placed on people in organizations, or locus of human value, which is shown as 'Humanistic' and 'Instrumental' cultural values in Figure 1.1, may be central to understanding at least one level of cross-cultural interaction within organizations in Africa. It may also be central to understanding many of the difficulties of managing people in organizations in Africa. It is to this level of analysis that we must turn to further understand the 'changing management systems' depicted in Figure 1.1.

## Levels of cultural analysis

The inter-continental cultural level is fundamental to a number of theories such as the 'disconnect' thesis (Dia, 1996; Carlsson, 1998). At the naïve level of theorizing this may be seen as a difference between 'developing' and 'developed' countries (Jaeger and Kanungo, 1990; Blunt and Jones, 1992). A number of studies have incorporated Hofstede's (1980a) cultural dimensions to explain some of the differences between African and 'Western' countries (Kanungo and Jaeger, 1990; Dia, 1996; Iguisi, 1997). The shortcomings of these approaches will be examined below. Recent cross-cultural studies have incorporated more sophisticated value constructs such as those of Schwartz (1994) (e.g. Munene *et al.*, 2000), or have tried to develop value constructs that incorporate 'African' values (Noorderhaven and Tidjani, 2001). An alternative or complementary approach is offered here which develops a theory of 'locus of human value' and helps in an understanding of management and organization systems operating in Africa that focuses on inter-continental cultural interactions: principally African cultures with Western countries.

Less developed is work on other levels of cultural analysis that often requires more sophisticated concepts and research tools. Hence understanding cross-cultural interaction at the regional and cross-national levels, which is becoming more important with the establishing of regional trading agreements (Mulat, 1998) and more inter-country interaction, is at very early stages. Some of the studies mentioned above in connection with inter-continent comparisons are suggesting differences among African countries (particularly Noorderhaven and Tidjani, 2001). However, the lack of sophistication of quantitative measurement instruments, and the lack of qualitative comparisons, has hampered understanding at this level. As a result of a country's unique interaction with a former colonial power, inter-continental interactions are likely to be bound up with inter-country differences and similarities.

Inter-ethnic cultural analysis has remained largely within the domain of social/cultural anthropology, and has been investigated or applied rarely to management and organization theory. This level of analysis is important for understanding potential and actual conflict in the workplace, and in addressing resulting issues of cross-cultural management in African countries. The inter-continental level of analysis is primarily focused upon here, as this has a direct bearing on a discussion of locus of human value, and on the changing management systems depicted in Figure 1.1.

### Inter-continental cultural level of interaction

Cross-cultural management theory has been criticized for its lack of theory that connects cultural values to management and work practices, particularly at the behavioural level (Cray and Mallory, 1998). The focus of interest in this book is at the level of management and organization systems, their cultural derivatives, how they are manifested particularly in the management of people, and how they operate in Africa. This focus has the most relevance to practising management in understanding the influence of cultural factors, and for management and organizational development practices. Although at the theoretical level these systems can only be constructed as *ideal types*, they can form the basis for cross-cultural investigation, as well as informing management practices in Africa which often have to reconcile these various systems. This approach is particularly useful in attempting to overcome and integrate some of the complexities of the effects of different cultures on African societies generally and management and organizational practices in particular. These systems are described as 'post-colonial', 'post-instrumental' and 'African renaissance'. Table 1.1 also includes a comparison of the three systems with that of a fourth ideal type: an East Asian/Japanese system. Table 1.2 postulates how these management systems may be manifested in different sets of management attributes.

### Post-colonial management systems

Description of management in Africa has largely been informed by the developed–developing world dichotomy as was noted above, and exemplified in the work of Blunt and Jones (1992), one of the most thorough descriptions, and that of Jaeger and Kanungo (1990) of management in 'developing' countries in general. This is particularly in the distinction made between 'Western' management styles (teamwork, empowerment, etc.) and 'African' styles (centralized, bureaucratic, authoritarian, etc.) (Blunt and Jones, 1997).

#### ORGANIZATIONAL SYSTEMS

However, systems of management identified in the literature as 'African' (Blunt and Jones, 1992; 1997) or as 'developing' (Jaeger and Kanungo, 1990) are mostly representative of a post-colonial heritage, reflecting a theory X style of management (from McGregor) which generally mistrusts human nature with a need to impose controls on workers, allowing little worker initiative, and rewarding a narrow set of skills simply by financial means. This system is identified in the literature as being 'tacked on' to African society originally by the colonial power (Dia, 1996; Carlsson, 1998), and being perpetuated after independence, perhaps as a result of vested political and economic interest, or purely because this was the way managers in the colonial era were trained (Table 1.1).

In terms of strategies there is an emphasis on inputs (particularly in the public sectors such as increasing expenditure on health, education and housing after independence) to the exclusion of outputs such as quantity, quality, service and client

*Table 1.1* Comparison of different organizational management systems in Africa

|  | Post-colonial | Post-instrumental |
|---|---|---|
| Main principles | • Theory X<br>• Western/post-independence African<br>• Instrumental | • Theory Y<br>• Western/'modern'<br>• Functionalist |
| Importance | • Continuing legacy through political and economic interests | • Looked to as alternative<br>• Influence from multi-nationals, management education and consultants |
| Strategy | • Inputs and process orientation<br>• Lack of results and objectives<br>• Risk aversive | • Results and market oriented<br>• Clear objectives<br>• Calculated risk taking |
| Structure | • Hierarchical<br>• Centralized | • Flatter hierarchy<br>• Often decentralized |
| Governance and decision-making | • Authoritarian<br>• Non-consultative | • Often consultative<br>• Increasing emphasis on 'empowerment' |
| Control | • Rule bound<br>• Lack of flexibility<br>• Outside influence or control (family, government) often seen as negative | • Clear rules of action<br>• Flexible<br>• Outside government influence decreasing |
| Character | • May not act ethically towards stakeholders<br>• Not very efficient<br>• Static<br>• Probably not foreign owned | • More ethically responsible<br>• Aims to be successful<br>• Change is a feature<br>• Probably foreign owned |
| Internal policies | • Discriminatory<br>• Employee policies aimed at duties rather than rights | • Non-discriminatory<br>• Access to equal opportunities and clear employee policies on responsibilities and rights |
| Internal climate | • Employee alienation common<br>• Weak trade unions<br>• Inter-ethnic friction<br>• Discourages diversity of opinions<br>• Promotion by ascription | • Emphasis on employee motivation<br>• Weak or co-operative unions<br>• Move towards inter-ethnic harmony<br>• Diverse opinions often encouraged<br>• Promotion based on achievement |
| External policies | • Lack of customer/client policies<br>• Lack of results orientation | • Clear policies on customers/clients<br>• Results orientation |
| Management expertise | • Educated management elite with low managerial expertise | • High, results oriented managerial expertise is aimed for |
| People orientation | • Control orientation | • People and results orientation |

| African renaissance | East Asian/Japanese |
|---|---|
| • Humanistic<br>• Ubuntu<br>• Community collectivism | • Humanistic<br>• Corporate collectivism |
| • Some elements may prevail in indigenous organizations<br>• Of growing interest internationally | • Developing importance through East Asian investment<br>• May be seen as alternative |
| • Stakeholder orientation | • Market and results orientation<br>• Clear objectives<br>• Low risk taking |
| • Flatter hierarchy<br>• Decentralized and closer to stakeholders | • Hierarchical and conformity |
| • Participative, consensus seeking (*indaba*) | • Consultative but authority from top |
| • Benign rules of action<br>• Outside influence (government, family) may be seen as more benign | • Consensus and harmony above formal rules<br>• May have a lack of flexibility |
| • Stakeholder interest may be more important than 'ethics'<br>• Success related to development and well being of its people<br>• Indigenous | • Harmony and face may be more important than ethics<br>• Efficiency<br>• May be slow to change |
| • Stake-holder interests<br>• Access to equal opportunities | • Can be discriminatory (towards women)<br>• Employee relations may be more implicit |
| • Motivation through participation important<br>• Unions protect rights<br>• Inter-ethnic harmony taken into consideration<br>• Everyone should be able to state their opinions<br>• Promotion based on legitimization of status | • Aims at employee commitment (job satisfaction may be low)<br>• Company trade unions<br>• Inter-ethnic relations may not be an issues<br>• Consensus rather than diversity of opinions stressed<br>• Promotion by seniority |
| • A clear awareness of and articulation of stakeholder interests | • A focus on business and customer networks rather than explicit policies |
| • Management expertise based on people orientation | • Management effectiveness based on collective skills |
| • People and stakeholder orientation | • People (in-group) orientation |

Table 1.2 Comparison of different management attributes in Africa

| | Post-colonial | Post-instrumental | African renaissance | East Asian/Japanese |
|---|---|---|---|---|
| Management motivators | • Economic security<br>• Control | • Managing uncertainty<br>• Self enhancement<br>• Autonomy<br>• Independence<br>• Achievement | • Belonging<br>• Development of person and group | • Belonging<br>• Development in corporate context<br>• Elements of economic security |
| Management commitment | • To business objectives<br>• To relatives<br>• To organization | • To self<br>• To results<br>• To ethical principles<br>• To work | • To group<br>• To people | • To business objectives (the corporate)<br>• To results<br>• To work<br>• To relatives |
| Management principles | • External locus of control<br>• Deontology<br>• Theory X<br>• Mistrust of human nature<br>• Status orientation | • Internal locus of control<br>• Teleology<br>• Theory Y<br>• Conditional trust of human nature<br>• Achievement orientation | • Internal and external locus of control<br>• Trust of human nature<br>• Status and achievement orientation | • External locus of control<br>• Theory Y (in-group), theory X (out-group)<br>• Trust of in-group members<br>• Relational and relativity aspects of decision-making<br>• Status through seniority |
| Management practices | • Reliance on hierarchy<br>• Use of rank<br>• Low egalitarianism<br>• Lack of open communication<br>• Lack of open information | • Some participation<br>• Mostly communicating openly<br>• Providing open information when necessary<br>• Confrontational | • Participation<br>• Egalitarianism<br>• Communicating openly<br>• Providing open communication | • Consultative (e.g. *ringi* system of consultation)<br>• Communicating and information giving to gain consensus<br>• Maintaining harmony |
| Main orientations | • Managing process<br>• Managing power relations | • Managing results (external focus)<br>• Managing people | • Managing people (internal stakeholder focus)<br>• Managing results (defined by stakeholder interests) | • Managing people (in-group/out-group relations)<br>• Managing results (defined by stakeholder interests) |

satisfaction (Blunt and Jones, 1992), or the supply side rather than the demand side of capacity-building (Dia, 1996). Best use is not being made of inputs or the supply to organizations (generated through improvement in education and training) through capacity utilization within organizations. Table 1.1 therefore indicates a lack of results and objectives orientation, and a possible associated risk aversion. Kiggundu (1989) adds that there is typically a lack of a clear mission statement or sense of direction.

He also characterizes organizational structures, in terms of their *governance and decision-making* as having top management that is overworked, having authoritarian and paternalistic decision styles with centralized control and decision-making (Kiggundu, 1989). This is also reflected in Blunt and Jones's (1997) view that leadership is highly centralized, hierarchical and authoritarian. They also add that there is an emphasis on control mechanisms, rules and procedures rather than performance (and a high reluctance to judge performance), a bureaucratic resistance to change and a high level of conservatism, and importance of kinship networks. These aspects are indicated as *control* factors in Table 1.1.

The *character* of such organizations may well reflect public sector, parastatal or recently privatized organizations that are not foreign owned. The public sector and state owned enterprises in 'developing' countries generally, and sub-Saharan Africa specifically have been widely criticized as being too large, bureaucratic and change resistant (Blunt and Jones, 1992). There is broad agreement concerning the poor performance of the public sector, which has engendered support for a reduction in its size (Balogun, 1989) and an assertion that it is detrimental to the development of entrepreneurship and competitive production (Kiggundu, 1988). Some of the inadequacies which Joergensen (1990) draws attention to in relation to state owned enterprises in East Africa, include lack of clear objectives, over-staffing, lack of job descriptions and job evaluation, lack of incentives, and political interference, as well as poor infrastructure and lack of systems. These all point to the inefficiencies indicated in Table 1.1. Yet there is little empirical evidence to suggest that private sector organizations are any better equipped to meet the challenges of change and development in Africa (Blunt and Jones, 1992). Montgomery's (1987) study among SADC countries suggests private sector organizations are no more rational in goal seeking than the public sector. Part of the inefficiency of post-colonial organizational systems may be the levels of corruption and 'unethical' behaviour towards their stakeholders (Table 1.1). This has been well documented in the literature (e.g. de Sardan, 1999).

*Internal policies* may be discriminatory as a result of preferences given to in-group or family members. Kanungo and Jaeger (1990) suggest that because of the associative thinking in developing countries, there is a tendency for behaviour in organizations to be context-dependent, rather than the developed country orientation towards context-independent behaviour orientation where explicit and universal rules apply to a situation rather than the situation and context determining the responses to it. This may lead to decisions based on relationships rather than the application of universal rules, and may therefore be regarded as discriminatory (Table 1.1). A reflection also of the theory X nature of management and general distrust of human nature, as well as a lack of organizational democracy may be revealed in employee policies aimed at duties of workers rather than of rights (Table 1.1).

The *internal climate* of organizations may be revealed in employee alienation (Table 1.1). Understaffing, poor motivation, risk aversion and unwillingness to take independent action; close supervision of subordinates with little delegation; operations which are often inefficient and high cost with low productivity, over-staffing, under-utilization, poor pay and poor morale indicated by high turnover and absenteeism, are all features which Kiggundu (1989) recounts (see also Chapter 7). Through the general underdevelopment of the economy and the tenuous status of many jobs, unions are likely to be weak and often subjugated to wider political interests (Fashoyin and Matanmi, 1996). Diversity, including ethnicity and gender does seem to be an issue (Merrill-Sands and Holvino, 2000; although this is inadequately treated in the literature except that pertaining to South Africa). This may also be a reflection of discriminatory policies based on context-dependency, and promotion by ascription (who you are rather than what you have achieved: see, for example, Trompenaars, 1993).

As a result of an inputs focus (Blunt and Jones, 1992; Dia, 1996) *external policies* regarding customers and clients are likely not to be overt, and lacking in results orientation. Kiggundu (1989), having suggested that top managers are likely to be overworked with a reluctance to delegate work, asserts that they are typically learned, articulate and well travelled. However, at middle management levels there are weak systems and controls, inadequate managerial skills and a lack of industrial knowledge. This is reflected in the general low levels of *managerial expertise* depicted in Table 1.1.

## MANAGEMENT ATTRIBUTES

Attributes of managers operating within this system would be expected to derive from the overall management system operating in an organization. With a control orientation of post-colonial systems, and a self-perpetuating inputs orientation, managers who fit in well could be expected to be motivated by control features of their jobs and economic security (Table 1.2). While little research has been undertaken on *management motivation* in Africa (discussed in more detail in Chapter 6), those few studies do seem to support this supposition (Blunt and Jones, 1992, report one study in Kenya by Blunt in 1976 and one undertaken in Malawi by Jones in 1986).

The direction of *management commitment* can also be derived from the above discussion. An indication of a commitment to 'business' objectives involves the pursuit of end results at the expense of means, although not reflecting an achievement orientation (Montgomery, 1987, noted a regard for internal aspects of the organization rather than policy issues, development goals or public welfare, remarking on an aloofness of managers in the public sector). This may reflect an ethical disregard for wider stakeholders, and a pursuit of corporate objectives as they dovetail with own objectives (Kiggundu, 1989, underlines the political nature of this agenda). For example, de Sardan (1999) argues that corruption is embedded in the logics of such practices as negotiation and gift giving, and is both conspicuous and generalized within the administration of organizations in Africa. There is also evidence, from the discussion above, of family influence in organizations, and commitment of managers may well be directed to these family connections (Table 1.2).

*Management principles* may be related to an external locus of control of 'developing' countries where events are considered not within the individual's control, where creative potential is regarded as being limited, and people are generally fixed in their ways and not malleable or changeable (Kanungo and Jaeger, 1990). This may well reflect also a mistrust of human nature, and a belief in the undisciplined nature of African workers to industrial life (Abudu, 1986). Decisions are focused in the past and present rather than the future (Montgomery, 1987; Kanungo and Jaeger, 1990) and therefore may be deontological in nature rather than teleological. Action is focused on the short term, and success orientation may be moralistic rather than pragmatic as a result. This may reflect a lack of achievement orientation and a status orientation as a management principle. A passive–reactive orientation (Kanungo and Jaeger, 1990) is assumed. Again, this may give rise to a theory X conception of management (Table 1.2).

The way these principles are manifested in *management practices* is widely accepted in the existing literature as in authoritarian management styles with reliance on the hierarchy, use of rank, low egalitarianism, and a lack of openness in communication and information giving (Montgomery, 1987; Blunt and Jones, 1992; Blunt and Jones, 1997). This may lead to conclusions that the *main management orientations* within post-colonial management systems are towards managing internal processes, and managing power relations (Table 1.2)

## AN HISTORICAL LEGACY

The perceptions created by this conceptualization of 'African management' within a developed–developing world paradigm may not be useful (fatalistic, resistant to change, reactive, short-termist, authoritarian, risk reducing, context dependent, associative and basing decisions on relationship criteria, rather than universalistic criteria) when directly contrasted with management in the 'developed' world. Implied within this conceptualization is that the developing world should be 'developed' to become more like the developed world. However, its positioning in Figure 1.1 is as an historical legacy from colonial involvement in Africa of the 'developed' world.

The developing–developed conceptualization often fails to recognize other (sometimes embryonic) management systems operating in Africa. It is also not sufficiently underpinned by cultural theory. The developing–developed world paradigm reflects a paucity of cultural analysis, and in management theory reflects the traditions of the convergence thesis (from Kerr *et al.*, 1960). Where this view of management in 'developing' countries is explained by cross-cultural theory, reference is often made to Hofstede's (1980a) value dimensions. Hence Kanungo and Jaeger (1990) depict the organizational situation in developing countries as relatively high in uncertainty avoidance (low tolerance for risk and ambiguity), low individualism, high power distance (reflected in a lack of consultative or participatory management), and low in masculinity (a lack of competitiveness and achievement orientation, and a low centrality of work). Hofstede's (1980a) own data is not very helpful on African culture as he had low sample sizes from West and East African countries that he combined into two regional samples, and a whites only sample from South Africa. The popular

South African management literature supports a view that African cultures have a collectivist propensity (Koopman, 1991). The academic work of Blunt and Jones (1992) indicates from the available literature that African societies are low on individualism. More recent studies that include African countries suggest lower levels of values associated with individualism (Munene *et al.*, 2000), and higher levels of those associated with collectivism (Smith *et al.*, 1996; Noorderhaven and Tidjani, 2001). Yet these say little about the nature of African collectivism, and provide little explanation of the 'disconnect' thesis.

## LOCUS OF HUMAN VALUE

At this level of inter-continental cross-cultural interaction, in historical perspective, the concept of locus of human value in distinguishing an antithesis between an *instrumental* view of people in organizations which perceived people as a means to an end, and a *humanistic* view of people which sees people as having a value in their own right, and being an end in themselves may be more usefully explored (Jackson, 1999). The Western concept of 'human resources' typifies the former approach in its view of people as another *resource* to meet the objectives of the organization. It is likely that this concept would predominate in post-colonial African organizations to a certain extent (Table 1.1). Blunt and Jones's (1992) assertion that African (post-colonial) organization is input- rather than output-dependent may lead to the conclusion that such organization is not functionalistic in the sense of objective seeking. Yet it is difficult to conceptualize such organization as humanistic. Organizations in Japan and other East Asian countries (and depicted in comparison in Tables 1.1 and 1.2) may have been more successful in harnessing the latter approach in order to obtain employee commitment to the organization (Allinson, 1993; and discussed in more detail in Chapter 7 of the current text), but organizations in Africa have largely not done this. Hence African workers themselves see work organizations as instrumental towards providing a contribution to their own livelihood (Blunt and Jones, 1992) and that of their communal group.

The *instrumental–humanistic* construct may avoid some of the pitfalls of applying a developing–developed dichotomy (as in Jaeger and Kanungo, 1990), and in applying a simplistic 'individualism–collectivism' model (Hofstede, 1991) to cultural analysis in explaining differences between indigenous and imported views of human relations. It may also explain the levels of inappropriateness of what is next termed post-instrumental management systems.

### Post-instrumental management systems

A belief, within the developing–developed world paradigm, reflecting the convergence theory of Kerr *et al.* (1960) and contingency theory of Hickson and Pugh (1995; and see also Cray and Mallory, 1998, for an overview), is that the developing world, through industrialization, should become more like the developed world. This is reflected in the trend for 'Western' approaches to management to be imported into African countries through multinational companies, and 'Western' approaches to be sought out by managers who are increasingly being educated within Western or Western-style management courses, and being trained in Western traditions. This may not only affect organizations in the private sector, but also those in the public and parastatal sectors and those recently privatized enterprises which are in the process of refocusing as a result of downsizing and other major organizational change. This may reflect also a disparaging of 'African' (i.e. post-colonial) ways of organizing and managing. This disparaging is reflected in much of the literature reviewed above.

It is unnecessary to go into the detail that is summarized in Tables 1.1 and 1.2, where 'post-instrumental' systems are contrasted with post-colonial systems, other than to outline the principles involved. It is unlikely that such a system, based on 'modern' management theory is blatantly instrumental, but will likely lack the humanism of what is here described as African renaissance.

A distinction has been made in the Anglo-American strategic human resource management literature between a 'hard' organizational perspective, reflecting utilitarian instrumentalism which sees people in the organization as a mere resource to achieve the ends of the organization, and a 'soft' developmental human relations approach which sees people more as valued assets capable of development, worthy of trust, and providing inputs through participation and informed choice (Beer and Spector, 1985; Tyson and Fell, 1986; Hendry and Pettigrew, 1990; Storey, 1992; Vaughan, 1994). Tayeb (2000) quite rightly states that the concept of human resource management is itself a product of a particular Anglo-American culture. It is likely that both the 'hard' and 'soft' approaches taken within Western organizations are both a reflection of an inherent cultural concept which perceives human beings in organizations as a means to an end (Blunt and Jones, 1997, use the term 'functionalism'). If this is the case, then it is likely that when Western companies, or managers educated in the Western tradition, try to implement 'Western' human resource practices in cultures which have a different concept of people, and a different regard for people in organizations, then incompatibilities will be manifested through lack of motivation and alienation leading to low productivity and labour strife.

The extent to which such manifestations are the case in foreign-owned, and Western management-oriented companies in Africa has been little researched. This remains at the moment as a hypothesis ripe for testing.

### African renaissance management systems

It may be somewhat idealistic to try to identify a particular African style or even philosophy of management (e.g. Human, 1996b), but it is worth pointing to aspects that it may include, so that in empirical studies those aspects may be discerned where they do exist (Tables 1.1 and 1.2). A useful framework is provided by the work of Binet (1970) on African economic psychology. Dia (1996) provides an account of this work. This can be supplemented and supported by popular African management texts (Mbigi and Maree, 1995; Boon, 1996; and Mbigi, 1997), as well as specific anthropological work (such as that of Gelfand, 1973, which is used here to illustrate specific aspects by reference to Shona values in Zimbabwe). Key values can be summarized as follows.

## SHARING

A need for security in the face of hardship has provided a commitment to helping one another. However, it is likely that this value is not based on simple exchange, but as a result of a network of social obligations based predominantly on kinship. More recently the concept of *ubuntu* has been prominent in the South African popular management literature, a value that is built on the assumption that people are only people through other people. Mbigi (1997), for example, suggests that collective trust is a large part of this value that should be developed in organizations before participation and empowerment initiatives can succeed. Certainly Gelfand (1973) suggests that trust (*ruvimbo*) is seen as an important virtue in Shona culture. Openness, sharing and welcome together form important components of *ubuntu* (Boon, 1996). These aspects are reflected in Table 1.1 in a wider community stakeholder orientation which also includes elements of family and other outside involvement, and a character that involves the development and well-being of its people, with a general people orientation (Table 1.1), and a sense of belongingness, trust and openness (Table 1.2).

## DEFERENCE TO RANK

Dia's (1996) assertion that this refers to power distance, particularly within the organizational context between employer and employee is probably rather simplistic. Although traditional rulers were such by their title to the senior lineage, they had to earn the respect of their followers, and rule by consensus. Political decision-making was through obtaining consensus, and through a system of checks and balances against autocratic rule. People were free to express opinions and dissension (Mbigi, 1997). At the same time taking one's proper place in the social scale (*kuzvipeta* in Shona) is an important aspect of the virtue of humility (*kuzvidukupisa*), and refers not only to deference to rank and seniority, but also to the senior person showing humility towards the younger person, and to the educated person not looking down on those less educated (Gelfand, 1973). This is reflected in Table 1.1 in a control that involves benign rules of action, and promotion based on the legitimization of status (reflecting management principles based on both a status and achievement orientation in Table 1.2).

## SANCTITY OF COMMITMENT

Commitment and mutual obligations stems from group pressures to meet one's promises, and to conform to social expectations. This is reflected in Table 1.1 in the obligations to stakeholders, for example in the external policies, as well as the commitment to the group in Table 1.2.

## REGARD FOR COMPROMISE AND CONSENSUS

This certainly involves the maintenance of harmony within the social context, but also qualifies a deference to rank discussed above. Boon (1996) for example summarizes the main characteristics of traditional African leadership by saying that the chief personifies the unity of the tribe and must live the values of his community in an exemplary way; not being an autocrat the chief must rely on representatives of the people, councillors to assist him (chiefs were and are male), to be guided by consensus. Failure to do so would result in his people ignoring his decisions and law. The people are strongly represented with a duty to attend court hearings, and all have a responsibility to each other, collectively to ensure the laws are upheld. As a result of this collective responsibility everyone has a right to question in open court. The concept of openness is an important value and implies that no one should receive retribution for anything said correctly in an open forum. If this is a latter day idealization of consensual authority, it was certainly a perception of early anthropologists working in Southern Africa (see, for example, Gluckman, 1956). In Table 1.1 this is reflected in structures that have flatter and more accessible hierarchies, consensus-seeking decision-making, and internal climate of participation and openness, and protection of rights. Management practice also reflect a participative, egalitarian and open approach (Table 1.2)

## GOOD SOCIAL AND PERSONAL RELATIONS

This stems from many of the aspects discussed above, particularly the commitment to social solidarity. Dia (1996) observes that the tensions of management–labour relations that have been a feature in African organizations can be attributed largely to a lack of a human dimension and the adversarial attitudes of colonial employment relations. In Table 1.1 this is reflected in an internal climate of inter-ethnic harmony (although group solidarity may also act against this as will be discussed under), and other aspects of people orientation generally, and a humanistic orientation.

This presents a different picture to that of Blunt and Jones (although this is partially recognized by them: Blunt and Jones, 1997) and other commentators on organizational management in African countries. Both this view, and an idealized view of what African management could have been (without colonial interference) is probably too simplistic as has been stated above. With the increase in interest in African approaches to management as indicated in the South African popular management press mentioned above, and the general call for a renaissance of African thinking, values, education and political transformation (Makgoba, 1999), any description of management systems within Africa should include a consideration of an 'indigenous' African management. Alongside this, a looking towards alternative management paradigms for inspiration and adaptation in Africa seems logical. Japanese management has provided systems of management in East Asia that appear to be successful in collectivistic societies (e.g. Chen, 1995) that may have some parallels with African societies. Aspects of this as a fourth system have been included in Tables 1.1 and 1.2 for comparison purposes.

Research and management understanding is necessary at the inter-continental level because of the extensive interaction not only between sub-Saharan Africa as a 'cultural entity' and European and other former colonial powers and present-day multinational companies, but also because of the unique interaction of each African country with organizations and institutions that are foreign to the African continent. This may give rise to differences between countries like Senegal and Gambia (formerly French and British respectively) that share the same language and tribal groups (Sow and Abdulaziz, 1999), on the basis of their interaction with colonial and former colonial countries, as well as any differences in indigenous cultures. This aspect, as well as others such as ethnicity, may explain some of the cultural differences among African countries.

### Changing management systems

The discussion above, and the typologies of Tables 1.1 and 1.2, and Figure 1.1 have presented three systems of management as 'ideal types' that are purported to be operating in African countries. It is unlikely that these are operating in a pure form. The 'hybridization' of management systems is an important consideration in Africa. Concepts of crossvergence have been operationalized and researched in other regions such as Hong Kong (Priem *et al.*, 2000). These studies indicate that rather than a tendency of convergence (the coming together of value systems) in regions and countries that have had high levels of influence from other cultures, there is rather a tendency of crossvergence (developing of hybrid value systems as a result of cultural interactions). The nature of change, and continued influences from different cultural sources in African countries may indicate the development of hybrid systems of various forms. Some of these may be highly adaptive and effective in managing cross-cultural dynamics, and in managing the different requirements of instrumental and humanistic perspectives. Some may be maladaptive. There is evidence from India (Rao, 1996) that hybrid 'human resource development' systems are being designed to manage the different Western (instrumental) and India (humanistic) orientations in organizations. Its applicability in other regions such as sub-Saharan Africa needs to be investigated, as well as good practice being developed in Africa (Cashbuild in South Africa may be such an example: Koopman, 1991).

A further aspect should also be considered with regard to locus of human value. A study by Jackson (2002b) over seven countries around the world suggests that a humanistic orientation is associated with collectivism. Hofstede (1991) makes the case that poorer societies (and perhaps disadvantaged sections of societies) are more collectivistic through the need for mutual self help. If this is the case, then people in African countries who are socially disadvantaged may be more likely to have a humanistic view of human worth, and those in a socially advantaged position may have a less humanistic locus (Figure 1.1). This may also be reflected in organizations, with managers having a less humanistic viewpoint than employees. If this is the case then this has important implications for employee–manager relations in practice. We take this up in Chapter 3 and in later chapters.

The inter-continental cultural level of analysis represents just one level. In order to obtain a more complete picture of cultural dynamics operating in sub-Saharan Africa, at least two other levels must be taken into consideration: the regional or inter-country level; and, the intra-country, inter-ethnic level. It is important to understand these levels, particularly in managing conflict and developing synergistic work teams (see also Chapter 8).

## Regional and inter-country cultural level of interaction

Although since the colonial era African countries have traded primarily with a European power rather than with other African countries (providing a unique interaction with a colonial power), the establishing of regional trading agreements is encouraging regional cooperation (Mulat, 1998). This, therefore, is increasing inter-country interaction: another level of cross-cultural management which is growing in importance to effective African management.

Yet the literature on management and organization in Africa mostly ignores cultural differences and interaction that may exist among African regions, among countries, (and indeed within African countries). Even studies that 'compare' African countries such as Akinnusi (1991) often largely ignore cross-cultural and cross-national differences. Wider studies that have incorporated a small number of African countries include the Chinese Cultural Connection (1987).

*Confucian dynamism*, which emerged as a cultural dimension among 23 nations, and subsequently re-labelled by Hofstede (1991) as *Long Term Orientation*, provides Zimbabwe with a score on his Long-term Orientation Index equal to that of the UK of 25 (maximum 118, minimum 0) and Nigeria a score of 16 second lowest to Pakistan's score of 0. Although both scores indicate a short-term orientation, Nigeria's lower score may provide a basis for further investigation. Smith *et al.*'s (1996) reanalysis of Trompenaars' (1993) data suggests that Ethiopia, Nigeria and Burkina Faso are relatively high on *loyal involvement*. The dimension *utilitarian involvement–loyal involvement* defines the way in which individuals relate to social entities in terms of a calculative involvement or an obligation-based commitment. Burkina Faso appears to be higher on loyal involvement and on *conservativism* (as opposed to the pole of egalitarian commitment which correlates positively with Schwartz's *egalitarian commitment* and Hofstede's *individualism*). In Trompenaars' (1993) original study there is an indication that Nigerian managers view their organizations more from a social rather than a task focus than do managers from the two other African countries of Burkina Faso and Ethiopia. Nigerian managers may also have a tendency to be more collectivist than managers from Burkina Faso, favour more low context relations than Burkina Faso managers and more high context relations than Ethiopian managers, and favour more paternalist management than their Ethiopian counterparts and slightly less paternal management than the Burkina Faso managers.

There does not appear to be a connection between the African countries with a French, British or independent heritage and the respective colonial power, but clearly this is an area which needs more systematic investigation. For example on the one measure of individualism–collectivism (Trompenaars, 1993) Nigerian managers appear to be more collectivist (at least in decision-making) than Japanese managers, and more so than Burkina Faso managers. However, Nigeria's percentage agreement with the 'collectivist' response is in line with that of France rather than that of the UK. Trompenaars (1993) results, based on single item variables, and based on a priori cultural dimensions can only be indicative, as they have not been successfully empirically validated. Another factor that may need to be taken into consideration is the influence on management and organization of post-independence political orientation, in particular between 'socialist' and non-socialist countries. Taylor (1992) suggests that although in theory 'socialism' may encourage centralized planning, bureaucracy and group conformity, and militate against individual initiative, countries such as Zimbabwe and Tanzania may only be nominally socialistic, with also a movement towards more liberalization of the economy (e.g. through Structural Adjustment Programmes). In Taylor's (1992) comparison of public sector personnel management in Tanzania, Zimbabwe and Kenya (a non-socialist country) he discounts this as an influencing factor in the nature of organizational administration.

What these inter-country comparisons do not tell us very much about are the interactions of managers among the different countries. The legitimacy and utility of cross-cultural study should be based on whether or not managers actually interact or are likely to interact. We now turn our attention to inter-ethnic level analysis.

### Inter-ethnic cultural level interaction

Most African countries themselves are multi-cultural. The colonial 'scramble for Africa' ensured this through dividing up the territory according to European claims rather than existing African ethnic divisions. The importance of understanding at this level, among other aspects, is in addressing the area of conflict resolution, and in the provision of equal opportunities: an issue not only highlighted in South Africa (Chapter 12), but also may other countries south of the Sahara. Expectations of one ethnic group may be different in the workplace to the expectations of another group. In Nigeria, whose main three language or tribal groupings (Hausa, Yoruba and Igbo) are fairly well documented even in the management literature (e.g. Adigun, 1995), it may be appropriate and feasible to undertake studies which consider cross-cultural differences within the country. In other countries with large 'settler' populations, differences between white and black groups may be an appropriate avenue for research (conflict resolution in, for example, South Africa, is not only a legitimate application of research findings, historical inter-ethnic conflict may also affect the way data is collected). This may be particularly the case as white managers may be closer to the instrumental approach of Western companies, which was discussed above, and black African managers closer to a humanistic approach.

The (mainly Western) approaches to studying cultural differences (Hofstede, 1980a; Schwartz, 1994; and Smith *et al.*, 1996) provides only 'thin' description which has severe limits in describing differences among African countries, let alone within African countries. 'Thick' description is more usefully employed to develop hypotheses. In Nigeria, for example, Adigun (1995) describes the Hausa as conservative, religiously orthodox (Islamic) with little education and urban sophistication. Achievement or striving for excellence is of no importance for the individual's societal standing. Values such as loyalty, obedience, servility and sensitivity to the demands of those in authority, as well as respect for tradition are important. Its members are trained in subordination, political intrigue and opportunistic choice of patrons. They are less interested in getting a steady job, being promoted and raising their living standards. He describes the Igbos as readily embracing Western education and Christianity. They attach importance to individual achievement, with personal effort and use of abilities leading to a rise in status. Obtaining occupational skills and using enterprise and initiative are valued. With entrepreneurial emphasis, there is a willingness to take any job, and live modestly while attaining wealth. The Yoruba (Adigun, 1995) also embraced Western Christianity and education and are the most urbanized of the three groups. Social status is derived from a combination of clientage and through occupational achievement. As a result of embracing urban life, and obtaining high educational standards Yoruba are often in managerial ranks. Social support and group solidarity are emphasized with the extended family being important for exerting social pressure, and providing patterns of mutual obligation. Status is important, and individual achievement also brings honour to the family.

This level of description enables Adigun (1995) to develop specific hypotheses regarding differences among these three groups within the workplace (see also Gannon's, 1994, use of the concept of cultural metaphors to provide 'thick' description of 'Nigerian' culture). Yet such 'thick' description also may tend towards stereotyping if not grounded in research. Thin description derived from questionnaire surveys, for example, may provide a basis of comparison, yet very little such comparisons actual exist within the literature on management in Africa.

### Other levels of analysis: gender and gender attitude differences

Cross-gender studies of management in Africa are also relevant as is cross-national differences on perspectives on and attitudes towards gender difference (Woodford-Berger, 1998). The extent to which management 'culture' involves an under-representation of women should be taken into account when comparing management in African countries. This of course is important to possible bias in comparative research, but research findings on the nature of different attitudes and gender discrimination are important to addressing subsequent development issues.

### Cross-cultural dynamics

Any investigation of management and organization in Africa must consider the different and overlapping management systems described above and tentatively labelled post-colonial, post-instrumental, African renaissance and others such as Japanese alternatives. It must consider how these systems vary, for example through different influences of post-colonial systems (e.g. Portuguese, French, Belgian, British and their different operating varieties), and multinationals (e.g. American, Australian, Swedish and various other Anglo-Saxon and European variants). It must also consider how these systems differ and combine in cross-cultural interaction at the various levels discussed above: inter-continental (predominantly African–Western, implying a need to also investigate outside Africa in Western companies), cross-national (e.g. Zimbabwean–Zambian within region, or South African–Nigerian across regions when such comparisons are appropriate and useful), and inter-ethnic (e.g. Hausa, Igbo, Yoruba in Nigeria).

However, an understanding of management in Africa that includes only these variables would remain at the descriptive and comparative levels. Investigation that is concerned with the effectiveness of organizations and management in Africa should include at least two other aspects: the dynamics of cross-cultural interaction (i.e. how can multicultural working, which is implicit in management in Africa, be effective or ineffective?), and change (i.e. how do organizational stakeholders' perceptions, values, decisions and actions affect change at micro and macro levels?). Jackson and Kotze's (in press) study of a major multicultural South African organization, the South African National Defence Force, employed integration–disintegration theory adapted from the literature on multicultural teams. Multiculturality may be both a disintegrative influence where members of cultural groups are tending to make in-group, out-group decisions (Tsui *et al.*, 1992), but also strengths may be drawn from cultural diversity in increasing creativity and better decision-making (Jackson, 1992; Lau and Murnighan, 1998).

It is likely that a predominant multiculturality in African organizations is leading to the former, disintegrative position, particularly as collectivist societies are more prone to make in-group, out-group decisions (Hui, 1990), leading to conflicts within the workplace, or in inter-organizational relations. Elron, Shamir and Ben-Ari (1999) in their study of cultural diversity in multinational peacekeeping forces note that recent work on multicultural teams suggest that highly heterogeneous teams develop a strong hybrid culture compared with those which are less heterogeneous (Early and Mosakowski, 1998; Hambrick *et al.*, 1998). An inability to revert back to previous identities and norms explains this. This necessitates the need to develop a new common culture when co-ordination and communication are required among a number of different participants. A common sense of identity within the emerging culture, which enhances internal communication, co-ordination and cohesiveness (Elron *et al.*, 1999) may be discernable through investigating such inferred variables as agreement on the perceptions of organizational and management attributes, in terms of what the current situation in the organization is, the ideal situation (what is desirable in terms of management styles and organizational factors such as level of hierarchy, decision-making process, and control) and how this contrasts with the way these aspects are likely to change.

Logically, organizations are likely to change in a positive way, if the perceptions of the various stakeholders concur about the present nature of the organization and its management, and the desirable character of change. Figure 1.1 attempts to draw together these elements, and identifies the nature of the relationships among variables.

## Developing effective management in Africa

For managers in Africa trying to make sense of the complexities inherent as a result of historical circumstance and different levels of cultural interaction, the developing–developed world paradigm has not been useful. The attempt by international agencies to influence effective governance in Africa by structural and economic measures that reflect a largely instrumental view at the macro level (see Jackson, 1999), has failed to address the real issues of developing people. In fact people are regarded as a 'resource' as we discussed above. By recognizing the interplay of the dynamics of locus of human value, at the inter-continental level of cross-cultural analysis, it may be possible to develop hybrid approaches (as seems to be happening in India: Rao, 1996) to the effective management of people, at the micro level.

At the regional cooperation level, involving cross-border working, the 'European' model of managing cross-culturally by developing synergies in cross-border teams, rather than the 'American' model of managing diversity by homogenization (e.g. Thurley and Wirdenius, 1989; Jackson, 1993) may be more appropriately considered.

Many other considerations are involved in developing inter-ethnic cross-cultural synergies within organizations apart from decreasing dis-integrating effects and increasing integrative effects, as depicted in Figure 1.1. These include addressing issues of patronage in some African countries, and continuing issues of discrimination in other countries.

However, much can be achieved by employing a cross-cultural paradigm which focuses on understanding these issues, and then addressing them by developing managers in Africa on a cross-cultural basis, learning through good practice and building on the deep-felt humanistic perspectives of African peoples. It should be remembered that organizations and managers have been managing these dynamics in Africa for many years. Lessons can be drawn from good practice not only for management in Africa, but also to contribute to global managing throughout the world.

We now start to address this in the next chapter. In the current chapter we have tried to show how the pejorative developing–developed world view hampers understanding and therefore the effective managing of organizations in Africa. In the next chapter we discuss how theory (which is sadly lacking in most texts on management in Africa) may be built, and how this may inform research in this area. Yet this is not just intended for academic researchers or students undertaking research projects as part of their studies. The adage 'there is nothing so practical as good theory' attributed to Kurt Lewin, we believe may become self-evident for the other stakeholder communities discussed in the Introduction of the current text. Chapter 2 therefore sets the scene for the rest of the book and continues with our quest to rethink management in Africa.

## Note

\*    This chapter is based on an article 'Reframing human resource management in Africa: a cross-cultural perspective' by the current author published in *International Journal of Human Resource Management* 2002, 13(7), 998–1018, which has been expanded and adapted for the purpose of this book.

# Chapter 2

# Developing cross-cultural theory and methods in Africa

'Mlendo ndiye adza n'kalumo kakuthwa' . . . [a Chewa proverb meaning literally: 'A visitor is the bringer of sharp razor blades'] . . . visitors or those new to a society are carriers and introducers of novel ideas, which may either be the solution to some vexing problems or phenomena, or may contribute very positively towards the search for solutions.

(Kaphagawani, 1998)

It might still be wondered . . . whether the ways of reasoning among the different peoples of the world might not be so incomprehensible as to render any cross-cultural evaluation of the truth or soundness of belief systems impossible in spite of the supposed universality of conceptual understanding. Putting it differently still, granted that there is enough mutuality of conceptual schemes for one culture to understand the intimations of another, does it follow that there must be enough commonality of cognitive criteria for the rationality of those intimations to be assessed from the viewpoint of an alien culture?

(Wiredu, 1995)

## Introduction: the relevance of cross-cultural theory

Over the last two decades a literature has grown on cross-cultural management research drawing mainly on cross-cultural psychology, but also in part on social/cultural anthropology. During this time little has been learned in cross-cultural management theory or methodology from studying management in Africa. This reflects general management theory that has ignored contributions that could have been made from studying organizations in Africa. This is a very serious gap in both cross-cultural and management theory: a field, like its parent the social sciences, that attempts to establish methods and concepts that can be employed worldwide.

Culturally, sub-Saharan Africa is very complex (e.g. Reader, 1998). This is not just in the number of ethnic groups that can be found in African countries, but in the different possible levels of cross-cultural interaction (Western/African, cross-border, inter-ethnic) as we saw in Chapter 1. This complexity is also exhibited in the degree of crossvergence of cultures, and through the process of hybridization of management systems as a result of cultural crossvergence (see Priem *et al.*, 2000), and the extent to which power and ideology are important influences in cultural interactions in

Africa. In the face of these complexities current cross-cultural theories such as Hofstede's (1980a) empirically derived cultural dimensions (and more recent empirically derived theories such as that of Schwartz, 1994), which have been used extensively in management research seem wholly inadequate in explaining cultural differences and interaction in Africa. The irony seems to be that now that members of the academic development community (e.g. Dia, 1996) and management scholars (e.g. Iguisi, 1997) are beginning to focus on cultural differences in management in Africa, they have turned directly to Hofstede's (1980a) theory. This may be through a lack of alternatives.

Having discussed the complexities of cross-cultural issues within Africa, it also seems very peculiar that previous studies of management in Africa have been either devoid of a consideration of culture and cross-cultural interaction as a relevant issue (e.g. Blunt and Jones, 1992, treat 'culture and organization' in a separate chapter as a separate subject, and not as an integral part of studying management in Africa), or they compare managers in different countries with little justification (for example it may be interesting to compare Ghana with Kenya, Kuada, 1994, but any such comparison should be fully justified).

Previous cross-cultural management studies that have included African countries have often done so to increase the range of country cultures, rather than to inform effective management in these countries (e.g. Smith *et al.*, 1996, include Zimbabwe rather incidentally; Munene, Schwartz and Smith, 2000, include African countries mainly as a comparison with Western countries; however Noorderhaven and Tidjani, 2001, provide African countries in their study to address issues of governance in Africa). Certainly, there have been few studies that empirically investigate cross-cultural management differences at the inter-ethnic level (Adigun, 1995, for example, discussed in Chapter 1, provides a view of ethnic differences in Nigeria rather than a systematic empirical analysis), and some only indirectly address the issue of inter-continental (Western/African) cross-cultural differences and their influences on management (Iguisi, 1997, partially addresses the issue of appropriateness of management practices in Africa).

This chapter, which builds on Chapter 1, therefore has the aim of developing a conceptual and methodological approach that focuses on cross-cultural content and processes in sub-Saharan Africa. Not only is it hoped that this will provide the basis for understanding issues of cross-cultural management in the sub-continent itself, but also to contribute to cross-cultural management theory by focusing on the issues and levels of analysis required to study complex cross-cultural interaction, cross-vergence and hybridization within post-colonial societies where power and ideological relations are major factors.

We attempt to do this by further clarifying the conceptual basis of management systems and culture in an interactive process that produces hybrid forms of management and organization within the context of sub-Saharan Africa (Figure 2.1).

We then go on to discuss issues of the legitimacy and utility of cross-cultural study in Africa. This has implications for the types of comparisons that can and should be made, and for the types of questions that can be asked, and how they can be asked, in order to take account of indigenous and exogenous frames of reference.

## Developing a conceptual model

Figure 2.1 presents a conceptual framework for studying the *products* of cultural crossvergence and hybridization. That is, the management systems that are influenced by and derived from cultural interactions, historically and currently, that provide the organizational strategies, structures, principles and characteristics; and in turn influence and interact with management styles, beliefs and competencies to provide control mechanism that are important to obtaining staff involvement comprising both current motivation and longer term commitment.

Yet using the term 'system' does not imply conceptually a Systems Theory perspective (for example, Katz and Kahn, 1978). Rather it assumes that different management systems operating in sub-Saharan Africa (and indeed in other regions) have different logics. So the system that is discussed in Chapter 2 under the ideal type of 'post-instrumental' may well have the teleological characteristics of Systems Theory, and be influenced by this conceptualization of an objective-seeking organization (that is, instrumental). Post-colonial management systems may not be results oriented, and be more influenced by the logic of bureaucratic control mechanisms. Where African renaissance systems operate, there may be more an emphasis on obligations to stakeholders and a humanistic logic.

In this way our use of the term 'ideal type' is in line with that of Weber:

> An ideal type is formed by the one-sided accentuation of one or more points of view and by the synthesis of a great many diffuse, discrete, more or less present and occasionally absent concrete individual phenomena, which are arranged according to those one-sidedly emphasized viewpoints into a unified analytical construct.
>
> (in Freund, 1972)

The ideal types that we have outlined in Chapter 1 are constructed from the literature and contain prevailing assumptions about what 'African' or 'developing' management is like (i.e. post-colonial), what 'Western' management is like (post-instrumental) and what a new indigenous African renaissance management might be like. As such, it is unlikely that these ideal types exist in these actual forms, but they can be used for analysis purposes where it is important to distinguish the different influences on actual management systems in Africa. We have also said that there may be influences from other ideal types such as Japanese/East Asian systems, and that, for example, French and Anglo-Saxon versions of post-colonial or post-instrumental systems may differ. We have also argued that the essence of such systems can be seen in a distinction between the way people are valued in organizations: instrumentally or humanistically. Hence the post-instrumental ideal type system is in essence instrumental. Despite a softening of instrumental approaches in modern HRM in mature industrial economies (see Jackson, 2002b), post-instrumental systems have not broken outside this box (otherwise they would no longer be post-instrumental). The African renaissance ideal type system would be in essence humanistic, and post-colonial systems are essentially instrumental, although containing in-group and out-group collectivist dynamics

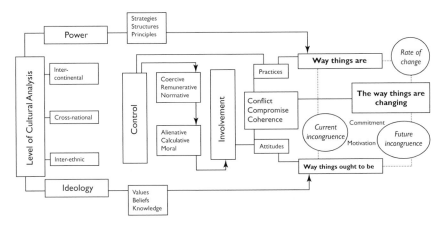

*Figure 2.1*  Cultural manifestations in management systems: the process of
hybridization.

(discussed in more detail in later chapters), may contain elements of selective humanism.

Looking at management systems as ideal types also recognizes multiple realities of a situation, whilst trying to make sense of these different realities and incorporate them into manageable categories. Systems Theory on the other hand tends to dehumanize the organization (Silverman, 1970). The conceptual and methodological approach taken here is to listen to the voices of individual managers, as members of organizations. This approach is requisite for a cross-cultural approach that recognizes these multiple perceptions of the same reality.

However, although cultural values per se may be important antecedents in cross-cultural research, the framework does not particularly focus on those aspects. Rather, it focuses on the systems as a whole (see Tables 1.1 and 1.2 in Chapter 1). This involves *the way things are in organizations*. Yet, not only do individuals make judgements about the way things are, they also make judgements about *the desirability of those manifestations*. Individuals may judge these differently as members of different organizations, as people with a particular cultural and/or national identity, and as of a gender group, of different levels in the organization, and as members of different types and sectors of organizations. Individuals may also make judgements about *the way things are going*: how are aspects of the management systems in the organization changing and what are they likely to be like in the future. From these three perspectives, it is possible to develop a series of measures that can be used in cross-cultural research.

1   the perceived nature of *current management systems* (the way things are in Figure 2.1);
2   the perceived nature of desired or *ideal management systems* (the way things ought to be in Figure 2.1);

3    the perceptions of the way things are changing or *future management systems* (the way things are changing in Figure 2.1);
4    the gap between perceived current management systems (1) and desired management systems (2) can be expressed as the level of *current management systems incongruence* (i.e. the wider the gap between what is there and what is seen as desirable, the higher the level of incongruence);
5    the gap between future management systems (3) and desired management systems (2) can be expressed as the level of *future management systems incongruence* (i.e. the wider the gap between the way things are going, and the way people would like them to go, the higher the level of incongruence);
6    the gap between current management systems (1) and future management systems (3): the level of *management systems change* (i.e. the wider the gap between the way things are now, and the way they will be in the future, the higher the perceived level of change).

Any of these measures may vary among cultural groups and between gender groups, as well as by organizational level. Variation among cultural groups is particularly important as an indication of the incongruence among relevant groups within organizations in Africa. In particular measures 2, 4 and 5 are important in this respect, and may reflect differences in the desirability of current and future management systems in terms of the different distribution of power among cultural groups in organizations. Table 2.1 shows this connection between power and different levels of cultural analysis. Organizational level may reflect variation by cultural group at an inter-ethnic level. For example, there may be more black individuals in lower organizational positions in organizations in South Africa (Breakwater Monitor, 2000) and this association of lower/higher organizational position with culture or ethnicity may be repeated in other African countries. Expatriate South Africans may hold higher positions than Zambians in a subsidiary of a South African organization in Zambia, at a cross-national level. American expatriates may hold higher positions than Kenyans in a subsidiary of an American bank in Nairobi. We believe that power relationships are fundamental to cross-cultural analysis in Africa, and this will be further developed later.

Yet this also involves the success of the dominant ideology within the organization (and at societal level). Ideology is concerned with issues of power and hegemony, and again this will be explored in more detail later. The measures proposed above also have importance as indicators of staff commitment and involvement in the organization. For example, if the level of *current management systems incongruence* is high (that is, management systems are not compatible with staff's expectations and desires) staff motivation and moral may be low. If the level of *future management systems incongruence* is high (that is, staff do not see things working out the way they would like in the future), their longer-term commitment to the organization may be low. This certainly reflects both the disconnect thesis (Dia, 1996; Carlsson, 1998), and the reported low motivation and commitment levels of African staff (e.g. Blunt and Jones, 1992), and these relationship are indicated in Figure 2.1. But this may also be an indication of the success of the dominant ideology in the organization.

It is first necessary therefore to focus on these aspects in more detail, by looking at different levels of cultural analysis (Figure 2.1), and focusing on the different aspects of the framework, and the connections between them, in order to describe how it is possible to study the manifestations of cultural crossvergence (or intermixing of cultural factors) and hybridization.

## Levels of cultural analysis and power relations

The multicultural context of Africa can (and should) be analysed at multiple cross-cultural levels (inter-continental, cross-national, and inter-ethnic) and time/change perspectives (past, present and future). In applying this approach, within the sub-Saharan African region, within the so-called developing regions and in global context, it is possible to challenge much of the accepted wisdom within cross-cultural management theory of comparing countries (as cultures) on the basis of simple variation on dimensions purporting to measure cultural values (Hofstede, 1980; Tompenaars, 1993; Schwartz, 1994).

Apart from a weakness in addressing the multiple levels of measurement of culture, this type of approach to cross-cultural study also lacks an appreciation of the dynamics of cross-cultural interaction (Cray and Mallory, 1998). This type of approach does not take into consideration the historical/change dynamic, and the interaction of the different levels of cross-cultural influence. It also does not provide an understanding of power relations (see Human, 1996) within this dynamic that so strongly influence the process of hybridization. In post-colonial countries, the influence of power within this dynamic is easily discernable (Ahluwalia, 2001). It is also an aspect that needs to be prominent in any social scientific investigation (Flynberg, 2001) not least cross-cultural studies. These aspects, within the context of Africa, are summarized in Table 2.1.

*Table 2.1* Cross-cultural dynamics in post-colonial societies

| Levels of analysis | Past | Present | Future |
|---|---|---|---|
| **Inter-continental** | Colonial/Indigenous | Post-colonial/Western/Indigenous | Future hybrid systems |
| *Power dynamic* | Economic, military and ideological | Economic, contractual and ideological | Contractual and obligatory |
| **Cross-border** | Restricted cross-national | Increased intra-regional | Increased intra-continental |
| *Power dynamic* | Political and military | Political and economic | Economic and cooperative |
| **Inter-ethnic** | Colonial 'divide and rule' | Political/power relations | Increased synergies |
| *Power dynamic* | Political and military | Political, economic and sometimes military | Multiculturalism |

### Inter-continental level

As we have seen in Chapter 1 interactions take place (across continents, so to speak) with Western powers, both historically as former colonial countries, and through the activities of modern multinational companies, and the predominance of Western education. These interactions were dominated economically, militarily and often ideologically by the colonial power (e.g. Reader, 1998). Today they are dominated economically through interactions with both multinational companies and multilateral agencies, particularly the World Bank and the IMF, and bilateral agencies of Western governments (e.g. Barratt-Brown, 1995). The predominance of Western education ensures an ideological disparaging of indigenous thought systems. Yet there is tremendous potential ('Future' in Table 2.1) to develop effective hybrid systems of management with admixtures of Western and indigenous thought systems and practices. It is likely that there has been a movement away from coercive control systems in organizations with the diminishing of colonial influences, toward a contractual/economic control system. Future or present hybrid systems may use a mixture of contractual and obligatory control mechanism (control mechanisms are discussed in more detail below).

### Cross-national level

Emerging trading blocs among countries, such as SADC, COMESA and ECOWAS, are encouraging intra-regional interaction, rather than between the African country and its former colonial master (e.g. Mulat, 1998). Colonial powers severely restricted communications among African countries. Transport infrastructure reflected this in roads and railways being built to link seaport with mineral source, rather than to link a country with its neighbour. Trade was restricted to include only that between colony and colonial power. Trading blocs are now encouraging more interaction, although often the legacy of colonial transport infrastructure restricts this. The growing requirement to work with managers and trading partners among African countries, often within regions, introduces another level of cross-cultural interaction, as we saw in Chapter 1. It is likely that such interactions are facilitated or restricted by political/governmental considerations, and motivated by economic factors that drive competition. Higher levels of mutual cooperation, on an intra-continental rather than just a regional basis, may well drive future interactions. Indeed, a view that many African states are not viable economic entities (Reader, 1998) may require higher levels of intra-regional and intra-continental cooperation for future economic and social prosperity. Understanding these differences are more important than ever, as interaction increases among different sub-Saharan countries.

### Inter-ethnic level

Most countries in sub-Saharan Africa are multi-ethnic, often by virtue of the fact that successive colonial powers have artificially divided up the sub-continent, ignoring indigenous identities; and by the sheer complexity of ethnicity in any one country.

South Africa has eleven official languages. Cameroon, a country that was successively ruled by Germany and then partitioned and jointly administered by France and Britain, has over 250 language groups, as well as the two official languages of French and English. This type of scenario is repeated in many different forms within Africa (see www.ethnologue.com). 'Divide and rule' was a common political strategy for colonial rulers, and resentments thus created have often extended into the inter-ethnic tensions witnessed today. Sometimes this has erupted into military action and civil war. Yet in organizations in post-colonial African countries there is great potential to create synergies from multiculturalism. However, this is likely to vary from country to country.

### Power and ideology

From the above discussion on levels of cultural analysis, it may be apparent that equal relations may not typify interaction at these three levels. Western multinational companies may have more power than local managers and indeed the staff they employ (inter-continental interactions). South African corporations, and managers, may dominate in trade or operations among SADC countries (cross-national interactions). White managers may dominate in a South Africa corporation. Managers of South Asian decent may dominate in particular organizations in Nairobi, while Kikuya managers may dominate in others (inter-ethnic interaction).

Power relations are translated into control mechanism within organizations, and reveal themselves in management systems. Rather than being a simple mediator where culture is the antecedent (independent variable) and the management system is the end result (dependent variable), power is an integral part of the way cross-cultural interaction gives rise to strategies, structures and principles of management, and how these are operated in an organization (the way things are: Figure 2.1). To be more specific:

- *Power* can be described as the ability (militarily, economically, politically, etc.) to impose one's will on others (see, for example, Dahl, 1957).
- *Ideology* (within the context of the framework in Figure 2.1) may be described as the hegemony of value, belief and knowledge systems created through education, media and dominant practices, that legitimize and sanction practices within organizations (a thorough examination of this concept can be found in Larrain, 1979).

Hence the dominance of colonial power before independence gave rise to the disparaging of indigenous value, belief and knowledge systems and created education based on a Western model. Since the Second World War the dominance of American economic influence has led to a proliferation of MBA programmes and textbooks, as well as American management practices, throughout the world (see Boyacigiller and Adler, 1991). Yet global convergence (from Kerr *et al.*, 1960) of principles and practices may not be happening. That is, the acceptance, for example, of Western styles of management may not be complete. There is a strong argument to suggest that crossvergence, rather than convergence is the dominant process within globalization (Beals, 1953; Ralston *et al.*, 1997; Priem *et al.*, 2000). This presupposes that indigenous value, belief and knowledge systems are present, but modified through the hegemony of globalizing power relations, which in turn may be modified through practice. This will be related to the direct nature of foreign and post-colonial influences. This also relates to public sector organizations, under the influence of Western education, and pressures to reform from IMF/World Bank initiatives.

The judgement of 'the way things ought to be' in an organization, that is, the perception of the desirability of aspects of management systems, may well vary by 'cultural' group (be it a national group or an ethnic group). However, this perception will also be influenced by the position of that group in an organization as a dominant or subordinate group, and the extent to which the dominant ideology has been accepted or not. Figure 1.1 suggests a relationship between an instrumental and a humanistic locus of human value, and advantaged and disadvantaged social positions respectively. This may relate in part to a relationship between humanism and collectivism (Jackson, 2002b). Collectivism is target specific, that is one relates to one's in-group as a collectivist (and in a humanistic way) and to one's out-groups in a non-collectivist way (that is, in an instrumental way). Dominant management and/or owner groups in organizations may therefore treat in-group members in a humanistic way (see Jackson, 2002b), and out-group members in the organization in an instrumental way. The extent to which there is a difference between a perception of the way things are, and a perception of the way things ought to be reflects the level of disparity between the power of the dominant group to enforce particular strategies, structures and principles, and its legitimizing ideology in the extent to which staff in the organization accepts the dominant management systems as they operate in the organization.

An overriding principle in the way in which management systems are conceived and operated, is that of control (Tannenbaum, 1974; Katz and Kahn, 1978). The nature of that control, and its perceived legitimacy, influence the level of involvement of staff and managers in the organization. Again, its perceived legitimacy may well reflect the values, beliefs and knowledge systems of a cultural group, and the integrity of that group in terms of acceptance or rejection of dominant ideology.

### Control and involvement

Control operates through organizational aspects that include strategic leadership and outcomes, structure, decision-making processes, rules and procedures and policies. It is reflected in aspects such as internal climate. These aspects of management systems and organizing have cross-cutting orientations that generally relate to the way power is wielded within work organizations. Etzioni (1975) categorized these as coercive, remunerative and normative power, as means of control in organizations, as follows:

- *Coercive power* operates by being able to punish or compel through physical or other means, and would be related to authoritarian management behaviour. The legitimacy of that behaviour may be based on political, economic or physical dominance with its source in colonial institutions representing military and economic coercion.

- *Remunerative power* is based on an ability to reward people through monetary means or withholding or supplying other tangible resources, or intangible resources related to remuneration, such as promotion. Its source in neo-colonial institutions (e.g. Ahluwalia, 2001) could be economic dominance and the proliferation of contractual work arrangements through Western style companies. This would normally be based on an instrumental relation, and on economic power.
- *Normative power* relates to the ability to use moral and symbolic influence, and is more likely to be based on obligatory or reciprocal relations. This may need more explanation beyond Etzioni's (1975) conceptualization, and placed within a cross-cultural frame of reference. Jackson (2002a), for example, examines the creation of obligation and shared values within motivational systems created by corporations in Japan, and to a lesser extent in Korea. Such organizations have been successful in 'capturing' the wider societal values of collectivism, and establishing shared values and commitment within the corporation (Jackson, 2002a). This is very much a humanistic and people centred perspective. It is within this perspective that Etzioni's concept of 'normative' control is taken within this text. Normative values have to be shared and internalized, and cannot be imposed. This suggests that people are involved in the corporation as people with a value in their own right, and part of the corporation, rather than as a means to an end as in an economic contractual relation, or a coercive relation with the corporation.

Etzioni (1975) suggested that these different forms of control influence the type of employee involvement with the organization (see also Chapter 7). Hence:

- coercive power would be associated with *alienative involvement* with a negative or lack of involvement in or commitment to the company;
- remunerative power would be associated with *calculative involvement* where people are committed explicitly as far as they are rewarded appropriately and as far as they lack alternative employment choices; and
- normative power would be associated with *moral involvement* where commitment is internalized and is implicit.

Although more recent research by Banai, 2002 (albeit limited within a study of kibbutzim in Israel), has failed to confirm such a simple relationship: it is possible that this relationship is culturally mediated such that cultures that are more accepting of high power distance (in Hofstede's, 1980a, terminology) are more likely to be accepting of coercive, authoritarian practices, and less alienated by them than employees in a culture that is less excepting of power distance and hierarchy. Individualistic cultures may be more accepting of contractual employment relationships with remunerative reward as the main motivator. If African communities are more collectivist, as the literature suggests (Chapter 1), relying on reciprocity and obligatory relations, it is likely that there is an ill fit between a coercive (authoritarian), or a remunerative (instrumental) control system and African employees' expectations. Hence a normative control system (providing it propagates and induces the appropriate values) may lead to moral involvement within organizations in Africa. From this perspective, given the mediating influences of culture, Etzioni's (1975) control–compliance theory may be useful for understanding the relationship between control orientations and employee involvement in Africa.

### Reconciling practices and attitudes

The implication of this is that the type of management system operating within a work organization will influence employee commitment, employee work relationships (e.g. with supervisors and co-workers): that is, 'the way things are'; and will interact with employee work values (e.g. motivators, work centrality, and orientation to the company and co-workers): that is, 'the way things should be'. This interaction will be either one of conflict, compromise or coherence (Figure 2.1). That is, values may conflict with current practices and organizational arrangement; or there will be consistency or congruence between *what is* and *what should be*. An alternative is that there may be a compromise between the two. These possibilities will also relate to the power relations and the type of control, and the type of involvement in the organization. Hence with an asymmetric power relationship (e.g. master–servant), it is more likely that conflicts between *what is* and *what should be* will not be resolved, leading to alienative involvement of employees with the organization. This type of relation is supportive of Dia's (1996) and others' (e.g. Carlsson, 1998) disconnect theses of colonial and post-colonial organizations. A cohesive relation between what is and what should be is more likely to be a product of an indigenous organization working in harmony with the community within which it operates. In other words, the organization will be in tune with its cultural context. The often contradictory relationship between home/community life and work life (which we suggested in Chapter 1, and develop in more detail in Chapter 7) may be reconciled. Such organizations in Africa are few and far between, and are suggestive of African renaissance or *ubuntu* (Mbigi, 1997) organizations (discussed in Chapter 1). The compromise possibility is likely to be a main driver of hybridization, where the outcome may either be an organization with a management system that is highly adaptive to the context, or may be a more negative outcome with a mal-adaptive management system.

Management systems will also relate to the specific attitudes, working principles and practices of managers. The way things are will interact with the way managers feel things ought to be. That is, interaction will either be one of conflict, compromise or cohesion. In addition, management attitudes, principles and practices may also be a function of the product of compromise: that is, hybridization. Yet it is more likely that managers, rather than staff will be susceptible to ideological influences in post-colonial societies that may be an important consideration in the interaction between management systems *as are* (which in large part are a function of the attitudes, principles and practices of managers) and (desirable) management systems that *should be*. This is through the prominence of Western style management education in African countries. This is not simply that the Africa elite has been or is being educated in Britain, the United States or France (Närman, 1998), but managers who attend post-experience MBA programmes, for example, at the University of Nairobi, or young students who do a pre-experience business certificate course at the Zimbabwe Institute of Management are more likely to be taught with American or British textbooks, and by teachers who have been educated within a Western tradition. This is in addition to the general disparaging of African culture in schools as a legacy of the colonial era (Chivaura, 1998; Gethaiga, 1998). The level of conflict between *what is* and *what should* be for managers in an organizational setting is likely to be a function of internal personal conflicting values between tradition and modernity, between African and Western.

We have therefore tried to outline the general theory that informs the work within this book. Thorough the following chapters we will be putting this theory to the test. We will also be developing the general theory in relation to specific aspects of the management systems outlined in Chapter 1. In particular, we will be relating this to the management of organizations within the uncertain environment of sub-Saharan Africa, to the decision processes in organizations, to leadership and management styles, to the motivation and reward systems and to employee commitment, and to the development issues of managing multiculturalism and management teams.

Underlining these aspects of management systems will be the issue of management control and how this operates differently in different ideal type management systems. We will be using the *ideal type* as a tool for cross-cultural analysis, which can cut through much of the prejudice and confusion about management in Africa, and sharpen our thinking and reanalysis of management in Africa.

With appropriate analytical tools, and a fresh perspective, it may be possible to cut through much of what has been hampering management in this complex cross-cultural environment. We might be able to provide the sharp razor blade suggested in the Chewa proverb quoted by Kaphagawani (1998) in our opening quotation. We are not, however, saying that this is purely the prerogative of the outsider looking in from the outside. These tools would very quickly become blunt if it were not for the insight and specialist knowledge of the insider. This is why we have tried to develop research methods that reflect the collaboration of insiders, and which enable us to listen to the voices of African managers and employees.

## Implications for management research in Africa

Within the current text we had to make some hard choices about what should be included, and what should not. This original chapter in draft form was a long one that detailed hypotheses, research considerations, and research methods. Although these aspects are important, it may seem somewhat unfair on the patient reader who may be far more interested in cutting to the chase and learning what the current author and the project team has learned about management and change in Africa. Another consideration was the static nature of a book of this sort, which goes against the dynamic and ongoing nature of this project. Although we hope that this project will produce a second edition of this book in a few years' time, we consider this book only one part, albeit an important part, of the ongoing project. We have therefore attempted to draw out the relevant research and methodological issues in the ensuing chapters. If you would like more specific details, for example on the questionnaires we used, interview checklists, as well as more technical consideration, please refer to the more dynamic outlet of this project: www.africamanagement.org. This website will also keep you up to date on progress of the project, future publications and resources for educators, trainers and developers. If you do not find what you are looking for email the current author: tjackson@africamanagement.org.

We have set out in this chapter the basis of the theory that we believe can better inform both research efforts in Africa, as well as informing the practice of cross-cultural and appropriate management in sub-Saharan Africa. We stated at the outset the assumption of the project and of this text, that effective and appropriate management in Africa can make a difference to the well-being of humankind; that appropriate and effective management in Africa is cross-cultural management; and that without the basic research being undertaken in a systematic way, based on a constructive rather than a pejorative theory, it will be difficult to inform management processes and to learn from current good practice, and indeed to improve this good practice.

Any methodology must be premised on an interactive orientation: that is, we are not just collecting information; we are feeding back the information into organizations and to managers. Reaction and feedback from managers is an essential part of the research process that converts theory into practice, and informs theory through practice. Hence, early in the project in 1998, we held two cross-cultural workshops in Zimbabwe, kindly funded by the British Council. Not only were these instructive to the managers who attended, particularly in our discussions from the results of our initial management survey in Zimbabwe (although then only comprising a sample of 100, no database on management of its sort had previously existing in Zimbabwe, as far as we were aware), but they were crucial in framing the project, and obtaining feedback on some of the methods adopted, and the making of necessary adaptations to methods as well as developing theory.

Since then we have also run workshops in South Africa, and at the time of writing plan to do so in Cameroon and Nigeria. Research is a dynamic, not a passive collection of information that is then written up in a book or articles. This is especially true in the context of sub-Saharan Africa. Research must be ongoing, and reflect an action dynamic that is able to make interventions into management processes, and which in their turn may inform our unfolding theory. We hope you will enter into this dialogue on our website.

We now turn to Part II of this book and proceed to more practical issues of managing competencies and capacities, drawing on from both theoretical discussion and results from our empirical studies.

# Managing competencies and capacities

# Chapter 3

# Managing complexity and uncertainty in the African environment

Africa was weak before the Europeans touched its coasts. Nature is not kind to it. This may be the birthplace of mankind, but it is hardly surprising that humans sought other continents to live in.

(From 'The heart of the matter', *The Economist*, 11 May 2000)

We look at Africa as the last emerging market. . . . People who invested in Japan after World War II when it was in ruins were viewed as quite radical, but they made a lot of money. That's the same argument we're making with Africa today.

(From an interview with Clifford Mpare and Justin Beckett of New Africa Advisors, *Fortune*, 19 February 1996)

Our vision of an African renaissance must have as one of its central aims the provision of a better life for these masses of the people whom we say must enjoy and exercise the right to determine their future. That renaissance must therefore address the critical question of sustainable development which impacts positively on the standard of living and the quality of life of the masses of our people.

(Thabo Mbeki, Address to the Africa Renaissance Conference, September 1998, Johannesburg (reproduced as the Prologue to Makgoba, 1999: xvi))

## Perceptions of the African context

There is no doubt that sub-Saharan Africa has suffered from a bad press. Perceptions in the West are mostly based on journalistic reports of humanitarian disasters: famines, civil war and genocide. Bad news always makes good news. Afro-pessimism seems to abound, with the opening quotation from *The Economist* being typical. Unfortunately this is often accompanied with an implicit suggestion that there is something inherent within sub-Saharan Africa, or within Africans, that makes the sub-continent unstable and unmanageable (often forgetting the recent history of Europe), rather than attempting to understand the different forces that have shaped, and are shaping the environment and indeed understand many of the positives, not to say opportunities, that exist in Africa. This is realized in part by more far-sighted comments such as the opening quotation from *Fortune*. Yet this is perhaps missing the point. Africa cannot now just be seen as a business opportunity. This has been its history, and now its legacy. President Thabo Mbeki's comments in the quotation at the beginning of this chapter underscore the need for a wider view, particularly of business organizations operating in Africa.

In this chapter we present a picture of management systems interacting with their African environment through the particular perceptions that managers (and other stakeholders) have of this environment. Traditional systems theories (e.g. Katz and Kahn, 1966) are usually missing this aspect and come under criticism from Action Theorists such as Silverman (1970).[1] Within our approach, culture, and cross-cultural perceptions, values and attitudes are important, but they are not the only factors. Of particular importance are the relationships to stakeholders that organizations have, and the purpose of the organization within the recognition of different stakeholder interests. The opening quotations at the beginning of this chapter underscore the importance of taking such an approach. The first position sees Africa as a hopeless case, the second sees Africa as a business opportunity, and the third sees people who live in Africa as the major stakeholders. This in part reflects the paradox we discussed in Chapter 1, between the need to make organizations lean and competitive, and the need to develop people within the work organization. This emphasises the importance of considering the perceptions of different stakeholders, even when examining a seemingly 'objective' subject such as the environment within which the organization operates. These views may be based on a particular cultural perspective, and those views that predominant result from the power relations among those different stakeholders (see Chapter 2). This is because we are considering the interactions between managers and their environment as a dynamic, rather than accepting the environment as a 'given'. Therefore the way managers see this environment is important to the way they act towards it, and the way they manage organizations accordingly.

The way managers act towards their environment in Africa (and this could be applied to any environment, but is particularly relevant to emerging or developing countries) involves an interaction between endogenous factors contained within the organization itself, and exogenous factors (both internal to the country and external to it) contained within the general environment (see Figure 3.1). Exogenous factors influence and reinforce managers' perceptions of the role of their organization within the environment, their perceptions of relevant stakeholders and their interaction with them, and environment constraints and opportunities and how they act toward them. Not only do exogenous factors affect managers' actions through their perceptions of these factors, management actions also affect exogenous factors. For example, if all managers in all organizations do not pay bribes, this will affect the operating environment (Utomi, 1998).

The framework in Figure 3.1 first points to the importance of understanding the perceptions that exist regarding constraints and opportunities in sub-Saharan Africa, and the way *exogenous* factors are seen. These factors, some of which are considered in more detail later, are:

- *Environmental*: such as climatic and terrain problems, as well as the land-locked nature of many countries;

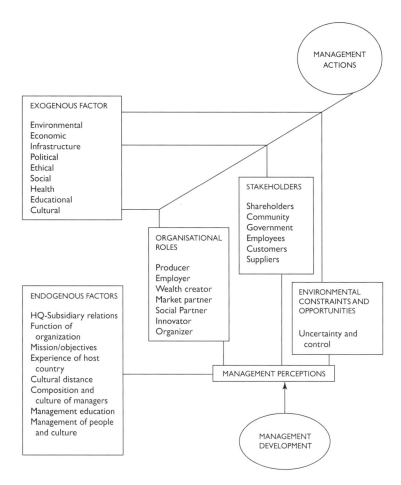

*Figure 3.1*  Organization and the African environment.

- *Economic*: particularly the poor state of the economy (illustrated in Table 3.1 by GDP per capita, but the negative image partly off-set by FDI as a percentage of GDP as we discuss later);
- *Infrastructural*: such as the level of technology (fixed-line and mobile telephones per 1000 people is a useful indicator, although the increased possession of mobile telephones may be indicative of the poor infrastructure for fixed line telecommunications: Table 3.1);
- *Political*: particularly the role of politics and its interaction with business as well as the issue of governance (an indication of one aspect is the combined political rights and civil liberties indices of Freedom House indicating the levels of freedom in these areas in each country: Table 3.1);

Table 3.1 Indicators of environmental constraint

| | Economic | | Infrastructure | Political | | | Ethical | Social | | | | Educational | | Cultural |
|---|---|---|---|---|---|---|---|---|---|---|---|---|---|---|
| Country | GDP/Capita[1] $ | FDI/GDP[2] % | Telephones Per 1000 people[3] | Political Rights and Civil Liberties[4] | Seats held by women in parliament[5] % | Inequality GINI[6] | CPI Scores[7] | HDI value 2001 (rank)[8] | Life Expectancy[9] | HIV/AIDS 15–49[10] % | Education Index[11] | Literacy rate 15+[12] % | ELF[13] |
| Botswana | 6,872 | 26.1 | 216 | 2.0 | 17.0 | — | 6.0 | 0.577 (114) | 41.9 | 35.80 | 0.74 | 76.4 | 0.399 |
| Cameroon | 1,573 | 13.7 | 7 | 6.5 | 5.6 | — | 2.0 | 0.506 (125) | 50.0 | 7.73 | 0.64 | 74.8 | 0.879 |
| Côte d'Ivoire | 1,654 | 24.2 | 48 | 5.0 | 8.5 | 36.7 | 2.4 | 0.426 (144) | 47.8 | 10.76 | 0.43 | 45.7 | 0.896 |
| D R Congo | 801 | 2.9 | 1 | 6.5 | — | — | — | 0.429 (142) | 51.0 | 5.07 | 0.51 | 60.3 | 0.902 |
| Ghana | 1,881 | 15.1 | 18 | 3.0 | 9.0 | 39.6 | 3.4 | 0.542 (119) | 56.6 | 3.60 | 0.61 | 70.3 | 0.874 |
| Kenya | 1,022 | 7.6 | 15 | 5.5 | 3.6 | 44.5 | 2.0 | 0.514 (123) | 51.3 | 13.95 | 0.71 | 81.5 | 0.882 |
| Malawi | 586 | 22.9 | 9 | 3.0 | 9.3 | — | 3.2 | 0.397 (151) | 40.3 | 15.96 | 0.64 | 59.2 | 0.606 |
| Mozambique | 861 | 14.4 | 7 | 3.5 | 30.0 | 39.6 | — | 0.323 (157) | 39.8 | 13.22 | 0.36 | 43.2 | 0.698 |
| Namibia | 5,468 | 48.0 | — | 2.5 | 20.4 | — | 5.4 | 0.601 (111) | 44.9 | 19.54 | 0.80 | 81.4 | 0.722 |
| Nigeria | 853 | 50.5 | 5 | 3.5 | 3.3 | 50.6 | 1.0 | 0.455 (136) | 51.5 | 5.06 | 0.57 | 62.6 | 0.857 |
| Rwanda | 885 | 11.8 | 7 | 6.5 | 25.7 | 28.9 | — | 0.395 (152) | 39.9 | 11.21 | 0.57 | 65.8 | 0.260 |
| South Africa | 8,908 | 13.4 | 304 | 1.5 | 27.9 | 59.3 | 4.8 | 0.702 (94) | 53.9 | 19.94 | 0.75 | 84.9 | 0.886 |
| Zambia | 756 | 52.8 | 17 | 4.5 | 10.1 | 52.6 | 2.6 | 0.427 (143) | 41.0 | 19.95 | 0.68 | 77.2 | 0.807 |
| Zimbabwe | 2,876 | 14.5 | 41 | 5.5 | 9.3 | 56.8 | 2.9 | 0.554 (117) | 42.9 | 25.06 | 0.80 | 88.0 | 0.472 |
| Sub-Saharan Africa | 1,640 | 27.7 | 32 | | | | | 0.467 | 48.8 | 8.70 | | 59.6 | |
| High Income OECD | 26,050 | 12.1[a] | — | 1.0[b] | 13.8[b] | 40.8[b] | 7.6[b] | 0.928 | 78.0 | 0.40 | | | |

Notes

1 Gross Domestic Product per capita, 1999 (UNDP Human Development Report, 2001).
2 Inward Foreign Direct Investment as a percentage of gross domestic product (UNCTAD World Investment Report, 2000).
3 Fixed line and mobile telephones per 1,000 people, 2000 (2002 World Development Indicators database, 20 April 2002).
4 Average of Freedom House ratings for political rights and civil liberties respectively, on a 1–7 scale (countries whose combined average rating fall between 1.0–2.5 are designated 'free', 3.0–5.5 'partly free', and 5.5–7.0 'not free').
5 These figures (with number of women in ministerial posts) are the only ones contained in the UNDP Human Development Report, 2001 relating to gender equality that cover the countries of interest, and provide a useful surrogate.
6 Gini index measure inequality over the entire distribution of income or consumption 0 = perfect equality, 100 = perfect inequality (UNDP Human Development Report, 2001).
7 Corruption Perception Index 2001 Scores (Transparency International) relate to perception of the degree of corruption (mainly of public officials) as seen by business people, academics and risk analysts, and range between 10 (highly clean) to 0 (highly corrupt).
8 Overall Human Development Index value (and rank out of 162 countries). HDI is a summary measure of human development that measures the average achievement of a country based on: (a) a long and healthy life measured by life expectancy at birth; (b) knowledge measured by adult literacy rate (2/3 weight) and the combined primary, secondary and tertiary gross enrolment rates (1/3 weight); and (c) a decent standard of living measured by GDP per capita. Performance is expressed as a value between 0 and 1 (UNDP Human Development Report, 2001).
9 Although incorporated within the HDI, this unbundled measure provides an easy to understand although crude social/health indicator (UNDP Human Development Report, 2001).
10 This provides an indication of the estimated percentage of people between the ages of 15 and 49 who are living with HIV/AIDS in 1999 (UNDP Human Development Report, 2001).
11 The Education Index is the 'knowledge' aspect of the HDI, combining adult literacy with school enrolments (see 8 above) (UNDP Human Development Report, 2001).
12 The crude literacy rate at age over 15 for 1999 (UNDP Human Development Report, 2001).
13 Ethnolinguistic Fractionalization is a measure of the probability that two randomly selected individuals in a country will not belong to the same ethnolinguistic group. The measure used here is Roeder's 1985 index (Roeder, 2001).
a 'Developed countries' has been used here as a substitute for High Income OECD countries b USA has been used as a substitute for High Income OECD countries.

- *Ethical*: particularly corruption and cronyism (Table 3.1 provides the corruption perception index of Transparency International);
- *Social*: which encompasses a whole range of issues including inequality (Table 3.1 provides measures on the GINI index of wealth inequality for some of the countries included in the current study, and seats held by women in parliament as a surrogate for gender inequality);
- *Health*: life expectancy and the estimated HIV/AIDS incidence are major considerations (Table 3.1);
- *Educational*: particularly levels of education and the skills available to work organization (Table 3.1 provides the UNDP's Education Index, and literacy rates for each country);
- *Cultural*: either through ethnic conflict or differences in cultural attitudes (Table 3.1 provides an ethnolinguistic fractionalization index).

However, it is often difficult to neatly compartmental these. Economic and infrastructural problems interact with social and health problems and are compounded by political actions. These may be exacerbated by, as well as contributing to the lack of educational and training opportunities (Table 3.1 also provides the UNDP's Human Development Index which combines measures for life expectancy, knowledge base including adult literacy and enrolment in primary, secondary and tertiary education, and GDP per capita).

Explanations of why certain perceptions exist may be found in the factors we describe as *endogenous*. These include the function and executive objectives of the organization; the relationship between the headquarters and the African subsidiary in the case of a foreign company, including its experience of operating in African countries; the cultural distance between management and employees, and between foreign management and local managers; the composition and cultures of managers; the type of management education received by managers (so often Western management education, which we argue may ill-equip managers for managing complexity in Africa); and, the nature of the management of people and culture (this was discussed in Chapter 1 as being based on a locus of human value: whether people are seen as a means to an end or an end in themselves within the organization). All these factors are important; not as individual explanations, but in how they combine in terms of the power relationships among stakeholders, and the different (often cultural) values that are brought to bear.

Endogenous factors play a main part in managers' perceptions of the role of the organization within the African environment, and the identification of an interaction with relevant stakeholders. This may go back to our three opening quotations and the views they represent. Organizations may see themselves as simply serving the ends of shareholders, or may see that they have a more overriding responsibility in developing the local community and the economy. The eight societal functions of business developed by the Battelle Project (Lessem, 1989) are seen as useful here and are outlined later. Different stakeholders may be seen at varying levels of importance depending on the perception of the role of the organization. Hence shareholders may be important as stakeholders for a company with only commercial interests, whereas the local community may be a high priority for a company such as Shell in Nigeria in the aftermath of community unrest following policies that were seen to go against local community interests.

For management to be effective within the African environment, managers should be aware of the different influences on their perceptions of this environment, the interaction between endogenous and exogenous factors, and the management actions they take.

## Exogenous factors and the perceptions of constraints and opportunities

The connection between cultural views, stakeholders and power discussed above was touched upon in Chapters 1 and 2. One representation of this is the apparent paradox between the need to develop the economy through developing skills and capacities to work in modern organizations, and the shorter term needs of making organizations 'meaner and leaner', often to meet externally set objectives such as public sector downsizing, and liberalizing the economy to make way for more competition. The nature of economic and social issues within this paradox often becomes embroiled in political and related issues. For example one Western managing director in Cameroon told us:

> The economy is being dictated from the IMF and World Bank. There are pressures on the government to collect more taxes from the companies they know will pay, rather than widening the tax base. They will reassess tax liability and backdate it for 30 years. They will reinterpret the tax laws to do this. We can contest this, but it takes time, and the collection arm still tries to collect the tax in the meantime, even coming down here and putting padlocks on the door to close down the factory. There is also a lot of shady dealing. So your documentation has to be in top order. If not, officials will fix it for you if you are prepared to deal with the problem in a pragmatic way. As a company we are not prepared to do this. It is against our code of practice. We know that other companies, whose MDs belong to certain political parties have less trouble than others.

This raises a whole number of issues of meeting short-term economic goals (often imposed by outside agencies), as well as corruption and cronyism. Other issues that are part of the paradox comprise a complexity of social, cultural, educational and health factors. For example, a consultant in Botswana remarked on the problem of productivity:

> It isn't the lack of educational opportunities and facilities. For example opportunities at the university are good and fully funded. People have the capacity to produce, but don't seem to want to. Maybe it is because people are closely knitted to their villages, and rush home at the weekends. This is, for example, typically for funerals. There are a lot of deaths in the villages. Some estimate the HIV infection rate to be 30 per cent of the population. Employers are now requiring prospective employees to take AIDS tests with implications for civil liberties.

During workshops in Zimbabwe run by the current author, managers remarked on the difficulty of responding to requests of employees to go to funerals, often requiring several days' to a week's leave. This was explained as relating to obligations within an extended family. Combining this with mortality rates through HIV/AIDS infection, this may be regarded as a serious constraint on productivity. Employers appear to be addressing the immediate problem of employing people who are HIV positive in different ways. Similar to the situation reported in Botswana, a medical officer of a mineral mining corporation in Kenya reported that Kenyan employers are addressing this issue through testing applicants. In Zimbabwe, one manager of an insurance company remarked that they had stopped spending training money. Often the company would spend money to train somebody up, and they would then become sick and die. Baruch and Clancy (2000) argue that these types of approaches to dealing with the employment of those infected with HIV is not helpful, particularly with skills shortages in many countries, and with the fact that those diagnosed as HIV positive may yet have a life expectancy of quite a few years. Again, policies towards HIV/AIDS are very much a matter of how this is perceived by top managers. Baruch and Clancy's (2000) findings indicate a lack of an established HRM policy for HIV/AIDS in organizations in Africa, and hence are not well equipped to deal with this sensitive issue.

### Afro-pessimism and investment

Given these few examples of the problems confronting managers in Africa, and anecdotes concerning them, operating constraints might seem overwhelming. It seems popular to talk about an Afro-pessimism. Certainly Western (and Eastern) companies are often wary of doing business and setting up operations in Africa despite the perceptions of the huge potential markets, unlimited human potential and natural resources in the sub-continent. Yet it depends on who is doing the telling, as to the perceptions created of corporate timidity to invest in Africa. Ayittey (1999: 9) reports that

> Africa has become unattractive to foreign investors. The net yearly flow of foreign direct investment (FDI) into developing countries quadrupled between 1990 and 1995 to over $90 billion. Meanwhile, Africa's share of FDI to developing countries fell from 3.5% to only 2.4%. According to the World Bank, in 1995 a record $231 billion in foreign investment flowed into the Third World. Singapore by itself attracted $5.8 billion. Africa's share, however, was a paltry one percent, about $2 billion, and less than the sum invested in Chile alone.

Yet in 2000 UNCTAD (United Nations Conference on Trade and Development) reported that 'Inflows of FDI into Africa (including South Africa) rose by 28 per cent, from $8 billion in 1998 to $10 billion in 1999. This growth rate is higher than that of other developing countries' (UNCTAD, 2000: 40). Of this

> Sub-Saharan Africa (including South Africa) had its share in total FDI inflows to Africa slightly reduced from 72 per cent in 1998 to 71 per cent in 1999.

However, the development in the sub-region was not uniform; some countries managed to attract rapidly increasing FDI inflows in recent years. Angola and Mozambique have been particularly successful.

(UNCTAD, 2000: 41)

It is perhaps misleading to compare FDI in Africa with Singapore as Ayittey (1999) and apparently the World Bank do. The UNCTAD (2000) report goes on to say

Measured against other indicators, such as GDP or gross domestic capital formation, FDI in a number of small African countries appears much more sizeable than figures for absolute inflows might suggest. Angola, Equatorial Guinea, Lesotho and Zambia rank high if FDI inflows are related to gross domestic capital formation. A similar ranking emerges when FDI inflows are related to GDP. The two rankings give different pictures of locational attractiveness.

(UNCTAD, 2000: 41)

In fact the four countries mentioned far exceed the investor attractiveness of Asia and the Pacific, as indeed does sub-Saharan Africa as a whole when expressed as a percentage of gross fixed capital formation (UNCTAD, 2000: 41, Figure II.11; see also Table 3.1 in the current text). This more positive image presented by UNCTAD does not finish there. The report goes on to say that there has become a bigger diversification of sources of FDI to Africa. While the United States maintained its position as most important investor in 1998 with outflows of $7.8 billion, France and the United Kingdom ranked second and third with outflows of $2.5 billion each. However, the combined share of the two have fallen over the last two decades and other countries, particularly Germany and the Netherlands, have increased their investment and gained in importance, with an increasing number of countries becoming important sources for FDI, including Japan (pp. 41 and 44). This seems to have been partly driven by privatization programmes that have been extensive, particularly in South Africa, Ghana, Nigeria, Zambia, and Côte d'Ivoire.

So, to what extent do perceptions reinforce the pessimism surrounding Africa? The well-told story of the representative from a Western shoe company who went to Africa to assess the market is instructive. He reported back to head office that people do not wear shoes here; therefore there is no market. A representative from another shoe company similarly went to Africa, and reported back: people do not have shoes here therefore the market is limitless. This representative, it is said, was from the Czech/ Canadian Bat'a Shoe Company, now one of the most successful shoe manufacturers and suppliers in Africa! A similar story might now be told for the mobile telephone market: the lack of surface telephone infrastructure in many African countries is providing good opportunities for companies such as Vodacom and MTN, often working their way northwards from South Africa.

## Perceptions of the 'African problem'

Our perception of the 'African problem' is often coloured by the developing–developed world paradigm as we discussed in Chapter 1. A United Nations Industrial Development Organization (UNIDO, 1999) report on African industry in 2000 identified the following factors, from the literature on empirical research, of the reasons for Africa's stagnation:

- adverse climatic and weather conditions with declining rainfall in some regions
- over-dependence on primary commodity exports with negative implications for long-term growth
- rapid population growth often having a negative influence on economic growth
- contagion effects from the weak performance of neighbouring countries and regional political stability
- the weak performance of 'pole' economies such as South Africa and Nigeria that may have been expected to drive regional economic expansions
- small markets which preclude companies exploiting economies of scale
- adverse terms of trade
- geographical position with many countries landlocked with higher costs and risks of trade
- low levels of investment and savings
- high levels of external indebtedness
- weak human capital with often deteriorating educational and health infrastructure
- underdeveloped physical infrastructure with resulting higher operating costs
- underdeveloped financial services sector resulting in high interest rates and high levels of risk aversion
- a weak private sector apart from a small number of countries such as South Africa, Zimbabwe, Botswana, Kenya and Côte d'Ivoire
- frequent political or military disruptions that discourages investment and entrepreneurship
- dependence on foreign assistance, which has declined since 1990
- failure to develop a business-friendly environment.

(UNIDO, 1999)

Rimmer (1991) explains that 'Africa is perceived as beset by intractable problems: runaway population growth, diminishing capacity to feed its people, deteriorating physical environment, crushing burdens of external debt'. Yet 'some bodies, including the World Bank, have interests entrenched in an African crisis; their importance, the resources they command, perhaps even their very existence, depend on a perceived need to rescue Africa from disaster'. This is not to say that the crisis is a myth but that 'our recognition of it owes much to the presence of various international economic institutions and aid-donating agencies' (Rimmer, 1991: 90–1). This vested interest in the African problem, no matter how well-intentioned, supports and perpetuates the developing–developed world paradigm. An additional problem may well be that African elites (who may stand to benefit from Western aid) may help to perpetuate this dependent image of Africa, and managers in Africa may sometimes find it difficult to see past this.

What is perhaps needed is a proper evaluation of constraints, as well as the opportunities within the sub-continent, particularly from the perspective of managers who operate in Africa and how these are addressed through the strategies of organizations. Also connected to this strategic perspective is the inclusion of different stakeholders in the formulation of strategies that interpret and respond to constraints and create opportunities (see also Chapter 4).

## Overcoming constraints: addressing exogenous factors

It is also the case that there are positive factors that provide the basis for growth in opportunities within sub-Saharan Africa that managers can capitalize on, and integrate within organizational strategies. However, like the example of the first shoe salesman, not all organizational managers so easily identify opportunities, and not all have a clear idea of how constraints may be successfully addressed. It is worth considering other human aspects that either have, or could be used in overcoming some of the difficulties and complexities of the sub-Saharan environment.

### Entrepreneurship and creativity

There are high levels and traditions of entrepreneurships in many African societies (e.g. Wild, 1997). This is glaringly obvious to any casual visitor to Africa who cares to walk around the often huge market areas of the large towns, but this is so often channelled into the unofficial sectors of the economy. Mbigi (1997: 32) reminds us that 'In Afrocentric cultures and tribes, individual entrepreneurship is encouraged, nurtured, harnessed, celebrated collectively and highly respected, almost to the point of canonization'. Barratt-Brown (1995) remarks that the real figure for intra-west African trade will be very much greater than the official statistics suggest, because of the almost equal amounts of goods that cross the frontiers illegally. Cameroon lost an estimated $285 million in the late 1980s through the illegal export of food crops into Nigeria in exchange for manufactured goods (Barratt-Brown, 1995). Prices in the supermarkets in Yaoundé are relatively high, even by Western standards, yet anything can be bought in the markets at much lower prices, and the unofficial economy is where most people will buy their consumer goods, where they can afford them. The Bamoun people of Cameroon, comprising one of the largest ethnic groups in Cameroon, do not figure in our data on managers for that country. This is because they are the artists and craftspeople who work and exercise their entrepreneurial skills largely outside the official economy. These examples of creativity and entrepreneurship often go unused in organizations in the official sectors.

### Humanism and collective responsibility

High levels of humanism, collective responsibility, community self-help and mutual assistance are manifest within many African societies. The collectivism of Japanese society has been successfully captured by corporations in Japan that are in tune with and grow out of the wider societal culture (Jackson, 2002a). However, Dia (1996) offers the 'disconnect' thesis (see Chapter 1) to suggest that organizations in sub-Saharan Africa are largely out of tune with the wider society in which they were implanted. In South Africa Mbigi (1997), among others, has been instrumental in developing the *ubuntu* movement that suggests a closer integration of African corporations with traditional African societal values and culture, while Koopman (1991) provides an indication of how this might be achieved in practice. Many larger organizations in South Africa have introduced programmes based on this concept (Swartz and Davies, 1997), although there is little evidence to suggest from our current study that this has been directly sustained in South Africa or is travelling up the continent. Yet similar sentiments have been vocalized in interviews with managers in other countries. The example of Afriland First Bank in Cameroon is instructive in this respect (see Chapter 10). Evidence also abounds on the margins of the informal economy of the mutual self-help aspects of humanism and collectivism in the many credit unions that exist throughout Africa (Barratt-Brown, 1995). While banks such as Afriland are beginning to work with communities in providing services that dovetail with such mutual help schemes, and political motivation has aided other such self-help movements such as 'Harambee' in Kenya (Wallis, 1994)

### Cultural heterogeneity

There is richness of cultural diversity and the potential for substantial creative inputs into organizations. A body of literature on cross-cultural management has developed across the world, yet little of this seems to have touched management education in Africa, at least outside South Africa. Even within South Africa, managers in some of the organizations in which interviews were conducted as part of the current study indicate that cross-cultural training was something that was undertaken in 1994 (the year of democratic elections) and is no longer relevant. Yet, often there was a realization that something should be done, particularly with the over-representation of a particular ethnic group (for example, Kikuyu in Davis and Shirtliff in Nairobi: Chapter 11; and Bamileke in Afriland First Bank in Yaoundé: Chapter 10). There is often a defensiveness toward the suggestion that culture affects the way managers manage. To our interview question, 'how does your culture influence the way you manage?' it was not unusual to obtain an immediate reply (before we could explain) that 'I treat everyone the same'.

Barr and Oduro (2001) look at the question of whether ethnic fractionalization gives rise to differentiation of treatment of employees from different ethnic groups in Ghanaian organizations (Table 3.1 provides a measure of ethnolinguistic fractionalization in the African countries included in the current study, and includes Ghana). They found that although earning differential could be attributed to variation in a standard set of workers' characteristics such as education and experience, the largest proportion of the differential is attributable to ethnic fractionalization in the labour market combined with different worker attributes. Hence workers who are related to their employers earn a premium, and there is evidence to suggest discrimination in favour of inexperienced co-ethnic employees.

The implication of this, if generalized to other ethnically fractionalized African countries (see Table 3.1), is that either there is a lack of cultural heterogeneity in any one organization because one particular ethnic group is favoured for recruitment (as in the case of Davis and Shirtliff in Kenya) or that cultural heterogeneity exists at the lower ends of the organization, but at the managerial, decision-making levels, one group is favoured (as is still the general case in South Africa, although legislation is in place to address this: Breakwater Monitor, 2000). Therefore it would seem that ethnic fractionalization is viewed more of a constraint rather than as an opportunity, and culturally diverse inputs are not being obtained. (There are exceptions in South Africa: for example, in the Group Schemes division of Old Mutual, one of the leading insurance and finance groups in the country and one which sees itself as operating within a diversified market, black as well as white managers provide insights and expertise.)

Exclusion politics may well play a role in creating culturally homogenous organizations in Africa. Yet the cross-cultural literature, such as Elron *et al.*'s (1999) study of United Nations peace-keeping forces, and Jackson and Kotze's (in press) study of the South African National Defence Force, suggests that synergies may be developed out of cultural heterogeneity. The basic thesis is that the higher the level of heterogeneity of cultures (in terms of ethnolinguistic fractionalization, the higher the indices: see Table 3.1) the more likely synergies will be developed from the multiple cultural groups. In fact a hybrid culture will develop, as organizational members will find it difficult to return directly to the values of their base culture. The less heterogeneous, the more likely it is that members can return to their base cultures and the less likely they are to develop common synergies.

If this can be applied to whole nations, this may in part provide some explanation of how a diverse country such as Nigeria, with many conflicting interests among its population and cultural groups, can hang together as a nation (Maier, 2000); whereas a country such as Rwanda, which with Swaziland shares the distinction that its boundaries more or less follow the frontiers of its former African kingdom, and may indeed fall outside Davidson's (1992) curse of the nation-state at least in that one respect, can be beset by such apparent ethnic conflict. (De Waal, 1994, repudiated at the time of the genocide the assumption that this was an expression of age-old tribal animosity, and that this was a crime perpetuated by a group of known individuals associated with two extreme political parties, tracing this back to the destruction by the Belgian colonial powers of the original reciprocal relations among the three strata of society with the same language and traditions, the Twa, Hutu and Tutsi: see also de Heusch, 1995.)

### Globalization and cultural crossvergence

Related to the level of cultural heterogeneity in African countries is the globalizing influence first of foreign trade (albeit often through slave-trading), then of colonization, and then through the neo-colonialism of 'modernization'. This has brought a whole number of different cultural influences to Africa, although not always on favourable terms. Institutions still reflect their colonial inheritance and are indicative of the 'disconnect' thesis (Dia, 1996). Management education mostly reflects the American MBA content and represents cultural imperialism. For example, it is instructive that not only management textbooks used in Anglophone Africa reinforce this content, but management books on Africa often begin with Anglo-America management theory, and then see how it can be applied to the African context (the classic scholarly book by Blunt and Jones, 1992, is an example of this, and more so the recent yet less erudite book edited by Waiguchu *et al.*, 1999).

These globalizing influences have had the effect of introducing another layer of cultural heterogeneity, both directly through a colonizing and then a settler population (particularly in South Africa, Zimbabwe, and less so in Kenya), and then a modern expatriate population; and indirectly through literature, education and training. Elsewhere, these types of influences have brought benefits through hybridization of management systems that are highly adaptive to their context, for example in the so-called K-type management systems in South Korea which borrow from both Japanese and American as well as indigenous Korean influences (Chen, 1995), and the hybrid forms developed through crossvergence of Chinese and Anglo-American influences in Hong Kong (Priem *et al.*, 2000). In India (Rao, 1996) an approach to human resource development is providing a synthesis of Western and Indian influences (see also Chapter 1: for a more detailed discussion see Jackson, 2002b).

So, if there are opportunities and positive aspects of the African context, why are organizations not making more of these? Explanations may be found in the way exogenous factors interact with endogenous ones: particularly in the way that uncertainty is perceived and managed.

## Understanding and managing uncertainty

Figure 3.1 indicates a relationship between endogenous and exogenous factors through managers' perceptions of environment constraints and opportunities, but also through organizational roles and how these relate to organizational stakeholders.

Here we are concerned with the nature of management perceptions of environment constraints and opportunities, particularly in the way that uncertainty is seen, and is managed through management actions. We believe this is a key issue in the relationship between endogenous and exogenous factors, and in the way managers act towards their environment. This has its antecedents in cultural factors.

### Environmental uncertainty and locus of control

Two of the environmental aspects discussed by Kanungo and Jaeger (1990) in connection with developing countries, *high uncertainty* and *external locus of control*, are particularly relevant. Uncertainty affects management in African countries, and the level of perceived control that managers have over their environment affects their responses and inputs into the environment. In looking at the responses of organizations to environmental factors, it is difficult to separate these two aspects, particularly as the latter has been seen in the cross-cultural literature as being influenced by culture (Smith *et al.*, 1994). We deal first with high uncertainty in the African context.

### The role of institutions in uncertainty

Utomi (1998) describes a situation in Nigeria where companies are reluctant to make many decisions between October and March. This is because the government's budget process creates a major source of uncertainty concerning aspects such as tariff changes. The outcome of the budget due on 1 January, which may be delayed as late as March may render a late year business decision unfruitful. For example, by October companies become reluctant to open letters of credit to import raw materials from abroad, as the goods may not arrive before January. The ensuing budget could ban the particular commodity's importation, in which case the company would have to bear the loss; or, the custom duty could be increased making the final product too expensive. It could also happen that tariffs on the final product are lowered so that local production of that particular product becomes uncompetitive. Utomi (1998) identifies the main problem as a weakness of institutions in post-colonial societies (largely through the disconnection between colonial institutions and colonized societies, and more latterly as a consequence of a post-colonial inheritance, the expropriation of the state for private gain rather than serving the needs of civil society).

The role of institutions in society is to reduce uncertainty by establishing agreed-upon rules that, for example, reduce the costs of transactions. He quotes North (1990: 54) in saying 'the inability of societies to develop effective, low cost enforcement of contracts is the most important source of both historical stagnation and contemporary underdevelopment in the Third World'. An example is the enforcement of property rights in courts of law. If there is uncertainty about the ability of a business to enforce such rights, as there are no stable rules about rights of property, and no effective and agreed upon way of enforcing such rights, this may lead to uncertainty in business transactions in the ability of an organization to deliver on its promises. Such uncertainty through weak institutions often gives rise to favouring in-groups (cronyism) or favouring those who are prepared to pay (corruption). Organizational responses to this type of uncertainty may vary, and Utomi (1998) argues that these responses also input into the environment. He provides the example of a bank that chooses in its strategy to make ethical conduct central to delivering quality service to customers. Its visionary leadership sees a weakening of service delivery by banks where 'playing according to the market' by making questionable payments has resulted in the corruption of bank staff and a lowering of morale of others. This policy can then be a major advantage as the environment changes and customers turn to what they perceive as the more reliable banks. This can then influence regulations as stronger institutions evolve to maintain these standards of ethics in banking.

From a perspective of management behaviour and decision-making, the response towards this type of environment by managers working to lower the level of uncertainty in a situation of movable and shifting rules of the game is governed by the extent to which they can influence events external to them (locus of control). Other influential factors might include: the extent to which they want to play the game as they see it (e.g. join the ruling party, pay the bribe); the extent to which they want to change the game (as the above banking example illustrates); or, the extent to which they want to opt out of the game (e.g. do not pay the bribe, or do not ingratiate one's self with the ruling party). These choices again may be a result of the extent to which a manager feels able to influence external events (locus of control, of which the second choice may require an internal locus of control, and the first an external locus of control). They may also result from the particular relationship of the subsidiary company with the parent company (for example, Guinness's policy of not dealing with transaction in a pragmatic way: Chapter 10).

### The role of culture in the perception of uncertainty

Although this area has been studied in the cross-cultural literature within major studies across countries, information on African countries is quite sketchy. As well as *locus of control* (Rotter, 1966; Smith *et al.*, 1995), high *uncertainty avoidance* (Hofstede, 1980a) is mentioned as a cultural factor in developing countries as a whole (Kanungo and Jaeger, 1990), and Africa specifically (Kiggundu, 1988; Blunt and Jones, 1992). Smith *et al.* (1995) also describe an association of internal–external locus of control with Schwartz's (1994) dimension of *mastery* over the environment versus *harmony* with the environment.

Both internal locus of control and mastery over the environment depict a perception that individuals can affect the environment and can control events by their own efforts. Of the three African countries included in Smith *et al.*'s (1995) study, Ethiopia and Nigeria are seen as having somewhat less of an internal locus of control than Western countries and Japan, yet not such an external locus as most other South and East Asian countries including China, Korea and Hong Kong. Yet Burkina Faso is seen to have a very high external locus of control, with a big difference with its near neighbour Nigeria. The only African country included in Schwartz's (1994) study, Zimbabwe, provides one of the higher scores for mastery and lowest scores for harmony. This may provide an indication that African countries have widely different cultures, or, because of a suggested association (from Smith *et al.*'s 1995, study) with GDP, this may reflect Zimbabwe's relative economic prosperity at the time the data were collected. Within Smith *et al.*'s (1995) samples, Burkina Faso is very poor, and its people may well feel a general helplessness towards the environment.

An unrelated cultural dimension, *uncertainty avoidance* (Hofstede, 1980a) may provide further insights into the way uncertainty is perceived by managers in Africa. Uncertainty avoidance refers to a preference for structured situations versus unstructured situations. The dimension runs from being comfortable with flexibility and ambiguity to a need for extreme rigidity and situations with a high degree of certainty. From our discussion above about the high level of uncertainty within the African context, it seems logical to assume that if Africans indeed do share a cultural propensity towards high uncertainty avoidance, there will be a major difficulty in managing such a high level of uncertainty. Hofstede's (1980a) original results are unfortunately not very helpful on this.

His results for West and East Africa, both of which combine data from small sample of countries, indicate a moderate to low uncertainty avoidance, whereas the South African (all white) sample indicates a lower uncertainty avoidance on a par with New Zealand, Canada and the USA. More recently a study by Thomas and Bendixen (2000) in South Africa using a version of Hofstede's instrument indicates differences among cultural groups for uncertainty avoidance. Although their results are similar to Hofstede's (1980a) for South Africa as a whole (their uncertainty avoidance score is 48 against Hofstede's 49, apparently reflecting the lower scores for white English, white Afrikaans and Coloured) their black Xhosa group has a high score of 76, their black Zulu group a score of 59, and their black Sotho group a much lower 47. This may indicate that in South Africa, black African groups have a higher intolerance of uncertainty than white and coloured groups.

Unfortunately they provide little or no explanation of this and the differences among the black groups (leaving one to doubt the construct validity of this result; they also do not explain how they arrived at culture level results simultaneously for culture group, gender group, and country), particularly in view of their parallel result for perceived management effectiveness, which unfortunately now lumps all black groups together (again, another level of analysis), and shows no significant differences among Asians, Black African, Coloureds and Whites.

Wentzel (1999) provides a more rigorously reported study in South Africa among thirteen different cultural groups with good sample sizes (from 1,006 for Afrikaans to 23 for Swazi). With a maximum uncertainty avoidance score of 69 and a minimum score of 28, the order of these groups from low to high uncertainty avoidance is: Afrikaans, Shangaan, English, Tswana, Coloured, Ndebele, Asian, South Sotho, Xhosa, North Sotho, Swazi Zulu, Venda. This still supports the general assumption that black Africans in South Africa are less tolerant of uncertainty than white managers. (Wentzel, 1999, however, does not provide any explanation based on the culture of each group within his study, particularly why Shangaan managers should have a lower uncertainty avoidance and why Venda should have a higher score.)

While Kanungo and Jaeger (1990) do not offer any explanation of why a high uncertainty avoidance in developing countries may be important in managing the uncertain environment, Blunt and Jones (1992) provide the basis of an explanation by linking it to organizational cultural characteristics of conservatism, depersonalization, isolationism and subordination. All these characteristics are concerned with the removal of one's persona from the work organizational context, to depersonalize the work situation, to keep one's head down without risking making decisions and accepting things as they are. They further discuss the instrumental regard that African workers have for their work, with low involvement and regarding it purely as a means to an end (we discuss this further in Chapter 7).

This may therefore be regarded as reinforcing the 'disconnect' thesis (e.g. Dia, 1996). If work organizations are at variance to the overall societal cultures within the communities from which employees and managers are drawn, it could be assumed that these respondents to questionnaires will present a higher uncertainty avoidance (that is, protecting themselves by disengaging). Again, uncertainty avoidance may well reflect characteristics of post-colonial management systems rather than cultural values of Africans per se. This being the case, the uncertainty within the African environment may be difficult to manage through post-colonial management systems, because the system (high uncertainty avoidance) and the environment (high uncertainty) are incompatible.

Rather than management systems being perpetuated that have an effect of disengaging managers from addressing issues presented by their environment (that is, assuming a position of high uncertainty avoidance – or avoiding the uncertainty in the environment), it may be more constructive to view the environment from a stakeholder position.

## Organizational roles and stakeholders

Viewing sub-Saharan Africa, its resources and people simply as a business opportunity, with its constraints and risks is perhaps a restrictive perception that may well be coloured by an instrumental locus of human value (see Chapter 1) with an emphasis on one stakeholder (often foreign shareholders), and therefore seen from a particular cultural perspective (or in the case of the permeation of Western management education, the adoption of Western values that are then applied to the perception of the sub-Saharan African context). In order to more fully understand the overall context, it is relevant to take a stakeholder approach. With the poor fit between community and institutions (e.g. Dia, 1996) this may be more important in Africa and post-colonial societies in general than in the industrialized high income countries.

An interesting division of eight societal functions of business was proposed by the Battelle project and recounted by Lessem (1989). It distinguishes eight societal functions of business. This suggests that a business organization acts towards its environment in terms of:

- a producer of goods and services to fulfil the needs of customers
- an employer to create and sustain jobs offering employment in both quantity and quality
- an economic unit to create and distribute wealth

- a market partner to participate in the maintenance and development of a healthy economy
- a social partner to participate in the maintenance and development of a healthy society
- an innovator to create new and better products, processes and services for particular customers and society in general
- an organizer to maintain and develop order, including orderly relationships amongst people in society.

Public sector organizations may also fulfil a number of these functions, and these may provide a useful classification to employ when describing both public and private sector organizations' relationships with the sub-Saharan African environment. These different roles that organizations might perform are inextricably linked with the stakeholders' perceptions of the organization. Hence consumers may see the organization as a provider of goods or services; employees and the local community as a provider of jobs; shareholders as a means of creating wealth; government as a means of developing the economy; governments and local community in developing a stable and healthy society; customers in providing innovation and better products or services; and governments and civil society in developing orderly relations among members of the society (see Figure 3.1).

Again this highlights the antithesis between an instrumental view of organizations as addressing the objectives of the executive, perhaps in maximizing profits; and a humanistic view of organizations serving the ends of multiple stakeholders. For example, in Chapter 12 we look at how some multinational companies in South Africa try to reflect the interests of shareholders and maintain a competitive position by reducing staff. The implication of staying in business is to minimize its impact in the local community as an employer. Contributing less to the local community in this respect is balanced by funding community projects. Yet while attempting to manage an uncertain environment, a company such as this may lose connection with local stakeholders. As we will discuss in the next chapter, a lack of involvement in decision processes with the various stakeholders may actually diminishing an organization's ability to manage within an uncertain environment.

## Implications for managers in Africa

It is unfortunate that management education and development in Africa has been caught up in a lack of recognition of the differences between the environment of sub-Saharan Africa and, say, the United States. Managers having undergone MBA-type training perhaps have to unlearn principles that work in one environment, but not in the environment in which they have to manage. From the account of managers' relationship with the African environment, and the issue of managing uncertainty, we can point to the following competency areas:

- an understanding of the relationship between endogenous factors and the perception of exogenous factors, particularly in the way culture and stakeholder values might influence the way the environment is seen and acted towards;

- an ability to capture within organizations the entrepreneurial traditions, flair and expertise;
- an ability to capture within organizations the wider societal collectivism and humanism through mutual self-help;
- an ability to develop synergies from cultural heterogeneity;
- an understanding of the different cultural influences of management systems in Africa and how to develop effective hybrid systems from these different influences that are highly adaptive to the African environment, rather than blindly adopting Western principles of management;
- a capacity to manage the relationship between uncertainty and uncertainty avoidance responses by being aware of what motivates uncertainty avoidance, and how perceptions of uncertainty are formulated;
- a capacity to include the different stakeholders in the decision process in order to be more in touch with the environment, and to manage it through making use of multiple perceptions.

Through the remaining chapters we will return to many of these aspects, in order to shed more light on them. We will particularly return to them in Chapter 8 when we focus more specifically on management development issues. We now turn in Chapter 4 to the final competency area on our list; that of including stakeholders in the decision processes of organization.

## Note

1   The theoretical approach that we have tried to build up throughout this book is that of the organizational systems being negotiated reality among various individual players as part of different cultural (and gender, age, professional, etc.) groups, within relationships of power. The systems approach (typified by Katz and Kahn, 1978) provides a basic concept of open systems theory but reifies the subject as object (see, for example, Townley, 1994). The Action approach (typified in the critical writing of Silverman, 1970), based on phenomenological principles, argues that organizations are negotiated reality among the different actors, but tends to downplay the role of power relations (as indeed does cross-cultural theory). This aspect is best informed by the classical literature on ideology, particularly from the writings of Marx, although Larrain (1979) provides a wider view of the historical roots of this concept which Putnam (1973) defines as 'a life-guarding system of beliefs, values and goals affecting political style and action', whereas Marx sees this more as a false consciousness arising from the hegemony of a dominant economic class. Our position here is that within power relations in post-colonial Africa there are dominant ideologies that are propagated, through education, the world press, etc., regarding the African situation, relations in organizations, and relations between organizational actors and community which result from and are affected by cross-cultural dynamics. The intellectual and management quest is to understand the different perceptions within these relationships, to take account of these different perceptions among the stakeholders concerned, and to thus understand and develop the ensuing (hybrid) organizational systems operating within these power relations, within different levels of cross-cultural interactions, within the context of Africa.

Chapter 4

# Managing decision-making in organizations in Africa

Most Africans favour absolute obedience to authorities. In Africa, authority is related to formal status rather than to knowledge and specialized skills.

(Beugré and Offodile, 2001: 538)

. . . participatory discourse and practices are part of a wider attempt to obscure the relations of power and influence between elite interests and less powerful groups such as . . . employees of organizations . . . giving the 'sense' and warm emotional pull of participation without its substance, and are thus an attempt to placate those without power and obscure the real levers of power inherent in the social relations of global capitalism.

(Taylor, 2002: 122, 125)

It was . . . in societies without chiefs or kings where African democracy was born and where the concept that the people are sovereign was as natural as breathing. And this is why in traditional Africa, the rights of the individual never came before the rights of the community.

(Williams, 1987: 170)

This chapter is about managing organization decision processes, through control and value systems. Managerial decision-making involves a combination of:

1   Organizational governance which structures the decision processes and determines who has access to these processes through power relations that involve the distribution of resources, including intangible ones such as information and career opportunities;
2   Human values, which influence the way people relate to the environment (see Chapter 3) and the way they relate to other people, as we explored in Chapter 1, concerning the perceived value of a person in terms of instrumentalism and humanism; and
3   Cognitive approaches, or the way problems are perceived, the search for information, the construction of alternatives, and the way choice is made among those alternatives.

All of these aspects are interconnected; either directly or indirectly and in part or in whole are influenced by culture, cross-cultural differences, and intercultural interactions (Figure 4.1). We explored in Chapter 3 the complexes of the African environment and the need to manage uncertainty. This can only be done successfully with effective and appropriate decision processes in place within the organization. The current chapter is therefore immediately connected with the previous one, with an assertion that it is difficult to understand the complexities of the environment without the involvement of different stakeholders. It may also be difficult to manage this uncertainty by employing concepts and principles of governance borrowed from Western management, through Western management education, and by employing Western practices. This is not to say that these principles must be rejected, but as we have already discussed in Chapter 1, they should be set within their cultural context, and be used together with other 'ideal type' management systems to develop effective hybrid forms of decision processes and mechanisms.

The way decision processes operate in organizations is also closely linked with leadership and management styles, the subject of the next chapter. The type of leadership and management styles adopted by managers will be linked to the type

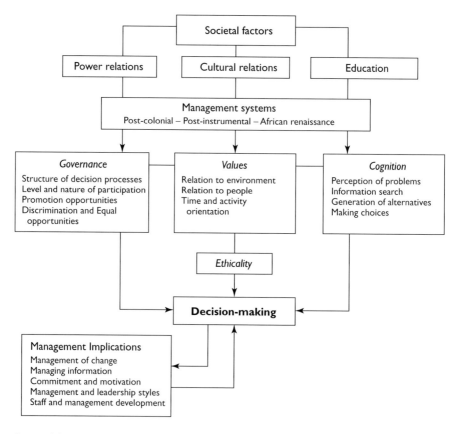

*Figure 4.1* Management decision-making in Africa: governance, values, cognition.

of governance within the organization. Hence if governance is autocratic, one could expect to see autocratic management styles. It is difficult to separate the person from the system. Yet sometimes there may be incongruence (particularly moving down the ranks) between a manager's values and the way he or she is expected to manage. We explore the relationship between control systems and management styles more fully in Chapter 5. In the current chapter we are more concerned with the decision process itself, and its three main aspects: organizational governance and how this relates to management and control systems, and to access of stakeholders to the decision process; values that operate within these systems that give rise, for example, to the ethicality of decisions; and cognitive processes that may differ across cultures.

These three aspects are inextricably linked with societal factors including power relations, cultural relations and educational influences. The way these aspects relate to 'ideal type' management systems has been discussed in the previous chapters. Cultural aspects play a key part in many respects. This includes, at inter-continental level, the relative influence of post-colonial, Western and African approaches; and the effect of education, including management education. At the inter-ethnic level it can also include the extent to which one ethnic group predominates within the organization, and the extent of exclusiveness and discrimination. It is to the issue of governance and control systems that we now turn.

## Governance and control

The decision-making process itself involves making sense of ambiguity and taking risks (Jackson, 1993). The first aspect is by necessity historical. The decision-maker is working on the information available about what has already happened; or, as may be the case with perceptions of the African environment as discussed in Chapter 3, what is assumed to have happened or is happening. The second aspect is future oriented (see, for example, Brady, 1990). A risk is being taken because one is applying a perspective based on (often assumed) knowledge of the past, and projecting this to what might happen in the future if a certain course of action is followed. The process itself takes place in a context. The immediate context is the organization, and the organization is situated in its environment. The overall governance of the organization is important to the way decisions are made as it influences how ambiguity is made sense of, and who makes sense of it, as well as the basis upon which risks are taken: that is, who benefits from the outcome of the decision, and how do they benefit?

For example, organizations that are control-oriented (Chapters 2) may restrict access to the decision process, by closely guarding information and not communicating openly to people lower down the hierarchy. Decisions may only benefit the elite of the organization, but they may be more risky because information that could have been obtained from other parts of the organization has not been sought and used. (This aspect of decision-making is illustrated for example by Vroom and Yetton's decision tree: see, for example, Vroom 1973; it is discussed in detail in Jackson, 1993.) This may be more typical of post-colonial systems of management. Those organizations that are perhaps more calculative, encouraging consultation and seeking information from other parts of the organization, and using this to reduce risks in decision-making may be more typical of post-instrumental (Western) management systems. Tactical participation may encourage staff lower down the hierarchy to implement decisions, and foster ownership of decisions, but may still have limited overall benefits for such staff and their wider communities.

Wider stakeholder participation of decision-making may further reduce the risks of making bad decisions, and broaden out the base of beneficiaries of decision outcomes. This type of decision-making requires a completely different type of organizational governance where the position of elites is not threatened. For post-colonial and post-instrumental management systems, this may pose major threats to governing elites.

As we suggested in Chapter 1, there is a tendency in the literature to assume that the post-colonial management system describes management in Africa generally. Certainly the description of high levels of autocracy and bureaucracy (Kiggundu, 1988; Blunt and Jones, 1992) are accounted for by reference to post-colonial systems. Post-instrumental systems may only introduce tactical participation within organizational systems (despite the rhetoric), and African renaissance systems (where they exist in this idealized form) may provide a more humanistic and community based stakeholder participation.

These different levels of autocracy and participation feed into the nature of access to the decision process in organizations. Not only does this involve who is party to decision-making, it also concerns the potential access to organizational decision processes through promotion opportunities, and to organizational resources. Levels of discrimination affect this. This may be based on the power relations in an organization that favour a particular ethnic group, and this may also be based on political affiliation or gender (for the latter see Merrill-Sands and Holvino, 2000).

### Tactical participation: the new tyranny?

Taylor (2002) argues that 'participatory discourse and practices are part of a wider attempt to obscure the relations of power and influence between elite interests and less powerful groups such as . . . employees of organizations' (p. 122). Further, participator discourses serve the purpose of 'giving the 'sense' and warm emotional pull of participation without its substance, and are thus an attempt to placate those without power and obscure the real levers of power inherent in the social relations of global capitalism' (p. 125). He suggests that 'managerialism' is spreading from the private sector in industrialized countries to all kinds of organizations across the globe including state bureaucracies and NGOs in developing countries, with a technocratic view that 'management' is a universal, rational process that can be applied anywhere. Thus participatory management principles and practices developed in the West are being spread to developing countries and to different types of organization (Taylor, 2002).

As we noted in Chapter 1, the Human Relations School tried to correct the overtly exploitative (instrumental) approaches of the earlier stages of industrialization in the West. This had close supervision, and top down authority structures that resulted in worker alienation and collective resistance. Yet Taylor (2002) asserts that the Human

Relations approach has not necessarily replaced earlier approaches, but is used in an opportunistic and contingent way to achieve optimum management results. Hence this does not represent a humanistic perception of the value of people within organizations (see Chapter 1 of the current text), but is still very much within the instrumental paradigm, which sees people as a resource, a means to an end. Our reference to Vroom and Yetton earlier is illustrative of the contingency approach used within Western management. Based on a decision tree they make recommendations about the best 'style' to adopt: autocratic, consultative or participative. This is dependent on: the quality of the decision to be made; the level of acceptability required by subordinates in order to implement the decision; and, the timescale of the decision-making process. Hence, an autocratic style can be adopted if a quick decision is needed (as participation may take a long time), if the full commitment of the workforce is not needed, and if the 'quality' of the decision is not important: that is, if the operating environment is not too complex and does not need a greater understanding involving different stakeholders.

Within the emerging or developing countries of sub-Saharan Africa, it may be appropriate for Western multinational (as well as other) organizations, to talk about (and even practice) participation and employee empowerment. There may be a whole number of reasons for doing this. In South Africa organizations are being encouraged through legislation and incentives to instigate empowerment programmes to involve employees in decision-making, as well as providing opportunities through career development, for people who have been disadvantaged, to have more access to the decision process. Here, some of the more enlightened companies are attempting to blend Western and 'African renaissance' systems while being mindful of commercial considerations. Because of the difficulties of achieving this hybridization, and the lessons that may be learned, it is instructive to consider the attempts of one company to do this.

## Towards hybrid forms of decision-making processes

It is possible to discern the three management systems within this example, and the successes and problems of hybridization. Post-colonial systems are represented as the past: autocratic, conservative and exclusive. Some managers note a hanging on to this past by those who have perhaps benefited from the old systems, with at least one manager reminiscing about how under this system people were at least singing the same song. Attempts at developing more participative and autonomous forms have led to some diversity in how this is achieved and how decisions are made across the organization. Post-instrumental systems are represented by both the apparent commercial consideration of the advantages of introducing empowerment, as well as the apparent tactical levels at which participative decision-making has been introduced; still leaving strategic decisions to be taken at the top. The African renaissance system within this company does go beyond the rhetoric. There is a serious attempt to redress past inequalities of access to decision processes, through broadening out their stakeholder base. Black managers are being encouraged up

## Empowerment and decision-making in Metropolitan, South Africa

Metropolitan's national and international headquarters is situated in an ultra-modern building some 20 km outside Cape Town in the pleasant suburb of Bellville. Visitors arriving at reception are prompted to look at a digital camera lens behind the receptionist, for the company's records for security purposes. On the way to the offices, the visitor is shown past first floor café areas, shops and restaurant, all within a light open lobby area. Architects have created a building in which staff can feel comfortable and secure in their surroundings.

Metropolitan started off life in 1897 when the African Homes Trust Syndicate was established as an informal association helping people to build their own homes. In 1954 this became a mutual insurance company. In 1979 African Homes Trust merged with Metropolitan Life, and in 1986 Metlife was listed on the Johannesburg stock exchange. In 1993 Methold, a black empowerment consortium obtained a 10 per cent stake in Metlife. Later Methold became New Africa Investments Limited (Nail) with a majority 51 per cent holding in Metropolitan. In 1995 the Group launched Metropolitan Health. That same year it obtained a listing on the Namibian Stock Exchange, launching the wholly owned subsidiary Metropolitan Life Namibia the following year. That same year the company launched Metropolitan Botswana. The business of the Commercial Union Group was acquired in 1998, and in 1999 Metropolitan took over the administration business of BankMed. In 2000 the group went through three months merger discussions with Sanlam, another of the major insurance companies in South Africa, which eventually folded after mutual agreement.

In 2001 Nail pursued its interests in the media sector, becoming a listed company, while Metropolitan de-listed. A holding company, New Africa Capital, has been created under which Metropolitan conducts all its different businesses.

Three companies dominate the life insurance market within South Africa. In a recent brand awareness survey by the *Sunday Times* (Johannesburg: Supplement to the *Sunday Times*, 7 October 2001, p. 7) Old Mutual was in first place for brand recognition and customer loyalty, Metropolitan second and Sanlam third.

In an elaborately produced internal publication entitled *A New Dawn*, complete with porcupine quill binding and distributed to all staff, the Group CEO Peter Doyle and Group Chairman Dikgang Moseneke take up the concept of the African renaissance that has been so publicized by South African President Thabo Mbeke. They write:

Metropolitan is at the beginning of a new dawn. A new era in the history of the company. For some time now, the company has been in a state of change. Firstly, Nail has been involved in its own restructuring over the last two years. Then we had the opportunity to enter into merger talks with Sanlam. When the merger was called off, we moved right into the transformation of Metropolitan, including the integration of Nail and Metropolitan. This was the start of Project renaissance. Project renaissance took a long, hard look at Metropolitan, identified its strengths and weaknesses, and also looked at its potential. . . . The word renaissance means a revival or a birth, and today is the day that our revival begins. For Metropolitan, today is the start of something new and something exciting.

The company is trying to create a workplace of enabled and accountable individuals as one manager interviewed said: 'There is a vision of empowerment, everyone employed with 'soulful' work: 'enterprising' and 'innovative' become natural. This will sustain both individuals and the organization. We are working towards this, but we are some way off.' However, the resistance to empowerment is seen by some as a constraint, as a result of baggage from the past. Hence the company is trying to address this through creating a new culture and changing mindsets. The main policy document on this is the above-mentioned publication *A New Dawn*.

Despite these intentions, some managers interviewed see as constraints the lack of information sharing and a lack of involvement in strategic decision-making. As one manager says:

there is a mystery about how we do our business. Things should be open. Managers who are going to implement strategy should be part of strategy making – things shouldn't be a mystery. This inhibits business here. There is a fear that white people's jobs will be flooded by hordes of black people. So people keep information to themselves. Information is power.

Although the company's policies encourage staff to become more 'empowered and entrepreneurial' this does not seem to be directly addressing the gap between implementing strategic decisions and being involved in strategic decision-making.

### Decision-making and the operating culture in Metropolitan

It has already been noted above that there may be a separation between inputting into strategic decision-making and having to implement strategy.

The way decisions are made in an organization is a key feature of its operating culture. Also the levels of control that constrain or facilitate input into the decision process, and the opportunities that different stakeholders have to participate in it, are all factors that make up the operating culture. Equal opportunities are part of this, with the inclusion or exclusion of groups in their access to the decision-making process through promotion opportunities, as well as levels of participation and democracy. These are important element in South African organizations' scrutiny of themselves.

Among the managers interviewed in Metropolitan there is consensus about the way things are in the company, and the way things are going, which was reflected in a recent communication audit undertaken company-wide.

> We had a focus communication audit. Results show a very autocratic style of management, very top down. The chief executive, Peter Doyle, operates in a very transparent way, but the executives around him don't. Therefore most people (80 per cent) don't know what is going on. . . . Certain managers are playing power games, because this is a weapon. The executive floor is seen as hallowed ground. The operating culture is not conducive to doing business in South Africa today. There is recognition that this needs to change. It needs to happen and is slowly doing so. There is a lack of communication which needs to change.

This is reflected in other managers' comments. For example, one manager explains that decisions are

> top down. Very few people would take decisions unless the guy up the top takes those decisions or would approve. There is a job grade division – the decisions a person can take are related to the job grade – for the whole group. There are tight controls on what you can do or not in each job grade. When the whole thing about entrepreneurs came in, there was a debate about how we can let people take their own decisions. There is an intention of entrepreneurship, but not the practice.

So there is recognition of a need to change, and a strong indication of the direction of changes, with the encouragement of entrepreneurship and empowering people, yet the old culture is strong.

Another manager explains:

> There is an open system, but this is not necessarily the way decisions are made. There is still hierarchy and autocracy. Still centrally based,

but there are opportunities to challenge the status quo. There is a need for a new leader, a facilitator leader. There to embrace change, to become a changing agent.

We will return to the question of leadership (an issue that is taken up more fully in Chapter 5). First we will explore a little about where this strong culture comes from, and how it is changing.

One HRM manager explained:

The company has changed significantly over the last four to five years. I struggled to accept and work within the company when I came here from [my last company]. It was very conservative and run by actuaries. They bring the norms and culture. I found it very centralized in decision-making. I initiated the values process – what should we let go of, etc. It wasn't fully accepted by the CEO and I went for a watered-down version. We 'work-shopped' what the values should be. We had a values *indaba* [tribal conference or meeting] and identified ten values. To live these, we discussed what should we do in terms of behaviours. We established a body to get people to live these values, and we could reward people who demonstrated these values. We had quarterly winners and a national champion. There is a legacy of an insurance company. . . . We are still rather centralized, but not as much.

A problem, as some managers pointed out, is the resistance to changing to a more entrepreneurial and empowerment culture. One manager said:

The culture has changed over the last year and a half. We are communicating. We always had a flexible, family culture when we were smaller. But it was always very hierarchical. This is being changed. We are not there yet. Next years we will see if things will change in practice. At the top, the company still has a white male domination. So we can't say they are valuing diversity in this respect. But there are more black representatives at top level. They always say they want participation and input, but they are not using the input of sales staff out there when designing products.

This resistance is reflected in one senior manager's reminiscence of the past:

The company is going through a lot of change – cultural issues and how do we manage. There is confusion as to how we should be doing things. There is a drive towards more decentralization and people taking ownership of their business area. This is working in pockets, but overall coordination isn't working very well. Before, when we were more autocratic, things went more smoothly. People are not singing from the same song.

This attitude is also reflected in some managers' perceptions of the lack of inclusiveness in the decision process. Hence:

it is still a 'boys' club'. So the female component is not encouraged. It is purely still an Afrikaans company – not even English. However they try to change that, it doesn't work. Decisions are still made on the golf club, by some people. Any attempt at changing this is just masking the other activity. [For example] they will bring in an Empowerment Manager, but they will make decisions at a braai [barbeque]. There is a contrast between the reality, and what is stated.

Another manager concurs with this:

The company is very autocratic. We have policy on the grounds that we have to address equity issues, but business decisions override that. The Empowerment Manager has an Employment Equity Committee, but this often gets bypassed. For example, people are being recruited without reference to the committee. . . . The intentions, for example on empowerment are good, but these are being hampered by people and decisions, and how decisions are being made.

However, the culture is not uniform throughout the company. One manager explained:

It is a diversified group. So you have participation to very authoritarian styles of management. My own style is inclusive, and I know that in other divisions, because I deal with the group, there is authoritarianism and people not wanting to take decisions. A move towards a more decentralized organization opens up risk, as there is still a culture of people afraid to take decisions. It will take a while for empowerment to work through.

This is corroborated by another manager who says:

The company has sub-cultures. It is different in different divisions. In Life Division there is a traditional and autocratic culture because of no real transformation. We are closing branches now. Medical and Employee Benefits [division] is more part of the new stream. This

> diversity of corporate cultures isn't a bad thing. But we still need some overriding principles. So we go from the conservative, Life division, to more modern.

This is suggestive of the question of leadership and how this variation across the company is dealt with. One manager who has recently joined the company remarks:

> Based on my limited time with the company, it is a male dominated organization. Information doesn't flow. And decisions are not quick enough. It is very bureaucratic, although a very flat organization. Communication doesn't go anywhere. You find individual pockets of 'lawlessness', because people are doing what they like. There is a culture of non-performance. We encourage non-performance. Problems are not addressed; people are simply moved into other jobs. They don't like letting people go.

(The full case study can be found on www.africamanagement.org)

through the ranks, and issues of empowerment at the lower levels, as well as trying to include different stakeholders, are being addressed. Hence:

> Our stakeholders include our shareholders, our clients, our own people at all levels of the organization, and the communities with whom we do business and from whom we draw our employees.
>
> (From *A New Dawn*)

> Newmet [i.e. the new company] will adopt empowerment policies to assist all the group's stakeholders in maximizing the economic and personal benefits that they derive from the business . . . these empowerment policies will be entrenched in the culture and business processes of the group and will incorporate specific initiatives targeting all those groups who have suffered discrimination.
>
> (From *A New Dawn*)

Yet there is still antagonism between the three different 'ideal type' management systems and how they address the issue of control through governance of the organization. In any organization undergoing such changes, it will take time to work through these.

### Levels of participation

Anther issue that this case raises is that of the level of participation. Taylor (2002, after Armstrong, 1999) proposes that this may happen at four organizational levels:

1   Job level: employees are able to influence decisions regarding how they do their job, and its immediate environment.
2   Management level: employees can influence the planning and allocation of work and other resources.
3   Policy-making level: employees can influence strategic level decisions.
4   Ownership level: employees own the business in part (through equity ownership along with external investors) or in whole (as in a worker cooperative).

Often where participation is being introduced in organizations in Africa, it is at the job level. As we mentioned above, there is much evidence in the literature that autocratic (post-colonial) systems have predominated (e.g. Kiggundu, 1988) and that where Western, 'modern' management and HRM systems are being introduced (e.g. Kamoche, 2000), participation is at what we have called the 'tactical' level, or at job level.

We would argue that each of the three 'ideal type' management systems, would employ different control mechanisms, that would facilitate different levels of involvement, and would encourage different types of management behaviour (Table 4.1).

We further explore these connections, together with findings from our empirical studies, in the context of leadership and management styles in Chapter 5. However, in order to fully understand why such connections exist, it is first necessary to focus on values (Figure 4.1) as a key element in decision-making in organizations.

*Table 4.1* Management systems, governance and decision-making

|  | *Post-colonial* | *Post-instrumental* | *African renaissance* |
|---|---|---|---|
| *Control mechanisms* | Coercive | Remunerative | Normative |
| *Levels of involvement* | Autocratic and bureaucratic | Tactical participation | Stakeholder participation |
| *Managerial behaviours* | Directive/exclusive | Tactical/contingent | Stakeholder/inclusive |
| *Time orientation* | Past (containing/controlling) | Future (doing, achieving) | Present (being) |
| *Decision principles* | Rules, procedures and precedence (deontology) | Results, costs and benefits (teleology) | Stakeholder benefit (respect for persons: past, present and future) |
| *Job performance* | Standardization of jobs and procedures | Encouragement of job autonomy/participation | Development of involvement in strategic decision processes |

## Values in managerial decision-making

Wider societal values, as we have seen in Chapter 3, such as locus of control and uncertainty avoidance may affect the way managers relate to their environment. Chapter 1 focused on the way managers may relate to and value people in organizations, in terms of instrumentalism and humanism. Deontology and teleology reflect managers' orientation towards human activity and how this relates to concepts of time, particularly in terms of past, present or future orientations, as well as the way they value people. For example, Lane *et al.* (1997) delineate cultural differences in terms of both time orientation and activity orientation. A past orientation may relate to a respect for tradition and proven ways, basing decisions on precedence and the need to maintain continuity. A present orientation may relate to current realities and spontaneous reactions to situations and change. This may reflect an orientation of 'being'. A future orientation may represent a longer-term approach, and an anticipation of change, taking a more proactive approach to decision-making and change. In Lane *et al.*'s (1997) terms, this may also reflect a 'doing' orientation involving striving for achievement, and an emphasis on performance and objective seeking.

We suggest that colonial (and perhaps post-colonial) management systems reflect a past-orientation based on deontological decisions; post-instrumental or Western systems reflect a future, objective and performance seeking orientation; and 'African' (if not an African renaissance) management systems reflect in part a state of being, but also referring to the past in terms of continuity with the past, as well as looking towards future benefits for a wider stakeholder base (rather than the narrow stakeholder/shareholder perspective of post-instrumental, teleological systems).

The two aspects of decision-making, making sense of ambiguity (historical) and taking risks (future oriented) may also reflect the type of values inherent in the decision-making process. An emphasis on the historical may imply a deontological approach (decisions are based on pre-set principles), while an emphasis on the future may imply a teleological decision approach (decisions are based on projections about likely outcomes). Pre-set principles may include laws, rules, company regulations, codes of practice, or particular philosophical principles (Kant's *categorical imperative* is the most cited example in Western literature on deontological ethical decision-making: see for example, Jackson, 2000). This may be the basis of decision-making in management systems that reflect a high level of bureaucracy. This may enable staff lower down the hierarchy to take decisions within a particular remit, by referring to a set of regulations. This is one way of reducing risk, where there is a relatively low level of uncertainty in the operating environment. This may well have been typical of colonial systems of governance. As we discussed in Chapter 1, this type of decision-making in the public sector led to a standardization of functions and low transferability of skills, and thus restricted the competency base of staff, and did not equip them for managing in a complex, uncertain, modern economy (Picard and Garrity, 1995; Carlsson, 1998).

Projections of likely outcome may be based on cost–benefit analysis in the general management literature (utilitarianism is the most widely cited principle in the Western literature on teleological ethical decision-making, which is based on a projection of a decision having the greatest good for the greatest number of people: Bentham, 1789/1970, in Brady, 1990). Although many Western companies have codes of practice, it is likely that decision-making predominantly is based on teleological projections about the likely outcome. This is the whole basis, for example of systems theory (e.g. Katz and Kahn, 1978) where organizations are goal seeking. Decisions, logically, are based on the contribution to the attainment of objectives. The consideration of what organizational objectives teleological decision-making actually serves is based on executive perceptions of the mission or strategic goals, which stakeholders are considered relevant or important, and who is (whose perceptions and aspirations are) included in the decision process.

## Ethics and decision-making: Shell in Nigeria

Whether decision-making is deontologically or teleologically based, they also contain within them an ethical element. This may range from a manager deciding to take a day off sick when not really ill, or using organizational material or time for personal use (Jackson, 2001), through to the type of decisions made by Shell in Nigeria concerning its relationship with the local community and the government (Hendry, 2000). Decision-making in organizations invariably involve an implication for people. They involve decisions about the relative importance of stakeholders, which stake-holders to include in the decision-making process, and the likely implications for each set of stakeholders.

The main focus of oil production in Nigeria is in the Delta region, one of the poorer areas of the country, and home to the Ogoni people, as well as around 20 other ethnic minority groups (we have mainly followed the account of Hendry, 2000, but also see the interesting account by Maier, 2000). These people appear to have been excluded from positions of power, and even victimized by members of dominant ethnic groups. Not only have they benefited least from the oil revenue, they have also had to suffer the environmental disruption that this has entailed. After 35 years of production the region was still without water, electricity and hospitals. Shell had done very little in terms of contributing to local well-being, or even jobs. Oil spills were frequent, contaminating land and rivers and having major consequences for subsistence farming and fishing. Pipelines passed over ground through villages exacerbating the effect of spills. Pipes were old and often corroded, with Shell being slow to replace with new pipelines. Shell also seemed to provide inadequate clean-up, using burn-off methods that left residue, or burying crude in the ground. Apart from spills, the main focus of opposition to Shell was gas flaring. Some gas flares were close to villages and had been burning non-stop for 30 years, leaving major pollution problems such as acid rain, quantities of methane and $CO_2$ that were a threat to health.

The opposition to this came to a head in the early 1990s. This was urged on by Ken Saro-Wiwa and the Ogoni elders drawing up a bill of rights aimed at the government and demanding autonomy for the region (the Nigerian government were major shareholders in SPDC, the operating company set up by Shell to exploit oil in the region). With no response either from the Nigerian government or Shell, a major demonstration against Shell ensued in October 1992. Police shot 80 demonstrators. Hostility grew with attacks and sabotage against staff and property. This was followed by brutal attacks on Ogoni villages, with homes destroyed, thousands beaten or detained and hundreds executed. Shell publicly went along with the government line that the police were quelling violence between the Ogoni and neighbouring people.

Despite Ken Saro-Wiwa's commitment to non-violence, he and other leaders were arrested in May 1994 and sentenced to death. Despite widespread international outcry, they were hanged. Shell took the line that they had no business in Nigeria's legal affairs and therefore should keep out of it. They put in a plea of clemency to the President, but did not challenge the legal process. They were condemned for this by Greenpeace, and Amnesty International. Shortly after that Shell announced a new commercial joint venture with the Nigerian Government for a liquefied gas project.

Although Shell committed itself to principles of fair trial, when the cases of nineteen other Ogoni leaders came up for trial, they continued to argue for non-interference. By the end of the 1990s Shell had doubled its spending on community projects to US$40 million a year, but was still subject to acts of protest, sabotage and kidnap, and had not resumed production in Ogoniland.

During this time, Shell had argued in its defence that reinvestment of oil revenues back into the region was the responsibility of the government, and stated that they had applied US$20–40 million a year to community projects, although they were under no moral obligation to do this. A high percentage of oil spills had been due to sabotage. They further argued that they had been the victim of changing international standards, and of inappropriate expectations of environmental standards in the Nigerian context. The pipelines and gas flares, they say, were considered acceptable when first installed. Maintenance is made difficult and dangerous because of local hostility. Internationally they also point to their minority stake in SPDC and to the independence of Shell operating companies. Further, they had little control, because they could not implement anything without the agreement of the Nigerian government majority shareholder and their financial contribution. Defending its position over the Saro-Wiwa case, they said it would be wrong to interfere in the legal processes of a sovereign state, or in Nigerian politics. If they pulled out of Nigeria it would mean the loss of many jobs, and the sound business practices and money spent on community projects would be lost.

The dilemma for Shell was how to manage different interests, both commercial and community based. It had to manage criticism from the international community as well as from the Ogoni people. It had to protect workers and property from sabotage, and it had to protect its position in Nigeria against its competitors, and against threats from the Nigerian President to nationalize SPDC.

Making ethical decisions, we have argued (after Allinson, 1993, who argues that it is a respect for persons), is about the inclusion of stakeholders. It was clear in this case that the main community stakeholders were excluded from the decision process, nor given much consideration in terms of the costs and benefits for them. Shell, like many other multinational corporations, publishes a code of conduct (General Business Principles: given as an appendix in Hendry, 2000). This represents a deontological approach in establishing preset rules of decision-making and conduct. The fact that for a company like Shell working in Nigeria it is difficult to adhere to these rules, may be because such codes of conduct or codes of ethical behaviour go against the essentially teleological perspective of post-instrumental management systems. Results are more important that rules (see Brady's, 1990, discussion of rules and results in ethical decision-making).

### Ethics across cultures

Corporate ethical decision-making has become a major issue in corporate America, and codes of ethics proliferate. Jackson (2000) argues that American multinational companies have mainly driven this tendency in other areas such as Europe. It would seem that the use of published codes of ethics is largely, although perhaps not entirely, a function of public relations both externally towards customers, and internally towards corporate identity. The cross-cultural literature on management ethics is growing. One of the aspects that this literature explores is the extent to which ethics is universal (based on principles that can be applied in any culture, and transcends cultural values), or is culturally relative (the judgement of the ethicality of a decision can only be based on the values within the particular culture). When an African manager employs a family member, in preference to advertising in the job market and recruiting a stranger based on a set of competencies that match the job description, Western managers may protest amid cries of nepotism. Yet it may be more logical to recruit someone you know, where it is possible to consult community leaders or family elders who can put pressure on a recruit who proves to be recalcitrant (Mutabazi, 2002).

The debate on cultural relativism versus ethical universalism may be academic in view of managing in the African context. A more useful approach may be the one taken here: that it is necessary to include diverse cultural groups and interests within the decision process in order to arrive at appropriate and effective decisions. For example, a Western company may arrive in Africa with 'universalistic' ideas about the way staff should be recruited. By including stakeholders within the host community, it may be possible to include other ideas about what may be ethical, appropriate, effective, as well as meeting some of the aspirations of community members.

In Chapter 1 we have already discussed the humanism of African cultures, and that it is this that may distinguish Western instrumental approaches to decision-making from African renaissance approaches. For example, Wiredu (1992) discusses this humanistic morality in connection with Akan (of Ghana) thought. The Akan saying *Onipa na obia* (it is a human being that has value) denotes that all value derives from human interest, and that human fellowship is the most important of human needs; and, indeed a human being is part of a social whole.

We argue therefore that African values, and concepts of morality are based on the primacy of the implicit value of human beings, as an end in itself, not as a means to an end. 'Being', rather than doing, is important. Although human society is linked to the past, this is not that prescribed rules are fixed as a means of containing and controlling (Table 4.1). Future orientation is linked to respect for the needs of persons (as indicated by Allinson, 1993, in Japanese society). As we summarize in Table 4.1, governance of organizations and the management of decision-making is linked to values. Cultural values provide the link between the different elements of decision-making as indicated in Table 4.1. This is why decision-making, both in terms of process and content, may vary among different national cultures and sub-cultures. These differences can also be understood by reference to our third aspect of decision-making: cognitive approaches.

## Cognition in decision-making across cultures

Not all commentators agree that decision-making varies across cultures. Berry *et al.* (1992) indicate the lack of positive conclusions that can be drawn from the cross-cultural research findings on decision-making. This seems to indicate that there are probably few differences in decision-making styles and methods between different countries. Hence Negandhi (1987: 194) concludes that:

> The convergence in organizational practices in general, and decision-making in particular, is taking place rapidly. This can be seen from the results of our recent study of United States, German, British, Japanese, and Swedish multinational companies. The results showed that United States management practices concerning decision-making are the norms being followed by other nations. Other countries' practices correlated strongly with those of United States practices.

With the strength of cultural hegemony that we discussed in Chapter 2, this is little surprising. Yet we have strongly argued for the crossvergence thesis. Despite a lack of empirical evidence from Africa, there may be some fundamental differences between African approaches and Western approaches to decision-making, not least as we have already seen, in the area of values upon which decisions may be based.

Adler (1991) indicates areas where there may be cultural differences generally in cognitive decision-making processes, by describing five basic steps in decision-making, and their cultural variations. These are:

1   Problem recognition: do managers from different cultures see problems in the same way?
2   Information search: do they gather similar types of information in order to investigate the problem?
3   Construction of alternatives: do they construct the same types of solutions?
4   Choice: do they employ the same types of choosing strategies in order to select a solution from different alternatives?
5   Implementation: do they implement decisions in the same ways?

Adler (1991) tells us that some cultures emphasize solving problems whilst others are more oriented to accepting the situation as it is. So, in the United States managers may see situations more as problems to be solved, whereas Thai, Indonesian or Malaysian managers (and perhaps African managers) are more likely to attempt to accept the situation for what it is. She refers to an example of a supplier who cannot make a delivery on time. The American manager may look for another supplier who could make the delivery. The Malaysian manager, for example, might accept that there will be a delay in the delivery, and therefore the project will be set back a day or two. Situation-accepting managers would not see a problem in this situation; they would accept that they could not change every situation that confronts them. This may also be combined with a belief that fate or God will intervene, and are more likely to attribute cause and effect to external circumstances rather than internal attributes that are within their control (see Chapter 3).

For the next stage in the decision process Adler (1991) refers to Jung's two modes of information gathering: sensing and intuition. The former mode is concerned with the collection of facts relevant to the decision and relies more on induction. The latter mode relies more on holistic images and ideas, and on deductive ways of thinking. Whilst she does not present any evidence to suggest that this may involve a cultural distinction, she does cite the example of the different type of decision-making during the Israeli–Arab war in 1973. The Americans based their assessment of the outcome on the overwhelming number of troops and arms that the Arab forces had; the Israelis based their predictions on strong beliefs and images of the future. Sogolo (1993) indicates that in African ideas of rationality and logic there may not be the kind of distinction made between knowing and believing as there is in Western systems of thought. The concept of evidence may therefore be more intuitive and holistic, also relating to the wider situation, as well as relationships within that situation.

The constructing alternatives stage in the decision-making process is concerned with either looking historically in order to solve problems or to looking for new ideas for the future. Adler (1991) uses the example of the differing attitudes towards selection and training, in order to adapt an organization for new developments like information technology. A (organizational) culture that stresses the changeability and development of individuals may look towards training in order to develop the workforce for the future. A culture which stresses the permanence of human nature may place an emphasis on initial selection: that it is more important to ensure that you select the right people for the job at the beginning, rather than trying to change them afterwards.

This attitude may also be reflected in other areas of decision-making alternatives, particularly in the type of solution offered in order to solve problems: they may be looking to the known and established or looking to alternatives which break new ground and are innovative. We have already discussed the possibility that African cultures may have a respect for the past, while making decisions based on both 'being', and the future benefits to persons, through social relations (Table 4.1).

The choice stage of decision-making involves a number of factors that reflect cultural preferences, and reflects some of the issues of governance and organizational decision process that we have already discussed:

- Are decisions made by individuals or collectively (individualism/collectivism)? Individualist societies such as the United States may see the individual with the primary responsibility to make the final decision. In a collectivist society such as Japan, it is the group or team that makes the decision after much consultation. In organizations in Africa, this may depend on the nature of the predominant management systems, and the level of hybridization.
- At what level of the organization are decisions made (power distance)? In a high power-distance society decisions tend to be made at the top of a specific hierarchy, whereas in a lower power-distance society such as Sweden, it is more likely that worker autonomy schemes such as that initiated in the Volvo Kalmar plant will be prevalent, where decisions are taken at a lower level. Again, this depends on the nature of the hybrid management system in organizations in Africa. As we have previously discussed it also depends on the level of participation (Taylor, 2002). The workers at Volvo were making decisions at the first (job) level, rather than at the higher policy-making or ownership levels.
- Are decisions made quickly or slowly (time orientation)? Some societies are more time conscious than others. Hence North American and Western European business people may often be frustrated by the time taken to make a decision in other cultures. This may be mixed in organizations in Africa. Bureaucracy and hierarchy may slow down the time to make decisions, yet this may often be, in a post-colonial management system, a delay in reaching the decision maker. On the other hand, in many 'developing' countries there may be a short-term perspective on the need to make decisions in order to obtain relatively quick results. Again, this may depend on the nature of hybridization.

- How much risk is considered too much (uncertainty avoidance)? In high uncertainty avoidance cultures, managers may be unwilling to deviate too much from accepted and proven patterns and alternatives in order to contain the amount of risk involved. This also applies to different industries within the same national cultures. For example, high street banking is far less risk taking than, for example, stock exchange securities dealing (see Chapter 3 for a discussion on uncertainty avoidance and risk in Africa).
- Are alternatives considered holistically or sequentially? Managers from some cultures such as China, are more likely to address and solve problems in a more holistic way, rather than in a sequential way that addresses each issue or sub-issue as it arises and attempts to solve it before proceeding to the next. Again, there is evidence that African traditional thought processes may be more holistic and less sequential than Western decision processes (e.g. Ugwuegbu, 2001).

The cultural differences in the implementation stage (Adler, 1991) are largely those already discussed such as whether the speed of implementation is fast or slow, whether responsibility is delegated downwards or managed from the top of the hierarchy, or whether it is a collective or individual responsibility.

## Implications for managers in Africa

There are implications for management and management development (Figure 4.1). Organizational governance and the decision process influence the way change is managed. Participation in change management in Western textbooks refers to providing an opportunity of staff to take ownership of the change process through participation. If Kiggundu's (1988) and Blunt and Jones' (1992) assertions are correct that African cultural groups are high in uncertainty avoidance and high in power distance (in Hofstede's, 1980a, terms), this may be entirely the wrong way to manage the change process in organizations in Africa. First, change ensures high levels of uncertainty. Asking people's views on how that change should be managed can only increase the uncertainty in the situation. Second, power distance refers mostly to the acceptance of inequalities and deference to authority. Participation in such circumstances may only lead to questions about the ability of the manager to manage and provide leadership. However, power distance may be an attribute that may only apply to post-colonial systems, and some indigenous African political/management systems, certainly not all. Perry (1997) points out the problems of applying uncertainty avoidance in the context of Africa. Some commentators such as Blunt and Jones (1992) have suggested a high uncertainty avoidance culture for Africa, whereas Hofstede's (1980a) original but limited study of West, East and South Africa suggests a low to medium uncertainty avoidance. The Chinese Cultural Connection (1987) points to the limited application of this concept in many non-Western cultures, because of the difficulties of the idea of absolute truth in those cultures. Certainly in Chinese culture this is problematic. We have already noted that the truth in African epistemology may differ from Western thought.

There are also important management implications for the way information is handed and communicated in organizations in Africa. The more information is used as a power lever the less it is shared. This also has implications for leadership and management styles, which we will be exploring in the next chapter. Similarly the implications, particularly of participatory management, for commitment and motivation are discussed more fully in Chapter 7.

From the current chapter it is possible to draw some conclusions about the competency areas and capacities that managers either have developed, or need to develop in order to manage appropriately and successfully.

- an understanding of the influence of culture on governance, values and cognitive process that affect decision-making and decision processes in Africa;
- an ability to involve a wider stakeholder base in decision processes at all levels of decision-making (not just at job level), in order to better inform decision-making and improve its quality, and in terms of the potential costs and benefits to different stakeholder groups;
- an understanding of the tactical nature of many current (Western) participatory practices, and a need to transcend these in developing effective hybrid management forms that are able to balance and manage the contradictions among the different 'ideal type' management systems operating in sub-Saharan Africa (the case of Metropolitan may help in trying to understand these antagonisms and the difficulty of their management);
- an ability to assess the different levels of participation within the organization (after Taylor, 2002) and to facilitate discussion and management of decision-making at these different levels;
- an ability to manage the value systems within decision-making, particularly with regard to the ethical content of decisions, and how involvement in the decision process of a wider stakeholder base (from different cultural perspectives and different interests and needs) can facilitate this (the case of Shell in Nigeria may be instructive);
- an understanding of the cognitive process involved in decision-making and how this might vary from culture to culture (after Adler, 1991), in order to both make allowances for such differences, as well as including such differences within the organizational decision process (Chapter 8 discusses developing synergies from culturally diverse teams, which has a relevance here).

We are aware that within this chapter we have only scratched the surface of decision-making in organizations in Africa. Much still needs to be done to explore each element that we have outlined. We have focused mainly on the organizational aspect of decision-making, and have connected this with the governance of organizations. In the next chapter we make connections between issues of governance and control within organizations, and leadership and management styles.

# Chapter 5

# Using appropriate leadership and management styles

> ... the general tone of management in Africa is prescriptive ... often authoritarian, inflexible, and insensitive ...
>
> (Choudhry, 1986: 92, although not quoted in its original but as cited by Blunt and Jones, 1992 and copied blindly by numerous authors ever since)

> Current theories of leadership, and leadership rhetoric, in the West place high value ... on teamwork, empowerment, performance management ... and learning. ... The problem is that the amount of hype surrounding such putative features implies it is a hard sell, even in its place of origin. ... Transformational leadership in the West ... is more a construct of the rhetoric of management consultants than it is the reality of management practice. It seems likely that – as with Coca-Cola – the less the worth of the product to the consumer the more one needs to envelop it in a promotional mystique ... and this helps to disguise its discordance with most of the cultures in which its tenets are applied.
>
> (Blunt and Jones, 1997: 11)

> Coercive powers were generally not employed by the chief to achieve unity. Unity of purpose was achieved through the process of consensus building. In addition, persuasion and appeals, rather than force, were used by the chief and councillors to win over recalcitrant members on an issue.
>
> (Ayittey, 1991: 100)

In this chapter we focus on the nature of management in organizations in Africa in terms of managers' styles and leadership attributes. The need to understand the principles upon which management styles are based, and their appropriateness in the African context is an important issue. The 'ideal type' management systems, and their foundations that we have been working with so far in this text, provide a means of understanding the bases of management principles and practices. This also has important implications for other aspects considered in this text, not least the motivation and commitment of staff (Chapter 7). The Globe Project, one of the most extensive cross-cultural studies of leadership currently being undertaken (including five sub-Saharan African countries: Namibia, Nigeria, South Africa, Zambia and Zimbabwe) defines organizational leadership as 'the ability of an individual to influence, motivate, and enable others to contribute towards the effectiveness and success of the organizations of which they are members' (Project Globe, 1999: 184). Assuming that those whom one seeks to motivate and mobilize towards contributing to organizational effectiveness have different expectations and aspirations depending on their cultural background, appropriateness in leadership and management styles is important. This is a cultural issue.

Yet there are confounding factors that militate against managing appropriately in organizations in Africa. First there is the factor of cultural hegemony. We saw in Chapter 1 that initially through power relations involving direct economic and military force, institutions were imposed on African communities during the colonial era. The remnants of such management systems that were created remain in elements of what we have termed post-colonial management systems. More latterly, with influences from Western multinationals, multilateral agencies and management education, the management system we have described as post-instrumental is often seen as the 'modern' way of managing. This is related to a results orientation where people are viewed as a resource to be used towards executive ends. The inappropriateness of both organizational leadership and management styles is beginning to be challenged in the context of Africa (e.g. Carlsson, 1998; Mutabazi, 2002).

The next confounding factor is that the African context cannot be seen simply as one uniformed culture such that, once discovered, leadership styles can then be suitably adapted. The African context is one of cross-cultural interactions at various levels. This raises the importance of managers first being aware of the cultural values upon which they base their own management principles and those that predominate in their organization. Then, second, it raises the issue of managers having the necessary cross-cultural leadership competencies to be able to manage effectively in a multicultural situation. This does not presuppose that African managers do not have these competencies. It is certain that many have honed these skills through years of practice in managing complex cross-cultural dynamics. It does, however, presuppose that this is not what is being taught to managers within MBA and executive courses throughout sub-Saharan Africa.

## Leadership: the cross-cultural perspective

That the success of leadership styles and management principles are contingent on their cultural appropriateness in any particular societal context is a truism that is widely accepted in the cross-cultural management literature, but seems to have been missed in many MBA curricula and even in recent textbooks about management in Africa. For example, Blunt and Jones (1992, Chapter 4), Ndongko (1999, Chapter 7 in Waiguchu et al., 1999) and Ugwuegbu (2001, Chapter 4) all devote most of their chapters on leadership on recounting Anglo-American theory, describing leadership styles in Africa as 'prescriptive . . . often authoritarian, inflexible, and insensitive' (quoting Choudury, 1986: 93, for example), and stating that there is a need for better leadership in Africa, either explicitly or implicitly providing the Western model rather than referring to the cross-cultural literature.

Before looking at Africa specifically, there is therefore a need to focus on the cross-cultural literature on leadership and management styles in order to provide models for analysis of leadership in Africa in both what exists and what is perceived to be needed. Of course, good cross-cultural theory integrates indigenous approaches (see Chapter 2), as well as the dynamics of cross-cultural leadership. This is the approach we take here.

Jackson (1993) has placed a cross-cultural consideration of leadership within a 3Cs model of Context, Content and Conduct. *Context* is defined as the framework of rules, culture, social structure, and technology within which people live and work. This can be both overt in the structures within which we work and live, and the technologies we use, and covert in the implicit nexus of societal rules that make up what Harré *et al.* (1985) call the social order, which is internalized in the 'deep structure' of the mind. They state, 'It is our conjecture that the structure of the mind and the social order have evolved along precisely these lines [that is, as a control hierarchy] in some kind of co-ordination with the evolution of the structure of language' (p. 27). There is an inexorable link between societal control systems of explicit and implicit rules ('social orders') that are internalized through socialization processes, the 'deep-structure' of the mind, that influence and control our conscious awareness that determine our behavioural routines, and indeed is reflected in the language we use to describe things (Harré *et al.*, 1985). This is illustrated in Durkheim's (1915/1971) account of totemism, which sees the social order being consolidated by both the same words used to describe the clan and the (religious) totem (he draws on the social anthropology of the day relating to small-scale societies around the world), and ceremonies used to socialize members in venerating both totem and social unit.

We have already considered the environmental context of sub-Saharan Africa in Chapter 3. We are more concerned here with the 'deep structure' particularly of the cultural context that may be quite different from country to country, and from society to society. It is likely that if the implicit aspect of this is conceptualized as social control/deep structure, then the societal culture in which a person was socialized is more likely to be an overriding and enduring factor no matter what organization or type of industry he or she works in. Hofstede's (1980a) research within IBM across some fifty countries pointed to the overriding nature of national culture over organizational culture. Also, the less the similarity or compatibility between the organizational 'culture' and the societal culture within which a person is socialized, the less likely it is that the former will exert an implicit or internalized control on the person, and be associated with the 'deep structure' (implicit rules that guide a person's actions) of the mind.

*Content* can be defined as the perceptions, motivations, attitudes and objectives of individuals that are prerequisite to acting in a particular way. These aspects, which are part of the person, have been acquired or generated through the experience of living and working in a particular cultural context. They relate to what Harré *et al.* call 'conscious awareness', but would also link with, influence and be influenced by the 'deep structure' of the mind. These aspects, therefore, may be quite different among people from different countries and even from different sub-cultures and different companies. Yet because people can rationalize these attitudes, ideals or objectives they may well reflect organizational culture, the way managers have been educated and in fact the way in which hybrid management systems have developed through different cultural influences on the organization and the manager.

Whilst the 'deep structure' *context* of societal culture, values and control may be discussed and theorized, it is the consciously aware *content* that may be discerned through empirical research methods such as questionnaire surveys.

*Conduct* is what you see. It is the behavioural aspects of communication: what people actually do. This can also be extended to include the skills that people acquire in order to communicate and interact effectively. These aspects may be quite different among individuals and groups from different cultural backgrounds. This is seen in the styles of leadership in organizations in terms of what people do.

These three aspects, Jackson (1993) has argued, must be considered when looking at cross-cultural differences.

## The cultural *context* of leadership in Africa

For leadership to be appropriate and effective it must be in tune with its cultural and organizational context. Jackson (1993) has typified the context of leadership in terms of authoritarian or participative control systems. We can relate these two simply to Hofstede's (1980a) high and low power distance. Hence, effective and appropriate leadership will reflect an authoritarian approach in a high power-distance culture (where people accept authority and inequalities between boss and subordinate), and participatory approaches in a low power-distance culture. Countries such as France, Belgium and Portugal, with (according to Hofstede, 1980a) high power distance will have subordinates with strong dependency needs, and expect superiors to act autocratically. The superior will be expected to act mainly as a benevolent autocrat, and privileges for superiors will be expected. In medium power-distance cultures such as in the USA and Canada, subordinates will have medium dependency needs. They will expected to be consulted but will accept autocratic behaviour. Mostly they will see their superior as a resourceful democrat, and privileges for superiors will be accepted to a degree. In low power-distance countries such as Denmark and other Scandinavian countries, subordinates will have weak dependency needs, and will expect to be consulted. Superiors will be seen as loyal democrats and privileges for them will not be acceptable. If we are to accept Kiggundu's (1988) and Blunt and Jones' (1992) assessment that African groups would mainly score high on power distance, and this is consistent with preferences of senior managers not to delegate and not to use participative and decentralized forms of management, we could only conclude that such styles are appropriate and effective within the African context. Yet this is probably inaccurate and too simplistic.

For example, within the African context we might typify post-colonial management as high in power distance, post-instrumental (being highly influenced by American beliefs and practices) as being of medium power distance, and African renaissance as

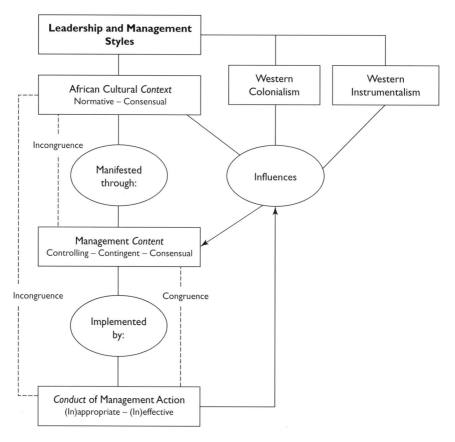

*Figure 5.1* Leadership and management styles in Africa: context, content and conduct.

being of lower power distance, if indeed it can be fitted into such a categorization. Although traditional African societies may well differ in their level of participation/authoritarianism, and this has a bearing on the current debate, the main point is what an indigenous management style is trying to become, not what it was like before colonial times. Having said this, the perception of traditional African leaders as despotic, Ayittey (1991: xxv) asserts, may well have been something of a colonial invention, he states:

> Clearly, such 'terrible' African rulers must have been generally those who gave the colonialists the most 'trouble'; that is, offered the stiffest resistance to European domination and conquest. Of course, to their people, such chiefs were not 'terrible' or 'despotic' at all but rather heroes who fought to resist the colonial subjugation.

Yet much of this mis-perception, he states, may have been not merely honest biases among anthropologists of the time, but difficulties in translation and interpretations of African languages. He quotes Williams (1987: 169) in saying:

> Africans . . . proudly speak of the freedom and absolute power of the chief or king. Some will even tell you that the king 'owned all the land' in the country. They are not trying to deceive. Words of another language often fail to translate the people's concept or meaning. When they say the king is supreme or has absolute power they mean that he has absolute power to carry out the will of the people. It is so well understood that supreme power rested in the people that it was never thought necessary to state such a fact. Likewise, they would say, and say proudly, the king 'owns all the land in the country' since everybody but a fool knew that he didn't, that nobody owned the land (in the Western sense), and that the king's role was that of custodian and overseer, his principle duty being to see that the land was fairly distributed among all families.

Ayittey (1991) goes further in saying that although Western scholars could be excused these biases and mis-interpretations, denigrating the African chief as 'despotic', yet modern African leaders redeem this image and use 'African tradition' to 'justify the imposition of all sorts of despotic regimes on their people' (p. xxvi). This may well apply, in part, to the justification of post-colonial styles of leadership in modern organizations in Africa.

However, the practicalities of modern organizations in Africa are that through a combination of these different (ideal type) management systems, hybrid systems are evolving. Where within these hybrid systems leadership better fulfils the aspiration, objectives and expectations of *followship* (an important addition to the Western vocabulary of leadership), it is likely that they will be more successful. Our argument throughout this text (following such as Dia, 1996, and Carlsson, 1998), is that management in Africa is seen as unsuccessful where it is not appropriate. This is mainly because colonial institutions were tacked onto African societies, and their post-colonial varieties remain inappropriate today. A similar argument may be made regarding the growing influence of post-instrumental management systems in both the private sector (influenced by Western multinationals) and in the public sector (influenced by multilateral agencies, mainly through structural adjustment programmes). Mutabazi (2002: 204) puts it thus:

> Africa has always been ruled by chiefs. However, African history since colonization has been stained by the disturbances of the traditional principles that govern sociability and intercommunal relations. Certain communities do not know which way to turn, so their leaders develop behavioural patterns in harmony with their own personal values – instead of being either *primus inter pares* [first among equals] or coconuts [black on the outside, white on the inside].

Given this intermixing of management systems within Africa, simply describing the context of leadership as relating to Hofstede's (1980a) power distance, or for that matter any other simplistic cultural dimension seems wholly inadequate. It is difficult to capture the cultural context of Africa in this way. The complexities of operating within a multicultural or multi-ethnic context similarly render such theory inadequate on two fronts. First, it may be tempting to compare ethnic groups in terms of power distance. Yet this does not account for differences in the influences of the cultural antecedents of different management systems on individuals from the different ethnic groups. Second, this theory does not allow for different outcomes of cultural crossvergence and its consequent hybridization of management systems in each organization. Third, it does not tell us very much about the cross-cultural dynamics of the situation in terms of interactions among the various players who may be influenced by these different factors in different ways.

It is more helpful to focus on manifestations of these different influences and processes through, for example, management control systems. For example, we have previously focused on coercive, remunerative and normative control mechanisms (Chapter 2). It is the crossvergence of cultural influences on control systems that form the *content* of the nature of leadership in organizations, and the management styles that are applied. Through these control systems (Figure 5.1) it is possible to gain insight into the different cultural influences on the management and leadership context in organizations in Africa.

## The cultural *content* of leadership in Africa

Hence in Chapter 2 we followed Etzioni (1975) in describing coercive power as referring to authoritarian systems that are able to compel or punish employees. Here we define a *controlling* management system as being hierarchical, authoritarian, centralized and having strict rules. Remunerative power (Etzioni, 1975) is based on an ability to reward people through supplying or withholding resources such as money and promotion. An indication of this would be strong orientation to the market and results focus, clear objectives, clear policies on client or customer relations, and clear rules of action. Organizations where this management system predominates may well see themselves as being successful in monetary terms, as well as having well trained and skilled managers. Normative power is based on an ability to use moral and symbolic influence, and based on mutual obligation and shared values (Etzioni, 1975). We argue that it is predominantly people-focused, and based on a belief that the organization works for its people, rather than people working to attain the objectives set by the executive. Organizations that predominate in this management system would have the well-being of its people as a major objective, with clear policies on employee relations, would focus on motivating employees, consulting employees, being flexible and encouraging diversity of opinions, while providing equal oppor-tunities and managing inter-ethnic harmony.

The *content* of leadership assumes particular orientations towards acting in certain ways, and incorporates values, aspirations, objectives and intentions. One of the debates in cross-cultural leadership theory centres on the contingency model of Fiedler (1967), which distinguishes a task-orientation and a relationship-, maintenance- or people-orientation. The first theory suggests that within each national culture managers will be predisposed towards one or the other of those orientations. For example Trompenaars (1993) asked managers across some fifty different countries how they see a company: as a system designed to perform functions and tasks in an efficient way, where people are hired and paid for the tasks they perform (task-orientation); or, as a group of people working together, having social relations with others and with the organization, with their functioning being dependent on these relations (relationship-orientation). He plotted the countries on a graph in terms of the percentage with a task orientation, with Hong Kong being the highest with 75 per cent and Malaysia being the lowest with 21 per cent. For the four sub-Saharan African countries included in the study, Burkina Faso has a high 69 per cent, Ethiopia a relatively high 66 per cent and Nigeria with a medium 56 per cent. It is difficult to draw conclusions from the results of South Africa (a low 25 per cent) without knowing something about the sample, and indeed Trompenaars himself does not draw conclusions from these results. Also, his results are drawn from one questionnaire item where managers are asked to choose between the two orientations. This does not provide for the subtleties of meaning that other studies have provided.

Thomas (2002) points out that this basic two-dimensional approach has been used to conduct studies in dozens of countries, often with the unsurprising result that relationship-oriented leaders increase subordinate satisfaction. Yet the task-orientation appears far more complex in its interpretations across cultures, and often conflicting results are obtained. This, Thomas (2002) suggests, requires a culture-specific interpretation of what constitutes task-orientation.

Smith *et al.* (1989) provide an indication of how the interpretation of these two orientations may differ among countries, through looking at differential factor structures across the UK, USA, Hong Kong and Japan. In the UK a high maintenance (relationship)-oriented manager is seen as more task-centred than the other countries, but also more consultative, explaining new tasks, consulting widely about change and looking for suggestions about work improvement and responding positively to them. A task (performance)-orientated manager is seen to be disapproving of members who regularly arrive late for work, and tends to evaluate the work of the group as a whole. America maintenance-oriented managers are seen to show most of the core maintenance behaviour as their British counterparts in consultative and participative behaviour, but are not task-centred as in the UK. They do not show disapproval of latecomers, do not meet socially outside work, and do not talk about immediate work problems with subordinates. US performance-oriented managers show core task behaviour. Although they dress like their subordinates, they are addressed formally by them, and do not meet subordinates socially.

It is the Asian managers who do not conform to type. Hong Kong maintenance-oriented managers discuss subordinates' personal problems in their absence, and also spend time socially with them as well as talk about work problems. Hong Kong performance-oriented managers exhibit all the same behaviour as their maintenance-oriented colleagues, but also discuss subordinate's career plans with them, and have more frequent meetings with subordinates, encouraging communication within the work group. Again, Japanese maintenance-oriented managers speak to others about a subordinate's problems rather than with the subordinate directly. They are seen to teach new job skills, and talk to subordinates about general work problems, as well as using written memos as a form of communication. Their performance-oriented colleagues meet their subordinates after working hours, arrange help with workloads if an employee has difficulties, and also check on work quality. They also teach new job skills, and also speak to others about a subordinate's problems rather than face-to-face.

The distinction between these two orientations does seem to blur when one goes outside the Anglo-American culture from which the theory emerged, and highlights the difficulty in transposing Western management conceptualizations to other cultures. In this case, the distinction becomes blurred when taking the theory from America to Britain, with the American group making the clearest distinction between these two orientations. It is likely that the distinction being made is between the 'soft' and 'hard' aspects of an instrumental orientation towards people (see Chapter 1 in the current text): that is, a 'tactical' distinction between different styles of management that are used on a contingency basis (see also this in relation to decision-making in organization: Chapter 4), rather than any real differences in the orientation towards people in organizations. Cultural differences are therefore being measured not against two dimensions, but against a variation on the same dimension.

A study of seven nations by Jackson (2002c) gave rise to a *humanism* scale indicating a dimension that reflects a valuing, fulfilment and involvement of people by the organization: seeing people as having a value in themselves (particularly the following items: 'A person in an organization should be valued mainly as a person in her or his own right'; 'The main objective of any organization should be the fulfilment of the people within it'; 'The whole point of an organization is to benefit its members'; and, 'An organization should be seen primarily as a means of obtaining the objectives of the people who work in it'). The items contributing to the *instrumental* scale indicated a results orientation as well as an instrumental view of people in achieving organizational results. Hence this scale was found to represent a dimension that reflects a value placed on people in organizations as a means to the ends of the organization (particularly the following items: 'The main value of a person in an organization is to achieve results for the organization'; and, 'An employee in an organization should be seen primarily as a means of obtaining the objectives of the organization'). Despite the cultural hegemony alluded to above, the manifestations of these orientations may be a fruitful way forward to understanding cultural differences in the *content* of management style and leadership orientation. This can be further honed by applying this within the three 'ideal type' management systems.

In Chapter 1 (Table 1.1) we depict post-colonial systems as essentially control oriented, post-instrumental as people and results oriented, and African renaissance as people and stakeholder oriented. It is likely that post-instrumental systems employing a 'hard' or 'soft' contingency approach to people management fits best with the Fiedler (1967) model, where task/relationship approaches are used as is seen appropriate from situation to situation.

### Post-colonial: control-oriented leadership

Noorderhaven, Vunderink and Lincoln (1996) present a good synopsis of many of the perceived leadership characteristics of 'African' management, and what we have called 'followship' characteristics, under a heading 'Power Distance', which in this case is seen as high. It is not necessary at this stage to go into detail of what we have called post-colonial management, as this has been adequately treated in Chapter 1. We can summarize these characteristics that constitute a control-orientation as follows:

- centralized decision-making at a high managerial level (Price, 1975; Mutizwa-Mangiza, 1991)
- unwillingness to delegate authority or to share information with subordinates (Vengroff et al., 1991; Blunt and Jones, 1992)
- consequently spending too much time on routine work and experiencing work overload (Onyemelukwe, 1973; Makoba, 1983)
- little autonomy and decision-making power at lower levels where jobs are narrowly defined (Onyemelukwe, 1973; Kiggundu, 1989; Blunt and Jones, 1992)
- consequently subordinates unwilling to act independently in the absence of a rule governing an action, and needing to check with superiors (Blunt and Jones, 1992)
- associated with this, little desire for subordinates to act independently as discretion can be a source of discomfort (Blunt and Jones, 1992; Odubogun, 1992)
- a predominant authoritarian style of African managers (Choudury, 1986; Kiggundu, 1989; Blunt and Jones, 1992), seeing familiarity with workers as eroding their power (Onyemelukwe, 1973; Odubogun, 1992), and at best being paternalistic rather than authoritarian (Onyemelukwe, 1973).

This perception of a control-orientation as something endemic to an African culture goes further. Noorderhaven et al. (1996) describe how a number of observers see the lack of initiative of African workers as a cultural factor (Onyemelukwe, 1973), as well as a function of poor education and dealing with unfamiliar technology. Further, they are seen as lacking a sense of individual responsibility, so that when a job is performed badly there is no feeling of guilt or failure (Dia, 1990). In addition African managers are seen as not to ascribe individual responsibility to employees and to forgive individual misdemeanours, with an attendant absence of a connection between performance and reward in the public sector (Brown, 1989)

Rather than being a cultural characteristic of African workers to shy away from responsibility, and to not take a pride in their work, it is likely that this is part of the low commitment and involvement of employees to organizations that are seen as contrary to African culture. This stems from the 'disconnect' thesis (Dia, 1996; Carlsson, 1998): employees are probably generally alienated from organizations (in the public or private sectors) that have a predominantly post-colonial management system (see also Chapter 7).

It may be for that reason, that, generally, control-based leadership styles have failed in Africa (if they were in tune with 'African culture' as suggested by some of the commentators above, they would indeed be successful, and there would be little need for a book such as this). Through the hegemony of Anglo-American principles of leadership, management education, the pressures for structural reform by multilateral agencies and the increased recognition that coercive management styles may not be appropriate, managers appear to be increasingly turning to Western theory and practice of leadership, and beginning to adopt management styles in line with this. If post-colonial management systems contained within them leadership styles that were not purely instrumental, objective seeking and results driven, and were sometimes paternalistic, post-instrumental systems are generally results driven. Leadership here employs tactical or contingency approaches as we discussed above, in order to motivate 'human resources' towards a particular end.

### Post-instrumental: contingency-oriented leadership

Yet such styles may be no more appropriate in the African situation than coercive-oriented styles. Leadership theories are big business in the West. Derr *et al.* (2002: using Amazon.com as their source) calculate that since 1995 3,947 books with the word leadership in the title have been published in English. Yet, Blunt and Jones (1997) are cynical of the fashionable leadership theories that often are only assessed by their intuitive appeal, rather than through 'repeated attempts to falsify predictions drawn from them, following conventional norms of scientific testing' (p. 10). Such a theory that comes under their scrutiny is transformational leadership, which is bound up with the importance of organizational culture and transforming this (inculcating through mission statements aspects such as fairness, trust, openness, commitment, productivity, quality and customer care), and with leaders that can build trust, ensuring reliability and predictability of employees' responses, thus reducing the need for close supervision and direct control.

Blunt and Jones (1997), say that such current theories of leadership place value on teamwork, empowerment, performance management and delegation, yet recognize as a problem the management consultant's rhetoric and hype:

> It seems likely that – as with Coca-Cola – the less the worth of the product to the consumer the more one needs to envelop it in a promotional mystique (Huczynski, 1993), and this helps to disguise its discordance with most of the cultures in which its tenets are applied.

> (p. 11)

They then go on to argue that these leadership approaches that reflect the predominant 'functionalist' view of management in the West may be inappropriate in Africa because of

> significant differences in value concerning authority, group loyalties and interpersonal harmony. Leadership in the West is follower- and performance-dependent, and therefore inclined to be more participatory. Concern for employee

welfare masks an overriding interest in the performance of the individual and of the organization.

(Blunt and Jones, 1997: 18)

The latter, that concern for employees masks an interest in performance, may well be true. As we have argued above, such approaches are based on contingency – if a hard instrumental approach does not work, a softer approach may be more appropriate in gaining the right commitment to the executive project. However, the former part of the reason for their doubting the appropriateness of such Western approach may be in part a result of focusing on characteristics of post-colonial management systems, rather than approaches to leadership that may be indigenous to Africa. It is to this that we now turn.

### African renaissance: consensus-oriented leadership

We have labelled the leadership orientation of African renaissance management systems as 'consensus'. This is not simply because leadership in traditional African societies was mainly consensus seeking (Ayittey, 1991), but also because of what Mutabazi (2002) calls 'essential values in African leadership' in embracing harmony in all parts of life (and death), and with community, environment, and in interpersonal relations with others.

Jackson (2002a) has argued that people management in organizations reflects a reconciling of the gap between work life and home/community life. Different cultures handle this differently. Hence the American approach is to provide a contract between organization and worker that acts purely in an instrumental and calculative way. A person is remunerated for the job he or she does. The contract can be ended at any time. A French approach is to separate the persona between home and work life. The worker's persona is protected by bureaucracy and formality, and kept separate from his or her private identity. Japanese management provides yet another model, where community and work life is better integrated. There is little separation between the two, as Japanese corporations have been successful in 'capturing' the wider societal collectivism.

The separation in Africa between home/community life and work life may be a huge problem where life is seen as integral. Mutabazi (2002: 208) argues that 'in African countries, life cannot be conceptualized and compartmentalized (into professional life, family life, life on Earth, afterlife, etc.) as it can be in the West'.

We can gain a picture of the basis of Africa leadership through Ayittey's (1991) description of the role of the chief, whom he asserts is more of a leader than a ruler. First, not all African societies had chiefs as such, and are termed 'stateless' by Ayittey. He quotes Yelpaala (1983: 357) in saying that it is apparent

from the way societies like the Tiv, the central Igbo, and the Dagaaba were organized, that they were well aware of the political structure of the centralized system, but tried to eliminate them as much as possible. For instance they recognized the tremendous advantage of power during war and used a limited form of it only then. Leaders were given power to command and carry out operations, but during peacetime, they became . . . common people and ceased to exercise that power.

This was generally the case, particularly among pastoralists. Yet societies such as the Igbo of eastern Nigeria do not necessarily conform to the semi-nomadic pastoralist societies such as the Fulani of northern Nigeria, and the San !Kung people of Southern Africa. Boahen and Webster (1970: 166, quoted by Ayittey, 1991) tell us that 'the Igbo were individualistic and egalitarian, every man considered himself as good as everyone else and demanding a voice in his local affairs. Since everyone had a right to rise in society Igbo culture emphasized competition, competition between families, between lineages and between clans'.

Social structure was based, as is common in Africa, on kinship, with policy-making bodies representative of lineages. Village government (the council) consisted of the ama-ala comprising the heads of extended families, and the 'village assembly of citizens'. The ceremonial head of the council was the head of the senior lineage, often the founding family of the village, yet his authority did not extend outside the council or outside his family group. The council was the controlling authority and performed all the functions of a chief. Ritual functionaries and age-grades helped also with the maintenance of day-to-day law and order. All adult Igbo males had a right to be present at the council meetings and voice their opinion freely. It was the function of the ama-ala to call together a village assembly to discuss important issues. If it acted arbitrarily, the people could demand a meeting and effectively bring the village to a halt. By ignoring unpopular elders they could exert social pressure to get the elder to bend to the popular will (Ayittey, 1991). Boahen and Webster (1970) describe the village assembly as 'the Igbo man's birthright, the guarantee of his rights, his shield against oppression, the expression of his individualism, and the means whereby the young progressive impressed their views upon the old and the conservative'.

Ayittey (1991) also describe the Fulani, the Somali, the !Kung, as well as the Kikuyu of Kenya (who overthrew their despot in the nineteenth century, to enact a new constitution affirming the rights of Kikuyu people in government), as having similar consensus seeking with 'leaders' taking the role of presiding over proceedings rather than taking arbitrary decisions without the involvement of the people.

In stateless societies, generally heredity alone did not play a large part in selecting headmen of villages. Gibbs (1965: 24, in Ayittey) tells us that 'for a man to be a respected and persuasive leader he must be an elder . . . he must be a good orator, and he must have established his claim to a position of leadership by his achievements.'

African societies that were structured as Kingdoms or states were generally not too different from stateless ones in the sense that 'according to traditional ideals, a chief could never force his people to do what they did not want to do; he was a leader rather than a ruler, relying for his position on influence rather than force' (Bourdillon, 1976, quoted in Ayittey, 1991). The chief was generally male, and was the political, social, judicial and religious head of the people. Yet, 'although the Bantu chief has the right of final decision, he always acts in council, i.e. machinery exists whereby he is assisted in his work as chief administrative and political organ by other members of the tribe' (Olivier, 1969, quoted in Ayittey, 1991). It is the job of the advisors to ensure that the chief rules properly, and to reprimand him when necessary, as well as to intercede on behalf of any person who lodges a complaint with the advisor. Advisors can be brought to task if they too fail in their duty. For example, Busia (1951) reported cases where two Asante elders lost their position and were heavily fined for failing to advise the chief of his wrong-doing. Ayittey (1991: 9) tells us that 'consensus was the cardinal feature of the indigenous African political system. Majority opinion did not count in the council of elders; traditionally, unanimity was the rule in most tribal systems; hence, the African political characteristic of debating, sometimes for days, to reach unanimity.' This required leadership of a particular type in this context: 'Coercive powers were generally not employed by the chief to achieve unity. Unity of purpose was achieved through the process of consensus building. In addition, persuasion and appeals, rather than force, were used by the chief and councillors to win over recalcitrant members on an issue' (p. 100).

This process of consensus seeking went also with a decentralized process of government. Heads of lineages had a voice in council, and the people directly represented themselves though assemblies, either at village level or at national (tribal) level (Olivier, 1969), where important issues such as law-making were debated and often given approval. Schapera (1955) for example identified four different levels of popular assembly among the Tswana of southern Africa, depending on the nature of the issue discussed.

Although there is no doubt that many a chief, 'as head of the tribe, occupies a position of unique privilege and authority' (Schapera, 1955: 62), yet it is difficult to sustain an argument that this represented large inequalities between leader and follower, as in the definition of Hofstede's (1980a) power distance, where inequalities are accepted by people in high power-distance countries. For example Ayittey (1991) (p. 121) tells us that

> the 'wealth of the chief' was misinterpreted as evidence of unequal distribution of income. It is true that some chiefs lived well and were better off than commoners, as custom required them to live 'royally' and to entertain guests in a manner that enhanced the stature of the tribe. However, the chief was wealthy in terms of *services* which he received but he could not accumulate capital for his personal use.

Often, resources were simply held, and protected, on behalf of the community, and not for the personal use of the chief, and wealth, for example in terms of cattle, was passed to the post-holder who succeeded the current chief.

### Management and leadership styles in hybrid management systems

We have therefore said that the implicit nature of the cultural *context* (used in terms of Harre *et al.*'s, 1985, 'deep structure of the mind' and 'social order') of leadership and management systems can be discerned through focusing on management systems in organizations, and how congruent they are with people's values and expectations. We have previously argued (Chapters 1 and 2) that the 'ideal type' management system can be used as a conceptual mechanism to understand the different influences on organizations and managers, to identify the different elements making up the ideal type, and compares this to the realities of the numerous hybrid forms of management system evolving as a result from these different influences. Each ideal type will have its cultural antecedence and will reflect cultural values such as instrumentalism or humanism. Incongruences may occur between the hybrid management system and managers and employees' values and expectations (see also Chapter 7 for an examination of employees values and expectations). The nature of management systems in organizations in sub-Saharan countries, and the extent to which this is at variance with managers' values, expectations and styles, can only be discerned through empirical investigation. It is to this that we now turn.

### Management and leadership styles in fifteen sub-Saharan African countries

Table 5.1 summarizes the results from our management survey across fifteen African countries. This focuses on controlling mechanisms involving control/coercion (termed 'controlling' incorporating the correlated items: very hierarchical, highly centralized, very authoritarian and many strict rules); people focus (motivates employees, clear policies on employee relations, has the well-being of its people as a major objective); consultative (consults employees, very flexible, encourages diversity of opinions); and diversity management (provides equal opportunities and inter-ethnic harmony). These sub-factors are combined into a dimensional factor (from an exploratory factor analysis of all sub-factors in Table 5.1) of Control–People Orientation. Controlling loads negatively (factor loading: –0.726) on a first factor with consultative (0.778), diversity (0.690) and people focus (0.623). The dimensional factor is formed by subtracting the sum of these three sub-factors from the controlling sub-factor to give a continuum score from negative (controlling) to positive (people focused). The other factor shown in Table 5.1 is Results Orientation. This is formed from factor 2 of the exploratory analysis and comprises: results focus (items: oriented towards the market and results oriented); clarity of objectives (clear objectives, clear policies on client or customer relations, and has clear and formal rules of action); and successful organization (very successful, high level of management expertise). The factor loadings are 0.744, 0.743 and 0.724 respectively.

We have also graphed the scores for the fifteen countries for these two factors, represented on two axes. Figure 5.2 shows their relative positions for 'my organization at the moment' (current); and Figure 5.3 shows a trajectory for each country, representing the distance between current and ideal ('the way I would like it to be'). Scores are shown in their standardized forms. Raw scores are standardized against the mean for all of an individual's scores for all items in the questionnaire. This was done to counter the effects of response set (i.e. individuals responding more highly or lowly on the 1–5 scale than other individuals). Zero represents the individual's mean score for all items. Score for items (as well as sub-factors and factors) are shown as deviations from the mean score.

These results from our survey indicate that:

- There is predominantly a *results* and *control* orientation among the African countries surveyed with variation among the countries such that DRC shows a higher *control* orientation, Côte d'Ivoire a lower *results* orientation, and both Mozambique and Rwanda a higher *people* orientation (Figure 5.2). This general orientation may be indicative of post-colonial systems (coercive control) combined with more 'modern' post-instrumental systems (remunerative control). Post-instrumental systems may be taking longer to penetrate in organizations in DRC, which may have a higher residue of past colonial systems. However, the lower results orientation of Côte d'Ivoire is not easily explained. From the late 1980s it has followed a number of structural adjustment programmes, and its free market economy is judged as being a relative success story (www.winne. com/CoteIvoire/B-politics.htm, 05/06/2002) in West Africa. Also with its moderately higher control orientation (Figure 5.2) this may well indicate a residue of its French colonial system. The reason why Mozambique and Rwanda show a higher people and results orientation is more difficult to explain, as both these countries have been subject to tight and formal colonial control systems. Yet Mozambique has shown a good recovery over the last few years, has privatized many industries, reduced inflation, and has implemented progressive political reforms since the end of the civil war (www.state.gov/pa/ei/bgn/ 7035pf.htm, 23/07/2002). Rwanda also undergone progressive political and social transformation including non-discrimination legislation. These aspects may partly explain the higher people and results orientation of organizations in these two countries, and explain the high ideal perception of managers on these two orientations (Figure 5.3).
- There is general desire among managers in the fifteen countries to be more *results* and *people* oriented although there is variation in the extent of this desire among the countries. Hence the Congolese show less desire to be *people* oriented perhaps indicating the entrenched nature of post-colonial systems; managers from Burkina Faso and Botswana indicate the largest distance between a current low *people* and *results* orientation, and a high ideal *people* and *results* orientation (Figure 5.3). However, for managers from both these countries, their perceptions of the future does not live up to this ideal (Table 5.1). Certainly the relative prosperity of Botswana may have raised expectations. However, it is difficult to explain directly why Burkina Faso's managers desire such a relatively high people and results orientation, and this may need further, qualitative, investigation.
- Generally the future perception of *people* orientation does not live up to the ideal, with a few exceptions. Table 5.1 shows that this is particularly the case for *people focus*, which is a sub-factor within control–people orientation. Of all the sub-factors this is the most indicative of a humanistic approach that we would expect to find in an African renaissance management system, as it reflects a centrality of

Table 5.1 Organizational control systems in Africa: scores from fifteen countries

| | | Bots | BuFa | Cam | Côte | DRC | Gha | Keny | Mala |
|---|---|---|---|---|---|---|---|---|---|
| Controlling | Current | 0.079 | 0.211 | −0.165 | 0.062 | 0.158 | −0.145 | −0.215 | −0.119 |
| | Ideal | −0.553 | −0.576 | −0.214 | −0.135 | 0.256 | −0.452 | −0.350 | −0.480 |
| | Future | −0.171 | 0.049 | −0.084 | 0.006 | 0.394 | −0.112 | −0.124 | −0.142 |
| People focus | Current | −0.416 | −0.437 | −0.363 | −0.214 | −0.433 | −0.387 | −0.306 | −0.345 |
| | Ideal | 0.776 | 0.943 | 0.547 | 0.278 | 0.033 | 0.606 | 0.629 | 0.668 |
| | Future | −0.069 | −0.069 | −0.066 | −0.109 | 0.061 | −0.144 | −0.123 | −0.155 |
| Consultative | Current | −0.469 | −0.490 | −0.381 | −0.235 | −0.584 | −0.383 | −0.309 | −0.348 |
| | Ideal | 0.670 | 0.536 | 0.363 | 0.239 | −0.214 | 0.555 | 0.627 | 0.598 |
| | Future | −0.110 | −0.297 | −0.113 | −0.048 | −0.152 | −0.097 | −0.105 | −0.124 |
| Diversity | Current | −0.052 | 0.197 | −0.191 | −0.073 | −0.302 | −0.073 | −0.060 | −0.141 |
| management | Ideal | 0.867 | 10.027 | 0.585 | 0.418 | −0.020 | 0.823 | 0.758 | 0.698 |
| | Future | 0.042 | 0.425 | 0.032 | −0.028 | 0.005 | 0.156 | 0.077 | 0.001 |
| **Control–** | **Current** | **−0.403** | **−0.449** | **−0.159** | **−0.250** | **−0.566** | **−0.134** | **−0.014** | **−0.155** |
| **People** | **Ideal** | **1.31** | **1.448** | **0.735** | **0.464** | **−0.296** | **1.172** | **1.05** | **1.172** |
| **Orientation** | **Future** | **−0.104** | **0.033** | **−0.066** | **0.024** | **0.399** | **−0.056** | **−0.092** | **−0.097** |
| Result focus | Current | 0.101 | 0.373 | 0.219 | −0.111 | 0.402 | 0.100 | 0.225 | 0.011 |
| | Ideal | 0.923 | 0.941 | 0.749 | 0.350 | 0.628 | 0.802 | 0.863 | 0.822 |
| | Future | 0.386 | 0.536 | 0.384 | 0.028 | 0.702 | 0.299 | 0.314 | 0.221 |
| Clarity of | Current | 0.015 | −0.111 | 0.090 | −0.104 | 0.316 | 0.023 | 0.110 | 0.090 |
| objectives | Ideal | 0.878 | 0.938 | 0.703 | 0.402 | 0.534 | 0.854 | 0.838 | 0.790 |
| | Future | 0.262 | 0.242 | 0.226 | 0.104 | 0.573 | 0.258 | 0.195 | 0.134 |
| Successful | Current | −0.019 | −0.243 | −0.114 | −0.129 | −0.342 | 0.037 | −0.017 | −0.086 |
| organization | Ideal | 0.950 | 0.936 | 0.713 | 0.305 | 0.172 | 0.968 | 0.856 | 0.861 |
| | Future | 0.271 | −0.049 | 0.175 | −0.012 | 0.250 | 0.318 | 0.196 | 0.121 |
| **Results** | **Current** | **0.009** | **−0.017** | **0.085** | **−0.115** | **0.111** | **0.058** | **0.115** | **0.009** |
| **Orientation** | **Ideal** | **0.958** | **1.006** | **0.739** | **0.362** | **0.440** | **0.879** | **0.858** | **0.835** |
| | **Future** | **0.320** | **0.242** | **0.291** | **0.059** | **0.504** | **0.306** | **0.239** | **0.162** |

| Moz | Nami | Nig | Rwa | SA | Zamb | Zim | All | SD | Fstat* |
|---|---|---|---|---|---|---|---|---|---|
| −0.363 | −0.080 | 0.043 | −0.541 | −0.071 | −0.200 | −0.035 | −0.098 | 0.702 | 90.29 |
| −0.370 | −0.278 | −0.087 | −0.195 | −0.532 | −0.436 | −0.641 | −0.332 | 0.656 | 26.30 |
| −0.168 | −0.1712 | 0.099 | −0.096 | −0.138 | −0.095 | −0.220 | −0.064 | 0.659 | 9.04 |
| | | | | | | | | | |
| −0.149 | −0.194 | −0.275 | −0.212 | −0.225 | −0.375 | −0.256 | −0.289 | 0.584 | 3.47 |
| 0.458 | 0.631 | 0.443 | 0.297 | 0.654 | 0.551 | 0.633 | 0.537 | 0.529 | 21.56 |
| −0.139 | −0.057 | −0.113 | 0.104 | −0.004 | −0.094 | −0.007 | −0.065 | 0.595 | 2.55 |
| | | | | | | | | | |
| −0.137 | −0.379 | −0.405 | −0.023 | −0.329 | −0.353 | −0.436 | −0.348 | 0.656 | 5.30 |
| 0.463 | 0.588 | 0.261 | 0.339 | 0.580 | 0.429 | 0.584 | 0.441 | 0.580 | 27.32 |
| −0.130 | −0.133 | −0.198 | 0.145 | −0.061 | −0.104 | −0.1622 | −0.110 | 0.652 | 2.21 |
| | | | | | | | | | |
| 0.010 | −0.054 | −0.203 | 0.143 | −0.112 | −0.068 | 0.062 | −0.101 | 0.757 | 3.67 |
| 0.614 | 0.760 | 0.513 | 0.550 | 0.791 | 0.660 | 0.795 | 0.644 | 0.655 | 20.44 |
| 0.028 | 0.133 | −0.020 | 0.367 | 0.110 | 0.074 | 0.205 | 0.077 | 0.743 | 3.18 |
| | | | | | | | | | |
| **0.268** | **−0.142** | **−0.359** | **0.461** | **−0.134** | **−0.082** | **−0.194** | **−0.153** | **1.025** | **7.24** |
| **0.912** | **0.938** | **0.508** | **0.593** | **1.213** | **0.971** | **1.330** | **0.898** | **0.910** | **40.67** |
| **−0.077** | **−0.148** | **0.206** | **−0.270** | **−0.172** | **−0.064** | **−0.268** | **−0.048** | **0.968** | **5.40** |
| | | | | | | | | | |
| 0.218 | 0.284 | 0.034 | 0.428 | 0.292 | 0.322 | 0.223 | 0.202 | 0.653 | 8.83 |
| 0.577 | 0.885 | 0.693 | 0.890 | 0.868 | 0.744 | 0.931 | 0.775 | 0.544 | 12.79 |
| 0.252 | 0.381 | 0.161 | 0.771 | 0.510 | 0.460 | 0.432 | 0.376 | 0.631 | 16.19 |
| | | | | | | | | | |
| 0.324 | −0.041 | 0.064 | 0.330 | 0.108 | 0.169 | 0.025 | 0.106 | 0.590 | 6.36 |
| 0.687 | 0.808 | 0.578 | 0.704 | 0.805 | 0.721 | 0.779 | 0.723 | 0.492 | 12.59 |
| 0.254 | 0.116 | 0.154 | 0.660 | 0.266 | 0.301 | 0.243 | 0.250 | 0.566 | 9.63 |
| | | | | | | | | | |
| 0.125 | 0.082 | 0.046 | −0.143 | −0.000 | 0.122 | −0.012 | −0.024 | 0.630 | 6.09 |
| 0.771 | 1.031 | 0.696 | 0.637 | 0.981 | 0.793 | 0.935 | 0.787 | 0.583 | 31.57 |
| 0.143 | 0.265 | 0.174 | 0.398 | 0.252 | 0.322 | 0.231 | 0.213 | 0.630 | 3.66 |
| | | | | | | | | | |
| **0.214** | **0.093** | **0.051** | **0.205** | **0.137** | **0.214** | **0.974** | **0.100** | **0.474** | **4.62** |
| **0.710** | **0.903** | **0.667** | **0.741** | **0.888** | **0.781** | **0.887** | **0.774** | **0.436** | **23.86** |
| **0.224** | **0.267** | **0.169** | **0.610** | **0.346** | **0.360** | **0.330** | **0.290** | **0.488** | **10.52** |

*Significant at 0.01 level

*Table 5.2* Other organizational characteristics: scores from fifteen countries

|  |  | Bots | BuFa | Cam | Côte | DRC | Gha | Keny | Mala |
|---|---|---|---|---|---|---|---|---|---|
| *Ethical* | Current | −0.368 | −0.048 | −0.164 | −0.118 | 0.338 | −0.137 | −0.011 | −0.006 |
|  | Ideal | 0.451 | 0.830 | 0.422 | 0.105 | 0.651 | 0.433 | 0.477 | 0.475 |
|  | Future | 0.028 | −0.004 | 0.081 | −0.150 | 0.611 | −0.005 | 0.086 | 0.046 |
| *Undergoing* | Current | −0.184 | −0.199 | −0.153 | −0.328 | −0.271 | 0.003 | 0.026 | 0.168 |
| *change* | Ideal | 0.595 | 0.066 | 0.218 | −0.212 | −0.703 | 0.552 | 0.401 | 0.366 |
|  | Future | 0.098 | 0.195 | −0.034 | −0.322 | −0.377 | 0.131 | 0.119 | 0.179 |
| *Strong trade* | Current | −1.196 | −0.540 | −0.970 | −0.210 | −1.424 | −0.676 | −0.988 | −1.192 |
| *union* | Ideal | −0.151 | 0.003 | −0.164 | −0.164 | −0.615 | −0.007 | −0.084 | 0.045 |
|  | Future | −0.899 | −0.520 | −0.710 | −0.238 | −0.748 | −0.521 | −0.808 | −0.865 |
| *Influence* | Current | −1.081 | −1.140 | −0.750 | −0.407 | −0.476 | −1.195 | −0.767 | −1.095 |
| *of family* | Ideal | −1.374 | −1.597 | −1.173 | −0.509 | −1.172 | −1.458 | −1.040 | −1.315 |
| *relations* | Future | −0.979 | −1.156 | −0.828 | −0.443 | −0.540 | −1.139 | −0.713 | −0.962 |
| *Bound by* | Current | 0.342 | 0.358 | −0.028 | 0.140 | 0.666 | 0.294 | 0.144 | 0.359 |
| *government* | Ideal | −0.303 | −0.946 | −0.109 | −0.408 | −0.476 | −0.049 | −0.230 | −0.159 |
| *regulations* | Future | −0.051 | −0.245 | −0.097 | −0.125 | 0.633 | 0.166 | −0.056 | 0.111 |
| *Risk taking* | Current | −0.575 | −0.540 | −0.361 | −0.278 | 0.627 | −0.432 | −0.386 | −0.454 |
|  | Ideal | 0.360 | 0.319 | −0.057 | 0.062 | 0.773 | 0.262 | 0.234 | 0.083 |
|  | Future | −0.094 | −0.561 | −0.21 | −0.164 | 0.836 | −0.214 | −0.127 | −0.318 |

| Moz | Nami | Nig | Rwa | SA | Zamb | Zim | All | SD | Fstat* |
|---|---|---|---|---|---|---|---|---|---|
| −0.062 | 0.134 | −0.064 | −0.144 | 0.229 | −0.014 | 0.241 | 0.029 | 0.924 | 6.81 |
| 0.134 | 0.749 | 0.248 | −0.289 | 0.679 | 0.505 | 0.639 | 0.448 | 0.927 | 13.73 |
| −0.072 | 0.276 | 0.053 | −0.108 | 0.261 | 0.207 | 0.336 | 0.138 | 0.908 | 7.47 |
| | | | | | | | | | |
| −0.306 | 0.253 | −0.157 | −0.336 | 0.384 | 0.217 | 0.200 | 0.025 | 0.950 | 15.36 |
| 0.110 | 0.417 | 0.403 | −0.152 | 0.327 | 0.505 | 0.421 | 0.267 | 0.876 | 24.60 |
| −0.249 | 0.308 | −0.031 | −0.083 | 0.403 | 0.334 | 0.189 | 0.098 | 0.763 | 14.73 |
| | | | | | | | | | |
| −0.448 | −0.940 | −0.542 | −0.826 | −0.266 | −0.966 | −0.688 | −0.703 | 1.092 | 23.32 |
| 0.189 | −0.441 | 0.079 | 0.143 | −0.414 | −0.289 | −0.254 | −0.168 | 1.076 | 9.01 |
| −0.302 | −0.822 | −0.450 | −0.241 | −0.230 | −0.694 | −0.476 | −0.515 | 1.042 | 10.52 |
| | | | | | | | | | |
| −1.070 | −1.173 | −0.733 | −0.861 | −0.943 | −1.066 | −1.056 | −0.877 | 1.138 | 6.92 |
| −1.066 | −1.190 | −0.858 | −0.960 | −0.908 | −1.187 | −1.039 | −1.39 | 1.064 | 8.06 |
| −0.972 | −0.986 | −0.589 | −0.875 | −0.905 | −0.904 | −1.039 | −0.824 | 1.090 | 5.98 |
| | | | | | | | | | |
| −0.383 | 0.327 | 0.188 | −0.598 | 0.077 | 0.124 | 0.018 | 0.113 | 1.023 | 11.66 |
| −0.158 | −0.160 | 0.100 | −0.789 | −0.422 | 0.234 | −0.575 | −0.230 | 1.024 | 14.62 |
| −0.255 | 0.022 | 0.197 | −0.784 | −0.006 | 0.090 | −0.219 | 0.003 | 0.987 | 12.83 |
| | | | | | | | | | |
| −0.307 | −0.183 | −0.471 | −0.777 | −0.405 | −0.277 | −0.270 | −0.344 | 0.902 | 16.72 |
| −0.667 | 0.099 | −0.024 | −0.415 | −0.031 | −0.097 | 0.185 | 0.034 | 0.907 | 20.29 |
| −0.301 | −0.109 | −0.201 | −0.068 | −0.235 | −0.246 | −0.041 | −0.147 | 0.899 | 15.88 |

*Significant at 0.01 level

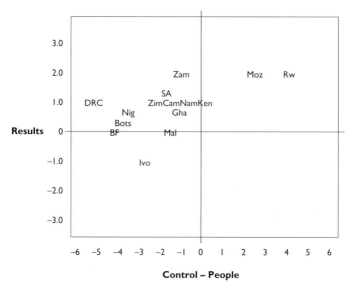

*Figure 5.2* Position of countries for current control systems.

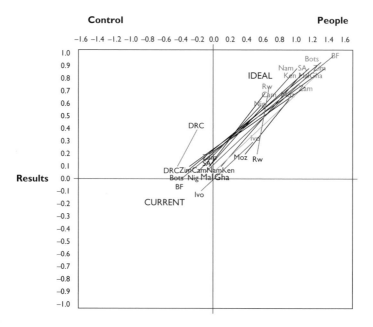

*Figure 5.3* Trajectory for countries from current to ideal control systems.

people in the organization. This result may indicate a need for organizations to take a more humanistic approach through normative control systems (see Chapter 2, and the discussion above).

- For managers in many of the countries surveyed their perceptions of future *results* orientation come closer to the ideal, although there is much variation among the countries (Table 5.1). This is perhaps closer to what organizations are trying to achieve through introduction of 'modern' (post-instrumental) management systems.

- Managers across the countries generally have a perception of medium to low (below their mean scores for all items) organizational success (Table 5.1) with DRC having the lowest score, and Mozambique and Zambia having the highest scores (slightly above the mean for all their individual scores). South Africa has a zero score, indicating only a perception of a moderate success, despite the many advances made by South African organizations over the last few years.

- Managers across the countries see their organizations as having a medium ethicality (Table 5.2), although this varies from a low for Botswana, and a relative high for DRC, South Africa and Zimbabwe. Yet the ideal is indicated as being higher than current scores, with only managers from DRC believing that organizations will live up to these expectations in the future. It cannot be concluded from this that organizations are very unethical, but it can be seen that they do not generally live up to the expectations that managers have.

- There is variation among the countries in managers' perceptions of change. However, scores are fairly low, indicating that most managers see a low rate of change. This may indicate a frustration with a lower than ideal level of change, and managers from many countries (Botswana, Ghana, Cameron, Kenya, Malawi, Mozambique, Nigeria, Namibia, Zambia and Zimbabwe) desire a higher level of change. It is only managers in South Africa that indicate a moderate level of current change, which reflects their ideal, and the future level of change. Managers in DRC appear to be averse to change.

- All scores for family influence are low, although it still appears to be present (i.e. managers are scoring above 1 = not like this at all). It appears to be slightly higher in DRC and Côte d'Ivoire.

- Managers see a medium to high influence of government controls on their organizations. This appears to be higher in Botswana, Burkina Faso, DRC, Ghana, Malawi and Namibia; and lower in Cameroon, Mozambique, and Rwanda. All, apart from managers in Zambia, appear to want lower levels of government controls.

- Trade unions appear to be weak in sub-Saharan Africa, especially so in Botswana, DRC, Cameroon, Kenya, Malawi, Namibia, Rwanda and Zambia. They appear to be less weak in Côte d'Ivoire and South Africa. Managers from all countries express a desire that they be stronger, but see no or little movement towards this in the future.

- Despite an indication that organizations are results oriented, they are not risk taking (a questionnaire item that did not correlate with other items making up the results orientation factor, nor loading on this factor), although generally managers express a wish that they were more so. Only DRC managers indicate that their organizations are risk taking.

From the results of our survey of managers across fifteen countries, these characteristics of organizations appear to provide the context of management styles and leadership. There appears to be a combination of coercive or 'controlling' mechanisms indicative of post-colonial management systems, and results oriented, 'remunerative' control systems indicative of the introduction of 'modern' post-instrumental management systems. This appears to support the view of, for example, Kamoche (1992) whose case study research indicates an introduction of Western practices, yet still reflects the views of, for example, Kiggundu (1988) and Blunt and Jones (1992) which see organizations in Africa as authoritarian and hierarchical; or, of predominantly post-colonial systems. Fashoyin and Matanmi's (1996) view that trade unions had become weak since independence because they were seen as competitors to the ruling elite, and suffered from repressive measure, is confirmed by these findings.

Yet despite a low people orientation across the fifteen countries, there appears to be a strong desire for managers to see a greater emphasis placed on a humanistic approach. With few exceptions, there appears to be a disparity between this ideal situation and the current one, and the situation that is projected for the future (Table 5.1). Yet with this particular orientation, where managers express the way they would like things to be, in its ideal form, there is greater variation among the countries than when they are expressing the way they see it at the moment, and the way it is going (from an inspection of the F statistics in Table 5.1). If we make the logical assumption that the way managers see things at the moment and they way they are going reflects the perceived *context*, their expression of an ideal can be seen as the *content* of leadership and management styles. It is the way managers would wish it to be, and reflects their own values and attitudes (although not necessarily reflecting their action or *conduct*). This may therefore explain why there is greater variance among the fifteen countries for the *ideal*. Structures and systems may well be similar across a number of countries, yet values and management attitudes may be quite different.

## The cultural *conduct* of leadership in Africa: implication for managers

We have focused predominantly on the cultural *content* of leadership and management styles in organizations. There is a discrepancy between the way organizations are seen and the way managers would like them to be. If managers acted according to their ideal, their organizations would be different. We can only assume that managers act more in accordance with the way they see their organizations as they are and the way they are becoming. We can perhaps glean something of the deep structure of the cultural *context* of leadership and management through the 'ideal' responses of managers. There is clearly an incongruence between such cultural values and expectations that may not only cause a disjuncture between work organizations and the wider society, but may also not enable organizations to work effectively through appropriate management actions. For example, it is clear that organizations are not very consultative (Table 5.1). From the available literature discussed above, African cultures appear to be far more consensual and democratic than recent observers have led us to believe. This is certainly reflected in our results. Managers generally show a desire for more consultation.

The question remains, why is this not converted to management action, and what are the implications for managers of our discussion on leadership and management styles, and our empirical findings? We can summarize as follows.

- The *content* of leadership and management in organizations is out of line with the African cultural *context*. As this involves power relations that are enforced through control systems, and which tend to be low in consultation and consensus, this does not allow attitudes and values stemming from the cultural context of Africa to be converted to management actions. In other words, generally, leadership in African organizations seem to be out of kilter with African cultures.
- Although there is some variation among African countries in the content of leadership and management styles in organizations, there appears to be greater variation in aspirations and ideals of managers among the countries. If this is a reflection of the cultural context in each country, we might assume that although the management influences on organizations in each country are similar, the cultural context is not. Generally speaking, it is unlikely that these differences are taken into account by organizations operating in different countries, for example by multinational organizations.
- In order to take account of the expectations and ideals of managers, organizations should be moving towards a people and results orientation and away from a controlling orientation (although with variation among the countries taken into consideration: e.g. DRC).
- Empirical information of the sort presented in this chapter is needed on an ongoing basis if organizations are to operate appropriately and effectively.
- Education and development of managers needs to reflect these findings, and to adopt a cross-cultural approach if appropriate and effective organizational leadership is to develop further in sub-Saharan Africa.

# Chapter 6

# Motivating and rewarding managers

Most people in post-independence African countries are not inspired to work, because they lack desire to accomplish something. The African bureaucrat is often motivated by material things he can gain from work. He engages in those activities of work that will result either in immediate financial gains or possessing the potential for such.

(Ankomah, 1985, quoted in Blunt and Jones, 1992)

Conflicts between African and Western values are evident in numerous aspects of managerial work. The African managerial style places greater emphasis on moral rather than on material incentives. Moral incentives are considered to be more meaningful and long-lasting. Indeed, wages are the property of the family not the individual; consequently, monetary incentives have little effect on performance, unless they are paid to the collectivity ... Western management approaches presume the desirability of taking risks, and value work motivation. In most African countries, the quality of life, and the value attached to personal time exceed any desire to accumulate wealth. Positive interpersonal relationships are valued above money.

(Grzeda and Assogbavi, 1999)

Most of our managers are motivated by the objective to build a country. This is an inner thing to motivate you.

(Manager, Afriland First Bank, Cameroon)

## Introduction

There is surprisingly little direct information in the literature on management motivation in Africa, although there is increasing documentation of the introduction of 'modern' reward systems, and evidence to suggest that many organizations are introducing pay and promotion systems that are related to performance (Kamoche, 2000). Often, when such systems are introduced, this is done first at managerial levels, with the expectation that this will then filter down through the organization to include all employees. However, there is also evidence to suggest there is still a lack of a system for pay and promotion in many organizations.

With a mixture of bureaucracy, or formal systems, and informal systems of pay and promotion, for example through favouring family or in-group members, this may well fit into the framework for the post-colonial 'ideal type' management systems that can be derived from much of the literature reviewed in Chapter 1. In Ghana, for example, Abdulai (2000) reports that in terms of compensation and benefits, the Ghanaian public sector is in a complete mess, with a 'lack of concrete and systematic policies and guidelines as well as the tendency to apply ad hoc measures and solutions to chronic compensation problems' (p. 455). Certainly, in many of the organizations that we investigated in our current study, compensation systems were variable, often not reflecting a systematic attempt to reward managers.

Reward systems should relate directly to the way managers are motivated. Motivation relates to the type of management systems operating within organizations and how managers perceive these. It also relates to the types of values systems that managers have. A lack of congruence between management systems and value systems may often imply inappropriate management systems (and logically it could be argued, inappropriate value systems) and a lack of motivation. There is a lack of empirical evidence about the fit between management and value systems in organizations in Africa, and for example, the appropriateness of Western 'modern' reward systems.

Although we do not expect this chapter to provide a comprehensive insight into these issues, we expect to be able to shed some light, and to provide some indication of how managers in Africa might be more appropriately motivated and rewarded. This is done by examining motivation within the three 'ideal type' management systems already discussed (Chapter 1). Findings are then presented from a survey of managers in fifteen sub-Saharan African countries, and then discuss the management implications of this for organizations in Africa.

Chapters 6 and 7 should be read in parallel, dealing as they both do with motivation. Chapter 6 addresses the current lack of information on management motivation in Africa and its centrality to effective management. The issues dealt with in this chapter dovetail neatly with those in the next chapter.

## Motivation and management systems in Africa

Much of the cross-cultural management literature on motivation is concerned with the problem of transferability of Western theories and principles to non-Western countries. Certainly in Africa, as we noted above, many organizations are looking towards the 'modern' management methods of Western human resource management (HRM) in motivating and rewarding managers. Even a company such as Afriland First Bank in Cameroon (featured in the quotation at the beginning of this chapter, and discussed in more detail in Chapter 10), which aims to be more in tune with African values and principles, looks towards Western principles in formalizing HRM reward practices. One member of the management team explained.

We have specific human resource management processes. At the beginning of the year everyone in each function has specific evaluation criteria. If I am a cashier the first evaluation might be the number of bank notes I have counted over the year, and the number of counterfeit notes I have taken. At the end you have the commercial criteria. At the beginning of the year you have norms. After that you set your own objectives depending on your own ambitions. At the end of each month you have to fill in a form to compare the difference between the norms and objectives and achievements. You send one copy to Human Resources, and you keep one copy. This gives you an opportunity to compare your performance, as well as being a form of control. We have a career profile for each function within the bank. According to that profile you know where you are and where you need to be. Promotion can be made in the same function but you can grow in grade. If you meet objectives three times you are promoted by rank. Also you can be promoted by function. We try as much as possible to have something quantifiable to treat everyone objectively. But qualitative actions are also taken into consideration. But there should be a relation between objectives and results. If you make an error this has to be explained, so there is an element of control in this.

Although this is only one example, we believe that a simple conclusion that Western motivational methods may be inappropriate is a gross over-simplification when looking at the realities of organizations in Africa. This is because these organizations are products of crossvergence of values and principles in a process of hybridization giving rise to a number of possibilities or solutions to the antagonism between home/community life and working life. Generally speaking, there is an antithesis between Western motivational theories and principles based on instrumental notions of the value of human beings in organizations, and African values based on humanistic notions of the value of people (such as the *ubuntu* concept that has gained some popularity in South Africa, deriving from the Xhosa proverb 'Ubuntu ungamntu ngabanye ubantu' or 'people are people through other people', and seeking to revive indigenous African humanistic principles in management). Yet in dealing with the realities of a colonial legacy and presence of Western multinationals and prevalence of Western management education in sub-Saharan Africa, as well as a weakness of African renaissance systems used in the management of organizations, expectation of managers may well be based, for example, on a direct relationship between performance and reward. For example, in the management promotion practices of Guinness in Cameroon:

We have a people management system. We look at all our senior managers. The appraisal system is the formal tip. We know how our managers are performing on a day-to-day basis. We have a profile of managers, we rank them by: What do they achieve? Do they meet and exceed our expectations? And we rank them in terms of management style: that is, how they achieve this. We look at how managers lead. We rank them informally and formally and see who has the potential to progress: people at the top, high potential managers will be promoted at least two grades over the next five years; then 'promotable' people capable of moving one grade; then those capable of development within their own grade; and, those at the bottom, the problem people. We look at the opportunities to develop these people: are they square pegs in round holes. If neither of these we have to make hard decisions. It is a hard decision if people

have to exit the organization because there isn't a lot to go to outside. Out of
40 managers last year we had to make this decision about four or five. We have
a development plan for each manager and we look at how we can help develop
people. but as in any organization the neck of the bottle becomes smaller.

(From interview with Managing Director, Guinness Cameroun)

We do indeed consider the main cross-cultural literature on the relevance of Western
theories to other cultural situations and their application to organizations in Africa,
because this is an important issue in Africa. Often these principles are accepted
uncritically, and this is also a problem (although the MD of Guinness Cameroun
states that 'sometimes these principles, coming from London, seem a bit academic.
We have to adapt them in a practical way to the situation'). But we consider this in
the context of the three ideal type management systems we have already examined
in detail.

The extract above from our interviews with managers of Afriland First Bank also
highlights the role of control in the use of motivational methods in organizations,
and promotion practices in Guinness also suggest this, with a final sanction of
dismissing managers if they do not perform. We therefore also consider motivation
in the context of management control (which we have discussed in previous chapters)
and how this might work in each of the three systems in connection with management
motivation. We do this by extending the control–compliance theory of Etzioni
(1975), the relevance of which we explored more fully in Chapter 2. Katz and Kahn's
(1978) theory of motivation based on 'rule enforcement', 'external rewards' and
'internalized motivation' has already been used to explain motivation in Chinese
enterprises (Tung, 1991; Child, 1994; Jackson and Bak, 1998). The importance of
these three motivational factors can be seen respectively in post-colonial (rule
enforcement), post-instrumental (external rewards) and African renaissance systems
(internalized motivation) (See Figure 6.1).

### Post-colonial motivational systems

Jackson and Bak (1998) discuss rule enforcement, or the acceptance of the legitimacy
of role prescription and organizational directives, as a motive in Chinese enterprises.
It is worth noting some of the parallels with organizations in Africa. The use of rules
and role prescriptions may be regarded as a form of role protection in the Chinese
context. Child (1994) provides the example of job descriptions carrying little
motivational content in terms of tasks or objectives to be achieved, but as an insurance
against being asked to take on additional and unknown duties and against being
overworked. This may also be indicative of the avoidance motive (McClelland's, 1987,
fourth motive after achievement, affiliation and power motives), in not wanting to
take risks because of a deep-seated fear of punishment.

However, the reverse side of the coin is the incentive to find ways around tightly
enforced regulations in state enterprises in order to facilitate their running. Therefore,
job descriptions may provide employees with a psychologically safe foundation from
which to work effectively. Jackson and Bak (1998) investigated role allocation and

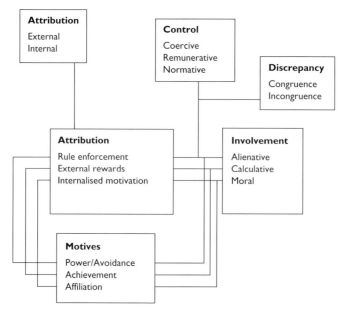

*Figure 6.1* Motivation and reward systems.

performance by looking at the way responsibility is given and the way performance is directed through goal setting and appraisal, and then enforcement through sanctions for non-performance, and reinforcement through praise. They found that there was a guarded attitude towards giving too much responsibility as workers appeared to like guidance and there was some fear of making mistakes resulting in inaction. Particularly older workers preferred clear instructions, although it was also evident that many younger Chinese workers preferred such an approach.

Yet motivation was also seen to rise when more responsibility was given to employees in their own area. However, this only came with experience, when more responsibility was given. There was little evidence of precise job descriptions being used, and instructions seemed to relate to the job at hand. General rules of conduct existed in some companies, and in one company these were made clear in a two-day induction session. These were quite specific: no spitting, no smoking, how to dress and cut your hair.

Several of the Chinese companies used goal setting extensively, and saw it as useful. This involved the setting of individual targets, face-to-face performance discussions, and weekly to annual appraisals, depending on the company.

Direct punishment was only found in the hotel sector where some of the companies punished their staff for bad behaviour and not working. Deductions from salary or bonuses were seen to give positive results. For some offences up to three warnings were given before dismissal. Penalty schemes for non-attendance at training sessions were also in operation. The use of pressure and punishment of this kind was not identified in companies outside the hotel industry. Yet companies seemed not to praise their employees very often. Individual praise in front of the group was not often used deliberately except in the hotel industry. A view elsewhere is that this may be negative or embarrassing.

Post-colonial or statist management systems in China may well have parallels with those in Africa, and indeed in other emerging regions, as rule enforcement as a motivator (or at least an avoidance motive) appears to be associated with security needs, and in reducing uncertainty within an uncertain environment (see Chapter 3). This is evident in Blunt and Jones' (1992) account of motivational needs in Africa. Howell *et al.*'s (1975) study of Liberian managers, Blunt's (1976) study of Kenyan managers, and Jones' (1988) study of Malawian managers all point to the importance of security needs among African managers. Although these studies are now somewhat dated, and questionnaire items derive from Maslow's theory (which we discuss in more detail in the next section on Western motivational theory) including items on financial rewards, they do indicate a need for more security and uncertainty in an uncertain environment.

Howell *et al.* (1975), for example, explain their findings in relation to the turbulent political climate in Liberia that created conditions of uncertainty in the community and in industrial organizations. As in China, role prescription and rule enforcement may well act as a motivator in sub-Saharan Africa as a form of role protection, with the addition of job protection, which as in China over the last decade or two, is getting more precarious in the light of structural adjustment programmes in Africa and accountability and privatization of the public sector in both regions.

### Motivating managers in post-colonial systems

We therefore argue that in statist or post-colonial systems security needs are important motivators, and control is used as a mechanism to motivate (sticks predominate over carrots). In Chapter 1 we noted that the colonial systems left an inheritance of management approaches that generally assumed that human nature is not to be trusted (e.g. McGregor's Theory X) with a need to impose controls on workers, allowing little worker initiative, and rewarding a narrow set of skills. This is in the context of authoritarian and paternalistic decision styles with centralized and hierarchical control and decision-making (Kiggundu, 1989; Blunt and Jones, 1997). Blunt and Jones (1997) also affirm that there is an emphasis on control mechanisms, rules and procedures rather than performance (with a reluctance to judge performance, as in the Chinese case), and high levels of conservatism and reluctance to change. Their highlighting of the importance of kingship networks also indicates the presence of a dual system. On the one hand there may well be high levels of hierarchy, bureaucracy and rules, but on the other hand, decisions about recruitment, reward and promotion may be made on an informal basis where preference is given to in-group members. We note this dual system in connection with some organizations in Cameroon (Chapter 10). For example, the Directeur Général of Caisse Nationale de Prévoyance Sociale explains that he was attempting to change the situation he found when first coming to his job:

The organization was ruled on a clan basis. You were close to the Directeur Général or you were not. People were motivated by what individual benefit they could obtain by this. People were not motivated by the desire to leave a mark, but only by the immediate return on their commitment to the Directeur Général.

Where this type of system prevails it would logically be senior managers who would predominantly benefit from the informal system operating for in-group family members, and more junior managers and staff who might be subject to the formal system of hierarchy, rules and control mechanism. For example, Asian run companies in Kenya provide an example of this dual system (formal and informal). In one organization in Nairobi that makes plastic moulding, we interviewed a succession of senior managers, all of Indian decent, and mostly having the same family name as the Managing Director. We asked what motivates managers. Responses included:

- 'The environment within the organization motivates managers.'
- 'I believe that one day the company will be big. I look forward to that moment. This is the same for most managers: to grow with the company.'
- 'Managers are very loyal to the company, they tend to stay.'
- 'There is no barrier to anything. There are open meetings, and open forums. This is motivating for everyone. When there is openness everyone is happy.'

When asked if reward was related to performance, these same managers answered:

- 'Performance appraisal is carried out every month. Employee targets are checked every month. There is an internal grading system for when someone has done a good job.'
- 'We have just introduced an appraisal form, with the timing of its use to be decided by management, but probably every six months. Employee and employer both grade and this is then agreed upon. Reward is directly related to performance, a person can be upgraded.'
- 'Reward is directly related to performance.' 'Appraisal is there, reward is related to performance.'

Yet the Kikuyu junior managers we interviewed told a different story. One manager told us: 'We are free to come to work to do a good job. Work conditions aren't bad. I am happy with this. The workforce needs more morale, although no manager has resigned recently.' On the subject of whether reward is related to performance he said: 'There is no agreement on appraisal. At the moment no-one is rewarding. There are no promotions.'

A second Kikuyu manager went into more detail:

I am motivated by my work; to make sure that the customer is getting good quality. I am not motivated by pay or promotion, but doing a good job, by internal satisfaction. There is no hope of going up the organization. Here, if you are made a manager they are expecting something from you, you cannot expect anything from them.

Asked whether reward is related to performance he said: 'I have never seen a performance appraisal system here. You are called a manager but you are not given any power. Things are being done to obtain ISO quality recognition, it is just one of the requirements.'

It is too simplistic therefore to conclude that control and rule enforcement prevails as a management motivator within post-colonial systems. This may well be the case for employees lower down the organization who are not part of the familial or 'clan' in-group. Yet for managers who are part of the in-group and have promotion prospects to higher levels, this may not be the predominant motivator. Motivators may then be a mixture of (in McClelland's, 1987, terms, which we discuss in more detail below) power, affiliation and achievement motive: a motivation to reach the top that is realistic; a motivation towards the affiliation of other in-group members at the exclusion of out-group members; and financial reward.

This may be reflected in both public sector organizations, and private sector companies where a particular group has ownership or predominates. Two solutions seem to be available for out-group members who wish to progress up the career ladder. The first is to change their tribal identity where this is a factor. We have seen this in Cameroon where members of smaller groups claim membership of larger more dominant groups (discussed in Chapter 10). This may present a more 'politically' acceptable face. The second way is for organizations to change through deliberate management policies. A number of companies in Kenya (for example, a water pump distributor which has been dominated by Kikuyus) and in Cameroon (for example, Afriland First Bank, which has been dominated by Bamilekes) were attempting to do this. As we noted above, one route that is often identified is to move over more towards 'modern' Western HRM methods. It is to this that we now turn our attention.

## Post-instrumental systems and the appropriateness of Western motivational theories

The static–content theories of motivation are standard reading in Western textbooks, and form the basis of management training programmes. They underline our assumptions about motivating employees in Western Anglo-Saxon countries which often emphasize external rewards within the Katz and Kahn schema introduced above (see Figure 6.1). The best known theories are those of Maslow (1958), Herzberg (1966), McClelland (1987) and McGregor (1960). They largely address the question 'What outcomes are attractive to an individual and why?' The development of incentive schemes within Western companies tends to focus on the satisfaction of such needs identified by Maslow and Herzberg through job design, participation in decision-making, promotion opportunities, working conditions and pay.

### Maslow's theory in the cross-cultural context

The classic cross-cultural study by Haire et al. (1966), which applied Maslow's model found differences in managerial need importance and need satisfaction across fourteen countries. For Italy, England and the United States the *need satisfaction* score was in the same order as Maslow's hierarchy of needs (security, social, esteem, autonomy and self-actualization), that is, security was the most satisfied need and self-actualization the least satisfied. Yet for *need importance* no country followed Maslow's order, although the United States came closest. Hofstede (1980b) argued that this result tells us more about Maslow (an American), and the human needs of US middle-class culture, than about need importance in different countries. He criticizes Maslow's theory as reflecting a particular individualist view of the world (Hofstede, 1980b) with 'self actualization' being at the top of the pyramid.

Yet Maslow's theory is extensively referred to in management textbooks and educational programmes throughout Anglophone Africa. Even in books that are purported to be written specifically for African managers, Maslow theory is accepted uncritically. For example, Ugwuegbu (2001: 47) writes 'Of the theories in this category [motive or need theory] the best known among African managers is Maslow's need hierarchy'. He then goes on to outline the theory without criticism, stating it is important for knowing where on the hierarchy an employee's need satisfaction has stopped so that the 'reinforcement system' can be manipulated to move the worker to the next level; satisfying all lower needs can liberate them to pursue creative achievement and self-actualization; and knowledge of workers' needs levels can aid selection and placement as well as the content of training programmes. Ndongko (1999) similarly outlines Maslow's theory uncritically and without referring to it later in her chapter when she develops more of a critique of prevailing (post-colonial in our terms) concepts of African employees.

Although other studies have found need hierarchies to be similar, but not identical, to Maslow's theory (for example, Steers and Sanchez-Runde, 2002, cite a number of studies), Hofstede's critique has tended to predominate in the cross-cultural management literature. Nevis (1983) suggests, for example, a revision of the need hierarchy in the Chinese situation to reflect group loyalty and national unity which may need to be addressed even before physiological needs; where self actualization is in the service of the community; where individual esteem (achievement, independence, reputation and prestige) may not be a relevant concept in a highly collectivist society; and, where 'face' is more related to belongingness than to individual esteem. As we saw above, Blunt and Jones (1992) also present evidence in the African situation that Maslow's hierarchy should be rethought. In particular, African managers place a higher importance on security needs, than on higher-order needs. We argued above that this may be a result of the uncertain environment that we discussed in Chapter 3.

These comments must also have implications for Herzberg's (1966) theory of hygiene factors where extrinsic factors such as adequate working conditions and money, when absent, may cause demotivation. Motivators or intrinsic factors include content of the task, achievement, responsibility and growth. Belongingness may well be a 'hygiene' factor in this sense, where if this is absent little else is particularly meaningful.

*Achievement motive in the cross-cultural context*

McClelland's (1987) motivation theory suggests that people are differently motivated towards achievement, power, affiliation and avoidance, where the achievement motive is key to McClelland's view of economic development. Such achievement involves the creation of more efficient ways of doing things and solving problems, the preference for tasks that reveal successful performance, and the taking of personal responsibility for performance. Yet the application of McClelland's theory in non-Western countries is even more ominous than other content theory. This is because of the purported relationship between high levels of achievement motive and economic growth. McClelland and Winter (1969) argue that as levels of achievement motive rise within a country, so does the level of entrepreneurial activity and economic development. This fits nicely with the modernization thesis implicit in the World Bank/IMF-led structural adjustment programmes in Africa and elsewhere. It fits well with the developing–developed world paradigm, where the objective of development is to be more like the developed world.

In this context, it is interesting to note a broad-brush comparison that Harris and Moran (1989) make between East Asian and Western values, which has a bearing on management motivation: respectively between equity (East Asian) and wealth (Western); group and individual, between saving and consumption; between extended family relations and nuclear and mobile family; between the importance of protocol, rank and status, and informality and personal competence; and between a need to avoid conflict and a need for conflict to be managed. Although not all the first values may apply to the African situation, this provides a clear indication of the foundation of the importance of the achievement motive in 'Western' culture. Again Hofstede (1980b and 1991) criticizes the concept of achievement motive as a product of American culture, and one that would have been unlikely to have been conceived by a Frenchman, Swede or Japanese (1991).

Indeed, when comparing McClelland's findings of a forty-one-country study on achievement motive in 1950, Hofstede finds that the level of achievement motive correlates positively with countries on his masculinity index, and negatively with countries on his uncertainty avoidance index. As low uncertainty avoidance means a greater willingness to take risks, and high masculinity means assertiveness or ambitiousness, Hofstede is not surprised by this correlation (1980b: 171). Those countries that score high on masculinity and low on uncertainty avoidance are the USA and other Anglo-Saxon countries including Britain, Canada, Australia and New Zealand.

It is also interesting that they include countries that have been under British rule, such as India and Jamaica. It is perhaps not surprising that South Africa also is included, in the light of the white only sample included in Hofstede's study. McClelland was particularly active in India with his achievement motive workshops, and these, Hofstede (1991) notes, found a ready audience, as a former British Commonwealth country; although we actually find this conclusion somewhat tenuous. This is particularly in light of our current analysis of the hybridization of post-colonial, post-instrumental and African renaissance management systems in Africa, which could equally apply in other post-colonial countries such as India. That is, although the introduction of Western principles cannot be dismissed totally, and may find a reception among Western educated managers, care should be taken in applying such theories downwards in the organization.

Achievement theories may also have application among small, independent entrepreneurs in India, as in Africa, where as Mbigi (1997: 33) reminds us that entrepreneurship is 'respected, encouraged, nurtured and collectively celebrated' and evidence for the development of entrepreneurs is well documented in countries such as Zimbabwe (Wild, 1997). It may well be an issue with management motivation that this entrepreneurial spirit is not well captured by larger private sector organizations in Africa.

Indeed, it may be the case that post-colonial organizations have repressed this spirit, and as Jackson and Bak (1998) note is the case in Chinese public enterprises, the avoidance motive (McClelland, 1987) may be high and may be a real problem for productivity as a fear of being punished for mistakes. Schermerhorn and Nyaw (1990) call this 'learned helplessness'. A person learns from an experience of past inadequacies to feel incapable of future success. A senior manager who is already a victim of learned helplessness does not expect initiative from middle managers. This may lead to passivity in the workplace and even a need for a high level of supervision. This is connected to a lack of achievement where taking risks is avoided, where there is a high level of uncertainty avoidance, and in McGregor's (1960) terms, a preponderance of management styles and techniques which favour Theory X, rather than Theory Y. The former assumes that most workers dislike work and therefore try to avoid it. They must be controlled and coerced into achieving organizational goals. The latter assumes that employees seek responsibility, can make decisions and will exercise self-control when properly motivated.

We believe this situation has parallels in organizations in Africa. For example, the Manager Director of Guinness Cameroun told us:

> People believe that the boss is there to make the decisions. We meet on a regular basis with managers. At my second meeting with the managers a second-tier manager asked what management was doing about a particular issue. I said, you are a manager, what are you doing about it. The managers here are more supervisors than managers. . . . We are trying to get people to take calculated risks, that is giving people the freedom to succeed, including making mistakes, and giving managers the opportunity to manage things the way they want.

Organizations such as Guinness recognize this as a problem and are trying to do something about it. We also noted earlier that the same company has been introducing measures that reward such behaviour by linking reward directly to performance, that is, getting managers to be motivated by making decisions and getting it right or learning by their mistakes and not getting punished for this. However, again we should note that punishment for getting things wrong may well have been for out-group members rather than in-group members who may have been better cosseted from the uncertainties of continuing employment.

We would argue that the power motive (McClelland, 1987) is the converse of the avoidance motive in post-colonial systems. The former, the need to influence and control, may be a motivator for in-group members, whereas the avoidance motive, an anxiety that motivates people to avoid certain experiences such as failure, rejection, and punishment, may be a (de-)motivator for out-group members in the same post-colonial organization. Gaining a position of power in an organization for an out-group member may not be an option, whereas avoiding getting the sack may well be. As we noted above, there may be a possibility of adopting the tribal identity of a more dominant group. In this case power motive may be present and a key motivator for individuals who follow this course.

Blunt and Jones (1992) agree with Kiggundu's (1988) assertion that many African cultural groups would score high on Hofstede's (1980a) power distance index, maintaining that this is consistent with the preferences of senior managers not to delegate and not to encourage participatory and decentralized management in Africa. Certainly we would agree that this would be the case in post-colonial management systems. This being so, progression up the hierarchy, enforcing controls, and directing people could be a motivator that perpetuates this system, where this is attainable for the individual. Where this is not an obtainable goal, alienation may be an issue or simply an acceptance of a hierarchical organizational system that seeks to control employees, although evidence from our management and employee (see Chapter 7) surveys suggests that this is generally not accepted.

Affiliation Motive (McClelland, 1987) concerns the need to develop interpersonal relations and may fit well with collectivist in-group social psychology. In Triandis' (e.g. 2002) terms post-colonial systems may reflect a vertical collectivism, whereas African renaissance systems may reflect a horizontal collectivism. Yet the work of Schwartz (1994) has shown that collegiality or 'egalitarian commitment' exists in individualistic societies as a voluntary affiliation rather than as the obligatory affiliation of collectivism. Egalitarian commitment also does not appear as an in-group/out-group situation.

Affiliation motive, if it can be applied in the way McClellend conceived it, may therefore be present in any of our three 'ideal type' management systems. However, by distinguishing between horizontal and vertical on the one hand and individualism and collectivism on the other, we may see that the affiliation motive as conceived by McClelland may not be directly relevant when looking at management motivation in a cross-cultural context. Triandis (2002) describes horizontal collectivism as including 'a sense of oneness with members of the in-group and social cohesiveness' (p. 26).

In horizontal societies there is a tradition of equality. Ayittey (1991) describes both stateless African societies such as those of the Igbo and Fulani of Nigeria, the Somali, Kikuyu of Kenya and the San !Kung of the Kalahari, as well as African kingdoms. Stateless societies, which Ayittey describes as more egalitarian and consensual could be described as horizontally collectivist.

Vertical societies, Triandis notes, assume that people are different from one another through an accepted hierarchy. Both traditional India and China constituted vertical societies with India's caste system emphasizing differences by birth, and China allocating resources according to a strict pecking order. African kingdoms, such as states of the Zulu and Swazi of southern Africa, the Ga of present day Ghana, and

Ife of southwestern Nigeria, may also be examples of vertical collectivism, although Ayittey warns that even with these types of African social organization the king has come into being by the will of the people, and that royal despotism rarely exists: the king being subject to consensual decision-making.

### Western motivational principles and collectivism–individualism

Triandis's (2002) concepts produce a typology of different kinds of culture: horizontal individualism such as, he suggests, in Sweden and Australia; vertical individualism such as in American corporations with the need to 'be the best'; horizontal collectivism such as in kibbutzim in Israel, and also we would suggests many African cultures; and vertical collectivism as in India and China, and also we suggest in Japanese and Korean corporations (see, for example, Chen, 1995). Hence Triandis suggests that in horizontal individualism people do not compete to do better, but are self-reliant, and with an emphasis on modesty. In vertical individualism people want to be the best, and inequality is seen as natural with large pay differentials ideally based on individual merit and performance.

Jackson (2002a) has discussed the problems of corporations from one such individualistic culture operating in another using the example of Sweden and America, and America and the Netherlands. The Swedish company IKEA, for example, had problems in the United States with local managers because progression was seen to be slow as it was largely based on experience, and there was a disparaging of self-promotion. Conversely, an American DIY company in the Netherlands found it difficult to implement an MBO (management by objectives) system tied to compensation as a way of incentivizing people. This was opposed by local managers and employees on the assumption that everyone gives 100 per cent of his or her effort all the time. Therefore they should be given 100 per cent as a normal exchange, and not given a bonus. Sales staff also refused to work on commission arrangements in order to work for less on a non-incentive basis.

In horizontal collectivism people merge with other members of their in-group, and are more or less equal with them. It includes a sense of oneness with in-group members and social cohesiveness. In vertical collectivism people are highly interdependent with their in-group and recognize the in-group authority as having the right answers. It combines with a sense of obligation to serving the in-group, and subordinating their needs, goals and aspirations to the requirements of the collective, even to the extent of this being oppressive. Triandis (2002) also suggests, through research evidence that authoritarianism is somewhat related to vertical but not horizontal collectivism.

This is why we suspect that vertical collectivism describes the prevailing culture in post-colonial management systems, and horizontal collectivism describes the situation in African renaissance systems. Western multinational companies (as well as Western education) would mainly represent vertical individualism, stressing achievement and pay differentials based on performance (such as the situation described in British-based Guinness Cameroun described in this chapter and in Chapter 10).

Lorenzen (2000) has described Danish firms working in sub-Saharan Africa. With

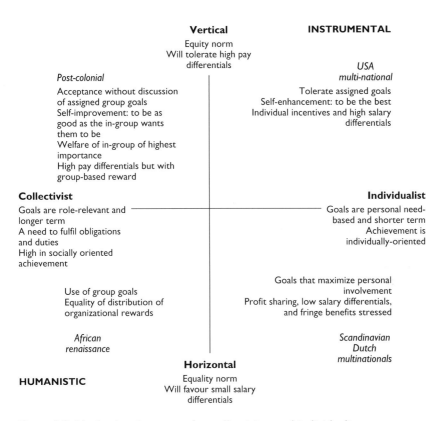

*Figure 6.2* Motivational patterns for collectivists and individualists.

Denmark scoring low on Hofstede's (1980a) power distance index (similar to Triandis' vertical concept), high on individualism, and low on masculinity (or achievement orientation), we would describe Denmark as a horizontal individualistic culture. One issue arising when working with African partners was the problem seen by Danish managers of the power distance of African organizations which the Danish saw as leading to inefficiencies. The main concern of the Danish managers she interviewed seemed to be the overcoming of inefficiencies and time wasting, rather than the introduction of performance systems that encourage individual reward and excellence (a theme not mentioned, but which was prominent in our own, perhaps British and therefore more vertically individualistic, research).

Our discussion of collectivism and individualism, cross cut with vertical and horizontal orientations has implications for management motivation and the way Western motivational principles are taught and accepted in management education and textbooks, and the way these are introduced in sub-Saharan Africa.

*Attribution theory in the cross-cultural context*

Another aspect of motivation that is important to consider across cultures (see, for example, Jackson, 1993) is attribution or locus of control (Rotter, 1966) which we first discussed in Chapter 3. This looks at the way people attribute cause and effect: either to internal causes that they themselves can affect through their own competencies and actions, or to external causes which cannot be controlled by us as they are external to us.

Rotter (1966) found that individuals differ on the extent to which they attribute cause and effect to either internal or external causes. In other words, people differ in the degree to which they believe they can control their environment and the things and events around them. Cross-cultural studies have shown that cultures vary on these two orientations (Smith *et al.* 1995). This is important to motivation, and the way incentive measures are transferred across cultures because it affects people's perception of what they can do to earn rewards.

Triandis (2002) reminds us that collectivists tend to attribute events to external causes, whereas individualists tend to attribute events to internal causes. Individual incentive schemes may therefore work well in individualist (and vertical) cultures, but not very well in cultures when people believe that they have very little effect on external events, which are attributed to luck, fate or God. Sales, production and levels of business may be due to causes outside their control. Individual incentives based on measurable performance may therefore be seen to be unfair in many African cultures that are collectivistic.

Hofstede (1991) maintains that collectivism predominates in poorer countries. People come together in situations of adversity, pooling their collective resources, and face the difficult and complex environment together. Influencing events in the outside world may be seen as beyond the individual, but with the help of the wider collective (including those who are now ancestors) one may harmonize and get on within the environment. This is why Triandis (2002) asserts that collectivists tend to change themselves to fit in rather than change their environment, yet individualists try to change their environment rather than to fit into it. It is unlikely that individualized incentive schemes can work very well in a collectivist situation. Yet we have to remember that organizations in Africa constitute various forms of hybridization, and that rarely has the wider societal collectivism been successfully captured by the corporation. In addition, managers, many of whom have been educated in the Western (predominately American) tradition, will be more likely to accept Western motivational methods than those lower down the organization.

*Expectancy theory and individualism–collectivism*

The predominance of external locus of control in collectivistic societies also places a rather different slant on expectancy theory of motivation (e.g. Porter and Lawler, 1968). Again, this is a theory that is widely taught and expounded in management textbooks. This theory supposes that performance equals ability *times* effort. However, in collectivist societies it is necessary to use a formulation of performance equals ability *plus* effort (Singh, 1981). Triandis (2002) explains this as follows. Individualists perceive performance as a personal quality. Therefore if a person does not expend any effort, and if he or she does not have the ability, they will not see performance. However, the collectivist sees performance as a group quality. It is therefore possible to show performance if one member of the group has the ability and other members expend a lot of effort.

We can take this further within the framework of external locus of control. Porter and Lawler (1968) propose that effort is dependent on *valence* or value of the envisaged reward as well as *perceived instrumentality* or probability that reward depends on effort. Within the African situation rewards such as additional pay through an MBO-type system may be attractive, but with a high external locus of control, a manager's connection between effort and outcome may be tentative, particularly if this is based on individual effort. This tentative connection may well be strengthened by the collective effort of a group.

Yet the problem appears to remain in many African organizations that in-group/out-group dynamics militate against the building of effective functional teams based on a collectivity and cohesiveness. There may be just two solutions to this. First base an entire organization on one in-group. This is increasingly difficult to do in a modern complex organization that requires talent from a broader section of the community, and is also increasingly politically difficult to justify. The second solution is to develop effective cross-cultural management within the organization in order to forge multicultural groups from which may be drawn high levels of synergy (that is 2 + 2 equals more than 4). This does seem to be the way organizations are moving. Although in some South African organizations top management is moving away from this in the belief that this has already been done in 1994 during the first democratic elections. When looking around the staff restaurant in one such organization it is easy to see the lack of integration of the different cultural groups. We discuss this option in detail in Chapter 8.

## Transferability of Western motivational principles

We can conclude that there are problems transferring Western principles across cultures, and much of the cross-cultural literature supports this, despite this being largely ignored by textbooks on management in Africa, and by the widespread use of Western textbooks in Africa. If post-colonial management systems are based on coercive control (from Etzioni, 1975) which translates into motivational principles based predominantly on rule enforcement (from Katz and Kahn, 1978) as we explained above, post-instrumental systems are based on remunerative control which translates into motivational principles based predominantly on external rewards (Figure 6.1). This is not to say that there is no overlap, and that internalized motivation is not an aspect of Western principles: from the literature it clearly is. We would like to argue that internalized motivation is more a factor in our third ideal type: African renaissance.

Yet simply arguing that Western principles are not applicable in organizations in Africa is too simplistic. This is because of the hybrid nature of organizations that have been subjected to different cultural influences. Yet different forms of hybrids have differing success in making a link between the world of home and community, and the world of work. Either the wider societal collectivism has not been successfully captured by many organizations in Africa, or its influences are so strong it warps the relationship within organizations by strong in-groups and negative attitudes towards out-group members. There is some evidence to suggest that organizations are addressing the in-group/out-group problem by taking an attitude of positive discrimination towards recruiting out-group members, but this may not be backed up by appropriate cross-cultural training (see Chapter 8), or in motivational and promotion practices. For example, in South Africa, with a legacy of exclusionist management policies, we met the following (demotivated) manager in a health-care product company that participated in our study. A Zulu by origin, he told us the following:

> There is no clear strategy to address inter-ethnic relations. Certain individuals from a particular ethnic group are seen to be more suitable for certain jobs. Does HRM look at colour? They do not address this. I have been with the company for five years. I sat down with my immediate superior. There are two grading committees for different levels. The superior was going to feed my case into the relevant grading committee, but my grade remains the same. I asked what criteria did they use – complexity, skills/knowledge, people management. I would score high on knowledge with my qualifications, and on people management, but apparently complexity of my job didn't warrant an upgrade. I asked for a definition of complexity, and this met exactly what I do. So it seems my case was not correctly presented to the committee? The committee is all white. This isn't even representative of managers in this organization, some of whom are black.

We now turn to motivation within Africa renaissance management systems in order to see how it may be possible to motivate managers using more indigenous principles that may better integrate home/community life and the world of work, and to develop synergies among different groups rather than forging unifying yet exclusionist tendencies in an in-group/out-group situation.

### *African renaissance motivational systems*

Any motivational system developed and employed within a work organization is a means of control. In Etzioni's (1975) terms African renaissance systems would use normative controls in order to develop shared values, to utilize motives of affiliations, to enhance internalized motivation, in order to develop moral commitment of managers and staff. Hence Koopman (1991) describes how in Cashbuild in South Africa, shared values were built mainly by getting people together in order to develop an understanding of values and principles upon which they wish to work. Metropolitan in our current study had also gone through a similar process in order to develop commonality and mutual understanding. One HR manager explains:

The company has changed significantly over the last four to five years. I struggled to accept the company and work within it when I first came here. It was very conservative and run by actuaries. They bring their own norms and culture. I found it very centralized in decision-making. I initiated the values process, which for example asked what should we let go of? . . . We work-shopped what the values should be. We had a values *indaba*, and identified ten values. We asked, to live these what should we do in terms of behaviours? We established a body to get people to live these values, and we could reward people who demonstrated these values. We had quarterly winners and a national champion.

Also as the quotation at the head of this chapter from a manager at Afriland First Bank in Cameroon suggests, common values that motivate may be created through a superordinate goal such as building the country. Shared superordinate values may be more likely to encourage a non-exclusive form of affiliation motive across cultural groups. The Directeur Général of Caisse Nationale de Prévoyance Sociale in Cameroon also recognizes this. He indicates that at the higher levels there are leaders who lack vision and are too concerned about the day-to-day business. They do not take the time to reflect on what they are doing and why. Managers do not have a clear understanding of the general mission. There is an attempt by top management to try to share the vision of social responsibilities toward the clients they serve, although there appears to be some resistance by managers lower down. He says: 'We lack vision and the knowledge of our mission; we have to constantly put it back on the agenda. It isn't easy . . . the influences of inter-ethnic relations in the organization are real, but you have to transcend them'.

Yet this may be more difficult in South Africa than in other countries such as Cameroon because it is more culturally complex across the collectivism–individualism divide. The best available data on this aspect is from Wentzel's (1999) study of management values across South African cultural groups.

In Figure 6.3 we have used levels of individualism and power distance as a surrogate for horizontal and vertical collectivism and individualism. It is only really possible to obtain an approximate comparison among these groups with these data. As it was not analysed at the 'ecological' level, we cannot compare this directly with Hofstede's data in different countries. Also because Wentzel (1999) did not standardize an individual's item scores against the individual's mean scores, it is difficult to interpret these scores in absolute terms. The data do appear to indicate that Afrikaans-speaking white managers, English-speaking white managers, Asian and Coloured managers are in comparison more vertically individualistic than the African groups. The Zulu, Tswana and Xhosa managers are more horizontally collectivistic. The Swazi group appears to be more horizontally individualistic. This tends to support an intuitive assumption that white South Africans will be more individualistic and hierarchical, and black South Africans will be less individualistic and less hierarchical.

Yet it is more difficult to explain why the Swazi group support a lower power distance in common with another Nguni group the Zulu, although this does lend support to Ayittey's (1991) argument that African kingdoms also are not the autocratic political institutions that the imperial authorities believed or created. He

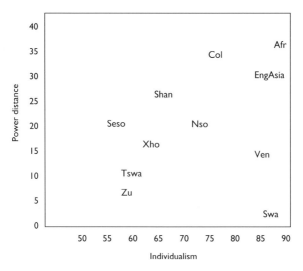

*Figure 6.3* Relative positions on power distance and individualism of South African cultural groups (derived from Wentzel's,1999, data).

Note
Afr (Afrikaans), Asia (Asian), Col (Coloured), Eng (English), Nso (North Sotho), Seso (South Sotho), Shan (Shangaan), Swa (Swazi) Tswa (Tswana), Ven (Venda), Xho (Xhosa), Zu (Zulu).

quotes Gibbs (1965: 499) in that among the Swazi 'The king is king by the people' and 'The king is ruled by his councillors'. In fact commoners participate in discussions with the king and the chiefs through regional forums called *Tinkhundlha*.

They also appear, with the Venda group, to be more individualistic than other African groups including the other Nguni groups (Zulu and Xhosa). Although slightly speculative, it may be that the Swazi who live in South Africa are away from in-groups in Swaziland, and may act more individualistically in work organizations where few if any colleagues will be Swazi. That they may have reached managerial rank on their own account may also be a factor. This again may highlight the difficulties of gaining synergies by using motivational principles that are more in line with collectivist orientations in South Africa. This may well be easier in Cameroon or other countries that may not have such a large collectivism–individualism divide.

Understanding differences in values orientation between individualism and collectivism (what Koopman, 1991, calls 'communalism', which is a reflection of Triandis's horizontal collectivism) is a prerequisite to designing management motivational policies and practices in African countries, including South Africa. Although Koopman's book predates the *ubuntu* movement in South Africa, the communalistic values are a useful account of *ubuntu* values, and aspects that we would include in our African renaissance ideal-type management system.

Given these differences between individualism and communalism, Koopman (1991) makes recommendations on how motivational systems may be developed, drawing on his experience in Cashbuild, in order to take account of the more communalistic orientation of managers and staff. Basing reward on a belief that people do not work purely for money, and that the need for dignity, pride, belonging and freedom should be fulfilled first, they addressed those needs first at Cashbuild before any additional rewards for money were introduced. Maintenance factors were also addressed as they were raised, such as funeral policies, housing loans and educational assistance, although these were only addressed once additional productivity and wealth, as well as 'human freedom' had been created. His recommendations from his experience were:

- Avoid rewarding staff for something they do not have control over. This involves avoiding long-term goals (over twelve months) and things beyond the workplace. This addresses the orientation towards an external locus of control.
- Only share profit if profitability is raised. If not this is tantamount to paternalism. Loyalty is difficult to buy in this way if staff see through this.
- Giving staff share ownership is not meaningful when, for example, food prices are a main concern in Africa. Their ability to sell their shares defeats the objective.
- Avoid rewarding communally oriented staff on an individual basis that will separate them into classes by money and grading systems, and avoid the principle of capitalistic meritocracy, as it does not apply in Africa.
- Develop communal reward schemes for communal effort, for example, by group, or section.
- Reward only those things that people feel they can control and measure themselves.
- Reward for upward movement of productivity indices.
- If share schemes are created, do so via a collective, with people gaining a meaningful proportion of shares that can directly influence their voting rights on issues within the organization.

These recommendations represent at least one organization's attempt to introduce motivational measures that address the issue of rewarding more communally minded managers. Although these are addressed to staff generally, and although we stated above that managers may well be more individualistically oriented than staff lower down the organization, Jackson's (1999) study in a number of South African organizations suggested that the predominantly black managers were more human-istically rather than instrumentally oriented. This study is discussed in Chapter 12.

## Management motivation in Africa: some results

So far in this chapter we have discussed management motivation from the perspective of our three ideal type management systems. We have however said that these ideal types combine in organizations in different hybrid forms. Cultural influences on motivation may be varied within organizations in Africa, yet little systematic information exists on the manifestations of values in motivational orientation. Within our general management questionnaire there was a need to keep the length to a limit that would not have an adverse effect on response rate. We therefore restricted the items relating directly to motivation to ten. This was a compromise, as single item measures of motivation are not as powerful as multi-item motivation scales. An individual's item scores were standardized against the mean of all the individual's item scores. This was done on the basis that some individuals may tend to score items at the higher end, some at the middle, and some at the lower end of the scale. By positioning all individuals' middle score at zero, which represents their mean score, it is possible to make a more reasonable comparison among all individuals completing the questionnaire. Managers were asked to rate 'me, as a manager' (self) on a five point Likert-type scale from 'not like me at all' to 'just like me', and 'managers generally in my organization' (others) on a five point Likert-type scale from 'not like them at all' to 'just like them'. On our standardized scores the more positive the score, the more positively the statement fits their assumptions about self or other. The more negative the score, the less the motivator fits their assumption.

Table 6.1 presents the scores for the groups of managers from each of fifteen different sub-Saharan African countries. Items are grouped according to an initial exploratory factor analysis. These factors are used only as a guide, as the factor analysis did not provide sufficiently high factor weightings to justify grouping the items in scales, nor did reliability analysis provide sufficiently high Cronbach's Alphas for any hypothesized scales. Individual item scores only are therefore shown.

### Attributing cause and effect: locus of control

Although the scores for locus of control are somewhat inconsistent (items 20 and 21 have a small but significant positive correlation for self, and a small but negative correlation for others: these items are therefore not direct opposites) this aspect of Table 6.1 provides some interesting results. The first is that managers differ in their scores according to country. The second is that managers generally assume that other managers believe less than them that if motivated enough anything can be achieved, and more that own achievement is based on outside forces.

However, the general trend is for managers (both manager's perceptions of themselves and of other managers) to believe less that achievement is based on external influences, and more that if motivated anything can be achieved. Where results for managers in each country show a consistency between these two items, we can conclude that managers from Botswana, Ghana, South Africa and Zambia see themselves as having a more internal locus of control than managers from Côte d'Ivoire, Nigeria and Zimbabwe who have a more external locus of control.

Yet the difference between the way they see themselves and others is very pronounced, particularly in South Africa and Zambia, showing that respondents believe that managers generally in their organization have a much lower internal locus of control and a higher external locus of control. The same general trend can be seen in Botswana and Ghana, and in the countries where managers have higher scores for external locus of control. When considering just the scores for 'others', managers from Burkina Faso, Malawi, Namibia and South Africa are also more of an external locus of control, and managers from Cameroon have a higher internal locus of control.

The only major inconsistency is South Africa. Managers here are telling us that they have more of an internal locus, but other managers have a higher external locus. We know that ratings for 'me, as manager' are somewhat idealistic as they show a positive correlation with a third way we ask managers to respond: 'the type of manager required for the future of the organization'. Because the correlations are so consistent we have tended not to display these results, as they are superfluous. They do show however, that managers tend to see the way they believe themselves to be as the future of the organization. This may be due to management education, of which, of all countries in Africa, South Africa has probable been the most exposed to the Western/American variety.

Generally, the level of external locus of control is not as high as has been supposed by previous authors (for example, Kanungo and Jaeger, 1990). There also does not appear to be a relationship between GDP (see Table 3.1) and external locus of control. Although by standardizing individuals' scores we have lessened the effects of socially desirable response set (i.e. a tendency to score higher or lower depending on a person's conformity with what they regard as a socially acceptable or desirable answer), but not entirely. This is also not likely to affect managers' perceptions of others.

### Security, autonomy and power needs

Managers expressing a relatively high level of need for security in their job are those from Ghana, Kenya, and Zambia. Those who express a low need for security are from Botswana, Burkina Faso, Côte d'Ivoire, Mozambique, South Africa and Zimbabwe. As such there are fairly wide differences among the countries, with the order being as follows:

*High security needs (GDP)*
Kenya (1,022)
Ghana (1,881)
Zambia (756)
Malawi (586)
Cameroon (1,573)
DRC (801)
Nigeria (853)
Namibia (5,468)
Rwanda (885)
Côte d'Ivoire (1,654)
Mozambique (861)
South Africa (8,908)
Zimbabwe (2,876)
Botswana (6,872)
Burkina Faso (965)
*Low security need*

It is difficult to provide a direct explanation for this order. GDP is a very rough guide, with many of the higher GDP countries reporting lower security needs as might be

Table 6.1 Comparison of scores on motivational items across African countries

| | | Bots | BuFa | Cam | Côte | DRC | Gha | Keny | Mala |
|---|---|---|---|---|---|---|---|---|---|
| **Security** | | | | | | | | | |
| 1 Prefers security of steady job | Self | 0.066 | −0.113 | 0.468 | 0.109 | 0.454 | 0.631 | 0.664 | 0.484 |
| | Others | 0.482 | 0.450 | 0.449 | 0.056 | 0.438 | 0.679 | 0.608 | 0.611 |
| 5 Eager for opportunities to learn and develop | Self | 0.990 | 0.932 | 0.545 | 0.132 | 0.746 | 1.044 | 0.882 | 0.967 |
| | Others | 0.130 | 0.561 | 0.150 | 0.112 | 0.753 | 0.304 | 0.227 | 0.126 |
| 7 Enjoying above all else to work as part of team | Self | 0.704 | 0.554 | 0.511 | 0.075 | 0.569 | 0.800 | 0.775 | 0.829 |
| | Others | 0.023 | −0.084 | 0.194 | 0.146 | 0.561 | 0.157 | 0.187 | 0.024 |
| 8 Preferring above all else to work alone (loads negatively) | Self | −1.160 | −1.168 | −1.089 | −0.359 | −1.182 | −1.224 | −1.044 | −1.008 |
| | Others | −0.706 | −0.496 | −0.604 | −0.195 | −0.970 | −0.629 | −0.666 | −0.417 |
| **Autonomy** | | | | | | | | | |
| 6 Setting self difficult goals | Self | 0.379 | 0.204 | 0.051 | 0.256 | −0.026 | 0.263 | 0.114 | 0.257 |
| | Others | −0.101 | −0.107 | −0.154 | 0.080 | 0.052 | −0.202 | −0.233 | −0.355 |
| 4 Freedom in job to adopt own approach | Self | 0.578 | 0.266 | −0.011 | −0.051 | 0.066 | 0.370 | 0.574 | 0.570 |
| | Others | 0.072 | −0.344 | −0.132 | −0.071 | 0.071 | 0.064 | 0.028 | −0.071 |
| 2 Preferring work to be unpredictable | Self | −0.496 | −0.820 | −0.885 | −0.290 | −0.494 | −0.861 | −0.697 | −0.453 |
| | Others | −0.687 | −0.760 | −0.634 | −0.205 | −0.434 | −0.761 | −0.626 | −0.633 |
| **Power** | | | | | | | | | |
| 9 Preferring above all else to direct others | Self | 0.027 | −0.271 | −0.053 | −0.376 | 0.225 | −0.009 | −0.330 | 0.062 |
| | Others | 0.162 | 0.028 | 0.095 | −0.043 | 0.302 | 0.077 | 0.072 | 0.039 |
| 3 Very ambitious to reach the top | Self | 0.339 | 0.561 | 0.622 | 0.400 | 0.834 | 0.714 | 0.584 | 0.865 |
| | Others | 0.230 | 0.232 | 0.549 | 0.285 | 0.870 | 0.496 | 0.417 | 0.468 |
| 10 Believing that work is the most important thing in life | Self | −0.071 | 0.077 | 0.305 | −0.067 | 0.094 | −0.198 | −0.191 | −0.048 |
| | Others | −0.084 | −0.183 | 0.315 | 0.002 | 0.062 | −0.166 | −0.070 | 0.021 |
| **Locus of control** | | | | | | | | | |
| 20 Believing that if one is motivated enough anything can be achieved (INTERNAL) | Self | 0.863 | 0.346 | 0.598 | 0.632 | 0.176 | 0.832 | 0.844 | 0.766 |
| | Others | 0.402 | −0.163 | 0.307 | 0.063 | 0.184 | 0.478 | 0.274 | 0.066 |
| 21 Believing that own achievement is based very much on outside forces (EXTERNAL) | Self | −0.643 | −0.729 | −0.616 | −0.231 | −10.061 | −0.634 | −0.466 | −0.503 |
| | Others | −0.308 | −0.175 | −0.422 | −0.246 | −0.878 | −0.371 | −0.341 | −0.314 |

* Significant at 0.01 level

| Moz | Nami | Nig | Rwa | SA | Zamb | Zim | All | SD | Fstat* |
|---|---|---|---|---|---|---|---|---|---|
| 0.174 | 0.397 | 0.453 | 0.309 | 0.096 | 0.521 | 0.068 | 0.347 | 0.896 | 12.72 |
| 0.264 | 0.542 | 0.457 | 0.238 | 0.438 | 0.641 | 0.340 | 0.456 | 0.740 | 7.79 |
| | | | | | | | | | |
| 0.539 | 0.930 | 0.623 | 0.618 | 0.927 | 0.894 | 0.883 | 0.770 | 0.690 | 21.59 |
| 0.345 | 0.077 | 0.303 | 0.217 | 0.160 | 0.296 | 0.244 | 0.247 | 0.762 | 7.40 |
| | | | | | | | | | |
| 0.272 | 0.751 | 0.388 | −0.054 | 0.571 | 0.760 | 0.617 | 0.546 | 0.817 | 15.62 |
| 0.124 | 0.035 | 0.129 | 0.043 | 0.014 | 0.144 | 0.051 | 0.123 | 0.797 | 4.95 |
| | | | | | | | | | |
| −0.966 | −0.990 | −0.824 | −0.801 | −0.894 | −1.236 | −0.793 | −0.956 | 0.997 | 7.70 |
| −0.571 | −0.599 | −0.518 | −0.765 | −0.557 | −0.783 | −0.462 | −0.586 | 0.946 | 5.13 |
| | | | | | | | | | |
| −0.202 | 0.671 | 0.002 | −0.191 | 0.469 | 0.315 | 0.544 | 0.209 | 0.890 | 15.00 |
| −0.073 | −0.131 | −0.207 | −0.171 | −0.178 | −0.189 | −0.073 | −0.158 | 0.808 | 2.77 |
| 0.203 | 0.729 | 0.257 | 0.034 | 0.695 | 0.475 | 0.746 | 0.400 | 0.845 | 23.90 |
| 0.180 | 0.081 | 0.090 | 0.260 | 0.030 | 0.071 | 0.116 | 0.038 | 0.784 | 3.09 |
| | | | | | | | | | |
| −0.657 | −0.248 | −0.468 | −0.819 | −0.125 | −0.709 | −0.187 | −0.491 | 1.03 | 14.91 |
| −0.595 | −0.482 | −0.427 | −0.518 | −0.547 | −0.737 | −0.343 | −0.543 | 0.946 | 4.15 |
| | | | | | | | | | |
| −0.440 | 0.160 | −0.138 | −0.012 | −0.054 | −0.257 | −0.115 | −0.118 | 0.934 | 6.32 |
| −0.157 | 0.057 | 0.046 | 0.172 | 0.087 | −0.026 | −0.011 | 0.059 | 0.819 | 2.33 |
| 0.322 | 0.698 | 0.358 | 0.770 | 0.483 | 0.645 | 0.584 | 0.554 | 0.798 | 8.25 |
| 0.334 | 0.443 | 0.426 | 0.686 | 0.253 | 0.378 | 0.279 | 0.410 | 0.760 | 8.77 |
| 0.298 | −0.289 | −0.143 | 0.566 | −0.543 | −0.048 | −0.209 | −0.119 | 0.970 | 20.45 |
| 0.162 | −0.296 | −0.080 | 0.504 | −0.395 | 0.061 | −0.260 | −0.068 | 0.835 | 18.06 |
| | | | | | | | | | |
| 0.391 | 0.856 | 0.547 | 0.040 | 0.806 | 0.796 | 0.630 | 0.651 | 0.748 | 17.82 |
| 0.307 | 0.171 | 0.319 | −0.008 | 0.183 | 0.286 | 0.141 | 0.230 | 0.785 | 4.49 |
| | | | | | | | | | |
| −0.591 | −0.468 | −0.510 | −0.727 | −0.642 | −0.855 | −0.521 | −0.584 | 0.951 | 5.15 |
| −0.303 | −0.389 | −0.293 | −0.679 | −0.390 | −0.432 | −0.240 | −0.382 | 0.840 | 6.07 |

expected. Yet the relationship is not straightforward, as higher security may be more on the agenda when this is actually obtainable such as in medium GDP countries, and those whose economies appear to be improving. However, it is difficult to explain the results from Burkina Faso.

Generally where managers have reported a low need for security in their job, they have also reported that managers generally in their organization have a higher need, yet where managers express a higher need for security they also report other managers having a similar level of need.

In our exploratory factor analysis, security needs (item 1) grouped more readily with affiliation and development needs, rather than with autonomy or power needs. Managers from most countries give a positive response to the motivation to learn and develop (item 5), but again there is wide variation among countries. Ghana, Botswana, Malawi, Burkina Faso, Namibia, South Africa, Zimbabwe, Zambia, Kenya and DRC all have relatively high scores. Yet in particular, managers from Côte d'Ivoire have a relatively low score. It is also interesting that almost consistently, managers give 'managers generally in my organization' a much lower score than themselves. The self-score does look to be rather an ideal, and as we have said above, the self-scores may often be regarded as such. For this item, managers from DRC appear to be the only group where this is not the case. It is clear that for most managers through Africa, the opportunities for learning and development is important, yet is not seen generally as a major priority in their organizations, although as we discuss in Chapter 8, many organizations in our study are addressing this issue.

Our results also show that managers generally prefer to work as part of a team rather than alone (items 7 and 8), but report that others in their organization do not share the same team spirit. Managers from Malawi, Ghana, Kenya, Botswana, Namibia, and Zambia express this higher team spirit for themselves, while Côte d'Ivoire, Rwanda and Mozambique managers appear to have a lower need to work as part of a team. We would have expected managers from South Africa to show a higher score for this ideal of working as a group in view of the levels of Western-style training that stresses team work. Yet it is notable that they provide a relatively low score for others indicating a low level of team spirit.

It may be possible to conclude therefore that there is a need for development and learning opportunities that is not being fulfilled. Similarly, the need to work as part of a cohesive team is not being adequately fulfilled. This may go hand-in-hand with security needs, although managers in many of the countries surveyed do not see this as a particularly important need. This may be because expectations are not high on this aspect. Clearly expectations are high with regard to learning and team work, and this is an area that needs to be addressed, and one which we look at in Chapter 8.

Another area that does not appear to be a top priority for managers is that of autonomy, personal goal setting and higher levels of uncertainty and unpredictability in the job. This may well go together with the value that Hofstede has described as uncertainty avoidance, and which Kiggundu (1988) and Blunt and Jones (1992) assert is high for African countries. Namibia, South Africa and Zimbabwe have the highest scores for a preference for 'setting self difficult goals', 'freedom in job to adopt own approach', and 'preferring work to be unpredictable', but also see other managers to favour far less autonomy and unpredictability than themselves. Managers from Burkina Faso, Ghana, Cameroon, Rwanda and Zambia seem to have the least tolerance for unpredictability in their work. Although generally autonomy in one's job does not appear to be a favoured motivator, three of the higher GDP countries appear to favour autonomy as an ideal more than the other countries.

The item that is more directly linked to power motive, 'preferring above all else to direct others' does not appear to be a high motivator among African managers, although there is variation among countries (DRC has the highest score for self and others). This somewhat contradicts the perception of (post-colonial) African management in the literature. Yet managers report that they are more highly motivated to reach the top (with DRC and Malawi having scores above the average for all managers). Most groups report that other managers are less ambitious than they.

The fact that work centrality appears to be low across the countries supports the disconnect thesis (Dia, 1996) and our assumption that there is a lack of connection between the world of work and home/community life. In fact it is lowest in South Africa, which is telling on the attempts of empowerment and development that aims to involve people more in organizations and decision-making. The relatively high score for Rwandan managers may need further investigation.

## Implications for managers in Africa

From this chapter, including the results from the management survey, it is possible to draw some conclusions about the types of capacities organizations need to develop in order to motivate managers more appropriately and effectively.

- The way managers are motivated in organizations in Africa is a function of the compatibility between management systems and managers' cultural values. Top management needs to comprehend these values if they are to successfully adopt systems that motivate managers at the various levels.
- Uncritically employing Western motivational theories and principles to motivate African managers may inappropriate and ineffective. An awareness of other motivational concepts and principles should be developed among top management.
- However, it is too simplistic to altogether dismiss Western HRM principles and practices in the African context. Crossvergence of cultures, hegemony of Western education and ideology, and the development of hybrid organizational and management forms have meant that different motivators may be effective or appropriate. For example, individualism and collectivism may both be influences in some African countries. Top managers should develop an understanding of these different influences in order to develop motivational systems that are appropriate to their country, organization and managers.
- Vertical collectivism in post-colonial management systems may lead to exclusionist in-group/out-group relations, where in-group members are favoured for promotion and reward. Top management should be aware of the de-motivational effects of this on out-group members, and develop methods that encourage inclusionism and synergies within management teams (see also Chapter 8).

- From our research results, factors that should be taken into account when developing management motivational systems are as follows:
  - Locus of control should be considered when designing individual reward systems, particularly those that provide reward for achieving individual targets. Internal organizational surveys may be inaccurate in gauging this, as an internal locus of control appears to be a socially acceptable response in some countries. Care should be taken in countries that return a self-assessment of an internal locus such as Botswana, Ghana, South Africa and Zambia. Such reward systems may be inappropriate in Burkina Faso, Côte d'Ivoire, Nigeria, Zimbabwe, Malawi and Namibia. There may be variations in the level of external locus of control in countries such as South Africa where the results from Wentzel's (1999) study for individualism and power distance may indicate a higher external locus of control for Shangaan, South Sotho and Xhosa managers who appear higher on vertical collectivism.
  - Security needs should also be considered in designing motivational systems that include reward for long service and loyalty while providing continuity of employment and low risk and uncertainty. For example, managers in Kenya, Ghana and Zambia may require higher security; and managers in Botswana, Zimbabwe and South Africa may not have such a strong need for security and stability.
  - Managers generally prefer to work as part of a team, but indicate that this need is lower than in others. As this reflects an ideal which needs developing, encouragement for team working should be incorporated within reward systems.
  - Work centrality is generally low across the countries surveyed, even despite efforts in South Africa to empower staff within organizations. Top managers have a choice of utilizing a Western contractual (instrumental) approach to employing managers, thus keeping work and home/community life separate, or integrating more fully the wider societal communalism into the workplace. Mutabazi (2002) describes one company in Rwanda that developed an approach to employment that trained up work substitutes from friends and family in the local community that drew more people into the life of the organization, and integrated it more with the local community. Koopman (1991) describes how in Cashbuild in South Africa the company developed ways of reflecting the wider societal communalism. Afriland First Bank developed superordinate values of developing the country and contributing to the wider community. There is therefore a growing store of knowledge of how the latter choice might be developed.

Developing managers in the organization is only half the story. Motivational systems that are first developed at managerial levels are often then filtered down through the organization. However, whilst managers have received some form of Western education, staff lower down may themselves be much closer to African values and communalistic needs and values. In the next chapter we examine the issue of gaining employee commitment.

# Chapter 7

# Gaining employee commitment
## Work attitudes and organizational climate

As compared with a white worker's output, that of a Negro varies between one-third and one-seventh or one-eighth, depending on the employer and the trade (or within a given trade). The usual proportion is about one-quarter. In other words, it takes a Negro four days to do what a white does in one. And this opinion was confirmed by all employees that we talked to.

(Dumont, 1960)

African organizations may be experiencing serious employee motivation problems. The sources of these problems are varied and not well understood because of lack of empirical research.

(Kiggundu, 1988)

This picture of a lazy, leisure-loving African does not stand rigorous examination. The flourishing agriculture, commerce, and industry of pre-colonial Africa belie the notion of the lazy African. . . . Others have spoken eloquently of the industriousness, not the laziness, of Africans. If African performance was different in industry, then an explanation for that difference must be sought.

(Abudu, 1986)

The attitudes of workers in Africa have been depicted variously as lazy (Dumont, 1960), lacking in motivation (Kiggundu, 1988 and Blunt and Jones, 1992) and having an instrumental regard towards work: that is, a high expectation of benefits to the worker and family but low commitment and loyalty to the organization (Jones, 1986). Yet taken alongside the industriousness (Abudu, 1986; Ayittey, 1991) and entrepreneurial attitudes (Mbigi, 1997; Wild, 1997) noted outside the organized workplace, this assumption bears closer examination.

Abudu (1986) proposes that the assumption of Europeans in the colonial period that Africans were lazy could be explained by racial arrogance and a failure to appreciate the socio-economic background prevailing at the time. The contrast between worker attitudes in industry, and the enterprise and effort that went into private entrepreneurship also explains the false notions towards African workers.

The African's reluctance to accept wage employment arose from his cherished independence in agriculture, his unwillingness to sever family ties because of the security offered, and fear of illness and death in urban areas. European failure to appreciate these latter fears spawned the notion of the 'lazy African'. When voluntary acceptance of wage employment failed, direct and veiled force was adopted to compel the African to accept wage employment; and since forced labour is unwilling labour, productivity was low.

(Abudu, 1986: 34)

This together with poor and inappropriate management is the explanation rather than any 'deficiencies in the indigenous culture' (p. 27). In Nigeria, of which Abudu specifically writes, he contends that the problem attitudes that still predominate in industry may be attributed to both the workplace and the wider society.

He cites the drive for success that characterizes self-employed Nigerians, in contrast to the lack of motivation of those within the industrial workforce. He particularly points to the reward system in industry where rewards are not related to effort, but based on 'unknown' factors such as ethnic background, age, sex, coupled with a perception of favouritism, corruption or just a lack of competence (writing mainly of the public sector). This, together with the high pay differentials among grades of employees, provides a disincentive, where progression up the ranks is seen as difficult as a result of such factors as favouritism through tribalism and corruption. He also points to other factors leading to unsatisfactory attitudes including faulty selection, training and placement. This combines with an organizational climate that encourages laxity in punctuality and effort.

Yet things have moved on since 1986 when Abudu was writing (although this work is still widely quoted). Reform in the public sector, and the adoption of reward-based systems in the private sector driven by Western multinationals and Western management education may well have provided a further basis of inappropriate management, and negative work attitudes.

One of the main challenges in the management of people in Africa, as elsewhere, is reconciling the differences between home and community life, and the world of work. Not untypical is a remark by one of the African managers we interviewed: 'when we go into work in the morning we step outside our culture and enter an alien one. When we go home at night we step back into our own culture'. Our basic premise has been an assumption that there are both tensions between an instrumental locus (seeing people in organizations as a means to an end) and a humanistic locus (seeing people as having a value in their own right – often as part of a community) of human value, and potential synergies. Through these tensions and synergies, hybrid solutions to this fundamental problem are developed. The extent to which people are committed to or alienated from the work processes they are involved in is an aspect that has been investigated in various guises since the Industrial Revolution in the West: from the concept of alienation in the Marxian literature through Etzioni's (1975) concepts of moral, calculative, compliant and alienative involvement.

In this chapter we focus on work attributes and attitudes (particularly from a cross-cultural perspective), and draw on our data from employees in South Africa, Kenya, Cameroon and Nigeria. Managers also in these countries were asked, within intensive interviews across organizations in different sectors, about the internal climate of the organization in terms of employee involvement, motivation and opportunities for staff progression and development. The extent to which managers and employees are in tune with each other is perhaps an indication of the level of commitment in an organization. The discrepancy between different perceptions of the work situation is an important element in our conceptual and methodological approach.

It may well be the case that African workers are not highly motivated within Western-style organizations, and post-colonial organizations, as much of the literature suggests (Kiggundu, 1988; Blunt and Jones, 1992). But simply looking at this issue from the perspective of Western theory (the approaches of Ndongko, 1999, and Ugwuegbu, 2001, which do little more than enumerate extant Western motivational theories, are perplexing) may not be an appropriate approach. A more fruitful approach is a cross-cultural one.

## Cross-cultural factors in employee commitment

In Chapter 2 we introduced the discrepancy concept of management and staff commitment, looking at motivation as a fairly short-term phenomenon related to a discrepancy between the perceived nature of current management systems in the organization and the desired nature of management systems. We saw commitment as being more future-oriented and a function of a discrepancy between the way management systems are seen to be going into the future, and what organizational staff desires. If things are not going the way staff would prefer, there is likely to be a low commitment to the organization in the future. This discrepancy concept is particularly pertinent to cross-cultural analysis that looks at the appropriateness of management techniques in different cultural situations (for example the relevance and appropriateness of Western management principles and techniques in African countries), mediated by power relations, and the ensuing dynamics of the interactions between the two or more cultures. In Figure 7.1 we have tried to capture those elements that may be encompassed within a concept of work attitudes and employee commitment. Here we have developed the model posited by Jackson (2002a) that incorporates incentives, needs and commitment in a more inclusive concept of employee motivation. The salient aspects of this are as follows.

### Incentives

These include task variables such as job design, technology and physical conditions of work; and, job variables such as pay and the level of autonomy of decision-making within the job. These are aspects that if they meet the expectations, needs or requirements of the job incumbent, will contribute to *job satisfaction*. However, this is only one part of the total satisfaction that one has within a job. Career variables, particularly the opportunities that one has to advance and develop, as well as organizational variables such as the level of participation, general conditions and opportunities, will contribute to *career satisfaction* depending on the extent to which these conditions and opportunities meet the needs, requirements and expectations of the employee. Career satisfaction is longer term than the immediacy of job satisfaction, and can enable employees to rise above dissatisfaction from a boring job. But career satisfaction may well have a bearing on commitment to the organization, if an employee feels that managers of the organization are looking after their career.

### Requirements

This is a general term used by Jackson (2002a) to encompass needs and expectations. They include cultural variables (such as those factors identified by Hofstede, 1980a) that may set the foundations of a person's need systems, over and above the need to sustain life. Affiliation, for example, may be a need that is influenced by collectivism. Security may well be influenced by the way ambiguity and uncertainty is dealt with in societies (uncertainty avoidance). They also include person variables, such as individual motivation, attitudes and ambitions, which may or may not be independent of cultural variables (it is likely that one's culture sets the boundaries of one's motivation, attitudes and ambitions).

### Needs satisfaction

The extent to which the total job, career and organization experience satisfies employees' requirements is a function of the discrepancy between these two sets of factors. In Figure 7.1 we have called the one set 'attributes' and the other set 'attitudes'. However, an attitude has been described as a predisposition to respond in a favourable or unfavourable way to objects or persons in one's environment (Allport, 1939) and therefore attitudes may be more accurately described as predispositions to respond in a particular way driven by the discrepancy between expectations, requirement or needs, and attributes of the situation. Thus individuals within a particular culture may respond in different ways, yet the aggregate of their likely responses may be described as a cultural phenomenon. Discrepancy between requirements and short-term attributes (particularly job and affiliation attributes) gives rise to a level of *job satisfaction*. Discrepancy between requirements and attributes of longer-term and more permanent features of the employment experiences gives rise to a level of *commitment to the organization*.

The shorter-term outcome, job satisfaction and work attitudes, is an aspect that has been treated more comprehensively within the cross-cultural management literature. It is this aspect that Hui (1990) looks at within the literature. He points to there being cultural differences in job satisfaction, which we explore below. However, this general approach to looking at cultural differences may well be an inadequate explanation of job satisfaction and work attitudes in the multicultural context of sub-Saharan African countries. Adigun (1995), for example, looks at the differences among Hausa, Igbo and Yoruba in work attitudes. He concludes that cultural background has little influence on perceptions of job motivation, yet, despite the title of his article, he does not really consider the effects of multiculturalism in Nigeria on work attitudes. The dynamics of multiculturalism in most African countries must have considerable influence on work attitudes and motivation. For example, in

Chapter 10 we look more closely at ethno-political dynamics in Cameroonian public sector organizations. Where, for example, career expectations depend on one's perceived ethno-political status within the organization, one's motivation must be affected either negatively or positively. Managers such as the Directeur Général of Caisse Nationale de Prévoyance Sociale are trying hard to overcome the effects of such an 'informal' influence on work attitudes by introducing formal mechanisms such as appraisal systems. Also many of the other aspects of the context of Africa that we explored in Chapter 3 have an impact on work attitudes. The issue of AIDS/HIV and its affects on job motivation is a subject that emerged very infrequently in our interviews. Yet this health and social issue alone must have a tremendous bearing on attitudes at work through workers' general well-being, taking time off for self and relatives, and attitudes of employers towards HIV-positive employees. As we saw in Chapter 3, there is evidence from Zimbabwe that employees are not spending money on training people, as they see this as a bad investment if a high proportion of employees are likely to die of AIDS. We also saw that organizations in Kenya and Botswana are screening recruits for HIV.

The general economic issues within a country, levels of education, and the health of the staff and their relatives must all influence the level of motivation and commitment to the organization. For example, Powertechnics in Kenya is only one company in our study that is providing employees with transport to work (because of problems with transport infrastructure), with subsidized meals at lunch time, and with health care, in order to counter some of the effects of context factors on employees' work attitudes, as well as inculcating a greater loyalty and commitment to the company (see Chapter 11). Magadi Soda, also in Kenya, and based within a Maasai community provides all essential services such as health and education for the people who work and live within this township community as well as the wider Maasai community (see African Context Attributes in Figure 7.1; and see also Chapter 11).

Steers and Sanchez-Runde (2002), for example, argue that work attitudes can also change over time as a result of structural changes in the political and economic context of a country. They cite Shin and Kim's (1994) study of Korean workers whose general job attitudes shifted negatively following a major industrial dispute in the late 1980s. In particular worker attitudes towards their supervisors and companies declined rapidly, as well as workers' willingness to follow supervisors' directions. The current author's visits to Zimbabwe took place in 1998 prior to land repatriation and internal sanctions. We are under no illusions that organizational factors must have changed in the intervening period because of the political and economic situation in the country.

In the remainder of the chapter we look at the literature on employee commitment and motivation across cultures and its bearing on the situation in Africa. We go further in examining inter-ethnic work attitude differences and similarities in African countries as far as this is possible within the existing literature and our own research data. We then look at the effects of the dynamics of multiculturalism on work attitudes (Cross-cultural Context in Figure 7.1). Drawing on Chapter 3, we then look at the influence of the African context on work attitudes and commitment (African Context Attributes in Figure 7.1). These interact with personal attributes and job attributes (Figure 7.1).

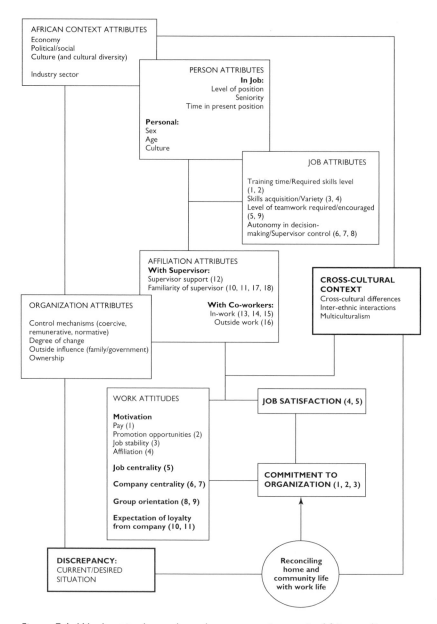

*Figure 7.1* Work attitudes and employee commitment in Africa: a discrepancy model.

African context attributes also have an influence on control mechanism used in organizations, the degree of change, and the nature of outside influences on the organization (Organizational Attributes in Figure 7.1) These factors, together with person and job attributes, influence interaction with supervisors and co-workers. All these aspects influence work attitudes (Figure 7.1) including employee motivation, the perceived centrality of work and the organization in one's total life, together with the orientation towards the group, and expectations of loyalty from the company. These aspects (Work Attributes in Figure 7.1) together with the perceived discrepancy between current organizational attributes and those desired are functions of levels of job satisfaction (in the short term) and commitment to the organization (in the longer term). We now consider these various aspects covered in Figure 7.1 in more detail.

## Cross-cultural differences in work attitudes

Hui (1990: 186) looks at job satisfaction across cultures, defining it as 'an employee's emotional and affective responses towards his or her job', and regarded as subsuming five independent components: satisfaction with work itself; supervision; pay; promotion; and co-workers. He notes that research across different countries has suggested different levels of job satisfaction among cultures and countries.

For example, he reports a study by Griffeth and Hom (1987) of managers of American corporations in fifteen Western countries. They group these countries into three clusters: Latin countries (Spain, Belgium, Italy, Portugal and Greece), which had lower satisfaction with co-workers, pay, supervision and promotion; English-speaking (England and Canada) with the highest satisfaction with promotion and workload; and Nordic and Central European countries (Norway, Sweden, Finland, Denmark, Germany, Austria and Switzerland), which had the highest satisfaction overall. Hui (1990) also reviews studies that show intra-country differences in work satisfaction including francophones and anglophones in Canada, with francophones showing the higher satisfaction; and Mexican, white and black Americans, with level of satisfaction running positively to negatively in that order. There are some indications in these studies that there are different levels of satisfaction with different aspects of work satisfaction in different cultural groups, possibly owing to different frames of reference. For example, O'Reilly and Roberts' (1973) study of white and black Americans indicates that blacks are more concerned with extrinsic job factors such as co-workers, and whites with both extrinsic and intrinsic factors of the work itself. So, there may not just be differences in terms of the level of work satisfaction across cultures, but also of the nature of work satisfaction.

De Boer's (1978) research indicated that 63 per cent of workers in Sweden were satisfied with their jobs, followed by the United Kingdom at 54 per cent, Brazil at 53 per cent, Switzerland at 50 per cent, and (among some ten countries) Japan at the lowest with 20 per cent. This low job satisfaction of Japanese workers has been noted in other studies and, for example, Cole (1979) explains this by the strong commitment and motivation of Japanese workers that enhances their expectations and therefore leads to dissatisfaction. Jackson, 2002a, explains this result for Japan as the difference between short-term job satisfaction, which can be low if the job is relatively boring, and commitment to the organization that can be correspondingly high where a longer term view is taken, because of aspects such as projected career progression, and inculcated mutual loyalty between employee and corporation. Supporting this view, in a later study of job attitudes and management practices among 8,000 workers in 106 factories in Japan and USA, Lincoln and Kalleberg (1990) conclude that Japanese workers are less satisfied but more committed than American workers. They deduced that the age and seniority system in Japanese companies reinforced a family-like relationship between workers and corporation which shows a concern for employee welfare that in turn is reciprocated by employees who show a strong commitment to the organization, even though their immediate job may not be to their liking. In comparison, the ethos in US firms is more transient, with a contractual basis for employment and lower commitment levels from employees. They also cited as a factor in commitment after-work socializing among Japanese workers that reinforced friendship ties and trust levels.

Bae and Chung's (1997) study of Korean workers took the lead from Lincoln and Kalleberg's (1990) study, using similar methods and comparing their results with those of the former from Japan and USA. They distinguish 'job attributes' (including task characteristic, social bonds, quality of ties with co-workers, and outside socializing); 'work values' (specific work values related to motivation such as good chances for promotion, work commitment, orientation towards the company, and company familism); organizational commitment (indicated by a professed willingness to work harder, stay in the company with less pay, and being proud of one's company); and job satisfaction (overall satisfaction with job, and a willingness to take one's job again knowing what is now known about the job). From this study Korean workers appear to evaluate their job complexity least among the three countries. This is in line with the lower level of industrialization of Korea compared with Japan and US. They also found that teamwork in the job is seen as important by Korean workers as their Japanese counterparts, and more so than the American. Also supervision styles are similar to Japan's in being more prone to unsolicited contact and vertically dependent providing less autonomy for Korean workers than their American counterparts. There is, however, a lower level of co-worker ties in Korean firms than in Japan and US. Differences also are shown to exist in attitudes to motivators among the three countries with Korean workers having the strongest achievement aspirations, and commitment to work. They also have the highest expectation of company familism, and expect to give loyalty to the company.

It is pertinent for a study of worker attitudes and commitment to dwell on such studies of 'collectivist' countries that have been successful in capturing the wider societal collectivism within the organization, in order to develop loyalty and commitment. This is one solution to the problem of how to reconcile home/community life and work life (Jackson, 2002a). It would seem from the literature (see quotations at the beginning of this chapter and preceding chapters) that organizations in sub-Saharan African countries have been unsuccessful in doing this. It could be postulated that owing to the very different colonial histories of Korea and Japan, when compared with African countries, the disconnect thesis of such as Dia (1996) would pertain in Africa but not in these two East Asian countries. Hence Japan developed organizations and institutions that were in tune with the wider society, and Korea blended various indigenous, American and Japanese corporate forms and management styles in the so-called K-Form management (Chen, 1995) in a way that was more in line with the requirements of developing an industrialized country as an extension of the wider society rather than as organizations and institutions tacked on to its host society.

If Japanese organizations have tackled the problem of reconciling home/ community life and working life by marrying them together, many Western countries such as America and Britain have handled this problem by keeping the two worlds mainly separate (Jackson, 2002a), by viewing work as a contract between employer and employee. However, this is not as simple as going to work to earn money to pay for the things one needs and enjoys. Work, profession, and the organization become part of one's identity within a highly individualistic (Hofstede, 1980a) achievement oriented (McClelland, 1987) society. This is really an extension of the instrumental/ humanism model presented in Chapter 1. In the instrumental view one's worth or value is determined by what one can do – that is, one's personal worth is determined by one's labour (a concept adopted by both Marx and Weber: Kanungo, 1990). Therefore, what one does as a job, and the prestige of the organization one works for is part of a person's persona and value in an individualistic society. This, type of 'solution' to the divide between home/community and work may not be appropriate to highly collectivistic, communalistic societies. Yet this seems to be the solution that has been foisted upon African communities. The outcome may well be one that Jones (1986: 208) has noted:

> There is among Malawian workers a generally instrumental orientation towards work, involving high expectations of the benefits, to the worker and his extended family, that employment brings, but less in the way of loyalty and commitment to the organization (or profession) that is said to typify the employer–employee relationship in the West.

One would therefore expect to find African workers having less commitment to the organization. As the level of industrializations is often low in many African countries, one could also expect lower training times, less skills requirements, less variety and autonomy, and less job satisfaction. Because of restricted job opportunities, with the addition of discrimination against less powerful ethnic groups, one might also expect to find lower career satisfaction.

However, these expectations may be too simplistic, particularly in view of our selecting employees in the current study from a wide variety of organizations, including low and high technology and finance where training times and skills requirements might be the same anywhere in the world. It may also be the case that to ameliorate this 'solution' to the divide between home/community and work, some organizations may have adopted management practices that are more paternalistic, such as those noted in the case of Powertechnics that provide a more protective environment for employees through provision of 'essential' services such as health care, transport and meals at work. It may be these types of practices that encourage more loyalty and commitment to the organization.

The studies undertaken by Bae and Chung (1997), and previously by Lincoln and Kalleberg (1990) forms the basis of our own study, and enables us to compare employees attitudes in Kenya, South Africa, Nigeria and Cameroon, with those in Korean, Japan and the United States.

## Work attributes in Africa

Work attributes include the context in which the organization operates, the attributes of the organization itself, particularly in terms of control mechanisms, affiliation attributes with supervisors and co-workers (often influenced by and influencing control mechanisms in organizations), and job attributes such as training and level of skills required, level of teamwork needed and encouraged, and the level of autonomy to do the job (see Figure 7.1). We have already briefly looked in this chapter at context attributes and at length in Chapter 3, and therefore do not intend to pursue this further other than when directly relevant to our discussion. Rather we focus on job attributes, supervisor relations, co-worker affiliation and organization attributes (Tables 7.1–7.3).

### Job attributes

Blunt and Jones (1992) decry the lack of deviation in organizations in Africa away from 'strict, hierarchical controls which effectively prevent workers from developing new skills and using their initiative' (p. 99). For example, they quote studies that compare the work operations in the Zambian copper mines in the 1970s and the British coal mines in the 1950s. These studies (Burawoy, 1972) describe an intensification of the division of labour, close supervision and disciplinary codes that promote frustrations among workers who are unhappy with a job that leaves no room for initiative and responsibility. The job, in fact, becomes devoid of meaning and is regarded only as a source of income. In so doing, the system discourages efficiency and productivity.

The main reason given for not introducing, for example, semi-autonomous, multi-skilled work groups was that management in the Zambian copper mines subscribed to the view of 'worker indolence'. However, a paper written later in the 1990s describes a very different system operating in the Zambia Consolidated Copper Mines Ltd (Chitiya, Undated) of open communications and job satisfaction following a lowering of expatriate managers and recruiting better educated managers and key employees. We noted in Chapter 1 that the colonial systems tacked onto African societies reflected a Theory X style of management (from McGregor) which generally mistrusts human nature with a need to impose controls on workers, allowing little worker initiative, and rewarding a narrow set of skills by financial means. Under-skilling has meant a narrow range of tasks, and skills that are not easily transferable. Within this view, the likes of autonomous work groups are not an option without a further up-skilling of the workforce. Yet the literature on Africa by and large does not reflect post-instrumental developments: organizations providing more consultative and participatory practices (we have discussed this in more detail in Chapter 4). Ndongko (1999) provides some fleeting evidence that employees within the Cameroon public service respond well to managers who exert lower controls, referring to her 1990 study, and asserting that these managers are in the minority.

However, more evidence in the recent literature suggests that organizations in Africa in both public and private sectors are embracing post-instrumental (Western) ideas regarding quality of work life and employee involvement. Although Kamoche (2000) reports that this is often fairly limited. Similarly he indicates in his study of companies in Kenya that attempts to improve training and a wider skills base have often been confined to managers. In fact, Kamoche's work (1992, 2000) is largely looking at the degree of introduction of Western models of human resource management in Africa (particularly Kenya) and its level of success. He concludes that the companies he investigated in Kenya have introduced Western HRM practice in varying degrees. Often measures such as semi-autonomous work groups amount only to tokenism and are confined to routine complaints and welfare (1992).

As we have seen in Chapter 4 of the present text, 'participation' is often confined to consultation and autonomous decision-making at a tactical level rather than at a strategic level: junior managers and key workers are given flexibility to make decisions about the way the job is done, rather than contributing to decisions at the strategic level concerning what jobs should be done. It is also likely that the further down the organization one goes, the less flexibility and autonomy the worker has. Our study was confined to workers who had a reasonable level of education that enabled them to complete a questionnaire. For many of the organizations we surveyed (e.g. financial companies and public sector organizations employing 'knowledge' workers) this would have captured all categories of workers. But for some of the manufacturing companies this may have excluded a number of manual workers.

So the more 'traditional' view may steer us towards expecting jobs in sub-Saharan Africa to be generally requiring low skills and little training time (through a lack of industrialization), having little autonomy (through post-colonial systems of management that restrict worker initiative, and through low skills level negating creativity and initiative), being low in team-work (through individualized jobs and where semi-autonomous work groups have not found a place), and with high supervisor control (through steep hierarchies, overbearing rules, and a stifling of worker initiative). Yet the more recent literature suggests the introduction of 'modern' HRM methods (Kamoche, 1992, in East Africa; Arthur *et al.*, 1995, in Western Africa). So we might expect to find up-skilling for jobs with more variety and autonomy, and more teamwork and less supervisory control. In fact our results show a mixture of these two systems, with variation among the four countries surveyed (Table 7.1).

Table 7.1 shows results for job attributes from samples of employees across a range of organizations in Cameroon (602 employees), Kenya (210), Nigeria (205) and South Africa (143). It also compares these results with samples in USA and Japan (Lincoln and Kallenberg, 1990) and South Korea (1997). Results from the latter three countries outside Africa provide a comparison with one Western country, USA,

Table 7.1 Comparisons of job attitudes

| | Corr./ Alpha[1] | F | Sig. | Tukey[2] | Cameroon | Kenya | Nigeria | South Africa | USA | Japan | Korea |
|---|---|---|---|---|---|---|---|---|---|---|---|
| A. Job Attributes | | | | | | | | | | | |
| Training time [1] (0=a few hours, 1 = a few days, 2=a few weeks, 3=2–5 months, 4=6 months to a year, 5=several years) | | 9.40 | 0.000 | CKS>N | 3.46 | 3.63 | 2.99 | 3.57 | 2.39 | 2.54 | 2.18 |
| Job/skills variety [2, 3, 4] | 0.700 Alpha | 15.50 | 0.000 | KNS>C | 3.77 | 4.08 | 4.04 | 4.16 | 3.59 | 3.26 | 3.34 |
| Teamwork [5, 9] | 0.340* | 7.39 | 0.000 | CKS>N | 4.12 | 4.07 | 3.82 | 4.07 | 3.37 | 3.70 | 3.68 |
| Autonomy [6, 8] (1=strongly disagree, 2=disagree, 3=neither agree or disagree, 4=agree, 5=strongly agree) | 0.382* | 10.32 | 0.000 | S>KN, C>N | 3.77 | 3.63 | 3.45 | 3.97 | 2.85 | 3.13 | 2.98 |
| Supervisor control [7] (0=I decide, 1=supervisor decides what and I decide how, 2=supervisor decides what and how) | | 61.55 | 0.000 | C>KNS, N>S | 1.35 | 0.87 | 0.97 | 0.75 | 1.07 | 1.08 | 1.07 |

Notes
* Significant at 0.01 level
1 Pearson correlation coefficient/Cronbach's Alpha.
2 Turkey multiple comparison test, where < or > denotes one country's score as being significantly smaller or greater than another country's score. Countries are denoted by their initial capital letter.

that is often provided as a standard; Japan as a contrast that may typify an economically successful 'collectivist' society; and, Korea, as a newly industrialized country which is depicted as a hybrid of Japanese and American management systems in a 'collectivist' society that is fairly economically successful (Chen, 1995). However, caution should be applied when making direct comparisons between results from the current study, and previous studies that may not have been conducted under the same conditions. Comparisons should be regarded only as an indication. Statistically significant differences are only computed among the four African countries included in the current study.

Training times vary among the countries. The results indicate that the jobs in the Nigerian organizations surveyed require significantly less training time (around 2–5 months) than in Cameroon, Kenya and South Africa (between 2–5 months and a year). However, results for Korea show training times closer to a few weeks, and in USA and Japan less than two months. It is likely that the African results are a function of the levels of employees surveyed, but is indicative of a modern economy with jobs that may be more challenging than indicated by the traditional literature depicting post-colonial management systems. Certainly the results for job/skills variety confirm a higher level of variety (even compared with the three non-Africa countries). Cameroon employees indicate a significantly lower level of job/skills variety than the other three African countries and this may well accompany lower levels of autonomy and higher levels of supervisor control in Cameroon as indicated in Table 7.1. However, it is Nigeria that comes lowest in job autonomy (significantly lower than Cameroon and South Africa), and also on teamwork (significantly lower than all three other countries). In fact teamwork scores highly for South Africa, Kenya and Cameroon, particularly in comparison with the three non-African countries. This may be explained either by the time differences between the studies (USA and Japan in the late 1980s), the level of introduction of Western practices such as semi-autonomous teams, or levels of group cohesion within the African workplace (in-work co-worker affiliation is indicated as high in the four African countries, and outside work co-worker association is indicated as low particularly in contrast to Japan and Korea (see Table 7.2)).

Finally, supervisor control is significantly higher for Cameroon (Table 7.1) than the three other African countries, and higher than for the three non-African countries. This indicates that on average the position is between 'supervisor decides what I do and I decide how' and 'supervisor decides what I do and how I do it'. Employees from the other countries indicate that generally the supervisor decides what they do and they decide how, with a number of employees in South Africa and Kenya deciding 'what' and 'how' themselves.

Job attributes in Cameroon therefore differ from those in the other African countries in that job/skills variety may be lower, and supervisory control is seen as higher, yet teamwork is on a par with South Africa and Kenya. Nigeria differs from the other countries in that training times are lower, teamwork is lower and job autonomy is lower. South Africa differs from the other countries in that job autonomy is higher and supervisory control is lower. Kenya is generally in the middle between Cameroon and Nigeria on the one hand and South Africa on the other. It is higher

Table 7.2 Comparisons of affiliation attributes

| | Corr./Alpha [1] | F | Sig. | Tukey [2] | Cameroon | Kenya | Nigeria | South Africa | USA | Japan | Korea |
|---|---|---|---|---|---|---|---|---|---|---|---|
| **A. Supervisor Relations** | | | | | | | | | | | |
| Frequency of talk with supervisor about work [11] | | 4.02 | 0.007 | N>C | 2.16 | 2.32 | 2.43 | 2.33 | 2.16 | 2.57 | 2.04 |
| Frequency of talk with supervisor about other than work [12] (0=seldom/never, 1=monthly, 2=weekly, 3=daily) | | 18.09 | 0.000 | S>KN>C | 0.76 | 1.07 | 1.15 | 1.51 | 1.63 | 2.15 | 1.43 |
| Frequency of getting together with supervisor outside work [17] | | 10.42 | 0.000 | N>CS, K>C | 0.39 | 0.67 | 0.77 | 0.49 | 0.20 | 1.37 | 1.25 |
| Frequency of getting together with manager outside work [18] (0=seldom/never, 1=several times a year, 2=several times a month, 3=once a week or more) | | 40.89 | 0.000 | KNS>C | 0.36 | 0.96 | 1.02 | 0.89 | 0.22 | 1.31 | 0.83 |
| Confide in supervisor about personal life [10] (1= strongly disagree, 2=disagree, 3=neither agree or disagree, 4=agree, 5=strongly agree) | | 5.19 | 0.001 | N>CK | 2.53 | 2.41 | 2.84 | 2.74 | 2.27 | 2.80 | 2.83 |
| **A. Co-worker Affiliation** | | | | | | | | | | | |
| In-work co-worker affiliation [13, 14, 15] (1= strongly disagree, 2=disagree, 3=neither agree or disagree, 4=agree, 5=strongly agree) | 0.794Alpha | 1.01 | 0.388 | ns. | 4.11 | 4.06 | 4.01 | 4.07 | 3.78 | 3.60 | 3.59 |
| Frequency of getting together with co-workers outside work [16] (0=seldom/never, 1=several times a year, 2=several times a month, 3=once a week or more) | | 6.45 | 0.000 | K>CS | 0.96 | 1.33 | 1.16 | 0.99 | 0.80 | 2.14 | 2.03 |

Notes

1 Pearson correlation coefficient/Cronbach's Alpha.

2 Turkey multiple comparison test, where < or > denotes one country's score as being significantly smaller or greater than another country's score. Countries are denoted by their initial capital letter.

on training time and teamwork than Nigeria and higher on job/skills variety than Cameroon. It is lower on supervisory control than Cameroon, and lower on autonomy than South Africa. The fact that the African countries score higher on training time, job/skills variety, teamwork, and autonomy, and lower on supervisory control indicates that there are no differences in response set between the current study and the two previous ones in non-African countries. It seems to indicate that in these African countries 'modern' approaches to managing jobs may well have moved on a pace over the last decade. Particularly in South Africa, the pace of change has been high, and the introduction of Western post-instrumental techniques may well be a factor in this. Differences among the African countries themselves may be a function of the colonial legacy, with differences between French and British colonial administrations. In Cameroon first the German and then the French rule tended to be based on centralized direct administration, and was bureaucratic and ruled by decree. British rule was often more laissez faire and even indirect (although considerable differences existed between and even within territories: Crowder, 1999). More coercive control mechanisms may pertain in Cameroon, and this is supported by our results on this (Table 7.3), which are discussed below. This is also developed in our chapter on Cameroon (Chapter 10).

### Affiliation attributes

Little specific literature exists on the nature of affiliation in organizations in Africa. A major reason for this may be that traditionally affiliation is seen as a motivational factor, and therefore is seen as an attitude rather than an attribute. For example, Blunt and Jones (1992) touch upon this aspect in relation to Maslow's hierarchy of needs, where it is treated under social needs. They remark that in Africa often this is focused on the relationship between employee and manager, which is a difficult relationship to manage in Africa. For example, workers in Malawi are reported to want to develop close personal relations with their supervisor, and that in a study of Ghanaian factory workers, employees complain that supervisors supervise too closely, making workers uneasy.

We have subsumed supervisor relations and co-worker affiliation under the heading of affiliation attributes. Supervisory relations is an aspect of management. The level and nature of supervision may be dependent on, as well as being a function of, the control mechanisms employed in an organization. Post-colonial management systems assume hierarchies, centralization and authoritarianism or paternalism. The formal system may therefore suggest distance between supervisor and worker, and impersonal relationships (see Table 1.1 and 1.2). Yet as we see in Chapter 10 through an examination of the Cameroonian public sector, there may be an informal system that favours in-group members. Collectivism, as Hui (1990) suggests, assumes an in-group and out-groups. A person is collectivistic towards in-group members, but not out-group members. Theory X applies to out-groups members who are not to be trusted, and Theory Y applies to in-group members who are to be trusted. Supervision may be different, and possibly more informal and less psychologically remote, for in-group members than out-group members.

We have already discussed the dilemma of reconciling the world of home and community with the world of work. Japanese corporations capture the wider societal collectivism by gaining commitment and loyalty from permanent employees. Contract workers are regarded as temporary and used as a buffer against redundancy in financially difficult times (Chen, 1995): they are out-group members. In Kenya, Powertechnics appear to be using contract workers in the same way to protect their permanent workers against lay-offs. Chinese companies appear to operate in a different way by incorporating family collectivism into business. Hence the in-group members are family members. They are the ones to be trusted, and those outside the family have low job security and low career prospects (Hui, 1990). Again, Powertechnics appear also to operate this type of collectivism within the organization by favouring family members at management level, or at least drawing from those well known to top management, and members of the same Indian ethnic group.

This in-group/out-group dynamic may work in different ways in different organizations. For example, in the past Davis and Shirtliff in Nairobi, a water pump distributing company owned by a family of English descent tended to recruit Kikuyu middle managers and below. They are well aware of this, and are trying to do something about it by introducing more formal recruitment systems. Senior managers in Afriland First Bank in Cameroon also were aware that they predominantly recruited Bamileke, and are trying to correct the balance. These last two examples suggest the introduction of Western (post-instrumental) HRM systems. In theory this should generate more open communication between supervisors and workers, and develop more approachability of supervisors. Yet hybrid systems emerging from open recruitment may well have the opposite affect: developing a larger out-group membership, and generating a more formal relationship between supervisor and worker.

If African renaissance systems develop from more traditional, family and neighbourhood collectivism, we could expect the informal systems of recruiting from these sources to prevail. Yet emerging values and principles such as *ubuntu* (Mbigi, 1997) suggest more inclusiveness, rather than the exclusiveness normally associated with in-group/out-group collectivism. This may well be more in line with Japanese corporate collectivism rather than Chinese family collectivism. That is, the corporation becomes the community, with links to the wider community of stakeholders as we discussed in Chapter 4. There is evidence that traditional African societies exhibit this characteristic of inclusionism by integrating different group and family members into the community through immigration, conquest, or marriage, which ensured the constant change, transition and flexibility of ethnic groupings (Thomson, 2000).

The nature of supervision in organizations in Africa may be a function of a combination of these different systems in different hybrid forms. So too will co-worker affiliation. With the dynamics of in-group/out-group collectivism operating in organization there may be high levels and low levels of affiliation at the same time. Open recruitment along Western lines may increase or decrease affiliation, while African renaissance principles should increase levels of co-worker affiliation. Work undertaken by Schwartz (1994) on Egalitarian Commitment, which is non-obligatory in nature and is associated with individualism, may well suggest higher levels of co-worker affiliation in Western organizations. The in-group nature of collectivism is based on mutual obligation. This may well lend itself to normative control systems where the corporation is successful in capturing the wider societal collectivism, and in effect becoming the collective. Obligations are established between corporate members. In individualistic systems, where contractual control systems prevail, egalitarian commitment may form a more informal level of affiliation, based not on obligation but voluntary association, or coming together for mutual benefit, such as in a trade union. It is therefore difficult to suggest the level of affiliation in any one organization in Africa, but the nature of such affiliation should be ascertained by looking at the types of control systems that predominate.

In Table 7.2 we can see that there are no significant differences among the four countries for in-work co-worker affiliation, yet all score highly on this aspect (in fact more highly than employees in the previous studies on USA, Japan and Korea). This scale is a composite of three items: 'People in my work unit are friendly and helpful'; 'I feel I am part of my work group'; and, 'I have confidence and trust in the people in my work group'. Perhaps a more telling measure is the frequency of getting together with co-workers outside work, in determining the level of collegiality or affiliation. Here there are significant differences among the four African countries with Kenyan employees reporting the highest level of outside work association compared with Cameroon (the lowest) and South Africa. Yet even the Kenyan employees' level of outside association is low compared with employees from Japan and Korea. This may well indicate that corporate collectivism is low in organizations in Africa. The fact that US employees produce the lowest score adds weight to this assertion, and may justify a tentative conclusion that the calculated nature of the work contract in individualistic/instrumental societies discourages outside work association. This is particularly in light of the US employees' relatively high score for in-work association. Correlation analysis also provides support. Frequency of getting together with co-workers outside work correlates significantly with the normative control (people) system shown in Table 7.3 (0.101 significant at 0.01), but there is no correlation with remunerative or coercive control systems. Moreover, in-work co-worker affiliation correlates significantly with the remunerative control system (0.226 significant at 0.01), with the normative (people) control system (0.214 significant at 0.01) and with coercive control system (0.151 significant at 0.01). The higher correlations with remunerative and normative control systems provide an indication that both these systems encourage in-work co-worker affiliation. Yet only normative control systems encourage outside work affiliation.

Relations and affiliation may be a function of the type of control systems operating, as we have already said. Nigerian employees appear to have more frequent contact with supervisors about work issues than their Cameroonian counterparts, but have less contact with supervisors about things other than work compared with their South African counterparts. Cameroon employees have the least frequent contact with supervisors for both work related and non-work related issues. Of the seven nations in the three studies included in Table 7.2, Japanese employees appear to spend most time with their supervisors for both work and non-work related aspects. To reinforce this view of a lack of affiliation with one's supervisor, Cameroon employees again indicate a lack of contact outside work with both supervisor and manager. Kenyans

Table 7.3 Comparisons of organization attributes

| | Corr./Alpha [1] | F | Sig. | Tukey [2] | Cameroon | Kenya | Nigeria | South Africa |
|---|---|---|---|---|---|---|---|---|
| **D. Organization Attributes** | | | | | | | | |
| *Coercive Control* [4, 5, 6, 7] | | | | | | | | |
| Current (employees) | 0.651Alpha | 26.73 | 0.000 | C>KNS | 3.88 | 3.32 | 3.42 | 3.43 |
| Current (managers) | 0.685Alpha | 10.72 | 0.000 | SN>CK | 3.16 | 3.07 | 3.45 | 3.35 |
| Ideal (employees) | 0.669Alpha | 19.12 | 0.000 | C>KNS | 3.63 | 3.11 | 3.22 | 3.02 |
| Ideal (managers) | 0.650Alpha | 26.87 | 0.000 | N>C>KS | 3.09 | 2.88 | 3.28 | 2.78 |
| *Remunerative Control* [1, 3, 17, 18, 22] | | | | | | | | |
| Current (employees) | 0.722Alpha | 19.18 | 0.000 | K>C>NS | 4.04 | 4.33 | 3.69 | 3.76 |
| Current (managers) | 0.730Alpha | 4.93 | 0.002 | S>N | 3.58 | 3.64 | 3.49 | 3.70 |
| Ideal (employees) | 0.737Alpha | 3.76 | 0.011 | C>N | 4.59 | 4.59 | 4.41 | 4.44 |
| Ideal (Managers) | 0.750Alpha | 22.98 | 0.000 | K>S>CN | 4.33 | 4.62 | 4.21 | 4.47 |
| *Normative Control (people)* [12, 13, 14, 16, 20, 21, 23, 26] | | | | | | | | |
| Current (employees) | 0.846Alpha | 7.91 | 0.000 | CK>N | 3.27 | 3.47 | 2.98 | 3.26 |
| Current (managers) | 0.836Alpha | 5.71 | 0.001 | S>CN | 2.97 | 3.06 | 2.97 | 3.18 |
| Ideal (employees) | 0.750Alpha | 1.97 | 0.118 | ns. | 4.38 | 4.52 | 4.31 | 4.50 |
| Ideal (managers) | 0.836Alpha | 14.18 | 0.000 | SK>CN | 4.06 | 4.44 | 4.01 | 4.34 |
| *Other Attributes* | | | | | | | | |
| Very successful [9] | | 9.57 | 0.000 | K>NS | 4.09 | 4.11 | 3.61 | 3.75 |
| High management skills [19] | | 10.31 | 0.000 | CK>SN | 3.95 | 4.18 | 3.58 | 3.60 |
| Very ethical [8] | | 7.51 | 0.000 | K>CNS, C>N | 3.64 | 3.94 | 3.30 | 3.54 |
| Undergoing rapid change [10] | | 4.14 | 0.006 | C>N | 3.98 | 3.93 | 3.64 | 3.78 |
| Family influence [25] | | 2.93 | 0.033 | ns. | 2.71 | 2.44 | 2.54 | 2.39 |
| Strong trade unions [15] | | 39.10 | 0.000 | S>C>KN | 3.28 | 2.29 | 2.64 | 3.72 |
| Bound by government regulations [24] | | 6.73 | 0.000 | KNS>C | 3.73 | 4.02 | 4.04 | 4.16 |

(1=not at all like this, 2=generally not like this, 3=neither like this nor unlike this, 4=somewhat like this, 5=exactly like this)

Notes

1 Pearson correlation coefficient/Cronbach's Alpha.

2 Turkey multiple comparison test, where < or > denotes one country's score as being significantly smaller or greater than another country's score. Countries are denoted by their initial capital letter.

and Nigerians appear to have a higher level of contact outside work although this is still only several times a year or below. United States employees have the least frequent contact outside work with supervisors, and Japanese employees the highest level of contact. Confiding in one's supervisor also appears not to happen across the seven countries, with Nigerian employees indicating the highest score on this aspect. Affiliation with one's supervisor appears therefore to be low among the four African countries and in the United States, but higher in Japan.

Across the four African countries, frequency of talking with supervisors about work is correlated positively with remunerative controls (0.087 significant at 0.01) and more highly with normative (people) controls (0.249 significant at 0.01 level). As one might expect, frequency of talk with one's supervisor about matters other than work is negatively correlated with coercive control ($\tilde{n}$0.075 significant at 0.05), as is frequency of getting together with one's manager outside work ($\tilde{n}$0.191 significant at 0.01). Yet the latter item is also negatively correlated with remunerative controls ($\tilde{n}$0.070 significant at 0.05). Frequency of getting together with supervisors outside work is positively correlated with normative (people) controls. Supervisor affiliation does therefore appear to be at least partially related to normative (people control systems), and negatively associated with coercive control systems. Remunerative systems may encourage contacts with one's supervisor about work issues, but not with outside issues, reinforcing contractual relations.

It is also interesting to see which of these aspects of affiliation associated with the three control systems are more associated with successful and skilful management in the minds of employees. In-work co-worker affiliation correlated positively with successful organization (0.191 significant at 0.01) and skilful management (0.242 significant at 0.01). Of supervisor affiliation, only frequency of talk with supervisor about work correlates positively with successful organization (0.098 significant at 0.01) and skilful management (0.166 significant at 0.01). Frequency of getting together with manager outside work is negatively correlated to successful organization ($\tilde{n}$0.073 significant at 0.05) and skilful management ($\tilde{n}$0.063 significant at 0.05). Clearly it is only affiliation concerning work aspects that are seen to be associated with successful organization and skilful management. Yet overall, it should be noted, successful organization and skilful management is associated in the minds of employees with both normative (people) control systems and remunerative control systems, as we now discuss.

## Organizational attributes

Our main focus of organizational attributes is the different control systems that operate in the organization: namely coercive, remunerative and normative. We have already discussed these at length in preceding chapters. We saw above that these are associated with some aspects of co-worker and supervisor affiliation and relations. We now discuss in more detail the relation between the perceptions of these control systems and national cultures and characteristics across the four African countries.

Table 7.3 indicates that Cameroonian employees see their organizations as more coercive control oriented than do employees from the other three countries;

Kenyan and Cameroonian employees see their organizations as more remunerative control oriented than do those from the other two countries, and Cameroonian and Kenyan employees see their organizations as more normative and people focused than employees from the other two countries. It is interesting that managers see organizations as less coercive control oriented than employees in Cameroon and Kenya, but not in Nigeria and nor significantly in South Africa. The same applies to remunerative and normative control orientations where managers in Cameroon and Kenya score lower than employees, but not in South Africa or Nigeria (Table 7.3). This may indicate incongruence between managers' and employees' perceptions in Cameroon and Nigeria.

We have argued previously in this chapter (and in Chapter 2) that incongruence between managers' and employees' perceptions on the attributes of their organization may well be indicative of a lack of understanding between the two groups, which may be a function of poor communication, poor relations or a lack of management awareness. A similar indication is the discrepancy between employees' perceptions of the current situation in the organization, and their ideal: what they would like to see. Generally employees (and managers) score their ideal for coercive control as less than the way they see it currently, and score both remunerative and normative control more ideally than they currently see the situation (across the data for the four countries differences are significant at the 0.001 level). Yet there is no significant difference between Nigerian employees' scores for current and idea for coercive control (paired samples t-test: t = 1.427, df = 100, sign. = 0.157). This may indicate that Nigerian employees are fairly happy with the levels of hierarchy, centralization, rules and authoritarianism within their organizations. Their perceptions also do not differ from the perceptions of managers. This appears to be a feature of the Nigerian employees in our sample, that there are no major discrepancies between the situation as they currently see it in the organization, the way they would like it to be, and the perceptions of managers.

There are other attributes of organizations in the four countries (Table 7.3) that show significant differences among the countries. Kenyan employees see their organization as more successful than do the Nigerians and South Africans. The Cameroonians and Kenyans see their managers as having higher skills than do the South Africans and Nigerians. The Kenyans and Cameroonians see their organizations as more ethical than do employees from the other two countries. Kenyans and Cameroonians also see a higher rate of change than do the employees in the other two countries. Of the four countries South African employees see their trades unions as stronger, followed by the Cameroonians. Yet it is Cameroon that records the lowest score for the level of government regulation that affects their organizations. Family influence in organizations appear to exist in much the same measure across the countries, although this is not reported to be high (between 2 'generally not like this' and 3 'neither like this or unlike this').

This therefore presents a picture of employees generally across the four countries seeing their organizations as more coercive control orientated than normative control oriented, and more remunerative control oriented than both coercive and normative control oriented. This is also reflected in the scores for perceptions of the managers.

This may well indicate a greater orientation towards Western post-instrumental principles in operation in the organizations surveyed. Ideally, across the countries, employees would like to see less coercive control (except in Nigeria), more remunerative controls, and more normative (people centred) controls. It is also interesting to note that there is a positive correlation between coercive and remunerative (0.167 significant at 0.001), and remunerative and normative control orientation (0.640 significant at 0.001), but not between coercive and normative control orientation. While employees see a fit between remunerative and normative or people orientations, coercive controls are not related to a centrality of people. These relate to the perception of the ideal in organizations. From our interviews it also reflects the general direction that managers are attempting to lead their organizations away from coercive control of the past, towards remunerative controls reflected in more formal HRM practices, yet being mindful of the people-centred aspects. Although it is possible that this is in respect of a soft instrumental approach that incorporates a concern for people as a valuable resource rather than as the target for development as an end in itself (see discussion in Chapter 1).

Remunerative and normative control systems are correlated more highly with successful organizations, high management skills, ethical organizations, and being bound by government regulations. They are correlated negatively with family influence. Normative control systems correlated highest with strong trade unions.

## Work attitudes

We have so far looked at work attributes: the perceived characteristics of organizations and work. We have also touched upon attitudes by comparing employees' perceptions of current attributes to desired attributes. The discrepancy between what is seen as the current situation and the desired situation, we have proposed, is an important aspect of job satisfaction and commitment to the organization. We now look at this discrepancy in relation to other work attitudes, including motivation, job and organization centrality, group orientation and expectations of loyalty from one's organization.

All motivators listed in Table 7.4 can be seen to be important to employees across the four African countries. There are no significant differences across these countries for pay as a motivator. It can be seen in the previous studies that this is a strong motivator for American employees, but Japanese employees have the lowest score for this of the seven countries.

Cameroon employees see promotion opportunities as significantly more important as a motivator than do employees in South Africa. The three non-African countries all show lower scores for this than the African ones, but Japanese employees score this particularly low. It may be because Japanese workers do not see this as an issue if they regard their career as taken care of by the corporation. If taken with job stability, it is clear that for Cameroonian employees promotion prospects may be a key issue in an uncertain job situation. Again, the scores recorded for Cameroonian employees for job stability as a motivator is significantly higher than that for South African employees. We noted (Table 7.3) that Cameroonian workers record a high

Table 7.4 Comparisons of work attitudes, job satisfaction and employee commitment

| | Corr./Alpha [1] | F | Sig. | Tukey [2] | Cameroon | Kenya | Nigeria | South Africa | USA | Japan | Korea |
|---|---|---|---|---|---|---|---|---|---|---|---|
| **B. Work Attitudes** | | | | | | | | | | | |
| Motivation – Pay [1] | | 2.58 | 0.052 | ns. | 2.71 | 2.61 | 2.66 | 2.57 | 2.80 | 2.33 | 2.55 |
| Motivation – Promotion opportunities [2] | | 3.17 | 0.024 | C>S | 2.66 | 2.62 | 2.65 | 2.46 | 2.36 | 1.58 | 2.41 |
| Motivation – Job stability [3] | | 2.76 | 0.041 | C>S | 2.69 | 2.70 | 2.65 | 2.51 | 2.84 | 2.22 | 2.63 |
| Motivation – Affiliation [4] | | 4.73 | 0.003 | K>CN | 2.62 | 2.74 | 2.54 | 2.70 | 2.72 | 2.18 | 2.64 |
| (0=not at all important, 1=a little important, 2=somewhat important, 3=very important) | | | | | | | | | | | |
| Job centrality (high score 1–5 = more important things than work) [5] | | 11.19 | 0.000 | S>CKN | 2.23 | 2.21 | 2.09 | 2.77 | 3.12 | 2.82 | 3.43 |
| Company centrality [6, 7] | 0.116* | 18.43 | 0.000 | KNS>C | 2.63 | 2.97 | 2.98 | 3.15 | 3.11 | 3.13 | 3.28 |
| Group orientation [8, 9] | 0.269* | 11.74 | 0.000 | C>KN | 3.57 | 3.30 | 3.20 | 3.41 | 3.12 | 3.40 | 3.90 |
| Expectation of loyalty from company [10,11] | 0.344* | 12.81 | 0.000 | C>NS,K>S | 4.47 | 4.39 | 4.29 | 4.12 | 4.44 | 3.54 | 4.66 |
| **C. Job Satisfaction [4, 5]** | 0.469• | 2.85 | 0.036 | ns. | 3.54 | 3.73 | 3.53 | 3.69 | | | |
| (1= strongly disagree, 2=disagree, 3=neither agree or disagree, 4=agree, 5=strongly agree) | | | | | | | | | | | |
| **C. Commitment to Organization [1, 2, 3]** | 0.563Alpha | 10.69 | 0.000 | KS>CN | 3.66 | 3.93 | 3.71 | 3.91 | | | |
| (1= strongly disagree, 2=disagree, 3=neither agree or disagree, 4=agree, 5=strongly agree) | | | | | | | | | | | |

Notes

* Significant at 0.01 level.
1 Pearson correlation coefficient/Cronbach's Alpha.
2 Turkey multiple comparison test, where < or > denotes one country's score as being significantly smaller or greater than another country's score. Countries are denoted by their initial capital letter.

score for undergoing rapid change for their organization. It may be that this contributes to the uncertainty within the country. In which case stability factors such as longer term prospects for promotion and job stability itself would be more at the forefront of employees' minds. South Africa has gone through a period of rapid change in the early and mid-1990s. Even though this may be ongoing, the pace of change is slowing down. Other African countries may be following in the wake of many of the developments in South Africa, and are still transforming public and private sectors through liberalization processes encouraged through structural development programmes of the 1990s. As we discuss in Chapter 10, Cameroon in particular is going through a period of public sector privatization. These, and other developments may explain why stability factors are important motivators in Cameroon.

Affiliation as a motivator may work in the opposite direction. We noted (Table 7.2) that although there were no significant differences among the African countries for in-work co-worker affiliation, Kenyan employees recorded significantly higher scores for the frequency of getting together with co-workers outside work (although much lower than scores recorded by Japanese and Korean employees in the previous study). In Table 7.4 Kenyans now record the highest score for affiliation as a motivator. This may reflect a situation that enables affiliation as a motivator rather than suppresses it. Supporting this assumption is the lower score for outside work co-worker affiliation for the Cameroonians, and their lower scores for affiliation as a motivator. We could interpret this in Herzberg's (Herzberg *et al.*, 1959) terms as pay, promotion prospects and stability in job as being 'hygiene' factors, (de)motivating in their absence; and, affiliation being a 'motivating' factor, motivating by its presence.

Motivators that relate more generally to life, work and company are also included in Table 7.4. South African employees' job centrality is significantly lower than the other three African countries (job centrality scores are reversed in Table 7.4, so the higher the score the lower the job centrality), that is they believe more highly that 'I have other activities more important than work'. Yet at the same time South African, Kenyan and Nigerian employees indicate a higher level of company centrality than Cameroonian employees. Despite Cameroonian employees' lower company centrality, they still believe more highly than employees from the other African countries that the company owes them loyalty (a similar attitude can be seen from the US employees). Cameroonian employees' loyalty and orientation is more towards their co-workers than the corporation (significantly more so than Kenyans and Nigerians). This reflects an in-work attitude, rather than a general attitude towards affiliation, as the two items which make up this scale are 'when I have a choice, I try to work in a group rather than by myself', and 'getting along with co-workers is more important to me than getting along with my bosses'. The high score for Cameroon also reflects the high score recorded by Cameroonian employees to the level of teamwork encouraged in their organizations (Table 7.1).

Despite these differences across the four countries, there is no significant difference among the four for job satisfaction. This is shown as generally medium to high. Yet there are significant differences across the four countries for commitment to the organization. This separates Kenya and South Africa from Cameroon and Nigeria, with the former two countries with higher commitment than the latter two countries. This in part reflects the scores shown for company centrality.

## Implications for managers in Africa

We have argued that the management of the relationship between working life and community and home life is crucial to the effectiveness of organizations. Jackson (2002a) has discussed the different ways this relationship is addressed in different countries, and has argued that culture is a main antecedent in how this is managed. One of the main conceptualizations for understanding this is that of locus of human value Jackson, 2002b). This distinguishes an instrumental and a humanistic regard for the value of people within organizations. Hence cultures that see human value instrumentally may see the relationship with the employee as contractual; effectively separating home/community life from working life. More humanistic cultures may not favour such separation and attempt to integrate working life with community and home life. While the literature suggests that African communities are communalistic and cultures regard people humanistically, organizations in Africa appear to manage the relationship with employees on a calculative, contractual basis. Unlike their counterparts in Western countries, they are more likely to reflect a coercive control system, that is more authoritarian, hierarchical and bureaucratic than the post-instrumental, 'soft HRM' practices adopted and refined by Western organizations operating in Western countries. Yet this may be changing in Africa with a move towards more results oriented organizations, but organization which, at the same time, adopt the contingency approaches of Western management in being more people oriented and more consultative. Yet there are dangers in adopting this approach, as we have seen previously in Chapter 4, where we were concerned with 'contingency' consultative decision-making processes used only on a tactical basis, and in Chapter 5 when we discussed management and leadership styles and how they may not be appropriate in the African context.

The task of management in organizations in Africa is to move away from the situation where employees are going into work in the morning and stepping outside their culture, and going back home in the evening and stepping back into their cultures. There should be a better compatibility between the two. The contractual arrangements in some Western, individualistic societies may work well as a separator between home and work life, because that is compatible with an individualistic and instrumental culture. This may not be compatible with a humanistic, communalistic culture. Certainly our results indicate that employees would favour more normative control systems, where people are the main focus, coupled with a results/remunerative focus and less coercive control systems. We saw this also with managers in Chapter 5, and in the current chapter in comparing employees' and managers' results. Yet employees appear to desire this more than managers. This may be a main reason why our results also show a low job centrality, as well as moderately low scores (below 3) for motivational attitudes. (Although scores for job satisfaction and commitment to the organization are moderately high, it may be that the latter reflects the general job market and a need for stability together with an expectation of being looked after by the organization as is shown in the score for expectations of loyalty from the organization (Table 7.4). The former may just reflect a general satisfaction with the job itself and the tasks performed.)

These results have implications for senior managers, and the type of organizational and employment arrangements that could be developed.

- Managers should be aware of the more humanistic and communalistic cultural attitudes of African employees that may not reflect the 'textbook' attitudes to be found in the Western management literature, and of the need to develop employment and motivational systems that better reflect these attitudes.
- They should be aware of the need for stability in employees' jobs and the expectations of loyalty from their employer, in return for employees' loyalty to the organization. Although employees indicate a moderately high loyalty to their organizations, they indicate a moderately low work centrality. The latter may be developed through integrating work more effectively and appropriately with community and home life. This may be best achieved through developing better links with community stakeholders in decision processes as we discussed in Chapter 3, and in adopting employment policies that involve the local community as we saw at the end of Chapter 6 in the example given by Mutabazi (2002) of the company in Kivu, Rwanda.
- The lower levels of co-worker and worker–supervisor association outside work is at odds with other communalistic and humanistic societies, and reflects a separation from work and home/community life. Although this may be a symptom rather than a cause, more attention could be placed on this aspect with the encouragement of out-of-work activity, and involvement in the local community, other than just funding community projects (as we discussed in Chapter 4).
- The levels of coercive controls are seen as being too high by employees, yet this may also be a factor in providing stability and low risk in organizations. Formal rules and other control aspects such as job descriptions may be better used to be seen to 'protect' employees (as seems to be the case in China as we discussed), rather than overtly to control. There needs to be a careful balance between the level of control, stability and security for employees, and the need for autonomy and flexibility in working.
- African employees appear to be team workers. Reward systems may be better developed that reflects this group orientation, and rewards team rather than individual effort.

In the next chapter we attempt to pull together the chapters in Part II that have focused on managing competencies and capacities. We do this by addressing more specifically developmental issues within the cross-cultural context that we have argued is a feature of the sub-Saharan African working environment. By developing managers, teams and organizations in this cross-cultural context, management may become more appropriate and more effective.

# Chapter 8

# Managing multiculturalism
## Developing managers

Adult training is often carried out in Africa in the same way it is delivered in the West and particularly in the United States. The underlying assumption . . . is that Africans learn in the same way that Americans or Westerners do.

(Sawadogo, 1995: 282)

Negotiations and cross-cultural communication skills are two related interpersonal competencies which have been neglected in management development in Africa, but which are becoming extremely important for dealing with the continent's domestic and international challenges of the 1990s.

(Kiggundu, 1991: 41)

## The cross-cultural imperative

The central tenet of this book has been the cross-cultural imperative for management within sub-Saharan Africa. Far from being an add-on (perhaps as the quote from Kiggundu (1991) above suggests, it is an integral aspect of the nature of management in Africa. Managers in Africa have accumulated a wealth of experience in managing across cultures. This is experience that, if articulated, can benefit global managers generally not least those operating in other emerging regions. Yet often managers in Africa, and perhaps African managers in particular, do not capitalize on this experience, and often turn to Western solutions for management education and training. We have come back repeatedly in this book to the issue of the prevalence of Western management education, and the dearth of an appropriate management literature that draws upon African experience, and which can be drawn upon to feed in to the management development process. It is certainly the major purpose of the project, of which this book is a part, to help develop such a literature, and to contribute to management development efforts in Africa, as well as assisting in the articulation of management experience (through systematic research) in Africa that may help managers managing in other parts of the world (see www.Africamanagement.org).

We take as our starting point in this chapter the following assumptions:

*   Good and appropriate management of resources and people is essential to the well-being of humankind in Africa as elsewhere.

- In Africa, as in many parts of the world, this implies the effective management of multicultural workforces, and of cross-cultural dynamics involving power relations at inter-continental, cross-national/intra-regional and inter-ethnic levels.
- Good management can be achieved with the help of appropriate management and organizational development.
- Such management development, if it is going to be appropriate and effective should be primarily cross-cultural in nature.
- Good management anywhere in the world can draw on cross-cultural experiences from other parts of the globe, as long as this does not take the form of 'intellectual imperialism': African experience is just as valuable as experience from any other part of the world in the pool of knowledge for global managers.

## Issues in cross-cultural management development

This chapter is designed as a more practical consolidation of Part II of this book, and as a bridge to Part III that draws on experience in specific countries in East, West, Central, and South Africa, within a theoretical framework of cross-cultural management. As such it deals with the issues of multicultural working in Africa at the three levels of interaction: *inter-continental, inter-country* and *inter-ethnic* (see Chapter 1). The first of these levels deals with the issue of hegemony of Western management principles, an issue that we first raised in detail in Chapter 2. Here power relations are important either directly through the interventions of multinational companies or educational institutions, or indirectly though the ideology of Western management texts and education which are seen as superior and authoritative, often debunking 'African' experience as not useful, and not 'modern'.

This raises the issues of what *methods* of management education and training in should be used in Africa, and what should be its *content*. For example, Sawadogo (1995: see the opening quotation at the head of this chapter) suggests that Western methods of instruction may be inappropriate for the African situation. This is an important aspect if management development efforts are going to have a serious and appropriate impact in sub-Saharan Africa. The content of training and educational programmes also has serious implications for the appropriateness and effectiveness of management development. By the early 1990s cross-cultural management was becoming an issue among commentators on management in Africa (Kiggundu, 1991: see the opening quotation at the head of this chapter; and Blunt and Jones, 1992, who devote a chapter to this issue), yet it was still seen very much as an 'add-on', rather than integral to what managers do, and how they should be trained.

We hope that the chapters that form Part II of the present text point the way to such content for understanding management in Africa. We discuss and reflect upon this content, and suggest why this is relevant and how it might form the basis of management development programmes.

At the second and third levels of analysis, inter-country and inter-ethnic, the issue of developing synergies in multicultural teams is key. Perhaps the need to address the inter-ethnic level in African countries is more urgent and pressing than at the inter-country level. Yet often the same principles apply to the latter in cross-cultural training, and this is a level that will increase in importance as organizations develop business and cooperation across borders on a relational basis in sub-Saharan Africa.

## Methods for management development in Africa

The way that management training and development is conceived and delivered is problematic across cultures, yet the introduction and extensive use of Western principles of education are assumed to work in Africa, without very much investigation and reflection. Western-style management programmes were the norm for managers who had attended training courses, whom we interviewed across the four countries of South Africa, Cameroon, Nigeria and Kenya. Over the last couple of decades a literature has developed on managers' learning styles across cultures. This focuses on differences in the preferences and expectations of managers in situations where they learn and receive instruction. Even the concept of management 'learning' is problematic (a concept that is difficult to translate into many other European languages other than English). This stems from a concept that the 'learner' is primary in the education and development process. Jackson (2002a) argues that this is very much an Anglo-Saxon product that reflects a process-based approach, rather than a content-based one (see Figure 8.1), and assumes that education is learner-led not instructor-led. It involves a notion of 'experiential' learning that does not always fit expectations of managers in other cultural contexts. This involves the concept of learning at both the individual level (action learning: Revans, 1965; Kolb, 1984) and at organizational level (the learning organization: Senge, 1990; Argyris, 1992)

Much of the (Anglo-Saxon) cross-cultural research in this area is based on Kolb's (1984) model of experiential learning. He saw this as a process or cycle comprising four stages:

- concrete experiences (providing an 'activist' learning style in Honey and Mumford (1982), as we see below), followed by
- observation and reflection (providing a 'reflector' style), leading to
- formation of abstract concepts and generalizations (providing a 'theorist' style), leading to
- testing of the implications of concepts for future action (providing a 'pragmatist' style), which then lead to new concrete experiences.

This process is governed largely by the pursuit of goals that are appropriate to our own needs. Thus we seek experiences that are related to these goals, we interpret the experiences in the light of these goals, and form concepts that are relevant to our needs and goals. As a result of personal preferences and inclinations, individuals tend to emphasize a particular aspect or stage of the learning cycle. Kolb (an American) uses the examples of different occupational groups: the mathematician who emphasizes abstract conceptualization; the poet who values concrete experience; the manager who is concerned with application of concepts, and the lover of nature who develops observational skills. This led to the idea of learning styles and has been extensively

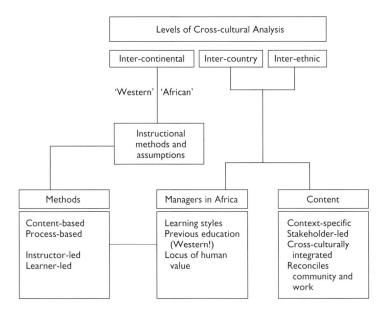

*Figure 8.1* Management development: managers, methods and content.

applied to management learning in Anglo-Saxon countries, where individuals have a preference for a particular stage in the process (Honey and Mumford, 1982).

Although this has been used extensively in the UK and US in management training, it is problematic when one moves across cultures. Hence Hughes-Weiner (1986) suggests that when looking across cultures at the different learning stages of Kolb we see the following:

- *Concrete experience*: people from different cultures are likely to have different backgrounds and different experiences. For example, their readiness for classroom learning may be quite different among different cultural backgrounds.
- *Reflective observation*: as a result of different behaviour patterns, socialization and institutional and work experiences, individuals from different cultures may make different assumptions about what they see and understand through their experiences. Therefore people from different societies are likely to acquire different bodies of knowledge.
- *Abstract conceptualization*: because people from different cultures may have different cognitive frameworks, this may lead to focusing on irrelevant information or misinterpretations in a particular cultural situation, and drawing wrong conclusions and theories when stepping outside their own culture.
- *Active experimentation*: behaviour differences between cultures may lead to misinterpretations and misattributions of the meanings of such behaviour outside individuals' own cultures, leading to confusion and frustration.

Allinson and Hayes (1988; and Hayes and Allinson, 1989) were interested in investigating this issue empirically using the Honey and Mumford questionnaire. They discovered cross-cultural differences among their British, Indian and East African samples of managers although their analysis did not confirm the four learning styles formulated by Honey and Mumford (1982). Rather, it gave rise to an *analysis* orientation (combining Honey and Mumford's 'theorist' and 'pragmatist' styles in a style that reflects the extent to which the manager adopts a theory-building and testing, rather than an intuitive, approach) and an *action* orientation (combining an 'activist' approach with a negative correlation with Honey and Mumford's 'reflector' approach, reflecting a trial and error orientation rather than a contemplative one).

This work by Allinson and Hayes provides us with a first clue of African managers' learning styles based on systematic cross-cultural research (albeit with limited samples sizes: 127 British, 40 Indian and 28 East African mid-career managers, and little explanation of the results). The East African managers appear to be lower on Analysis than those from India, and on a par with the British managers. They score lower on Action than either the British or Indian managers. This may mean that the East African managers are more intuitive, rather than employing the more 'scientific' approach of hypothesis formulation and testing in their learning style; and, a more reflective approach (Kolb's example of the lover of nature who develops observational skills).

The concept of learning styles, and how these differ across cultures have important consequences for educational and training methods. Triandis *et al.* (1988), for example, challenge prevalent Anglo-American approaches to training on the basis of cross-cultural differences between 'collectivism' and the 'individualism' of Western cultures. Training approaches are also questioned by empirical findings in an Australian–Asian empirical study (Niles, 1995). This suggests differences in motivation for learning based on McClelland's (1987) concept of 'Achievement Motive' (see Chapter 6 in the current text), where social approval is important for Asian students and achievement important for Australian students.

In the context of sub-Saharan Africa, Sawadogo (1995) calls into question the relevance of Western training concepts, such as that of the independent learner, the teacher as facilitator and the role of feedback; suggesting that Western training methods are largely inappropriate. This particularly calls into question the concept of *experiential* learning upon which is based many of the practices of Western-based (Anglo-Saxon, but not for example French, as we will see below) training and development. He examines four principles that are often applied to (Western) training in sub-Saharan Africa:

- People learn best when they actively participate in the learning process.
- People are independent learners with responsibility for their own learning and teachers act as facilitators.
- Feedback is a central tool in guiding the learner and the facilitator towards training objectives and optimizing results.
- The use of Western languages (normally English or French) in training is appropriate and effective.

To this we would like to add what may be regarded as an over-riding principle derived from our concept of instrumentalism–humanism: that the competencies approach to management development is seen as appropriate and effective in sub-Saharan Africa. Western (Anglo-Saxon) management training is based on a principle of management competencies. That is, from the strategic objectives of an organization, it is possible to identify more specific operational objectives. From this, job profiles are constructed for the positions an organization needs to fill in order to meet those operational objectives. Competencies can then be identified for each job, and this forms part of the job description. People are then selected for each job on the basis of best fit between actual competencies of the selected person, and the requirements of the job. Where there is a disparity between new or existing job incumbents and the competencies requirements of their job, this is made good by training. The requirements for the job, in order to meet organizational objectives, dictate the content of the training (for a fuller discussion of the competencies approach, its cultural origins within an individualistic, achievement culture, and its implication, see Jackson, 2002a, Chapter 3). We discuss *content* in more detail later (see Figure 8.1).

This also applies to management 'development', which is directed more towards the future requirements of the organization (although often ostensibly towards the 'development' of the individual): the requirements of the organization in terms of succession and career planning influence the content of the programme. Selection, appraisal, reward and promotion are based on the identification of relevant (to organizational objectives) competencies and the demonstration of such competencies in behaviours and results. This approach, based on an instrumental paradigm may be inappropriate for a culture that reflects a humanistic locus of human value (see Chapter 1). It tends not to be used in organizations in Japan, for example, where the organization is directed developmentally towards people within the corporation: individuals are not fitted into particular positions; organizational resources are used to develop people flexibly in a number of positions and functions (see, for example, Jackson, 2002a, Chapter 5). We have also looked at the inappropriateness of this approach within the development imperatives of South African society (see Chapter 12, and Jackson, 1999), and suggested an inherent antithesis between the need to make companies mean and lean and to employ only the minimum of staff in order to fulfil the operational objectives of the organization, and to use organizations developmentally in order to further the needs of the wider community. The latter approach does not therefore take an instrumental, competencies approach to development. This fifth principle (in addition to Sawadogo's, 1995, fourth) is an overarching one, and represents the basis paradigm which is taken for granted within Western approaches to training and development.

Sawadogo (1995), in order to investigate the appropriateness of the four principles he proposes, looks at learning in the traditional African context which is guided by an assumption that learning is a passive process and knowledge is respected. Learning as a passive process, Sawadogo (1995) asserts, is based heavily on extensive observation. This supports Allinson and Hayes' (1988) finding for East African managers that learning styles are more observational, with a reflective style. Children are expected to be passive learners and to ask a minimum of questions. They undergo deductive processes as well as using observations that they make of their experiences. This contrasts sharply with the more active learning style in the West, which looks at passivity as indicating a lack of energy and resourcefulness. Yet passivity, Sawadogo (1995) suggests, is a valued quality in the African context. He uses the example of a dispute between two people where the passive one is seen as the victim and the one who is right. It is a sign of wisdom and self-control, and a sign of a person seeking refuge in a higher (religious) power. In a learning situation it reflects a view that no one has the whole truth, and therefore one should not rush to make a choice or a statement. Therefore a long period of observation and reflection should precede action. Questions also are considered socially intrusive and often a challenge to the ways things are. Questions are therefore often phrased indirectly, and are used to increase one's understanding, not as often is the case in the West to challenge and check facts. Sawadogo (1995) suggests that because of the tradition of observation and oral transmission of knowledge, the skill of memorization is important. This may mean that the lecture format is more appropriate than group interaction, as we discuss below.

The second aspect of learning in the African context (Sawadogo, 1995) is that knowledge is respected, highly valued and almost feared. As a result of this the learner becomes very dependent on the trainer as the source of knowledge and wisdom, and cannot be thought of as an 'independent learner' as in the Western view. Sawadogo (1995) asserts that this dependency relationship is associated with the negative connotation of questioning, and that several commentators believe that this is cultivated in order to keep society's members in conformance with its rules: as a means of social control. Independence of learning is discouraged, and those adopting this form of expression tend to be marginal and rejected from the society. This view coincides with that taken in Chapter 2 in the current text, that control in 'African renaissance' management systems is largely normative (rather than coercive or contractual as in post-colonial or post-instrumental systems respectively).

The exception to the discouraging of independent thought and learning is within age sets of many African societies. People freely question and interact with peers in homogeneous groups. Group training sessions with people who barely know each other, and of different ages and seniority may be unsuccessful according to Sawadogo (1995). This may lead to one person dominating discussion. Rather, it may be better to start with small homogenous groups, and moving to medium-sized groups still taking account of gender, age and social or organizational position. Yet even so, Sawadogo, as we have seen above, suggests that the tradition of observation, together with memorization within the oral tradition, favour lecture methods. These two aspects, respect for knowledge and learning as a passive process, are contrary to the two Western principles of the independent learner, and the active nature of learning.

Sawadogo also discusses the role of feedback which is so important in the Western tradition in order to guide the attainment of objectives. Rather, in the African tradition of passive learning and respect for knowledge and the trainer, accurate feedback may not be forthcoming. It is rare to get negative feedback in a training session in Africa and normal to get positive feedback that may seem complimentary but not very helpful. People who see themselves as recipients of knowledge might find it strange that the trainer is soliciting suggestions and feedback from them. Sawadogo (1995) also suggests that because African society tends to be high context where it is difficult to separate the actor from the actions, people do not criticize others openly. Intermediaries may help to channel more accurate feedback therefore. We may add that this has parallels in the lack of success of 360 degrees feedback in appraisal exercises introduced by Western managers. Giving direct feedback to superiors, or even those on the same organizational level may be inappropriate.

Sawadogo (1995) finally directs his attention to the English and French language as an inappropriate medium of instruction when they are based on cognitive processes that are inductive and linear cause–effect reasoning, rather than deductive (based on observation) and less linear thought processes. Using the Mossi (Burkina Faso) language as an example he characterizes African languages as conveying a message structure of narrative, critical incident and high repetition, contrasted with the sequential, categorical and analytical structure of French and English. Message transmission is by interpersonal interaction in the Mossi situation but by multiple media in the French and English situations and therefore may be more context specific. Message retention is by memory and observation in the Mossi situation rather than through multiple media and through an action or doing process. In the Mossi situation communication patterns are through the power of oral words, listening and group based, whereas in French and English situations through the written word, through discussion, questioning and on an individual basis. Hence the word 'imitation' in English may have a negative connotation, yet in the Mossi language 'zamse' means both 'to imitate' and 'to learn and teach'. Similarly the word 'passivity' expresses a lack of initiative (we could add that 'proactive' is a major buzzword in Anglo-Saxon management circles), yet in the Mossi language it means 'good heart' (ne bugsego) or 'a person who proceeds cautiously' (ne maasgaa) (p. 291). He suggests that the word 'feedback' is particularly difficult to translate into Mossi, and the closest words, which tend to connote criticism, are viewed negatively. He discusses other similar problems in order to build his case for the inappropriateness of European languages in incorporating African traditions into training practices and methods.

The main problem in transposing Western (post-instrumental) training methods to sub-Saharan Africa therefore appears to be the assumption of an internationally universal experiential learning style. In order to partly overcome the problems of simply superimposing the experiential model onto other cultures, Jackson (1995, 1996) reformulated the Kolb model along the lines suggested by Hughes-Weiner (1986) and tested this empirically across different cultures. He proposes four learning modalities as follows:

- **Receptivity**: learners are predominantly receptive to *practical* stimuli or *theoretical* stimuli for learning depending on their cultural backgrounds and their experiences in educational systems. This could involve either on-the-job learning or off-job theoretical study.
- **Perceptual**: learners are more *intuitive* about sorting and judging information, or are *rational* in a step-by-step approach to judging the quality of information that is the basis for making decisions. This represents the difference between

being responsive to new and untried ideas in a holistic way, and being responsive to facts and details and proven approaches. This again reflects experience within their culture.

- **Cognitive**: learners are more *subjective* in the way they make decisions and solve problems based on personal judgements, or base their decision-making more on *logic* and scientific approaches. This represents a distinction between a preference to scientific approaches and subjects that provide definite answers, and a preference for more judgmental or subjective approaches of the humanities, and can be influenced by cultural differences.
- **Behaviour/Control**: learners prefer to rely on their *own initiative*, or on the *direction* of an instructor. This has implications for the level of control required or expected from the learner. This is likely to reflect prior educational experience in national systems that reflect either a controlled instructor lead approach, or a more facilitative learner–initiative approach.

Although African countries were not included in the ensuing empirical study, the results from a survey of management students and managers across the six countries of Britain, France, Germany, Poland, Taiwan, Lithuania are instructive. This is particularly the case in the differences between France and Britain, and generally the differences among European countries. As with European studies of Africa, Europeans lump African countries together. So with African commentators, there is a tendency to lump European countries together in a homogeneous group, when considering the effects of European principles and practices on organizations in Africa: a fault that can perhaps be seen in Sawadogo's work above. In the following results we therefore focus particularly on differences between French and British learning styles.

In the *practical–theoretical* dimension the French learners have a comparatively theoretical preference. This contrasts with the Polish learners who have a preference for practical class activity, learning by doing, learning from simulations in the class, but with a strong preference to learn alone. The learners from Taiwan are the most socially oriented in their learning, expressing a preference for learning with others. The British contrast with the French in being social learners with a preference for practical activity and learning by doing. The French are the most theoretical in comparative terms. The German learners express a preference for learning by doing and learning from simulations in the classroom, but are generally less practical if compared with the learners from Taiwan and Poland. This distinction between the theoretical and content-driven education style of the French and the more practical, process-driven, experiential nature of the British is well documented. Experiential learning is mainly an Anglo-Saxon invention, and reflects well this style, yet is at odds with the French system of education, and the types of systems transferred to Africa during colonial times.

There does not appear to be major differences between French and British for the *intuitive–rational* dimension. Although the British learners express a preference for intuition most strongly compared with other nationalities. For the cognitive modality the learners from France, Britain and Taiwan appear to be the most subjective in their decision approaches. The German learners show a preference for a logical approach rather than dealing with beliefs, feelings or what seems right. It would seem that at least on this dimension French and British coincide.

In the behaviour/control modality among the Europeans, the French have the least preference for *self-initiated* learning, with the Germans and then British preferring a self-initiated approach. The German sample, of all the national groups believe more that they should question a teacher's proficiency if need be. The Polish indicate that they are the least likely to do this. The Lithuanians believe strongly that teachers should be regarded as equals, with the learners from France and Taiwan believing more that teachers should be treated as superiors. This may again reflect a content-based approach to learning within the French system that is much closer to Sawadogo's principle of passive learning and respect for knowledge in the African situation. In this case the French approach may coincide more closely with African approaches than the British, and may well be more appropriate if we accept Sawadogo's thesis. British management 'learners' appear to favour practical and social learning activities, are intuitive, subjective and favour taking their own initiative in their learning. Yet it is not just at the individual level that Anglo-Saxon learning concepts are propagated in Africa. It is also at the organizational level, with concepts of the 'learning organization' being taken up by management development and organization development specialists in sub-Saharan Africa.

### The organizational learning and its appropriateness in Africa

It is mainly such Anglo-Saxon approaches to experiential learning that have given rise to the cultural product of the concept of Organizational Learning. Organizational learning may be regarded as experiential learning at the corporate level. Hence Argyris's (1992) single- and double-loop learning represent a cyclical process where actions (single-loop) or governing variables (double-loop) are adapted or changed within the organization. Single-loop learning takes place when mismatches between the outcomes that are intended and those that actually occur are corrected by simply changing the actions that were initiated in the preceding cycle. Double-loop learning occurs when these mismatches are corrected by examining and altering governing variables and then actions. Governing variables are sets of beliefs and values that can be seen to drive and guide people's action as agents for the organization. Organizational learning is said to occur when the solution to a new problem is actually implemented, rather than simply discovering problems and inventing solutions.

This model is comparable to an open systems model that explains how organizations as systems receive feedback from their environment from consequences of their outputs (e.g. Kolb *et al.*, 1991). Such an open systems model in organizational theory has been much criticized by people such as Silverman, 1970, over the last 30 years. This is because of the reification of organizations as entities separate from the people who comprise them, the perceived rationalistic cause–end relationship, and an instrumentalism based on 'executive goals'.

As was seen above, Kolb (1984) suggests that individual learning is governed by people's needs and goals. Thus people seek experiences that are related to their goals. They interpret them in relation to these goals and test their implications that are relevant to their needs. Organizations, however, pursue goals that are related to such as short-term profit, long-term survival or the achievement of social goals as in the case of public institutions (Bovin, 1998). Such goals can more accurately be referred to as executive goals rather than organizational goals (Silverman, 1970).

Senge (1990), who has had much influence in developing and propagating worldwide the concept of the learning organization, proposes five 'component technologies' that contribute towards developing learning organizations: *systems thinking* (an ability to see above the isolated parts of the system, and to see how it all fits together); *personal mastery* (continually clarifying and deepening personal vision, to focus on energies and developing patience in order to see reality objectively and to provide a commitment to develop mastery); *mental models* (an ability to understand and change shared mental models which are pervasive within the organization and which prevent change); *building shared vision* (developing an ability to unearth shared vision and foster commitment rather than compliance); and *team learning* (a capacity of members of a team to suspend judgement and starting to think together, and to recognize the patterns of interaction within a team that militate against learning). Senge (1990) also contends that teams are fundamental learning units in an organization.

It is understandable that on a superficial level the learning organization concept may be an attractive one to organizations in Africa. Yet the learning organization concept is based firmly on a systems model with a focus on the purpose of the system pursuing executive goals. Although many of the assumptions about this model are taken from ideas about the developmental nature of Japanese organizations (see Lessem, 1989) and what makes them successful, it is firmly grounded in an Anglo-Saxon concept of the commercial organization based on the maximization of resources: particularly in economically unfavourable conditions and a need to downsize, delay and empower; in uncertain commercial conditions; and in conditions of rapid change. Although these are conditions that need to be addressed in Africa (see Chapter 3), there is a tendency in the organizational learning concept to reflect an instrumental approach to people in the organization rather than a truly developmental approach in the humanistic sense.

Hence many organizations in Africa are going through a process of downsizing and massive societal changes. The concept of the learning organization is an appealing one as the message is that this can help to transform an organization, to make it more responsive to change in the wider environment and global competition. Yet in order to build a 'learning society' there is a need to develop more people inside organizations, not fewer. It is unlikely that the (Anglo-Saxon) model of the learning organization can cope with the wider societal need to develop people in Africa where countries are going through major transitions.

The model is also based on the concept of participation, empowerment and responsibility of training resting more firmly on the individual (often as part of the group). This may be difficult to implement in view of Sawadogo's assertions of the nature of traditional African learning, and perhaps also in the higher power distance of post-colonial management systems. It may also be inappropriate to the more collectivistic and emerging humanistic African renaissance systems.

These needs, which we have until now discussed in the context of the methods of training and management development in sub-Saharan Africa, should also be reflected in the content of management development. Part II of this book provides the basis for this content. It is to this that we now turn.

## The content of management development in Africa

Here we start from the position, developed within the chapters of Part II of the current text, that managers in Africa have either demonstrated competencies and capacities in a number of areas in order to manage successfully and they can share these with other managers; or, they are in need of developing these areas, and can benefit from the experiences of managers who have indeed demonstrated competencies in these areas. Developing effective and appropriate management in sub-Saharan Africa is key to building responsive and responsible organizations and institutions. This is particularly the case in a sub-continent that has been slated as having incompetent and corrupt leaders, that has weak ineffective institutions that are inappropriate to producing wealth, except for a minority of citizens, and incapable of addressing the needs of a wider stakeholder base in civil society.

The research is demonstrating that:

- The perceptions of the efficacy of management methods and styles, the way these are changing, and the desirability of these changes vary among ethnic and gender groups within countries, among African countries, and according to the relative influences of Western, African and post-colonial principles and practices. Hence:
  - There is a need to be aware of, and manage these differences within a complex and rapidly changing multicultural context, if management is going to be effective.
- Historical, cultural and power influences are leading to the development of different hybrid forms of management and organizations. Some are highly adaptive to the context in which they operate, some are mal-adaptive. Hence:
  - To develop effective management, there is a need to understand the dynamics of hybridization and to learn from the successes of those adaptive organizations, and from the shortcomings of those that are mal-adaptive.
- For employees and managers there is often a split between the world of work and community/home life, whereby staff going into work in the morning step out of their own culture and enter a different one. This is not being managed well in many organizations, often leading to low levels of employee morale and alienation from the work place.
  - To develop effective and appropriate organizations within which to work, people management principles and practices should reconcile this split between work and community/home life.
- Organizations in Africa have to operate within a complexity of different stakeholder interests. Often the interests of different stakeholder groups are not adequately recognized and incorporated within the wider decision processes of the organization. Often attempts at developing a more democratic organization

(for example, from Western principles) do not include a wider stakeholder base. Similarly, attempts at corporate responsibility programmes are not inclusive of community stakeholder interests, and sometime simply appear as cynical marketing ploys by foreign companies.

- In order to develop effective organizations in Africa, there is a need to incorporate a wider stakeholder base into a truly participative decision process.
- Within organizations, cultural differences are not adequately managed within the different power relationships that operate. Different cultural groups may not have the same access to resources and decision processes.
    - There is a need to positively manage cross-cultural relationships within organizations in Africa, and to take account of power relations and unequal access to organizational resources. This could include programmes of equal opportunities and positive discrimination, as well as training programmes to ensure managers are aware and sensitized to the issues, and can develop appropriate competencies.

From this, it is possible to develop seven main themes or competency areas that need to be attended to by managers, their organizations, and in their training and development:

1   constraints and opportunities: understanding the complexity of operating constraints within Africa and turning these into opportunities (Chapter 3);
2   multiple stakeholders: accommodating the interests of multiple stakeholders (Chapters 3 and 4);
3   decision processes: developing effective decision-making processes that give voice to these interests (Chapter 4);
4   motivation and commitment: obtaining commitment and motivation by reconciling conflicts between work and home/community life (Chapters 6 and 7);
5   appropriate management principles: assessing the appropriateness of management techniques in different socio-cultural contexts (Chapter 5);
6   multiculturalism: managing the dynamics of multiculturalism (Chapters 3–6);
7   cross-cultural development: developing an awareness of own cultural values and the way they influence the management of people (Chapters 3–7).

We now discuss these seven themes briefly, drawing on the discussion in Part II of the current text, and using these themes as examples of what should be incorporated into management development programmes, and which should be developed as capacities within management in Africa.

### Constraints and opportunities

Developing awareness amongst the management team of the broader operating constraints (political, economic, legislative, social and cultural) within a complex operating environment, and how these may be turned into opportunities.

The research is beginning to show a need for management not only to be aware of operating constraints, but also to develop an awareness of how these may be turned into opportunities amongst its management team. Sub-Saharan African countries' original economic development was based on extraction and agriculture aimed at an export rather than a domestic market and the contemporary export ratios reflect this. According to the African Development Report (2000: 136) Africa's share in global exports fell from 4.5 per cent in 1977 to 2 per cent in 1997 (in US dollars, 2000) This focus on export-led production had the effects of negating the need to develop a consumer-based economy, leading to the underdevelopment of processing and service industries, and skills associated with the secondary and tertiary sectors.

The inequalities of the past have ensured the under-education and under-skilling of many people who are ill-equipped for jobs in a highly competitive global market-place. Even in South Africa, its 1999 gross national product per capita (GNP) of US$3,170 places it in the upper-middle income group of semi-industrialized economies and one of the most prosperous countries in Southern Africa, yet it performs more in line with the typical lower-middle income countries, considering its social indicators (African Development Indicators, 2001: 5). A high dependency ratio among the population has been exacerbated by the pandemic of AIDS. The way this issue is being addressed in sub-Saharan African countries by Human Resource departments varies from decreasing expenditure on training (from interviews in Zimbabwe, suggesting that because of the number of employees falling ill after training, money spent on training was largely seen as a waste), to AIDS/HIV testing in countries including Kenya and Botswana (from personal interviews).

Long lists of constraints can be drawn up for other African countries, yet it is management who are able to turn these around into opportunities that may make the difference between a mal-adaptive management system and a highly adaptive system Organizations do thrive and prosper under adverse conditions. and the research is beginning to throw up such examples.

### Strategies and stakeholder interests

> Incorporating the interests of its multiple stakeholders including employees and their representatives, managers, community, government, suppliers, and customers into its strategic objectives, and not merely those of its shareholders in the case of private sector enterprises.

Many sub-Saharan African countries have been launched into a competitive global marketplace where the overriding trend for organizations in industrial countries is to downsize and delay to make the organization more competitive. Like South Africa other countries such as Kenya, Nigeria and even Cameroon, particularly under conditions from Structural Adjustment Programmes, may be becoming increasingly results-focused, and along with that have shareholder value as their main strategic driver.

In South Africa, for example, Jackson (1999) found that managers perceived their organizations as having a low priority towards employees, managers and local community as stakeholders. Quality and growth are the primary key success factors while job satisfaction and success of affirmative action was regarded as less important success factors. A big challenge in South Africa and other African countries, is how to reconcile the need to grow people within the wider society, thereby contributing to employment equity and providing development opportunities within the organization; and, on the other hand the need to be globally competitive, to be 'mean and lean' and to develop a profit focus. There is a need for organizations to be a means to developing people for the future (Jackson, 1999). To be effective in sub-Saharan Africa organizations may have to reflect the multiple interests of a broader base of stakeholders, and incorporate these within the strategic objectives of the organization. It may also be in this way that managers can interpret wider the ways in which constraints may be turned into opportunities.

Jackson's (1999) study concluded that organizations were driven by downsizing to respond to financial constraints and commercial imperatives and, responding to the social and developmental needs for affirmative action: hence, a managing of interests from different stakeholders. But the study also warned that the current nature of managers and organizations in South Africa might militate against reconciling such differences. Managers were asked to indicate the level of importance given by their organization to its various stakeholders (defined as 'those who have an interest in the organization'). The most important were customers, shareholders and government. The least important included suppliers, employees, managers and the local community (Jackson, 1999). Managers perceive their organizations as being focused towards their business, rather than their internal stakeholders (employees and managers) and the local community. Although this specific study was not repeated in other sub-Saharan countries, the current research project is indicating a lack of inclusiveness often along ethnic lines. For example, South Asian-run companies in Kenya do not necessarily reflect the interests of African managers and employees; companies run by a dominant Kikuyu management do not always reflect the interests (and reflect equitable access to decision-making processes and job opportunities) of other African ethnic groups. Foreign-run companies (for example, American multinational) do not always reflect the needs and aspirations of the wider community within which they operate.

It would seem logical that organizations must have effective means to give voice to those diverse interests, and incorporate them within the dialogue of the organization, its strategy, objectives, policies and practices. Hence, it is likely also that top managers will have to incorporate different stakeholders into the decision-making processes of the organization.

### Decision-making and access to decision-making processes

> Developing real and effective internal means for incorporating the perceptions, expectations, strengths and interests of stakeholders and different cultural and gender groups into the decision-making process and the management of change, through active participation at the strategic level.

The research results presented in Chapter 5 indicate that organizations are still relatively authoritarian and hierarchical, employing a coercive form of control. From the available literature this seems to be repeated in sub-Saharan countries generally (Blunt and Jones, 1992). Yet this may be more reflective of a post-colonial management system, rather than anything that is indigenous to Africa.

With the influence of democratic processes, Western approaches to management and perhaps even African approaches (see African renaissance management systems), organizations may well be looking towards more involvement of its people in the decision-making process. Yet only lip-service may be being paid to participative management in organizations. Often downsizing and delayering leads to 'empowerment' of managers and staff at lower levels of the organization than was previously required. This may well lead to the impression of participative management. Yet participative management may only arise through the active empowerment of the diverse interest groups in African countries. For example, in South Africa, a country for which the statistics are available, with more than 79 per cent of the management population being white, and over 78 per cent of all managers being male (Breakwater Monitor, 2000) full participation in decision-making of all members of the stakeholder populations of organizations may be some way off.

In African societies, as in many communalistic societies, the barriers between community life and organizational life must be broken down in order to provide a context for commitment and motivation of the workforce. This may go hand in hand with bringing in a form of participation that involves stakeholder interests from the community and within the organization (organizations are starting to do this and we have provided some case study examples in Chapter 4). Hence, it is likely also that organizations will have to develop this wider community stakeholder involvement in order to build employee commitment and motivation.

### *Motivation and commitment*

> Obtaining commitment and motivation by developing understanding of the relationship between community/family life and work life, and the way this relationship is differently perceived by different cultural perspectives.

Blunt and Jones (1992) indicated that African employees (in sub-Saharan African countries) work in order to earn money to pay for what they need in life. There is an indication of a lack of commitment to the organization by employees. Jackson (2002a) proposes that of collectivistic societies such as Japan, organizations have been successful in harnessing the wider societal collectivism to corporate life, to foster commitment by employees in a reciprocal relationship. Organizations in most other collectivistic societies (South Asia, Africa) have failed to do so mainly due to the legacies of colonial institutions and their failure to integrate with their host societies.

Our research presented in Chapter 7 indicates a low work centrality, yet a higher work satisfaction and commitment to the organization. The concomitant of this is the expectation that the organization will provide stability and will in fact be loyal to the employee.

This reflects Jackson's (1999) earlier study in South Africa, where managers (from a predominantly black sample) were asked to rank those aspects that are important in their total life. In order of importance the following ranking was given: (1) giving plenty of time to my family; (2) making work central in my life; (3) being actively involved in the community; (4) pursuing my religion; and (5) pursuing my leisure activities. This indicates, not an alienation from the workplace, but a primacy of family life. Jackson's (1999) study also included an organizational climate survey of 200 employees in three organizations in South Africa. This indicated that there was generally higher satisfaction with working conditions, content of job and job security, yet lower satisfaction with appraisal systems, recognition of employee worth, union–management relations among other factors and the extent to which employees felt involved in matters that affected them.

The way an organization pays attention to employee commitment and motivation through integrating the links between organization and community, the bringing in of different stakeholder interests and the regard for its people, is driven by its management systems. In Africa these systems are culturally influenced through an admixture of post-colonial, Western (and perhaps Eastern) and African inputs. The management of these inputs in hybrid systems of management that are likely to be adaptive, rather than mal-adaptive, to their African context may depend to a large extent on managers' abilities to recognize and articulate these cultural influences. Hence, it is likely also that organizations will have to encourage and maintain a level of awareness of the influences on management principles employed.

### Management principles

> Maintaining a high level of awareness of the contributing factors to the way the organization is managed through principles, policies and practices, and their appropriateness to the socio-cultural contexts within which the organization operates.

One of the concerns of the study by Jackson (1999) in South Africa was the apparent antithesis between Western and non-Western ideas of organization and management: between an idea of people as a resource (human resource management) and people with a value in themselves (reflected in the word *ubuntu*, from a Xhosa proverb 'Ubuntu ungamntu ngabanye abantu' – people are people through other people). It may be possible to reconcile this antithesis, but it would seem logical that before this can happen, managers should be aware of these different perspectives. In Jackson's (1999) study the consensus was that people should be valued in their own right, they should be consulted, and they should be treated fairly and ethically in an organization that is not merely concerned with short-term results and making profits. However, the general perception was that the organization regarded people as a valuable resource above the well-being of people in the organization. Results from the current study (Chapter 5) show that management principles employed are generally out of line with the African cultural context. African managers would like to see their organizations more people- and results-focused and less coercive or control-focused.

Whilst the 1999 study indicated that organizations are addressing the developmental aspects of people, there still seems to be a gap between humanistic and developmental intentions of organizations and their instrumental orientation. It may also be that there is still a low articulation of an 'African' approach. This may be in part due to a lack of conscious management of multiculturalism at the level of managing a culturally diverse workforce with different expectations. Hence, it is also likely that organizations will have to improve their management of multiculturalism in Africa.

## Managing multiculturalism

> Consciously manage the dynamics of multiculturalism in order to develop strengths and synergies from these, including the management of equal opportunities of individuals from different ethnic and gender groups to influence the direction of the organization.

This can be undertaken from a number of perspectives. This would involve not only managing differences in culture and gender from the point of view of understanding different cultures. It would also involve managing the power relations among people of different cultures (Human, 1996b). In South Africa, managing such relationships involves compliance to employment equity legislation on the one hand in order to redress the imbalances both at corporate and regional level, and consciously managing the process of multicultural working on the other hand. There is little evidence from the current research project that multiculturalism is being consciously managed in Kenya, Cameroon or Nigeria. In South Africa, cross-cultural workshops seem to have been undertaken in the mid-1990s, but have faded away (perhaps through a belief that the job is now done). Recent figures from the Breakwater Monitor (2000) which monitors employment equity in South Africa through some 200 voluntarily participating organizations, indicates that in 2000 African managers comprised 9.52 per cent of all managers, 5.53 per cent were Indian, 5.31 per cent were coloured and 79.64 per cent were white. Of the total 78.66 per cent were male and 21.34 per cent were female. There still appears to be considerable room for further redressing the power balances in corporations among the racial groupings, and in further developing awareness sessions and cross-cultural workshops.

Although training courses in intercultural management, and awareness sessions address issues of interaction, they may add very little directly to addressing issues arising from power imbalances within corporations that are culturally related. Nor do they address imbalances within the total stakeholder population. With these imbalances, it is difficult for organizations to argue that simply complying with the legislation is sufficient. Proactively managing across cultures would seem necessary in order to redress some of the power imbalances by building awareness, and developing general cross-cultural competencies. African management in general seems highly placed to take a lead in developing innovative ways to manage multiculturalism. The multicultural nature of most African societies and organizations in Africa in fact demands such an approach. Even apparently mono-cultural Botswana has a surprising diversity of cultural groups that are recognized as being quite distinct, and in the small community of Alice in the former Transkei in South Africa, the all-Xhosa community recognize differences between Xhosa from the locality and Xhosa who are not – favouring those clan-groups that were from the immediate locality.

One conclusion that may be drawn is that in order to effectively manage across cultures, it is necessary to have an awareness of the types of stereotypes that one is working with, to overcome some of the negatives, and focus on the positive aspect of cross-cultural working: to see multiculturalism as a positive aspects whereby different stakeholders from different cultural perspectives can make a variety of contributions, and where this input is not simply desirable, it is necessary to economic and social prosperity. A starting point in this is for individuals to have a high awareness of their own cultural background, its values, and the contribution that their values, perceptions and expectations can make.

Only recently has there been an articulation of the relation of African culture to management through the work of Mbigi (1997; Mbigi and Maree, 1995) in South Africa. Other African countries may be lagging behind in this articulation. Hence, it is also likely that organizations will have to provide development initiatives on an ongoing basis in this area.

### Cross-cultural training and development

> Providing appropriate training programmes to address cultural diversity.

In a multicultural context, the lack of understanding and articulation of the nature and influence of one's culture may be a serious stumbling block to building synergies from cultural diversity. Yet Human (1996b) argues that this is not enough. A clear understanding of the way power relations influence the stereotyping of groups and the perceptions of individuals and the expectation one has of such individuals is necessary. Thus she suggested that managers should be trained to be aware of the negative impact that the maintenance of inaccurate stereotypes has, and of the resulting expectations based on power relations that are transmitted through ideas relating to culture. Second, such training should make managers understand themselves. Third, it should provide the communication skills that are needed to minimize the impact of negative stereotypes and expectations, and to reinforce the process by which more accurate (and presumably more positive) stereotypes may occur. This is all dependent on a high level of awareness of one's self and other's culture, and the perceptions and expectations that have occurred as a result of the legacies of the past. This may involve grappling with many of the legacies of colonialism, and its impact on cultural perceptions and stereotypes. In order to incorporate these elements, it may be necessary, among other measures to integrate them within a development process.

By way of summary of the content of training and management development we can re-iterate the above, in terms of what we assert as the prerequisites to effective and appropriate management in sub-Saharan, but also what African managers can offer the global management community as a whole:

- awareness amongst the management team of the broader operating constraints (political, economic, legislative, social and cultural) within a complex operating environment, and how these may be turned into opportunities;

- incorporation of the interests of its multiple stakeholders including employees and their representatives, managers, the community, government, suppliers and customers into its strategic objectives, and not merely those of its shareholders in the case of private sector enterprises;
- development of real and effective internal means for incorporating the perceptions, expectations, strengths and interests of stakeholders and different cultural and gender groups into the decision-making process and the management of change, through active participation;
- obtaining of commitment and motivation by developing an understanding of the relationship between community/family life and work life, and the way this relationship is differently perceived by different cultural perspectives;
- maintenance of a high level of awareness of the contributing factors to the way the organization is managed through principles, policies and practices, and their appropriateness to the socio-cultural contexts within which the organization operates;
- conscious management of the dynamics of multiculturalism in order to develop strengths and synergies from these, including the management of equal opportunities of individuals from different ethnic and gender groups to influence the direction of the organization.

In Part III, we now explore how these themes have been addressed in specific countries, and in specific organizations.

# Learning from countries and cases

# Chapter 9

# Nigeria

## Managing cross-cultural differences and similarities

The trouble with Nigeria is simply and squarely a failure of leadership. There is nothing basically wrong with the Nigerian character. There is nothing wrong with the Nigerian land or climate or water or air or anything else. The Nigerian problem is the unwillingness or inability of its leaders to rise to the responsibility, to the challenge of personal example which are the hallmarks of true leadership.

(Chinua Achebe, *The Trouble With Nigeria*, 1983, and quoted widely)

The resilience, the wonderfulness, the energy – Nigeria can be compared favourably with the United States of America. I put it crudely sometimes that if you know how to package shit, you can sell it in Nigeria. I want this country to be the first black superpower.

(Bola Ige, Minister of Power and Steel, Nigeria, at the time of quoting in Maier, 2000)

Traditional philosophies of life in many Nigeria cultures reject the negative attitude towards work currently displayed by Nigerian workers. Each household member was expected to contribute fairly to work on the household farm. Indolence met with social disapproval and ridicule. Honest work for a day's pay was expected and received from employed persons. The image of the hardworking Igbirra, Wawa and Tiv migrant farmers of Nigeria is incongruent with present day observations concerning wage earners. Selfless service to the community was emphasised and enforced by different age groups, and this promoted a sense of commitment to public work.

(Abudu, 1986)

## Introduction

Nigeria more than any country in Africa has suffered from a bad press, from political turmoil to email scams. Perhaps the wonder of Nigeria is that from being a colonial invention, and through numerous ethnic conflicts including a major civil war, it has managed to hang together as a nation. For example, Maier (2000: 7–8) writes:

Nigeria . . . was the bastard child of imperialism, its rich mosaic of peoples locked into a nation-state they had no part in designing. Before the European conquest,

Nigeria was home to an estimated three hundred ethnic groups of sometimes widely differing languages and systems of internal rule. Although its constituents had traded and often lived among each other for centuries, the land of Nigeria had never existed as one political unit. The peoples gathered within its borders had different cultures and stood at very unequal levels of development.

This state of affairs is reflected in work organizations. For example, Abudu (1986: 31–2) states that:

> Unsatisfactory attitudes towards work may also be traced to lack of patriotism among Nigeria's citizens. The concept of 'the Nigerian nation' is, for most citizens, a sentimental one to be exploited for personal advantage. Moreover, since the emergence of a strong nation-state has been hampered by centrifugal ethnic forces in Nigeria, many employees in the public sector owe more loyalty to their ethnic roots than to the Nigerian state which has little meaning beyond a geographical expression for many workers in public employment.

## Western influence and indigenous management development

Despite the size and importance of Nigeria, it seems that little original management thought has emerged there in the same way perhaps as South African *ubuntu*. Eze (1989) provides one example of embryonic African renaissance thought when he proposed 'New patriotic management techniques' in order to meet the requirements for improving black African management in Nigeria, while contributing to national development and 'people's emancipation in Africa' (p. 55). As they address many of the management issues to be met in Nigeria, it is worth recounting these 'techniques'. They are as follows:

1 Management by self-revolution: a critical self examination of weaknesses of the black race in order to develop qualities of self acceptance, self knowledge, self trust, self pride, self protection and self reliance, not least to become free from foreign manipulation and become an independent self.
2 Management by ethnic group integration: through workshops, to break down ethnic differences, hostilities and prejudices, and to narrow social distances by forging new cultural elements at national and organizational levels.
3 Management by attitude change: through workshops in order to develop a more positive attitude and a willingness to change.
4 Management by patriotism: instilling a patriotic pride and esteem through orientation activities, laboratories and successful leadership acts.
5 Management by incentives conversion: again, through workshops designed to reorient black African workers away from spiritual-world incentives to material-world incentives; away from religious–social motives to scientific and factual goals.
6 Management by non-corruption: attitudinal change programmes aimed at changing African managers' corrupt practices by reorienting to corporate and national goals.

7 Management by impartiality and meritocracy: in order to counter authoritarianism and to inculcate fairer management practices through impartiality particularly in personnel issues.
8 Management by accountability: encouraging managers to be accountable.
9 Management by performance appraisal: using objective methods of appraisal.
10 Management by free zones: encourage the free transfer of indigenous knowledge by creating foreign-, multinational- and expatriate-free zones where ideas can be tried, tested out and shared. He suggests that other nations such as Japan and Korea, have applied this to the whole country, and suggests this for Nigeria.
11 Management by risk taking: to overcome one of the main sources of black under-development, the unwillingness to take risks. This is also connected to the previous activity of creating foreign-free zones.
12 Management by research and development: to counter the reluctance of multinational companies in Nigeria and other developing countries to establish R&D departments. Indigenous talents can be encouraged and developed by developing such capabilities in a foreign-free zone.
13 Management by basic revolutions: to galvanize the collective energies of the entire population and their creative skills and talents, 'not for the maximization of profit margins of private firms, but for the spiritual and material development of the society as a whole' (p. 47 May/June). These basic revolutions should be aimed at the self, psychological, nationalistic, language, cultural, agricultural and educational aspects. These are necessary to prevent another ' "partition of Africa" by foreign creditors and international financial institutions'.
14 Management by planned adaptation: there is a need not to adopt Western management principles and techniques but to successfully adapt modern methods in an environment that is conducive to this and free from foreign interests, and requiring many of the aspects outlined in the previous thirteen points.
15 Management by human relationships: this is to overcome the authoritarianism of current management, which is mainly supported by foreign interests and a situation that is not conducive to developing a more human relationship-based management that reflects seeing the 'worker as a fellow citizen to be led, trained and developed into a useful contributor to the growth of their company . . . [and] national economic growth' (p. 48).

Eze's (1989) approach is based on giving indigenous management self-confidence to reflect national and indigenous interests, rather than those of multinational companies. We have presented this at length because it is illustrative of some of the issues of management in Nigeria. It touches on what appears to be a sensitive issue of what we have termed cross-cultural interaction at the inter-continental level. The lack of confidence in African culture and principles applied to management is palpable; while the degree of Western influence is a sensitive issue that has led to indigenization legislation from the federal government, for example in the 1970s.

## Managing uncertainty

Utomi (1998) maintains that one of the challenges of organizations in developing countries, and he is writing primarily of Nigeria, is to manage uncertainty. He particularly points to the problem of weak institutions, and his example of the vagaries of the Nigerian budget-setting processes (discussed in Chapter 3 of the current text) is illustrative of this. Eze's (1989) programme is perhaps illustrative of many of the constraints and opportunities within the Nigerian operating context.

Nigeria has a population of some 130 million. Similarly to most African economies this is mostly an agrarian country with 70 per cent of the working population employed in agriculture, 10 per cent in industry, and 20 per cent in services 20 per cent (1999 estimates: CIA World Factbook). The main industries in order of importance are: crude oil, coal, tin, columbite, palm oil, peanuts, cotton, rubber, wood, hides and skins, textiles, cement and other construction materials, food products, footwear, chemicals, fertilizer, printing, ceramics, steel. Nigeria is oil rich, yet according to the CIA World Factbook is 'long hobbled by political instability, corruption, and poor macroeconomic management' although the civilian government of President Obasanja has initiated a number of economic reforms (re-elected in 2003 amid widespread accusations of vote rigging: *The Economist*, 22 April 2003, which report believes that probably the least corrupt candidate won the election as all parties were involved in vote rigging).

According to the CIA World Factbook: 'Nigeria's former military rulers failed to diversify the economy away from overdependence on the capital-intensive oil sector, which provides 20 per cent of GDP, 95 per cent of foreign exchange earnings, and about 65 per cent of budgetary revenues. The largely subsistence agricultural sector has failed to keep up with rapid population growth, and Nigeria, once a large net exporter of food, now must import food. Following the signing of an IMF stand-by agreement in August 2000, Nigeria received a debt-restructuring deal from the Paris Club and a $1 billion credit from the IMF, both contingent on economic reforms. The agreement was allowed to expire by the IMF in November 2001, however, and Nigeria appeared unlikely to receive substantial multilateral assistance in future years. Nonetheless, 'increases in foreign oil investment and oil production should push growth over 4 per cent in 2002' (CIA World Factbook, 2003, 19 March).

In fact despite President Obasanjo ensuring far more freedom of speech, a side effect (according to *The Economist*) has been a rise in ethnic conflict. The same report also maintains that he has made little progress in reforming the economy and over-coming poverty. There has been a small amount of privatization and liberalization, which the report says has led more noticeably to the rise in the number of mobile telephones. Diversification of the economy has not happened, and it is still over-dependent on oil. Its economy has tended to slide backwards over the last few years (*The Economist*, 22 April 2003). A main criticism has been the lack of the benefits of oil, which makes up a major part of Nigeria's economy, to the people of Nigeria. There are fuel shortages at the petrol pumps despite a vibrant black market (*The Economist*, 26 April 2003). Disputes with indigenous peoples in the oil-producing Delta region still continue. Again, little if any local benefit has been gained for living in the richest oil-producing region of Africa (*The Economist*, 22 April 2003; and see Chapter 4). There may well be a connection between interactions at the intercontinental level, between foreign companies and government, and between foreign companies and local people, and the ongoing ethnic clashes in the Delta region (see Chapter 4).

## Cross-cultural management

Our main purpose for this chapter is not to highlight the constraints and weaknesses of the country, as there is a large literature on this, but to focus on the possibilities of cross-cultural management. We have maintained that multiculturalism can be a force either of dis-integration of an organization, community or nation, or a force for integration and for developing strengths and synergies. We have argued within this book that effective and appropriate management in Africa means cross-cultural management. This entails an understanding of the dynamics of cultural interaction, and then a capacity to bring this understanding to bear in developing synergies through cross-cultural working and development. Here we look at how our management survey results may inform the understanding of cross-cultural dynamics, and how this might be used to manage multicultural influences and interaction more effectively, as an integral and major part of effective management in Nigeria.

## Cross-cultural management studies of Nigeria

Despite Nigeria's size, population and importance not only within Africa, but also as a major oil producer in the world, it does not feature in many wide-scale cross-cultural studies. Hofstede (1980a) did not obtain sufficient sample sizes in West Africa to provide separate country scores, although the later Chinese Cultural Connection (1987) study from which Hofstede (1991) derives his Long-Term Orientation (LTO) or Confucian Dynamism identified Nigeria as ranking 22 out of 23 countries for LTO with a very short-term orientation with Pakistan, and lower than the Anglo-Saxon countries of Australia, New Zealand, USA and Great Britain, and indeed lower than Zimbabwe. This compares at the higher end of the scale with countries such as China, Hong Kong, Taiwan, Japan and South Korea. Yet this is a somewhat ambiguous concept. The 'long-term orientation' pole comprises values of persistence or perseverance, ordering of relationships by status and observing order, thrift and having a sense of shame. The opposite 'short-term orientation' pole includes values of personal steadiness and stability, protecting your 'face', respect for tradition, and reciprocity of greetings, favours and gifts. Although both poles are claimed to reflect Confucian values, Hofstede (1991) maintains that the long-term pole reflects a more dynamic, future-oriented focus, whereas the short-term pole is more oriented to the past and present and altogether more static. Short-termism does appear to depict many developing countries (Kanungo and Jaeger, 1990), and this may well reflect Nigeria's position. Yet in the Chinese Cultural Connection (1987) study both Brazil and India appear in sixth and seventh rank (to South Korea's fifth position). It may be difficult to generalize on the basis of Kanungo and Jaeger's (1990) thesis.

A far more detailed wide-scale study is that of Trompenaars (1993) which includes Nigeria. Trompenaars' (1993) work was conceptually built on Parsons and Shils (1951) and Kluckholm and Strodtbeck's (1961) formulations of cultural differences, and other dimensions drawn from Rotter (1966) and Hall (1959). These conceptualizations include the values dimensions: regard for rules or relations (universalism–particularism), individualism–collectivism, low and high context societies (specific–diffuse) and the way status is accorded (achievement–ascription). Trompenaars (1993) also considers relation to nature (external–internal locus of control). His results are presented in terms of the percentage of positive (or negative) responses to each of several questions for each of some 50 different nationalities. His information was gathered through administering a questionnaire to attendees of management seminars in the various countries surveyed (Trompenaars, 1993).

The concepts that Trompenaars' items are purported to capture, are as follows.

- **Universalism–particularism** (Trompenaars, 1993)   In some cultures people see rules and regulations as applying universally to everyone, regardless of whom they are. In cultures that are more particularist, people see relationships as more important than applying the same rules for everyone. There is an inclination to apply the rules according to friendship and kinship relations. Nigeria appears to be moderately particularistic. This may have implications for recruitment and promotion policies in organizations that may be at variance to practices in counties such as the United States and Britain. This is consistent with Abudu's (1986) observations, with Eze's (1989) assertions regarding the need for impartiality, which may be based on ethnicity or kinship (see also Iguisi 1994), and with Adigun's (1995) finding that interpersonal relationships are a major work motivator in Nigeria, although Arthur *et al.* (1995) found in their study in Nigeria and Ghana that Western HRM had made main inroads into organizations in these two countries.

- **Achievement–ascription** (Trompenaars, 1993)   Status is accorded to people on the basis of what they achieve in their jobs and their lives (achievement) or who they are and where they come from, such as family background, their school or some other prior factor (ascription). Quite often more traditional societies accord status according to the latter precept. Nigeria appears to be highly ascriptive based on family background. Again, this may influence recruitment and promotion policies, which may be at variance to practices in some (but not all) Western cultures.

- **Locus of control** (Trompenaars, 1993)   People tend to believe that what happens to them in life is their own doing (internal locus of control), or they have no or little control over what happens to them (external locus of control), the causes of which are external to them. Kanungo and Jaeger (1990) believe that external locus of control is a characteristic value of people in developing countries, and we previously discussed this in Chapter 3 of the current text. Trompenaars' (1993) results indicate that Nigeria is high on external locus of control (higher than Ethiopia) and much higher than the Anglo-Saxon and most European countries. This aspect, as we discussed in Chapter 3 may influence the way managers perceive and act towards their environment. This is assumed within

Eze's (1989) proposals for addressing the low self-confidence of Nigerians, low risk-taking, and a move towards fact-based rather than spiritual-based incentives and goals.

- **Individualism–collectivism** Trompenaars (1993) takes Parsons and Shils' (1951) definition that individualism is 'a prime orientation to the self' and collectivism 'a prime orientation to common goals and objectives'. On at least one question, on working alone versus working in a group together (which may be quite a narrow aspect of collectivism), Nigeria scores highly on collectivism (higher than Burkina Faso, and much higher than the Anglo-Saxon countries).

- **Specific–diffuse** In a specific-oriented culture managers differentiate different parts of their life, such as work and family life, whereas in diffuse-oriented cultures this distinction is not made and people are involved in different areas of one's life such as family, leisure, community, and work. From Trompenaars' (1993) findings Nigeria appears to be a fairly diffuse culture. This may have implications for expectations of the areas in which the organization should be involved, such as providing housing and other social benefits to employees, and the type of encroachment on outside work time that can be expected.

Yet many of these value dimensions have overlaps. Smith, Dugan and Trompenaars (1996) undertook a rigorous statistical reanalysis of Trompenaars database, which provides two major value dimensions (through multidimensional scaling): utilitarian involvement–loyal involvement and conservatism–egalitarian commitment.

Utilitarian involvement involves aspects of individualism that stress individual credit and responsibility. It correlates positively with Hofstede's (1980a) individualism and low power distance. Loyal involvement comprises aspects of collectivism which stress loyalty and obligation to the group, and corporate loyalty and obligation. This correlates positively with Hofstede's collectivism and high power distance.

Conservatism comprises ascribed status, particularistic orientation, with an expectation of paternalistic employers together with a formalized organizational hierarchy. It correlates positively with Hofstede's collectivism and high power distance and with an external locus of control. Egalitarian commitment comprises achieved status, a universalistic orientation and a functional organizational hierarchy. It correlates positively with Hofstede's individualism and low power distance, with an internal locus of control, and also with Schwartz's (1994) egalitarian commitment, a dimension derived from his wide-scale cross-cultural research, which does not feature Nigeria. The dimension is similar to the current one being discussed, transcending selfish interests, and reflecting a voluntary commitment to promoting the welfare of others, rather than through obligation and kinship ties. This correlates positively with Hofstede's (1980a) individualism.

Nigeria is positioned moderately high on loyal involvement with the two other African countries in this study (although not as high as Burkina Faso) and between the two poles of conservatism and egalitarian commitment. It groups with India, Japan and Spain on both these dimensions. It is higher on egalitarian commitment than Burkina Faso. It is distinct from the Anglo-Saxon countries (UK, Australia, USA) in being higher in conservatism and loyal involvement. If we compare Nigeria therefore with the results for UK and USA in this study, we could conclude that Nigerian managers favour more ascribed status based on family background, they are more particularistic, again reflecting a relationship basis for such aspects as recruitment and promotion, and a higher obligation to one's group. These are mostly aspects that are associated with medium to higher levels of collectivism, which as we discussed in Chapter 6, may have a different logic to individualistic, achievement based and universalistic societies. It may be more logical to employ someone that you know, and if he or she does not perform to put pressure on them through family affiliations and obligations, rather than employing a complete stranger based on an objective set of competencies that conforms to a particular (instrumental) model of organizations and the value of people (see Chapter 1).

Iguisi (1994) provides more information on the management culture of Nigeria based on a study of three cement producing companies using Hofstede's value survey model. One company was based in the Netherlands while two were based in Nigeria. His results, albeit small scale, indicate that Nigeria has a higher power distance than the Netherlands, a lower individualism, a higher masculinity (although still a fairly feministic society, as the Netherlands is particularly low in masculinity) and lower in uncertainty avoidance than the Netherlands. Iguisi's (1994) results from an additional questionnaire indicate that as with Dutch managers, family is more important than work for Nigeria managers. Yet position rather than accomplishment is seen as a source of respect by the Nigerians. These results also indicate that Nigerian managers favour paternalistic management as compared to the Dutch managers, and reject consultative management more than the Dutch. Although these are fairly limited results, and they compare with a European country culture that is seen by Hofstede's (1980a) data as being lower in power distance, and higher in femininity, than the Anglo-Saxon countries. These results also go some way in disabusing Kiggundu's (1988), and Blunt and Jones' (1992) assumption that African countries are high in uncertainty avoidance (see also Chapter 3 of the current text).

These studies begin to provide a picture of management in Nigeria somewhat at variance with an Anglo-Saxon model. Studies such as that of Arthur *et al.* (1995) on the prevalence of Western HRM techniques in Nigeria, hardly give a second thought to the appropriateness of such techniques and principles. We have argued throughout this text that if such 'modern' management techniques are appropriate to African countries, why have they not led to highly adaptive and effective organizations that are conducive to operating in a complex environment. Evidence in other chapters (see Chapters 10 and 12 for example) suggests that Western organizations can be successful in Africa; otherwise they would not continue to operate. Yet they are successful by defining this success within the interests of a very narrow stakeholder base (predominantly foreign shareholders), and we have argued that this definition may not only be somewhat limiting, it may also not be appropriate to the African context (see, for example, Chapter 4).

In particular, results from previous studies that we reviewed above suggest that organizational practices may be out of line with Nigerian managers' expectations, values and ideals. (This was the focus of our current study that we presented in Chapter 5).

## Leadership and management styles in Nigeria

Our results from our management survey of fifteen sub-Saharan African countries (Chapter 5) indicate that Nigerian managers, relative to managers in other African countries, see their organizations as control- rather than people-oriented, with a moderate results focus. Ideally they would like to see their organizations more results- and more people-oriented in common with most of the other African countries (Figures 5.2 and 5.3). In particular (Tables 5.1 and 5.2):

- Nigerian managers see their organizations as more control focused than managers in most other countries, but less so than those in DRC and Burkina Faso. Ideally they would like it less so, but see little change for the future. There are some small (F = 2.697; significance = 0.031) differences among ethnic groups within our samples. In particular managers from the Delta region (standardized score = –0.193) appear to desire a less controlling focus, and managers from the Midbelt appear to desire a more controlling focus (standardized score = 0.111), although this should be seen within the context of a generally moderately low score (mean = –0.078: see Table 5.1, Chapter 5). We discuss inter-ethnic differences in more detail below, where we also explain our ethnic groupings.

- Nigerian managers see their organizations as not focused towards people (in common with all other countries), and would like to see a reverse of this, but only see a small movement towards this for the future.

- Nigerian managers see their organizations as not consultative (less so compared with managers in Rwanda, Mozambique, but on a par with most other countries); they want their organizations more so, but only see a little change for the future.

- They see their organization as not managing diversity (the only country to have a lower score is DRC), and having a strong desire to see this reversed, but seeing little movement for the future. There are small differences (F = 2.722; significance = 0.029) among the ethnic grouping within our samples. In particular managers from the Hausa-Fulani grouping appear to have a stronger desire (standardized score = 0.667) than those from the Midbelt grouping (standardized score = 0.316) for better management of diversity (mean standardized score is 0.520: see Table 5.1; see discussion below of inter-ethnic differences).

- They see their organizations as having little results focus (only Côte d'Ivoire, and Malawi have a lower score for this sub-factor), and wish to see a much higher results focus, and only see a little movement towards this for the future. This trend is also reflected in the sub-factors that comprise the results-orientation (Table 5.1): clarity of objectives, and successful organization. Although for the later they do have a small positive score, and this contrasts favourably with the other countries apart from Mozambique, Namibia and Zambia.

- They do not see their organizations as undergoing rapid change. Although this is in common with a number of other countries in the study including the west and central African countries, this contrasts sharply with South Africa, as well as with most of the other southern African countries (Zambia, Zimbabwe, Namibia, but not Botswana). There is a desire for change, but managers see organizations changing less in the future than they are currently.

- In common with the other countries, Nigerian managers present a picture of weak trade unions, with a desire that they be less weak, but see no change for the future.

- Despite what some of the literature reviewed above may suggest, managers indicate that there is little or no family influence in their organizations, that this is their ideal, and it is not likely to change.

- There is a moderate amount of restriction through government legislation, and there is no desire for this to change, and no perception that it is likely to change. This is more so than compared with South Africa, for example, but far less than is seen by managers in DRC. Within our samples there are significant differences in the perceptions of the extent to which managers see their organizations currently being bound by government regulation. Managers from the Delta (standardize score = 0.440) and Hausa-Fulani (0.420) groupings see their organization bound more by such regulations than managers from the Igbo (score = −0.030) grouping (Tukey multiple comparison test; F = 3.551; significance = 0.007)

- Managers indicate a low level of risk taking, in common with all other countries. Managers also indicate that they do not have a particular appetite for risk taking, although indicate that they would accept slightly more than they perceive is likely to be the case in the future. Managers from the Igbo and Midbelt groupings see their organizations as more risk taking than their counterparts from the Hausa-Fulani grouping (Tukey multiple comparison test; F = 3.649; significance = 0.006).

- There are few and small differences among the different ethnic groupings included in this study (Delta, Hausa-Fulani, Igbo, Midbelt and Yoruba), and we discuss this in more detail in the section 'Cross-ethnic differences in Nigeria' below.

This study therefore confirms many of the characteristics of organizations and its managers presented in the literature. Many of the features of a post-colonial management can be seen, with some movement towards a results orientation through the influence of post-instrumental (Western) management systems. The view that managers desire a much more definite people focus may indicate a preference for a valuing of people that may be more in line with our 'ideal type' African renaissance management. This lack of congruence between what is and what managers would like it to be may indicate lower levels of motivation and commitment on the part of managers and staff. We now look at management motivation in Nigeria.

## Management motivation in Nigeria

In Chapter 6 we focused on different aspects of motivation in order to shed light on those facets that were important for African managers across the fifteen countries surveyed. From Table 6.1, we can rank order the particular motivators for Nigerian managers (for self) as follows:

*Positive motivators*
Eager for opportunities to learn (security)
Prefers security of a steady job (security)
Enjoys above all else to work as part of a team (security)
Very ambitious to reach the top (power)
Freedom to adopt own approach (autonomy)
Setting self difficult goals (autonomy)
\* \* \*
Preferring above all else to direct others (power)
Believing that work is the most important thing in life (power)
Preferring work to be unpredictable (autonomy)
Preferring above all else to work alone (security: negative)
*Negative motivators*

There appears to be a strong motivation towards aspects that we have loosely grouped under security motivators (see Table 6.1 and Chapter 6), and a lower (or negative) motivation towards 'autonomy' and then 'power' motivators. We can look at these motivators in relation to the other national groups within our survey.

- The desire for opportunities to learn, although the highest motivator for Nigerian managers, in relative terms this is a moderately low score (0.623), although Côte d'Ivoire managers score a low 0.132, and is lower than most other countries. It is on a par with Rwandan managers (0.618), Mozambiquan managers (0.539) and Cameroonian managers (0.545), but the desire for opportunities to learn appears to be much stronger for managers for Botswana, Burkina Faso, Ghana, Kenya, Malawi, Namibia, South Africa, Zimbabwe and South Africa (see Table 6.1).
- Moderate scores are returned for most of the motivational items in our survey when compared with other national groups, with security items scoring around the average for all managers across the countries; although the autonomy items 'setting self difficult goals', and 'freedom in the job to adopt own approach' are lower than the average. Nigerian managers appear to have a moderately high need for security along with managers from other African nations, although neighbouring Ghanaian managers appear to have a higher security need, as do Kenyans; and South Africans have a much lower need for security than Nigerian managers when looking at the one item 'prefers security of a steady job' which may reflect the higher uncertainty in the economy and job market of Nigeria. Also when looking at this one job security item, there are differences among managers from the different ethnic groupings in Nigeria. Managers from the Delta region grouping (standardized score = 0.806) have a significantly higher security need than managers from the Hausa-Fulani grouping (0.270; Tukey multiple comparison test; F = 2.595; significance = 0.036). This may, however, reflect economic issues, particularly in the Delta region, which is the main oil producing region and yet provides little security or job opportunities for locals in one of the poorer areas of Nigeria (see discussion above and in Chapter 4).

- Centrality of work in one's life appears to be low down on the list of Nigerian managers, not only relative to other motivators, but also relative to managers from many other of the countries: lower than Burkina Faso, DRC, Cameroon, Mozambique and Rwanda; but higher than South Africa and Namibia.

- The power motivation item 'very ambitious to reach the top' score for Nigerian managers is below the average score for all managers across the fifteen nations. This is, however, one of only two of the motivational items that indicate significant differences among the different ethnic groupings within the country (Tukey multiple comparison test; $F = 4.773$; significance $= 0.001$). Managers from the Delta grouping score significantly higher than Yoruba managers, who score significantly higher than Hausa-Fulani managers. The Igbo managers also score significantly higher than the Hausa-Fulani managers. In order, the ambition to reach the top appears to be strongest among Delta managers (standardized score $= 0.750$), then Midbelt ($0.422$) and Igbo ($0.419$) managers, then Yoruba managers ($0.313$), and finally Hausa-Fulani managers ($0.070$). As often happens in cross-national studies, the average standardized score of $0.358$ for Nigerian managers does not provide an indication of the differences that exist across different cultural groupings within the country. We discuss this result in more detail below.

- For locus of control (Table 6.1) Nigerian managers reflect the average score for external and locus of control, with no differences among the ethnic groupings. In particular, managers from Ghana, Botswana and South Africa appear to have a higher internal locus of control and lower external locus, reflecting a higher score than Nigeria managers that they believe that if one is motivated enough one can achieve anything, and believing less than Nigeria managers that one's own achievement is based on outside forces.

## Employee commitment in Nigeria

We have previously reviewed the literature on employee commitment and work attitudes in Africa, and much of this relates to Nigeria (Chapter 7). For example, writing in 1986, Abudu characterized Nigerian workers as being seen to be lazy and generally having a negative attitude to work. This could be attributed to inequities in the reward systems with patronage playing a significant part. It could also be attributed to the government's use of employment as a welfare service, and a reliance on non-meritocratic criteria in recruitment, placement and training. Underlying social causes, he also contends, may be the effects of corruption, lack of patriotism and the 'cultural flux in which the contemporary Nigerian worker is caught' (Abudu, 1986: 34–5).

In our study of employees in a cross section of organizations across Nigeria, Kenya, Cameroon and South Africa (see Chapter 7), we sought to provide a thorough picture of work attributes and worker attitudes. We, like Adigun (1995), hypothesized that there would be differences in the attitudes towards work among the different cultural groups in Nigeria. Similar to Adigun who found only a few small differences, we found none. This is a somewhat surprising result that was also reflected in our results in our management survey. We discuss cross-ethnic differences and the implication of these results for Nigeria in more detail in the next section. Here, it is worth reminding the reader of our general results for Nigeria for work attributes and attitudes of Nigerian employees. These are as follows:

- Training time for jobs in Nigeria was less than for employees in the other three countries.
- The requirement for teamwork appears to be lower in Nigeria than the other countries.
- Job autonomy appears to be lower in Nigeria.
- Nigerian workers have more frequent contact with supervisors on non-work issues than their Cameroonian counterparts, but less than employees in South Africa.
- Nigerian workers are more likely to confide in their supervisors than their counterparts in the other countries although the likelihood is still quite low.
- Nigerian workers may be fairly happy with the levels of coercive controls (hierarchy, authoritarianism and centralization) as there appears to be an agreement on scores for coercive control between ideal and current for employees, and agreement between the scores for managers and employees. This distinguishes them from the other three countries whose employees wish to have lower levels of coercive control.
- Nigerian employees appear to be in accord with their managers in terms of the current and ideal levels of remunerative and normative control. Both appear to want more of both these control systems.
- Nigerian employees, with their counterparts in South Africa, see their organizations as less successful than employees in Kenya, and having less skilled managers compared with Cameroon and Kenya.
- Again, with the South Africans, Nigerians see their organizations as less ethical, and having a lower rate of change than the Kenyans and Cameroonians.
- Nigerian and Cameroonian employees indicate a lower commitment to their organizations than employees in Kenya and South Africa.

There is an inference from these results that Nigerian workers are more accepting of the prevailing management system within their organization, but are more disconnected from the work situation than counterparts in the other three countries. Whilst they are in accord with their managers, and somewhat accepting of a moderate coercive control, they also ideally would like to see more results and normative/people orientation. In this they appear to agree with managers. Yet they have a lower commitment to the organization than counterparts in the three other countries.

## Cross-ethnic differences in Nigeria

One surprising result in our management and employee surveys for Nigeria was the absence of significant differences among the different ethnic groupings. Although little systematic cross-cultural studies have been undertaken in organizations in Nigeria, political and social information on the country, of the sort reviewed at the beginning of this chapter presents a picture of a deeply ethnically divided nation that was artificially created through the whims of a colonial power and ignoring previous traditional territories and ethnic and language divisions. Yet at the same time Nigeria as a nation has managed to cohere throughout its short history after independence. There are also strong arguments in the politico-social literature that ethnicity has been used first as a divide-and-rule strategy of colonial powers, and then after independence as a means of domination by ethno-political groups that are able to use ethnicity and multiculturalism around which to gain allegiance, while using homogeneity of nationhood and coherence of the nation-state around which to dominate other ethno-political groups (Oha, 1999).

Thomson (2000) argues that current ethnic groups are a creation of colonialism. The Hausa-Fulani, Yoruba and Igbo of Nigeria were the dominant groups in three regions of post-independence Nigeria: northern, western and eastern respectively. Here 'tribes' were encouraged to develop in order to work with the colonial authorities for distributing resources. Ethnic groups that had previously only had loose and changing affiliations came together as 'tribes', otherwise they had little power in dealing with the authorities and gaining resources. He takes the example of the Yoruba, which he claims is a modern social and political construct. Previous to colonial rule the term Yoruba did not exist. People of the region identified themselves as Oyo, Ketu, Egba, Ijebu, Ijesa, Ekiti, Ondon or members of other smaller groupings, although they were aware of each other and had links through trade, social contacts or war. They had a common language, but with different dialects that were not always mutually understandable. The colonial authorities wanted larger communities to deal with, as did the missionaries who consequently invented a standard Yoruba vernacular based on the Oyo dialect, and printed a Yoruba bible. If people wanted access to Western education they had to adopt this common language.

We have also seen in Chapter 4 the 'ethnic' conflicts appearing to result in the Delta region from issues arising from domination by the oil companies. Again this may be in part a result of 'divide and rule' type strategies where smaller less dominant groups come into conflict. There is also evidence of dominant groups coming into conflict with minor or less dominant groups (Maier, 2000).

Within this context, we identified in our management survey five cultural groupings (three in our employee survey). These grouping were Igbo (mainly through respondents identifying themselves as such; Yoruba (mainly through respondents identifying themselves as a member of one of the subgroup that would normally be grouped under Yoruba: Oyo, Kabba, Ekiti, Egba, Ife, Ond, Ijebu); Hausa-Fulani (including Manga and Kanuri speakers, from cities of Kan, Zaria, Katsina, Maiduguri and states of Kano, Yobe, Bornu, Katsina and Sokoto); Midbelt (including Nupe, Tiv, Gwari, Mumuye, Mende and Chadic speakers; and from Kwara, Niger, Kogi, Plateau, Taraba states); and Delta (Ijaw, Ibibio, Aneng, Efik, Bini, Ogoni). Within the management survey for Nigeria (n = 435) the Igbo (n = 147) and Yoruba (n = 110) groupings are less contentious, although being mindful of Thomson's (2000) remarks and the fact that people we grouped under 'Yoruba' tended to identify their ethnicity through a smaller subgrouping. With the Hausa-Fulani grouping (n = 78) we also included managers who identified themselves as Kanuri (one of our samples was taken in Maiduguri). While Hausa, Fulani and Kanuri may be distinct groups they share much common history, tend to be Muslims and have been more isolated from the more Westernized south and west of the country. More contentious are the two grouping of Midbelt (n = 31), and Delta (n = 51) where it would be impossible to consider all the small minority groups separately when considering sample size. Yet the peoples that we thus grouped have shared much common history, interaction and as minority groups the same types of struggles with more dominant groups (e.g. Maier, 2000).

In the employee survey in Nigeria (n = 205) we only included in cross-ethnic analysis three groups: Yoruba (n = 53), Igbo (n = 74) and Delta (n = 23), due to limitations of sample sizes and because organizations within the study were located in the Delta region and the south west mainly around Lagos.

In Chapter 1 we saw that Adigun (1995) describes the Yoruba as having embraced Western Christianity and education and are the most urbanized of the three groups. Social status is derived from a combination of clientage and through occupational achievement. As a result of embracing urban life, and obtaining high educational standards Yoruba are often in managerial ranks. Social support and group solidarity are emphasized with the extended family being important for exerting social pressure, and providing patterns of mutual obligation. Status is important, and individual achievement also brings honour to the family. He describes the Igbos as also readily embracing Western education and Christianity. They attach importance to individual achievement, with personal effort and use of abilities leading to a rise in status. Obtaining occupational skills and using enterprize and initiative are valued. With entrepreneurial emphasis, there is a willingness to take any job, and live modestly while attaining wealth. He describes the Hausa as conservative, religiously orthodox (Islamic) with little education and urban sophistication. Achievement or striving for excellence is of no importance for the individual's societal standing. Values such as loyalty, obedience, servility and sensitivity to the demands of those in authority, as well as respect for tradition are important. Its members are trained in subordination, political intrigue and opportunistic choice of patrons. They are less interested in getting a steady job, being promoted and raising their living standards.

This obedience and servility may explain why Hausa-Fulani managers in our study were more accepting of a coercive control than the Yoruba and Igbo managers. Their lack of interest in a steady job and getting promoted is reflected in their having the lowest scores for 'preferring the security of a steady job' and 'very ambitious to reach the top'. The Yoruba and Igbo managers' higher scores for 'very ambitious to reach the top' also reflect the description that Adigun (1995) presents of ambition for these two groupings. The Delta grouping, who have a history of struggle against the more dominant groups, have higher scores for both these motivational items exceeding that of the other groups. This may reflect the needs of minority groups to be secure and recognized.

The Hausa-Fulani also see their organizations as being subject to more government controls and less risk taking than other groups. This may reflect the geographic location of their organizations, and that organizations in the north generally are less risk taking and more subject to government controls. Similarly in the Delta region where managers also see their organizations as being more subject to government regulations, respondents may reflect a higher level of control (perhaps higher environmental controls).

Yet the issue remains that generally there is a lack of differences among the different cultural or ethnic groups within our study, for both managers and employees. Although no empirical study can claim to be conclusive, this may provide a strong indication (along with Adigun's, 1995, study that produced similar results) that at least for Nigeria, there are few cultural differences that manifest themselves in organizational and managerial characteristics and attitudes (both from managers and employees). This could be explained by a prevalence in Nigeria of Western management methods that have been adopted by managers, and accepted by both managers and employees. However, this may be too simplistic an explanation.

The predominant management system appears be a mixture of coercive control, that may represent a post-colonial system of management (see Chapter 1), and moderate results orientation (remunerative control), with low people orientation (normative control. This can be seen graphically in Figure 5.2 in Chapter 5. There is a desire to move more towards a higher results orientation and people orientation (see Figure 5.3), and employees share this desire. It would seem therefore that there is still a major influence from post-colonial systems, with a lower influence than many other sub-Saharan countries from Western (remunerative control) systems.

A better explanation of the lack of differences among the ethnic groups may therefore be the cultural similarity of these groups, that share a common humanistic orientation, but have some influence from Western management approaches. We have noted at the beginning of this chapter the lack of articulation of an African renaissance approach to management, and we cited Eze (1989) as an exception to this. Despite the apparent similarities of the different cultural groups in organizational life, there does not appear to be any unifying concepts or management philosophy that can be drawn on to consolidate this unity. Yet organizations in Nigeria continue to engender a low commitment and reflect a perception of low efficiency.

## Implications for managers in Nigeria

We stated as one of the main purposes of this chapter to look at the possibilities for cross-cultural management in Nigeria. It would appear that the main issue is not to understand specific cross-ethnic differences in order to better manage inter-ethnic conflicts and differences in the work place, but to understand better the differences between Western management influences and African ones in order to manage more appropriately and to develop more commitment to the organization. However, this may well entail developing multicultural teams (incorporating a range of stakeholders in the decision process) in order to develop better understanding towards issues concerning the management of a multicultural workforce and the management of a complex and uncertain environment. In our results there is evidence of a lack of managing diversity, and this may entail discrimination (particularly against managers from the Hausa-Fulani grouping as they appear to have a stronger desire for better management of diversity) rather than a lack of cross-cultural understanding. It may be this area that needs to be more fully addressed. We can therefore conclude that:

- Managers need to develop more inclusive decision processes involving multicultural and wider stakeholder interests in order to better manage within an uncertain and complex environment.
- Cross-cultural management should reflect the need to develop an understanding of the differences between Western management approaches and African expectations and ideals; to focus on inter-ethnic similarities rather than differences; and, to address issues of ethnic discrimination.
- Many of Eze's (1989) proposals could be usefully adopted to address issues such as lack of confidence in African approaches, corruption, short-termism, slow rate of change, and differences between instrumentalism and humanism; many of these issues being identified within our management and employee surveys in Nigeria.
- Organizational change and development should reflect the desire expressed in the results of our management survey to move away from a low results and moderate coercive control, towards management systems that are more results- and people-focused; and to thus encourage a stronger commitment to the organization.
- At the different levels of the organization team-working should be more expressly encouraged to reflect a more group-focused approach of employees and managers, and to overcome the apparent negative supervisory attitudes to teamwork.

# Chapter 10

# Cameroon

## Managing cultural complexity and power

With *Olivier Nana Nzepa*

---

I found here an insane situation. The organization was ruled on a clan basis. You were close to the Directeur Général or you were not. People were motivated by what individual benefit they could obtain by this. People were not motivated by the desire to leave a mark, but only by the immediate return on their commitment to the Directeur Général. I am trying my best to be a guiding force in motivating people by the desire to succeed.

(Directeur Général, Caisse Nationale de Prévoyance Sociale)

People believe that the boss is there to make the decisions. The managers here are more supervisors than managers. It comes out of African culture and respect for elders and authority. We are trying to get people to take calculated risks, that is giving people the freedom to succeed.

(Managing Director, Guinness Cameroun)

In traditional culture it isn't the chief who makes the decision. Every stone is turned, by bringing people together. With individual decision-making there is a chance that you will make a mistake. So decisions are taken at the group level. We are like an African family that is trying to ensure our stability for the longer period.

(Manager, Afriland First Bank)

## Introduction

Davidson (1992) writes about the burden of the nation-state in neo-colonial Africa, as being a legacy of the political and military intrigues of the European nations through the period of imperial enclosures, and then independence. These intrigues have left behind in Cameroon a complex legacy from three colonial powers, where there are two official (European) languages and around 250 languages grouped into 24 African language groups. For most of the country the common language is French. To the west, which borders on Nigeria, the common language is English (about 20 per cent of the population). The currency (CFA – Communauté Financière Africaine – Franc) has in recent years been tied to the French Franc, and many of the multinational companies present in the country are French. Indeed, its main import partner is France (29 per cent of imports) and its second export market (18 per cent) (CIA World Factbook, 2003). Much of the political, administrative and legal systems are inherited from or modelled on the French, with just a smattering of British (World Investment News, 2002).

Hybrid management systems abound in infinite variety. The three quotations at the head of this chapter attest to this. Broadly, the first represents an attempt to break out from a post-colonial public administration system that has been characterized by the strength of its informal system, by introducing such formal systems of management as appraisal processes. The second represents a Western company's attempt to introduce post-instrumental performance-based management systems. The third is a rare example of an emergent African renaissance style of management modelled on traditional systems. These three quite different organizations are used as examples as we focus on management and change in a country that may well be regarded as a microcosm and possibly the epitome of sub-Saharan Africa: a unique country, but having many of the features of other African countries, and indeed many post-colonial societies.

## Managing complexity and uncertainty in Cameroon

Cameroon is unusual as a country whose borders were not set in stone immediately independence was won, and there is still an outstanding border dispute with Nigeria. Following the Portuguese slave trade as early as 1436, and an agreement with the British government to prohibit the slave trade in 1852, the kings and chiefs of Douala signed an assistance treaty with the German government on 12 July 1884. Two days later German sovereignty over Cameroon was proclaimed. After much local resistance to German rule, the conclusion of the First World War put an end to German occupation in 1919. In July of that year the country was partitioned by France and Britain and first administered on behalf of the League of Nations. After the Second World War the UNO granted trusteeship to France (over about 80 per cent of the territory) and Britain. French Cameroon obtained its independence on 1 January 1960, with British Cameroon remaining under the administrative jurisdiction of the Nigerian Federation. Following a plebiscite and much protest and debate, the northern part of British Cameroon joined Nigeria, and the southern part (known as Western Cameroon) reunified with the Cameroon Republic to become the Federal Republic of Cameroon on 1 October 1961. On 20 May 1972, following a referendum, the federation structure ended, and Cameroon became a United Republic (World Investment News, 2002).

Cameroon is perhaps in the unique position of being at the interface between Francophone and Anglophone sub-Saharan Africa, and at the crossroads between Central and Western Africa. Because of its oil resources and favourable agricultural conditions (it has one of the best-endowed primary commodity economies according to the CIA World Factbook, 2003), it is an important country to consider, not only within its immediate region, but also within sub-Saharan Africa as a whole.

However, Cameroon has largely maintained its colonial inheritance as a primary commodity producer. As Barratt-Brown (1995: 26) puts it:

> the colonies existed for the colonial trade; and it was in the very nature of the
> colonial trade that not only was wealth drawn from African produce to be spent

in Europe and not in Africa, but also that most of the consumer goods in African cities had to be imported from Europe. Exports were of primary products with little or no local processing, refining or manufacturing.

Cameroon's export concentration ratio reflects this in being a producer mainly of three primary products: oil, coffee and cocoa (Barratt-Brown, 1995, argues that most African countries' economies, because of colonial exploitation, are built on one, two, three or four primary products which are exported, to the exclusion of building an internal consumer market), although the country has diversified more in recent years. So, although the country is a member of CEMAC (Communauté Economique et Monétaire de l'Afrique Central, formally UDEAC, comprising: Gabon, Cameroon, Congo, Equatorial Guinea, Central African Republic and Chad), which as UDEAC was founded with the aim of establishing a common external tariff and to reduce internal tariffs and promoting harmonized development policies, Cameroon's focus is, with the other oil producers of Gabon and Congo, overwhelmingly outside Africa. Again, Barratt-Brown (1995) notes that there was a lack of projects within UDEAC to promote specialization within the region and encourage internal trade among the member countries, despite a single tax regime on products coming from within the region and a small compensation fund. The fact that all member countries are within the CFA franc zone has given some cohesion, but also a very strong outward orientation. He also adds that these countries have performed better than the sub-Saharan average for economic growth, but this is arguably due to oil revenues rather than regional cooperation (Barratt-Brown, 1995).

However, the propensity toward trade with former colonizers does not account for informal regional 'cooperation', perhaps a trade that has gone on noticed or unnoticed since ethnic groups were sliced in half with the advent of nation-state borders before and during independence. An estimated US$285 million was lost to Cameroon in the late 1980s due to the smuggling of food crops into Nigeria in exchange for manufactured goods (Barratt-Brown, 1995, tells of similar examples in other parts of sub-Saharan Africa).

## Strengths and opportunities

Cameroon has a totals area of 475,442 square kilometres and a population of 15.8 million. Its GNP is US$8,110 million. This, and its relative political stability compares very favourably with its neighbours Chad, Central Africa Republic, Republic of the Congo; is on a par with its smaller neighbour Gabon (with 268,000 km$^2$; 1,125,000 million inhabitants and a GNP of US$4,400 million); yet is dwarfed by Nigeria's economy with a 114,568,100 population and GNP of US$35,680 million within an area of just over twice the size at 923,768 square kilometres. Yet with a GDP per capita of $1,573, it compares well with Nigeria's $853 (see Table 3.1, Chapter 3).

Generally its economic indicators are reckoned to be good with a GDP growth rate of 4.6 per cent. Consumer price inflation was 3 per cent for 2001, up from the previous year's 2.1 per cent due to higher food prices (IMF, 2002). It has one of the best-endowed primary commodity economies (CIA World Factbook, 2003) because of its oil resources and favourable agricultural conditions: a factor in maintaining its role as a primary commodity producer, and trade predominantly with its former colonial masters, reflecting the high level of financial and political interest still shown in the country by France. Foreign investment generally declined by 72.66 per cent between 1984 and 1998. Yet this appears to be changing as the gross investment rate in Cameroon has increased from 18.8 per cent in 1997/8 to 20.1 per cent in 1998/9 with French companies very prominent investors (World Investment News, 2002).

There is no doubt that some managers recognize such strengths and opportunities within the country. We have argued in Chapter 3 that a key competence in managing uncertainty and complexity in Africa and other emerging regions is to be able to make a realistic assessment of the opportunities and strengths, and to maximize these while overcoming weaknesses and constraints. Guinness Cameroun, for example, is very successful in Cameroon. It sees its strengths both in its people, who are very flexible and open to new ideas, and an ability on the part of the company to communicate its objectives to the workforce.

Afriland First Bank has been successful in generating products for the local, African, markets, accepting that much business goes on through the informal economy and generating bank lending products that can be taken to the community. By doing this the company sees itself as developing a class of entrepreneurs in Cameroon.

## Constraints and weaknesses

Yet Cameroon has factors that are not conducive to developing an effective management climate. Of the 91 countries around the globe that are included in Transparency International's Corruption Perceptions Index for 2001, it is ranked eighty-fourth alongside Azerbaijan, Bolivia and Kenya (Table 3.1). Within Africa, only Uganda (ranked 88) and Nigeria (ranked 90) do worse. A national observatory was created in Cameroon at the end of the 1990s to fight corruption. A top-heavy civil service is seen as a major problem by the political economic orthodoxy of the IMF (see CIA World Factbook, 2003). In 1988 the government sought aid from the IMF and structural adjustment measures were put in place. Since then the economy has been liberalized with the abolition of non-tariff barriers and elimination of import quotas, the scrapping of price harmonization and administrative control of profit margins. During the three-year programme 2000–3 the government aims to complete its privatization programme. The ten commercial banks in Cameroon have been privatized since 2000. Similarly the telecommunications industry (Camtel) is due to be privatized. Other areas for privatization include road construction, rail and air transport, the utilities, as well as agriculture. The Cameroon Development Corporation, for example, which is the largest single employer after the state administration, with 25,000 employees, and producing palm oil, tea, rubber and bananas, is due for privatization.

Currently, agriculture accounts for 43.4 per cent of GDP and 70 per cent of the workforce; industry accounts for 20.1 per cent of GDP and services 36.5 per cent of GDP. Only 13 per cent of the workforce is estimated to work in industry and commerce. Estimates vary for unemployment from the official rate of 23 per cent to the 1998 estimate of 30 per cent (CIA World Factbook, 2002) to in-country unofficial estimates of around 40 per cent.

With the majority of the population concentrated in the South, Cameroon has a youthful age structure in common with most Africa countries (42.37 per cent under 15 years, and only 3.35 per cent of the population being 65 and over: based on 2001 estimates), and a population growth rate of 2.41 per cent. The HIV/AIDS adult prevalence rate is estimated at 7.73 per cent (in Table 3.1 this compares as 'favourable' with South Africa and other southern African countries) with 540,000 people living with HIV/AIDS and 52,000 deaths (estimates for 1999: UNDP Human Development Report, 2002/CIA World Factbook, 2002). The UNDP Human Development Index for 2001, which measures a country's achievement in terms of life expectancy, educational attainment and adjusted real income, gives Cameroon a ranking of 125 (out of 162 countries). This places the country at the lower end of the medium human development countries together with Kenya and Cameroon's neighbour Republic of the Congo, and substantially higher than Nigeria (ranked 136 and ranked amongst the low human development countries). Of its other neighbours, Gabon and small Equatorial Guinea do better at 109 and 110 respectively; Central African Republic and Chad do worse at 154 and 155 respectively (UNDP, 2002). In other areas indicated in Table 3.1, Cameroon does not fare well in our one indicator of level of technical infrastructure (7 telephones per 1,000 persons). Yet Cameroon does reasonably well for political rights compared with South Africa, and does considerably better in general literacy and educational levels than Nigeria (Table 3.1).

Contextual aspects, as well as cross-cultural ones, influence the level of discrepancy perceived by employees between 'what is' and 'what should be' at work. Hence low technical infrastructure may influence satisfaction with the job itself, where adequate technology is not available. Political and civil liberties may influence people's commitment and satisfaction generally within the work situation, and may lead to differences among countries that enjoy differential levels of liberties.

So, although the country has a number of strengths, it also has weaknesses and constraints that managers have to address strategically. In common with other companies in Cameroon, Guinness has difficulties with the administrative authorities within the country. This includes issues of constraints from outside the country, responses within the country that try to address these by, for example, collecting more taxes from those companies that currently pay in the absence of a broader taxpayer base, responses by companies in order to cope with such constraints, and unofficial practices that can fix the problem in a 'pragmatic' way. Managers in Afriland First Bank also recognize the difficulties of pressures from the IMF and World Bank (see below, p. 225).

Other constraints have more direct implications for people issues inside the organization. For example, managers from the three organizations described in the case studies below recognize the level and nature of education as a problem. For one of the public sector organizations included in our study, Caisse Nationale de Prévoyance Sociale (CNPS), this is simply a lack of education and skills of staff to do the job adequately. For Guinness it is the output of university education for administration rather than for management that seems problematic.

Another constraint, that may also be the basis of an opportunity and strength for the organization, is multiculturalism.

## Managing the dynamics of multiculturalism

The complexity of the origin of the Republic of Cameroon also overlays its ethnic complexity. Most African countries score high on ethnolinguistic fractionalization (Roeder, 2001). As we have seen in Chapter 3 this is a measure of the probability that two randomly selected individuals in a country will not belong to the same ethnolinguistic group. Cameroon, although culturally complex, is no more complex than many other African countries, including Kenya, Nigeria and South Africa (see Table 3.1). Yet unlike these countries, there is little information from the literature on cultural and work values in Cameroon. An exception is the work by Noorderhaven and Tidjani (2001) on African values. This compares a number of African countries and Western countries, but, as with other such studies that include African countries, it provides more of a comparison of African with Western countries rather than African with other African countries.

It can be seen that Cameroon scores relatively low on what Noorderhaven and Tidjani (2001) term Human Goodness (Table 10.1). African countries score lower generally than Western countries on this dimension. Cameroon's score is on a par with Tanzania, lower than Ghana, yet higher than Senegal. On Rules and Hierarchy, Cameroon scores highly with Tanzania and Zimbabwe. All the African countries score highly on importance of religion compared with the Western countries. It is difficult to make comparisons for Traditional Wisdom, as all countries score highly on this. Cameroon scores highly on Sharing, even compared with the other African countries with the exception of Senegal. Again, it has one of the higher scores for Jealousy, but has a relatively low score for Collectivism (which the authors admit does not reflect the classic concept of collectivism in the literature). For Social Responsibility Cameroon scores 0. Noorderhaven and Tidjani (2001) provide little in terms of post-hoc explanation of these differences, and this latter score for Cameroon needs further explanation. Yet it is possible to look more closely at these results for Cameroon.

The Human Goodness factor includes items 'The people of my society are hard working', and 'In general people can be trusted'. It could well be that a lack of belief in these aspects could lead to a lower score for Cameroon (this is perhaps in part reflected in Cameroon's low CPI score: Table 3.1). A high score for Rules and Hierarchy reflects our own findings (discussed below) that employees in Cameroon see their organizations as having significantly higher coercive control, compared with employees in Kenya, Nigeria and South Africa (Table 5.1). Higher scores for Sharing and for Jealously may indicate a higher level of communalism. Our results show both a higher score for Cameroon employees for normative control/people orientation, as well as for group orientation, and this may well indicate higher levels of communalism than other countries in the study (Table 5.1). The Social Responsibility factor incorporates two items: 'Citizens should feel responsible for helping build their society' and 'People with different ethnic backgrounds should be able to cooperate

Table 10.1 Position of Cameroon compared with other countries on Noorderhaven and Tidjani's (2001) African Values dimensions

| | Sample n | Human goodness | Rules and hierarchy | Importance of religion | Traditional wisdom | Sharing | Jealousy | Collectivism | Social responsibility |
|---|---|---|---|---|---|---|---|---|---|
| **Cameroon** | **105** | **17** | **100** | **81** | **89** | **74** | **68** | **54** | **0** |
| Ghana | 87 | 50 | 88 | 99 | 94 | 62 | 45 | 58 | 87 |
| Senegal | 111 | 0 | 79 | 90 | 100 | 100 | 100 | 51 | 66 |
| Tanzania | 87 | 18 | 100 | 85 | 100 | 63 | 30 | 73 | 25 |
| Zimbabwe | 63 | 35 | 100 | 94 | 97 | 45 | 0 | 53 | 82 |
| | | | | | | | | | |
| United Kingdom | 104 | 100 | 34 | 23 | 100 | 63 | 43 | 61 | 86 |
| USA | 126 | 77 | 42 | 58 | 89 | 45 | 35 | 53 | 82 |
| Belgium | 28 | 60 | 46 | 0 | 76 | 74 | 68 | 54 | 0 |
| Netherlands | 86 | 95 | 33 | 15 | 83 | 44 | 76 | 83 | 68 |

Note
Range 0–100. Human goodness: a positive view of people and a belief that such a positive view should be the foundation of organizations (African countries score low on this). Rules and hierarchy: indicates a higher power distance, and deference to superiors (African countries score high on this). Importance of religion: contrasts religiosity and hedonism (religious values are important in African countries). Traditional wisdom: reflecting a traditional view on wisdom and its sources. Sharing: a favouring of the sharing of wealth. Jealousy: reflecting mainly a fear of standing out, as it may cause jealousy. Collectivism: reflecting elements of collectivism combined with fatalism (and deviousness). Social responsibility: indicating an adherence to citizenship.

for the good of their society'. Clearly Noorderhaven and Tidjani's (2001) sample disagreed with these two statements.

The results on this last factor may well be indicative of the cultural complexities of the country. This is why it is difficult to see Cameroon as a complete cultural entity. Although there are some 130 ethnic groups (and around 250 languages and dialects) there are five major ones: Bamiléké and Bamoun in the west; Fulani and Kirdi in the north; and Ewondo around Yaoundé who together with other such groups as Bene, Bulu and Fong, belong to one of the largest ethnic groups in West Africa, the Fang and collectively known in Cameroon as Beti, the most dominant group in the public sector, government and military. The Bamiléké form one of the largest communities in Douala (the foremost industrial centre and port) and within the Western Highlands. They tend to dominate within much of the economy of the private sector of Cameroon. The Bamoun, who are mainly Moslem, are not generally found within the formal private or public sectors. Many of the artists and craftspeople are drawn from the Bamoun group.

The south of the country has been in contact with Europe for more than 500 years, and Christianity is common alongside traditional beliefs. The north was part of the Muslim Fulani kingdoms until the twentieth century. This has had the effect of keeping Western-style development to a minimum in the north, with main industrial developments in the south.

A consideration of cultural complexity involves two aspects: cultural differences and similarities, and cultural interactions. The first of these aspects has been treated well in the extant literature, and Hofstede's (1980a) work is a classic example of this. As we have seen above, large-scale international studies of this genre have tended largely to ignore Africa, and Noorderhaven and Tidjani's (2001) work is exceptional in that it includes Cameroon. Cultural comparisons within African countries (that is, inter-ethnic) are even more rare. The second of these aspects has been treated under the area of 'ethnicity'. For example, Nyambegera (2002) provides a good summary of this area, pointing out the impact of ethnicity on areas such as recruitment and promotion opportunities. This is bound up with power relations within inter-ethnic interactions in the workplace, where an ethnic group tends to predominate, as we discussed briefly above (see also Figure 10.1). Although also apparent in the private sector in Cameroon, it is particularly evident in the public sector, where it also becomes embroiled in national politics, which has a profound effect on how organizations and people are managed. It is to this area that we now turn.

## Politics, ethnicity and informal people management systems

To illustrate the connection between politics, ethnicity and management, on the first author's visit to Cameroon in June 2002, municipal and legislature elections were scheduled for the following Sunday. In the week leading up to this, there were very few chief executives of government departments, parastatal organizations or even some of the large commercial companies to be found in their offices for interviews. They were out campaigning for the ruling party.

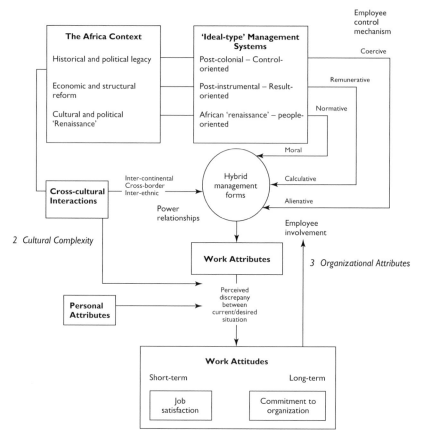

*Figure 10.1* Management of people in Africa.

The Public Service is by far the biggest employer in Cameroon employing more than 160,000 employees. In addition around 40,000 are employed by the parastatal organizations. The public sector as a whole accounts directly or indirectly for more than 70 per cent of the workforce outside the agricultural sector. With such a major role the public sector also affects management and HRM practices in the other sectors of the economy.

The degree of political influence (and by a tendency of political polarizations by ethnicity as we will explore below) on HRM can be discerned first by the results of a survey undertaken by Nana Nzepa (in press) in five ministerial departments, managed by three political parties. Three of these ministerial departments were managed by heads from the ruling party (CPDM). Two departments were managed by two different opposition parties (UNDPC and UCP). An analysis of political affiliation according to appointment shows that for top-level managers (director to under-minister) 80 per cent were politically motivated out of a total of 78 appointments made within the five ministries: top jobs in Finance (MINEFI), Post (MINPOST) and External Affairs (MINREX) were held by people from the ruling RDPC; Industry and Commerce Ministry (MINIC) was directed by the president of the UNDPC party; and Scientific and Technical Research Ministry was headed by a member of UPC party (Figure 10.2).

This position explains the situation confronting the first author in finding such managers campaigning rather than being at their posts during the lead-up to the election. The implication of this may be the exclusion of talents not belonging to appropriate political parties. The public service also experiences a relatively high turnover of managers, as people fall out of favour and others fall into favour. Again, being seen to be actively campaigning, and indeed returning the ruling party back to power is a means of safe-guarding one's job. Yet this situation may also give rise to inequity, frustrations and low motivation at managerial levels. It also provides evidence of what another study pointed out to be a dual system: a formal system put in place by French colonialism and an informal system (*Le Messager*, 1998). Again this has implications for power relations within inter-ethnic interactions.

The informal system, generally established and used in preference to the formal system, has as its main function the dominance and preservation of the power of the dominant group and its allies (*Le Messager*, 1998: 7–8). Hence, formal power through the administrative influences of HRM systems (e.g. formal selection, appraisal and promotion procedures) is weak in terms of challenging the interests of the dominant group. This 'tribalization' of the managerial workforce appears not to relate to any inherent ethnic antagonisms, but simply to political polarization along apparent ethnic lines.

At the level of recruitment and promotions, political patronage may not only affect who is favoured. The process of ethnic phagocytosis (smaller groups being swallowed

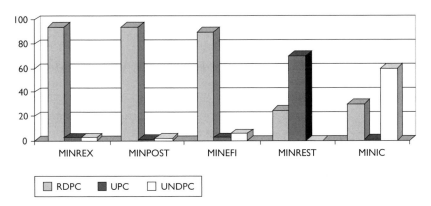

*Figure 10.2* Percentage of top management post holders according to political affiliation (Nana Nzepa, in press).

up by dominant groups) that this stimulates may actually be having an effect on the apparent ethnic composition of the country. It is therefore not unusual in the private sector of the economy, for a Bakoko or Yabassi (both minority ethnic groupings) to present themselves as the more prestigious and influential Douala in the commercial city and port of the same name. Similarly, within the public sector, members of the various small minority groups around the Central Province may present themselves as the politically dominant Beti. This tendency is understandable in the light of Figure 10.3, which reflects the ethnic composition among top-ranking managers in the public sector (Nana Nzepa, in press).

These aspects of politicization and tribalization affect the way people are managed in public sector organizations. This particularly results in a lack of formal rules of recruitment and career progression. The report quoted above (*Le Messager*, 1998) underlines the fact that no promotion at the higher managerial levels in the public sector can be accepted if not approved within the informal system. The real decision makers are not the leaders or managers of the formal system, but rather the king-makers of the informal system who appear to be motivated along political/ethnic lines.

The principle of decentralization of decision-making within the public sector put forward by the new Constitution, appears to have been largely ignored by the informal group, seeing this as a threat to their dominant position. Internally this may be leading to general inefficiencies and misplaced motivation, as we will see later by the example of the public organization CNPS. In addition, externally the public loses confidence in the public sector to deliver its services.

Although Dia (1996) proposes that colonial institutions imposed on colonized societies were disconnected from the wider civil society, it is likely that such institutions' formal systems were predominant. In post-colonial societies, such as Cameroon, it does seem that 'tribalism' through cronyism and political patronage has introduced an informal structure that tends to predominate within many African public sectors (e.g. Utomi, 1998). There are other problems that this type of system appears to exacerbate rather than address. Skills levels, for example, are a problem. The adult literacy rate for Cameroon is 74.8 per cent (Table 5.1). Although this

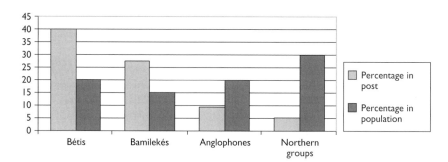

*Figure 10.3* Ethnic representation in high-ranking management posts in the public service (Nana Nzepa, in press).

compares favourably with countries such as Côte d'Ivoire at 45.7 per cent and Nigeria at 62.6 per cent, this compares unfavourably with countries such as Kenya, South Africa and Zimbabwe. Coupled with advances in technology, this situation quickly renders old skills redundant. Also the feeling of powerlessness felt by employees in the face of this informal system has been discussed by Courade (2000).

Courade proposes that due to the lack of a clear and transparent system of managing people, everyone is afraid of everyone else, with the result that people spend time and energy in trying to accommodate themselves to the people they see as important. Motivation may well be misplaced from a drive to increase productivity, to a desire to be seen to please and appease the right people. This may be concomitant with both support of a particular political group, coupled with the process of ethnic phagocytosis discussed above.

These types of processes involved with ethnic interactions and political power have implications for organizational and work attributes (our third theme: see Figure 10.1), and we discuss these implications on attributes within organizations in Cameroon further. We do this partly through reference to case study material drawn from interviews with managers as part of the general research project, in order to investigate how organizations are dealing with the difficult issue of ethnicity, power and the informal system. We also refer to findings from our surveys of employees and managers in Cameroon. The other aspect of cultural complexity mentioned above is that of cultural difference and similarity, and in particular the way cultural factors influence reactions to organizational attributes and work attitudes. We discuss this aspect later in a section on work attitudes, and with reference to findings from our survey of employees and managers within Cameroon.

## Organizational attributes in Cameroon

We have discussed in Chapters 1 and 2 that hybrid forms of management result from influences from different systems that emerge from combinations of historical and current influences, and from foreign and indigenous sources. Through cross-cultural interactions (including the politico-ethnic processes discussed in the last section), organizational attributes evolve. The operating environment also has a profound affect on the types of hybrid forms that evolve, and as we argued in the Introduction, some forms are highly adaptive to their environment, and some are not.

Although it is possible to gain a general view of such attributes prevailing in organizations in any one country though survey techniques, case studies provide more in-depth knowledge of these attributes and what managers are actively doing to address the issues involved: that is, what they are doing to provide more adaptive organizational forms that can operate effectively within the context of Cameroon.

## Caisse Nationale de Prévoyance Sociale: dealing with politico-ethnic issues

An example is Caisse Nationale de Prévoyance Sociale. CNPS administers social security payments under a national social insurance scheme, as an agency of the government. Here the Directeur Général (DG) describes as problematic the low levels of skills of employees who lack basic training and sufficient education levels for the job. This, as we have seen, is a general problem through low levels of education (although this compares favourably with the other countries shown in Table 3.1). At the higher levels there are leaders who lack vision and are too concerned about the day-to-day business. They do not take the time to reflect on what they are doing and why. Managers do not have a clear understanding of the general mission. There is an attempt by top management to try to share the vision of social responsibilities toward the clients they serve, although there appears to be some resistance by managers lower down.

Yet without sharing the mission, the DG believes, managers cannot be involved in the decision process. He says

> there is a tendency to rely on the DG as far as decisions are concerned, but decision-making has to be a collaborative process. I consult a lot, although in the end I make the decision when it is something for which I have responsibility. Some decisions are taken within committees, others are taken at lower levels because they are too technical or relate to operational use of resources.

One of the issues appears to be that some people are only motivated by money and see a refusal of management to respond to their money demands as a form of punishment, and this affects their engagement to their work. Those who have understood the message of what is trying to be achieved are more prepared to make the necessary sacrifices. The DG explains one of the problems of management motivation.

> I found here an insane situation. The organization was ruled on a clan basis. You were close to the DG or you were not. People were motivated by what individual benefit they could obtain by this. People were not motivated by the desire to leave a mark, but only by the immediate return on their commitment to the DG. I am trying my best to be a guiding force in motivating people by the desire to succeed.

This issue, which is illustrative of misplaced motivation through adherence to politico-ethnic loyalties, has implications for the reward system in the organization. The DG explains that the reward system we have here is in line with public sector practices, that is reward and monetary advantage is gained through promotion. Therefore people spend a great deal of energy in fighting for promotion. I am in the process of putting an appraisal system in place. Such a system, with measurable criteria will make it easier to assess the performance of each individual. This is going to take quite a time to implement, but finally we may have a proper appraisal system.

This appears to be a drive to assert a formal system, rather that be driven by an informal system. Yet this is difficult because

here people try to impress you by the supposed relationship they have with decision-makers. You have to be very careful. We have some problems in the management of our organization. The controls are loose. They are purely formal. Yet you also have to rely on feelings and Africa wisdom.

The process of change they are in, involving the questioning of what they are, and what they are trying to become causes a lot of resentment because 'we lack vision and the knowledge of our mission, we have to constantly put it back on the agenda. It isn't easy.' This is in part because

the influences of inter-ethnic relations in the organization are real, but you have to transcend them. The principal of ethnic equilibrium exists, but you have to refuse to encapsulate yourself in tribal logic. People who tend to use the tribal card are those who do not have the quality of their performance to fall back on. As DG you have to do your best to stay above all that.

The DG coming from the Bulu group, asserts that he tries not to let that influence his duty. Yet he admits still, 'the tribal reflex does exist'.

In this case, politico-ethnic issues have moved the organization towards an informal system of favouring certain groups, and encouraging motivation towards currying favour rather than towards organizational output. Post-colonial systems of management (see Figure 10.1) here combine both formal and informal systems of control, although top management is attempting to move away from this towards more results-oriented organizational forms. Coercive control mechanisms may well give way to more remunerative control mechanisms (Figure 10.1). Although mentioned, indigenous approaches are looked upon warily. This situation may well be repeated in the private sector, particular among foreign (Western) companies, which are attempting to develop productivity-focused management systems along Western lines, moving away from coercive forms of management control, yet being mindful (although still wary) of indigenous influences. Such an example is Guinness Cameroun.

## Guinness Cameroun: adapting Western techniques

Guinness Cameroun has seen a continued expansion in Cameroon. From offering a range of products, including lager and 'black products' (that is 'Guinness' proper and a non-alcoholic drink Guinness Malta), they have focused on the latter class of products. In the *Guinness Cameroun News* circulated to all employees the Managing Director declares the year ended June 2001 as the most successful in the 30 years history of the company. Malta sales increased by 21 per cent while Guinness itself saw a 19 per cent growth. Although not one of the highest paying companies in Cameroon, employees appear to stay. It is also unusual in Douala, the commercial heart of Cameroon, as the company is predominantly anglophone. However, the MD believes that more emphasis should be placed on recruiting francophones in order to get a better cultural balance.

### Developing a performance culture

Guinness Cameroun is a Western company with Western principles. Yet the MD states that 'although sometimes these principles, coming from London, seem a bit academic. We have to adapt them in a practical way to the situation'. With a workforce of 1,300 people, 'for the second year running we are putting in a performance culture, that is not Cameroon' says the HR Director.

> We have a target of 530 thousand hectolitres for our black products. If reached we pay out a bonus of two months' salary. Managers also have a bonus for, among other things, managing their cost. Managers have 15 months' salary here, and workers about 13 months' salary.

### Educational constraints

However, top management recognize that there are a number of constraints that have to be addressed. In particular they relate to the lower levels of education and the shallowness of the talent pool. For example the MD says that in areas of functional expertise there is not a great depth in the country. Although people will go to university, the general standard isn't high. The engineering expertise is okay, but in marketing and sales it is lacking. So we try to find bright graduates and put them through our programmes.

This also reflects the general emphasis of higher education in training graduates for administration rather than for management. At the lower artisan and trades levels standards are good, but the HR director believes that people are not taught to 'think outside the box. People are trained to be subordinates'. This leads on to the next constraint.

### 'Cultural' constraints

People expect a boss/subordinate relationship. According to the MD 'people won't address me by my first name, I am "patron"'. But they are working to change this.

People believe that the boss is there to make the decisions. We meet on a regular basis with managers. At my second meeting with the managers a second-tier manager asked what management was doing about a particular issue. I said, you are a manager, what are **you** doing about it. The managers here are more supervisors than managers.

Yet there is a belief by this Western manager that 'it comes out of African culture and respect for elders and authority', and states that 'we are more trying to change the culture of a country rather than just a company'. He explains that they have people there who have authority within their community, and will not tolerate being challenged in their own community. 'So, in a junior position in the company, they will not challenge authority here'. They are attempting to change that, the HR Director explains. 'We are trying to get people to take calculated risks, that is giving people the freedom to succeed, including making mistakes, and giving managers the opportunity to manage things the way they want'.

### Political and ethical constraints

In addition, in common with other companies in Cameroon, they have difficulties with the administrative authorities within the country.

The economy is being dictated from the IMF and World Bank. There are pressures on the government to collect more taxes from the companies they know will pay, rather than widening the tax base. They will reassess tax liability and backdate it for 30 years. They will reinterpret the tax laws to do this. We can contest this, but it takes time, and the collection arm still tries to collect the tax in the meantime, even coming down here and putting padlocks on the door to close down the factory. There is also a lot of shady dealing. So your documentation has to be in top order. If not, officials will fix it for you if you are prepared to deal with the problem in a pragmatic way. As a company we are not prepared to do this. It is against our code of practice. We know that other companies, whose MDs belong to certain political parties have less trouble than others.

### Opportunities through change

Internally, the MD explains that the company used to be very directive and run on an expatriate basis, 'following the pattern of a colonial master, copying the French way of working'. The company then introduced a programme to transform the culture and business in the early 1990s. The HR Director added that 'Top managers now have to lead by "walking the talk"'. But there have been problems with this. In 1994, when the CFA Franc was devalued, half the staff was laid off. This has left an element of cynicism that the company is trying hard to change. Fortunately, 'Cameroonian people are very open, and open to change and experimentation. We just need leaders to capitalize on this'. However, this may well be a two-edged sword, as people live for today. There is little forward planning.

### Employee benefits

This is being partly addressed through the structure of employee benefits, as the HR director reports.

> This [lack of forward planning] has a positive impact as people are ready to change, but also a negative effect as people may run out of money. This puts pressure on, as they make no provision, no contingency for future problems. So as managers we have to introduce practical things like pensions and saving schemes.

The other aspect of this short-termism is that 'you cannot run a business on this basis: people don't think what the long term may bring'. This company therefore appears to be adapting Western techniques of performance management, but adapting them in addressing environmental constrains, such as lack of educational opportunities, the nature of educational opportunities, uncertainty in political and ethical dealings, and a lack of performance culture including a perceived deference to authority and short-termism. Yet at the same time the top management appears to view indigenous culture in a negative light, largely ignoring any benefits to be drawn from it. This is in sharp distinction to the approach of Afriland First Bank.

## Afriland First Bank: developing indigenous approaches to people management

Adapting Western HRM principles to the Cameroonian situation may be one way among foreign multinationals. There also appears to be a new generation of indigenous firms that are now beginning to get past the 'small' stage and establishing themselves as players among medium-sized firms. Such an example is Afriland First Bank.

When Afriland First Bank was set up in Cameroon in 1987 it was with a mission to promote a class of entrepreneurs in Africa. This had begun in 1987 with five people, and today they have a staff of 300, including 50 trainees and around 100 managers. They now have a subsidiary company in Equatorial Guinea, and offices in Congo, Paris and Beijing. We interviewed the senior management team as a group, and we have tried to select statements that represent the collective views expressed, and which convey a picture of the approaches being used to forge what we belief to be one of the closest examples to the African 'renaissance' management system (albeit, of course, in a hybrid form).

### Reaching out to the community

When the company was first being put together

the question was put: how can we contribute to the development of our community. Here [in Cameroon] the community rather than individuals influence processes. We decided to create a tool to create wealth through business promotion. This would deliver new products suited to our environment and would fit in this culture.

So, for example, micro-finance is a key issue that is linked to the development process in Cameroon. 'We don't go into an area to open a branch, but to help people to develop themselves, so this can be linked to the development of the country. It is a community approach.' This is based in part on the fact that 70 per cent of the economy is in the informal sector, so to develop this they needed to create a link to the formal sector. 'When you want to promote African entrepreneurs you face the problem of lack of capital. So we have promoted venture capital for micro businesses'.

'At the strategic level we are building a new country. The country we find ourselves in was not built for us.' According to the management team, this artificially created country is only one of the constraints they find themselves confronting. 'It is difficult to build the [work] group as the boundaries of the country are artificial'. This has led to tremendous ethnic diversity within the country. 'People are going back to their roots all the time, we need cross-cultural management.'

### Environmental and operating constraints

In addition, other constraints are numerous. These include the importance of the state and an ethos of the civil service in the country that operates against the spirit of entrepreneurship. There is also a spirit of consumption rather than production in the country. There is a problem of rules, where these rules are dictated by the operating and strategic constraints. 'It is easy also to talk about corruption,' says one senior manager. This group of managers also pointed to the judicial and legal system. 'You can't do business unless this is effective, it is difficult where you have an arbitrary system.' The lack of infrastructure is also seen as a problem. This includes the telecommunications industry, electricity and the education system. The latter 'does not prepare people for technical or managerial jobs; it prepares people to be civil servants. Business people are not celebrated in this country, and there is a lack of political will to develop business.'

One manager suggested that after the country came out of its financial crisis during the 1990s 'our internal resources were limited. You therefore need outside sources to help you.' However, a fundamental problem is that 'the leader in our country is the IMF and World Bank'. It is they who are making the rules that fundamentally affect business in the country. So, although the immediate environment of relative social and political peace and stability and the economy present opportunities, it is still difficult to utilize these opportunities. There is a need to have plans and objectives. 'But these are strongly influenced by external forces.' This is not only the IMF and World Bank. 'We also have the strong influence of France.'

## Decision-making and the African culture

Despite these difficulties, there appears to be a strong motivation to address these issues from an African perspective. This first involves decision-making. This, in Afriland First Bank is a group process, unless a quick decision has to be made as an emergency case.

> This comes from our African culture. We set up a college to take decisions. In traditional culture it isn't the chief who makes the decision. Every stone is turned, by bringing people together. With individual decision-making there is a chance that you will make a mistake. So decisions are taken at the group level. We are like an African family that is trying to ensure our stability for the longer period. We don't think African is best, if we can obtain value from, for example, Japanese ways we will take it. But in our family the chief cannot always see that he is doing wrong. If he is doing wrong he is punished. You listen to your brother if he is telling you that you are making a mistake. We have noticed that working in committees is a collegiate way. This is a very strong training ground. We have been trained within those committees. Our philosophy is that we are a family and no one has an advantage. We all contribute. You have an opportunity to say what you think. If you are a member of a family you have to put controls first at your own personal level. You are the first level of control. You are then acting for the family. The family is the next level of control. In the bank we have levels of control at branch and headquarter levels. But the most important is at the personal level. Everyone in the bank is a controller. We have an evaluation process that ensures this.

Normative control systems therefore appear to be important within the bank.

Within the bank there is a discussion forum.

> In the north of the country you have isolated big trees in savannah areas. So people gather around the tree. They solve community matters, preventing small problems becoming destructive. This is the model here. Every month people gather without consideration of rank, to discuss internal matters. There is no general manager present. We look at good news. We discuss things that are not right. We ask people what they think and to decide upon the issue in respect of their individual operating unit. For the entire bank we meet informally once or twice a year, to develop a spirit of togetherness. Everyone can open the door of the Managing Director, and put an important problem to him.

### Internal climate, motivation and normative control mechanisms

So, there is

> fraternity and respect, solidarity, communication and a high critical feeling. You can't just do what you want. Everyone is looking at you. You may be the best in one way, but equal opportunities are not an individual matter. We are going to share the bonus. The climate is that you have to be able to stay in your place, or I am going to take your place tomorrow.

However, there may be a problem of size now that the company has grown bigger from it origins. 'If there is a death of a relative for example, we can't all go to the funeral as we used to, as we would be travelling to such things the whole time.'

One of the managers thought that it is obtaining results that get noticed that motivates managers. But he suggests that the question should be asked 'What kind of results?' 'As a family you have opportunities and you have the environment to stimulate motivation. But this is strongly linked to the individual's ambitions. Pay, for example, is just an incentive. The true motivation is the driving force of the individual.' But management motivation may also be driven by higher ideas. 'Most of our managers are motivated by the objective to build a country. This is an inner thing to motivate you.'

> We have specific human resource management processes. At the beginning of the year everyone in each function has specific evaluation criteria. If I am a cashier the first evaluation might be the number of bank notes I have counted over the year, and the number of counterfeit notes I have taken. At the end you have the commercial criteria. At the beginning of the year you have norms. After that you set your own objectives depending on your own ambitions. At the end of each month you have to fill in a form to compare the difference between the norms and objectives and achievements. You send one copy to Human Resources, and you keep one copy. This gives you an opportunity to compare your performance, as well as being a form of control.

> We have a career profile for each function within the bank. According to that profile you know where you are and where you need to be. Promotion can be made in the same function but you can grow in grade. If you meet objectives three times you are promoted by rank.

Also you can be promoted by function. We try as much as possible to have something quantifiable to treat everyone objectively. But qualitative actions are also taken into consideration. But there should be a relation between objectives and results.

As discussed above, this evaluation process is also considered a part of an element of control. 'If you make an error this has to be explained: so there is an element of control in this.'

So, although other control mechanisms are in place, mainly through remunerative incentives, emphasis is placed on normative control with the moral involvement of employees and managers who share a common vision. Hence,

the inner force is an African culture, but it is also strongly influenced by state and government controls. Also foreign countries controlling Cameroon influence the industry. As we are a francophone culture we try to take an Anglo-Saxon approach that is more specific. The French approach is less specific. Indirectly, there may be a Japanese influence, but this is only through the US influence.

Things are changing within the country and this affects the management of the bank. 'The country is becoming more liberalized and democratic. It is moving slowly, but in the right direction. There is a sort of African renaissance, but we have also to remove the negative things.' Yet managing with African principles is not always easy.

It is not easy in the African culture to manage more than about 300 people. The richness of the company is in its human resources. But we have to invest a lot to meet the challenges presented to us. As we are no longer a very small bank we are looking at human resource management. We have more democracy in the country, so this affects the way we talk to staff and do things.

Yet, one of the stumbling blocks to developing the business and changing people is that 'to do things you have to be good in your own head. This is a colonial thing. Black people don't think they are good enough, so how can black people build and run a good bank? People didn't use to talk about these things, but now they are more in the open.' However, within this Africa perspective there are still problems of ethnicity.

### Managing ethnic diversity and recruitment

For example, one manager said that

> since being in the bank I have never had to discuss the inter-ethnic aspect. But in meetings when people take the floor you see people are doing this from their own cultural education. In the north you have a big hierarchy and people behave according to their position in the hierarchy. It is similar for people from the west. In the centre and the east there is not this hierarchy. People come with their culture. But this isn't very direct.

This diversity can be both negative and positive.

> There are more than 200 ethnic groups in the country, so we are representative of the whole of Africa in our diversity. This is the problem of this country, but it can also be a source of progress. We are moving in the company to cultural diversity. First we are addressing the francophone/anglophone issue by giving first preference to new recruits who are English-speaking in order to obtain an equilibrium between English and French speakers, as well as helping us to operate internationally. Secondly, we are mainly a Bamileke culture, so we are taking people from other ethnic groups to bring diversity and to bring in other mentalities. By asking a person from another ethnic group, you may get a different perspective, and therefore arrive at a good answer.

However, the company avoids using a quota system, and the quality of the recruit is paramount in a recruitment decision.

Afriland First Bank, despite problems of managing environment constraints, and the problems associated with the growing size of the organization, has made a conscious decision to develop in an African direction. This is in distinction to both Guinness, which predominantly employs Western techniques yet adapts them to the local environment, and to CNPS who are attempting to overcome politico-ethnic issues by negating the informal system, and strengthening the formal HRM systems in echoes of Western approaches.

Through these three cases, it is possible also to discern the type of control mechanisms being employed. CNPS is attempting to change from a predominantly coercive system of control via both formal and informal means by employing aspects of remunerative control systems. Guinness is attempting this same transformation, yet is introducing a more thoroughgoing productivity based system by using more directly Western post-instrumental approaches. Here the issue is not to defeat an informal system, but to strengthen a results focus in order to make the company efficient and competitive. Afriland First Bank appears to be strengthening its normative control system through developing a moral basis for employee involvement, where people share a sense of community (whilst trying to retain this in the face of a growing organization).

These case studies look at the specific and the detail. It is difficult to draw generalizations from them and to obtain an appreciation of the situation as a whole in the country, and how this compares with other countries. We can only offer them as examples of the issues being addressed, and the way management is addressing them. In order to provide a more general picture, we now turn to results from our surveys of employees and managers in Cameroon and other countries.

## Work attitudes in Cameroon

Results of our organization survey in Cameroon, South Africa, Kenya and Nigeria (Chapter 7: Table 7.1) show that Cameroonian employees see their organizations as more coercive control focused than employees from the other three countries. They also see their organizations more focused in this way than the managers surveyed. Although the ideal is seen as oriented more towards coercive control than employees from the other countries, there is still a discrepancy between what is the current state of affairs and what is desired. All country employees show a desire for less coercive control (this being more pronounced in South Africa). However, the strength of the movement towards remunerative controls can particularly be seen from these results. Both managers and employees express a desire for a greater focus on results and remunerative orientation, with employees seeming particularly enthusiastic. Cameroonian employees score their organizations higher on this scale than their counterparts in Nigeria and South Africa. It is only employees in Kenya that rate their organizations higher in this regard.

Employees across the four countries express a strong desire for far more normative controls (expressing a centrality of a people perspective) yet rate the current situation in their organizations lower. However, in comparison with employees in Nigeria, Cameroonian employees (together with Kenyan employees) rate their organizations more people focused. It may well be that this is a reflection of the efforts that are being made by organizations such as the three above, to focus more on people. However, managers do not seem to share this view, and those in Cameroon see organizations as less people focused than the employee sample (particularly compared with South Africa).

So, how is this situation reflected in job satisfaction and employee commitment? Cameroonian employees indicate that they desire less coercive control than they perceive is the current state of affairs in their organization, more remunerative control, and more normative control mechanisms. Yet these discrepancies are not reflected in low job satisfaction (Table 7.1 shows moderate job satisfaction, with no significant differences among the four countries). However, Cameroonian employees report a significantly lower commitment to their organizations (together with Nigerian employees) compared to their counterparts in Kenya and South Africa. This cannot be wholly explained in terms of discrepancy in the types of control mechanism employed and expectations of employees, as similar discrepancies exist across the four countries.

Other results from our survey of employees indicate that job centrality is relatively low in Cameroon; company centrality is the lowest in Cameroon of the four countries, yet expectation of loyalty from the company is highest in Cameroon (Table 7.1). Also in terms of job attributes, job and skills variety is reported to be lowest in Cameroon, and supervisory control is highest in Cameroon out of the four countries.

Commitment to the organization appears to be the only area where inter-ethnic differences are significant in Cameroon (F statistic = 3.64 and significance = 0.006). The Central minorities group's (sample size [n] = 36) score for this item (see also Table 7.4) is 3.81; the group's Beti [n = 132] is 3.77; the group's Bassa [n = 73] score is 3.69; the score for the Duala/Littoral province group [n = 57] is 3.64; and the Bamileke group's [n = 166] score is 3.50. The Tukey multiple comparison test indicates that the Beti group's score for commitment is significantly higher than that of the Bamileke group. This may reflect the level of representation of the Beti group in the survey, together with traditionally more job security in the public sector where the Beti group is dominant. It may also reflect the dominance itself of this particular group within public sector organizations, with a greater loyalty to the organization because of the politico-ethnic patronage discussed above (see Figure 7.1). The lower ratings of the Bamileke group in the private sector may reflect the relative job insecurity in the sector.

## Implications for managers

There is very little information on management in Cameroon in the international literature. We have referred to that which does exist in order to provide a glimpse of the issues that affect the management of people. This presents a picture of constraints that are mainly political in nature, but which have also been attributed to ethnic issues. Above all, the available information points mainly to post-colonial management systems (in common with much of the literature on African Management: Jackson, 2002c), within the context of the public sector and the way the colonial system has been distorted by an informal system that predominates as a process of political patronage.

The shallowness of the literature is revealed through presenting actual case studies of three organizations: one in the public sector, one a Western multinational organization, and the other an indigenous medium-size organization in the private sector. Through the three cases it is easier to obtain an impression of the actual practice of the management of people and change. This can be seen as an attempt to address the issues of patronage in the public sector, and of trying to adapt Western approaches in the multinational sector, and to develop an African approach to managing people in the indigenous private sector.

Case studies are useful for developing insights into good practice, and the successful adaptation of hybrid systems of management. What the three illustrative cases show is that there is no one way. There is no simple development route for organizations in Cameroon, nor in sub-Saharan Africa as a whole, led by Western management principles or fledgling African 'renaissance' approaches. From our surveys, we can see that there is a general motivation (for both employees and managers) away from the post-colonial coercive control management systems, towards both results orientation (remunerative control) and people centred (normative control) systems of management.

Within this general driving force for change, for CNPS the main task is to put in place a formal appraisal systems that will negate the informal system of promotion and reward and lead to a meritocratic means of managing people. For Guinness the main task is in adapting an overtly performance led system to the African environment. This may well involve marrying remunerative controls with more people-oriented normative controls, in order to further inculcate employee loyalty. This may currently involve elements of paternalism (itself an element that can be discerned in post-colonial management systems). Yet an over-reliance on being taken care of by the company may also encourage a lack of individual initiative on the part of managers and employees. This is also an aspect that Guinness is trying to address. It may just be a matter of getting the balance right. For Afriland First Bank the challenge has been establishing a company along African lines; now its challenge is to maintain this in the face of the bank's own success and its growing number of employees.

# Chapter 11

# Kenya

## A bridge between Africa and Asia?

Kenya is still standing up to independence better than any other country south of the Sahara. There has been no breakdown of law and order, no revolution or military coup, no economic collapse. . . . Provided they keep their mouths shut and a suitcase packed, Europeans can live there with great pleasure and a fair profit.

(*Blackwards Magazine*, March 1971, quoted in Leys, 1975: 273–84)

One of the major factors accounting for lack of development in Africa is the existence of conflicting value systems, or more precisely, the imposition of the Western individualistic ethic on the existing African collectivistic ethic. This incongruity which is often characterized by a veneration of the Western and a distain for African value systems begins at school where individuals rather than group effort is recognized and rewarded.

(Maphosa, 1998: 150)

Human resource development is both a means and an end. Balance should be maintained between the two. If a choice between these two aspects has to be made, it should be in treating HRD as an end rather than a means, since ultimately what is important is human satisfaction and quality of life.

(Rao, 1996: 40, on Indian HRD)

### Introduction: Asians in Africa

So far in this book we have referred to a mainly trichotomous distinction among the 'ideal type' management systems of post-colonial, post-instrumental and African renaissance. In Chapter 1, we also included the possibility of other management systems that might contribute to hybridization of management systems (either adaptive or non-adaptive) such as East Asian or Japanese systems. In Chapter 12 we discuss this influence in connection with a Japanese company in South Africa, and note the increased interest in sub-Saharan Africa of Japanese corporations. Yet there are much older influences on East African societies and more recently on corporate life and management. Pre-dating European influences was the influx of traders from the Arabian peninsula who intermarried with the local population, giving rise to the Islamic-influenced towns of modern day coastal Kenya and the official language of Kenya: KiSwahili and the predominantly Moslem Swahili people (WaSwahili).

Of particular importance in Kenya is the influence on the management culture of Asian Kenyans, mostly descendents of Indian immigrants, within small- and medium-sized businesses (SMEs).

## Power Technics

In 1982 Mr Naresh S. Mehta established Power Technics in Nairobi as a 'cross-cultural' business. He had previously found his racial identity was a problem during a period when Kenya was undergoing Africanization. He held an engineering degree from India, at a time when Indian education was not highly respected, and British education was sought after. It was politically wrong to hire an Indian graduate when an African engineer could be hired. He therefore decided to set up on his own. He got family help to do this. He started with 300,000 Kenyan Shillings (ksh) (around US$500), mainly selling electrical parts. Now he has a half million ksh turnover. He also has three brothers who are doing well in other businesses which together form a group of companies on the same site, and which help each other.

He now employs 160 people, and manufactures switch gear, using sheet metals, as well as lighting and cable support systems such as trunking. They have their own training facility, and have been given awards from the Kenya Bureau of Standards and from UNIDO for innovation and excellence. They partner with a number of companies from Western countries, the biggest being Schneider Electrics incorporating their switch gear into control panels and switchboards, and Thorn Electric for whom they are the official distributor of lighting equipment in East Africa. The company is well known and respected and can frequently be encountered as an exemplory company on business information websites (e.g. www.winne.com/Kenya/C-Industry.htm, 09/05/2002). A walk around the factory which is modern, spacious, comfortable and computerized, confirms that it is on a par with any in the West.

South Asian immigrants, mostly from Punjab and Gujarat, were brought to Africa, predominantly to East and Southern Africa, by the British colonial authorities at the end of the nineteenth century (work began on the Mombassa to Lake Victoria line in 1896: www.nationaidio.com/kenyafiles/people.htm, 30/07/2001) to help build the railways, and to overcome the perceived problem of a shortage of reliable African labour. In East Africa (Kenya, Tanzania, Uganda, and also in Malawi and Zambia) there were estimated to be around 350,000 'Asian Africans', and in South Africa nearly 800,000 (Yakan, 1999). Notably in East Africa many have acquired positions of influence in the trading and services sectors.

In our studies of South African organizations we found managers of Indian descent typically in middle management positions in the Durban area, frustrated in going further by being 'too black' under apartheid, and 'not black enough' since democracy in the early 1990s. As we saw above, in Kenya, Africanization since independence may have led other Asian Africans to the same route as Mr Mehta in setting up businesses, and utilizing family connections and networks to succeed.

Three Asian African-owned and managed companies participated in our organization studies in Kenya. They mostly had strong links with India, through family relations, through employing managers from India, and through hiring managers who had undertaken management education in India, and indeed sometimes sending managers on short management or MBA programmes in India.

## Indian management and hybridization

Jackson (2002a) proposed that the more conscious hybridization of management systems in India, may well point the way to future adaptations in Africa and other 'developing' countries. We now briefly examine this process in relation to Indian management culture before looking at this in the Kenyan context.

England's (1975) study of the personal value systems of over 2,500 managers in five countries that included India, distinguished between *pragmatists* who have an economic and organizational competence orientation, and *moralists* who exhibit a humanistic and bureaucratic orientation. The study reported that the percentage of pragmatists was 67 per cent in Japan, 57 per cent in the United States, 53 per cent in Korea, 40 per cent in Australia, and only 34 per cent in India. The degree of moralistic orientation was 9 per cent in Korea, 10 per cent in Japan, 30 per cent in the United States, 40 per cent in Australia and a relatively high 44 per cent in India.

The values associated with Indian managers in England's (1975) study included a high degree of moralistic orientation; a valuing of stable organizations with minimum or steady change; valuing of a status orientation; and valuing a blend of organizational compliance and organizational competence. Indian managers appear to be more responsive to the human and bureaucratic consequences of their actions; they are more influenced by positions and approaches that utilize philosophical and moral justifications; they are more responsive to internal rewards and controls; and, because India has a larger proportion of moralistic managers, change in managers is likely to be slower and more difficult.

Smith and Thomas (1972) also undertook a cross-cultural study that looked at attitudinal differences between American and Indian managers. They identified differences in the area of authority and influence. They found that Indian managers at both middle and senior levels in organizations profess a belief in group-based, participative decision-making, but have little faith in the capacity of workers for taking initiative and responsibility. American managers on the other hand place a relatively higher faith in the capacity of individuals to take responsibility, and a lower faith in group-oriented participative decision-making. In contrast to American managers, Indian managers favour labour and government interventions in the affairs of the organization. Middle level managers in India espouse a greater belief in change and are less conservative then their American counterparts at this level.

Hofstede's (1980a) results place Indian managers high on power distance (same as West Africa, and higher than East Africa: certainly much higher than the Anglo-Saxon countries); of medium collectivism (interestingly on the same level as Japan and much higher than the Anglo-Saxon countries, yet not as collectivist as East Africa); of medium masculinity (with a score not far below the United States, but higher than East Africa); and low on uncertainty avoidance (on par with the USA, slightly lower than East Africa). He places India at a medium high score of 61 out of 118 for long-term orientation (Hofstede, 1991). This is much higher than the Anglo-Saxon countries and the only African countries included in this study: Nigeria and Zimbabwe. Smith *et al.* (1996) places India mid-way on their conservatism–egalitarian commitment dimension, and towards loyal involvement rather than utilitarian involvement (these dimensions are discussed in Chapter 9). These scores are close to those of Nigeria and Ethiopia. Kenya was not included in this study. We can see from Hofstede's results, despite limitations on his data from East Africa (comprising small samples from more than one country), that Indian cultures may be higher on vertical collectivism and lower on horizontal collectivism (see discussion on Triandis', 2002, concepts in Chapter 6). This may indicate that Indian managers may take an authoritarian yet paternalistic approach to management yet mindful of the human dimension and implicit value of people. This seems to be confirmed by Aycan *et al.*'s (1999) study that compares India with Canadian managers and employees. This indicates that Indians are higher in paternalism, power distance, uncertainty avoidance, loyalty to the community, reactivity (rather than proactivity) and futuristic orientation. Indian employees, incidentally, reported having less enriched jobs than their Canadian counterparts.

In contrast to the higher power distance and vertical collectivism of India:

> Traditionally, almost all of Kenya's ethnic groups were characterized by what has become known as 'egalitarian–segmentarian' structures in contrast to more hierarchical forms of social and political organization as, for example, the chieftainships and kingdoms in neighbouring Uganda.
>
> (Berg-Schlosser, 1994: 249)

Vertical divisions were, and often are, by age sets into which young people were initiated. Horizontally the social structure was defined by membership of clans and lineages (Berg-Schlosser, 1994).

In India, management practitioners and academics have developed a hybrid approach to managing people by distancing themselves from Anglo-Saxon practices that emphasize the human being merely as a *resource* (e.g. Sparrow and Budhwar, 1995). These hybrid approaches (although retaining the term 'human resources' in what appears to be the preferred phrase of Human Resource Development: HRD rather than HRM) are increasingly playing a role in organizational responses to issues arising from liberalization of the economy in India: a 'developing' country that has undergone similar processes to many sub-Saharan countries. Accustomed to operating in protected markets, organizations are having to learn to manage by combining the relative merits of conflicting paradigms, rather than relying exclusively on a single set of pre-conditioned theoretically correct policies. HRD therefore addresses the need to arrest deteriorating values, building up organizational and cultural strengths, broadening the philosophy of tolerance and sacrifice and displaying deep concern for people (Rohmetra, 1998). HRD is a 'humanistic' concept and a subsuming norm that informs the management of employees. It has come to assume a critical role in Indian management thought and practice. As a management philosophy, HRD involves a paradigm shift from the old approach of control to the new approach of involvement and self-development (Silvera, 1988).

Rohmetra (1998) suggests that it is similar to the concept of the rights and duties of human beings which democratic constitutions the world over consider inalienable and inseparable in human nature, and has similarities to the United National Development Programme's concept of a nation's human development. She asserts therefore that HRD is a humanistic concept that places a premium on the dignity and respect of people and based on a belief in the limitless potential of human beings. It emphasizes that people should not be treated as mere cogs in the wheel of production, but with respect as human beings.

As a humanistic concept it proposes that human beings should be valued as human beings, independent of their contribution to corporate productivity or profit. The various underlying attitudes symbolizing respect for people's dignity, trust in their basic integrity and belief in their potential, should lead to the creation of a climate in companies where individuals should find fulfilment in work and seek newer horizons for themselves and the enterprise (Rohmetra, 1998).

HRD practices in companies in India therefore attempt to blend Western and Eastern ideas and systems of people management. This concept of HRD (from Pareek and Rao, 1992) attempts to be more comprehensive and meaningful than utilitarian concepts evolved in Anglo-Saxon countries (see our discussion of post-instrumental management systems in Chapter 1). It has come to denote a planned way of developing and multiplying competencies, and the creation of an organizational climate that promotes the utilization and development of new competencies. Culture building is seen as a part of its agenda (Pareek and Rao, 1992).

## The Kenyan context

Kenya's population is rapidly approaching 30 million, with 50 per cent being under 15 years of age. The majority of people live in the central highlands and western part of the country. There is high unemployment, high crime rates in the big cities, and following relative prosperity after independence from the British authorities in 1963, is suffering from zero and negative economic growth. This deep recession may be due in part to corruption, mismanagement, deviation of funds, excessive borrowing and the suspension of all financial support from the Bretton Woods institutions which froze all new aid programmes in 1992. Informal employment has grown at higher levels than formal employment, with an estimated 3.3 million working in the informal sector (see for example www.winne.com/Kenya, 09/05/2002). The year 1992 also saw the liberalization of the economy following structural reform programmes imposed by the World Bank and IMF. Interest rates have been reduced, price controls and import licences have been eliminated, subsidies removed and some parastatal

## Bidco

Certainly, those values expressed by Bidco, a vegetable oil refining company, reflect those humanistic and community centred values. Bidco's origin goes back to 1970 when Mr Bhimji Depar Shar founded Bidco Clothing Factory in Nairobi. In 1985 Bidco soap manufacturing plant was opened, followed in 1991 by the opening of Bidco Oil Refineries in Thika. It is recognized today as one of the successful companies in Kenya, receiving awards from Kenya Institute of Management, Kenya Bureau of Standards among others, and being listed in PricewaterhouseCoopers Top 20 Most Highly Respected Companies. It is now the largest and fastest growing manufacturer of vegetable oils, fats, margarine, soaps and protein concentrates in East and Central Africa. It states within its community values:

- Bidco values its human resources above all others. The company has built its reputation on the work, skill and expertise of its staff.
- Bidco has developed and maintained an excellent relationship with its workforce. With programmes in place for both staff welfare and training, the company is continually finding ways to improve the lives of its employees.
- The company provides full medical insurance for its staff, as well as protective clothing and excellent on-site facilities.
- Bidco also plays a significant role in supporting the local community, and the company has contributed to a number of community based projects.
- Bidco products are regularly donated to children's homes, church organizations and schools throughout the country. The company actively supports several charitable community organizations.
- Bidco has a major programme to provide industrial attachment training to institutional graduates.
- Bidco believes that building a better society is an important part of developing economic growth and a better future.

Certainly this also contains elements of an instrumental approach. Such community sponsorship projects may be found in Western multinational corporations operating in Kenya such as Citibank. Bidco were also not alone in Asian African companies in Kenya in introducing Japanese techniques such as 5S and Kaisen, in order to combine different sources, both humanistic and instrumental, in developing management principles. Central to Bidco's stated vision is also its faith in Africa, and the fact that it is African: 'African born and proud of its African Heritage, Bidco believes in the future of Africa' (www.bidco-oil.com/profile/whoweare.asp, p.1, 07/05/2002). Asian African-run companies appear to be adept at adaptation and the hybridization of management influences and cultural sources, and this may well reflect such approaches as HRD in India.

organizations have been sold in an ongoing privatization programme. Despite its problems, Kenya still remains relatively peaceful and stable. Yet any visitor to Kenya will confirm the lack of maintenance of the infrastructure, most immediately manifest in the necessity to drive around huge potholes in the roads.

## Constraints and opportunities

An appreciation of the concerns of management in Kenya can be obtained by an examination of the May–July 2001 issue of one of the leading management practitioner journals in Kenya *Management: A Journal of the Kenya Institute of Management*. Raphael G. Mwai (2001), chair of the Association of Professional Societies in East Africa, states that the growth in real GDP has declined from 1.8 per cent in 1998 to –0.3 per cent in 2000. This continues the negative trend in economic growth over the last ten years. With a population growth rate of 2.8 per cent over the last ten years, this has accelerated the level of poverty in the country. So, over 50 per cent of Kenyans are classified as 'poor' living on less than US$1 per day. The role of the private sector was seen as the 'engine of growth' in the Sessional Paper No. 1 of 1986 ('Economic management for renewed growth'). The government policy was focused on the growth and development of the private sector. 'So what has gone wrong?' he asks.

His view is that the 'major role of the private sector is wealth creation. . . . Sustained wealth creation can only be achieved through sustained growth and market share. In a competitive and liberalized global market, the private sector must achieve global competitiveness. The constraints to this in Kenya are: low technology base, with most industries operating on obsolete technology and with fairly rudimentary IT; high cost production and delivery processes and systems, mainly due to low technology base, as well as inappropriate structures and systems of business management, capacity under-utilization (estimated to be 45 per cent) and weak innovation and creativity in business management practices and culture; inadequate systems of human resource development with the role of knowledge not clearly appreciated (this is particularly critical in small and medium enterprises); weak access to regional and international market information with Kenyan businesses not reaching out sufficiently, and connectivity to world wide web.

He contends that government has got a key role to play in developing the private sectors as currently enterprises are challenged by high interest rates, limited access to financial services, especially credit, high taxation levels and multiplicity of taxes, an unfavourable business environment characterized by over-regulation of business and unfair competition, costly physical infrastructure, insecurity of persons and property, and unstable exchange rates. He suggests that government should provide: a balanced macro-economic environment with implications for high interest rates and taxation levels; enhanced security of persons and property for improved investor confidence; improvement of physical and social infrastructure; protection of the environment; and protection of vulnerable members of society to ensure equity for all.

For Mule (2001, in the same publication), 'Poverty is high, and development indices, including life expectancy, child mortality, nutrition status, and education are deteriorating. Growth of the economy has come to a halt, and per capita incomes are falling with public institutions being rendered dysfunctional. The solutions suggested are:

> To eradicate poverty, the country must attain sustained growth with equity.

> As a nation, we should go back to [the] basics of nation building: What sort of nation and society do we want? What is our vision of Kenya? What is our common future? The logical starting point is the constitution, which must fully take into account the yearning, the fears and aspirations of Kenyans.

> On the economic front, we as a national must devise sound trade policies, which enable Kenya to participate constructively in the global economy. . . . Good trade policy must be rooted in sound development policy, which in turn, must make strategic choices of where we want to be in the future.

Specifically,

> Agriculture, rural development, development of small-scale enterprises, and human development must be the centrepiece of such strategy, which must also recognize the primacy of industrialization as a vehicle for long term growth. Successful industrialization will call for provision of efficient infrastructure and supporting institutions and policies.

Also,

> There must be a clear and agreed definition of the role of the state. At independence, contraction of power in the government and allied institutions was considered the appropriate reaction to both political and economic challenges. However, lack of competition lowered economic efficiency and, with it, growth.

> The state must be transparent. In Kenya we have fared badly on that score. Corruption is widespread and deeply rooted.

(Note that Kenya is number four in Transparency International's league of most corrupt countries: see Table 3.1.)

## Cultural factors

The 'cradle of mankind' has seen a whole number of waves of immigration of Africans and non-Africans, as well as interaction among the indigenous people. As with most other African countries the boundaries of the country were set without much regard for the indigenous people of the area and their traditional borders. Yet in the few management studies of Kenya little distinction is made among the different African peoples, nor in the differences between Asian Kenyans and their African counterparts in management positions. Yet this may be as a result of a number of reasons:

- low sample sizes in empirical studies (although, for example, Kuada, 1994, has a total sample of 287 Kenyans in his comparison of Kenyan and Ghanaian managers yet does not compare nor even mention different ethnic groups);
- little actual differences among the different cultural/ethnic groups (we discuss this shortly in relation to the current management survey);
- lack of basis for comparison (for example, Europeans managing large multi-nationals, Asians managing SME and African managing informal small and micro businesses).

Dondo and Ngumo (1998) argue that African culture has tended to constrain the development of entrepreneurship. These include:

- Respect for seniority and authority. They argue that this is a result of age, education, official rank and economic status. Power distance is accepted and this creates 'seniors' with autocratic tendencies and obsequious 'juniors'.
- Short-term planning horizons. A lack of planning after a consideration of risk, and a short-term mentality goes against the qualities of successful entrepreneurship, they argue.
- Interaction of land and entrepreneurial activities. The acquisition of land is often seen as an end in itself, and often Kenyans will work, or extract money from a business to buy a plot of land, no matter how unsuitable, as security for later life. The availability of such land coupled with this attitude towards it, they argue, militates against entrepreneurial activity as an end in itself.
- Belief in God and other extraterrestrial forces. They maintain that a belief in witchcraft is still prominent in Kenya. This takes the responsibility away from the individual and places ill fortune at the hands of the supernatural. This reluctance to accept responsibilities for one's own fortunes, they suggest, militates against successful entrepreneurship.
- Communalism. They suggest that the collective nature of traditional African life, where activity is approached collectively and the weak and destitute are helped by family members and where income is shared out among the extended family (particularly in a country where fewer than 20 per cent of people are in employment), has the effect of limiting the capital available to invest in businesses. It has the effect of involving the community in decision-making that can be a long process, and often irrelevant to the business. It has led to 'corrupt practices' in considering one's own people first for tenders and contracts. It has led to favouritism in employment practices by giving jobs to those you know.

Although mentioned by Dondo and Ngumo (1998) this does tend to ignore the level of entrepreneurship in the informal economy. For example, Ogonda (1992) explains that:

> African entrepreneurship has played an insignificant role in the whole manufacturing sector both in colonial and post-colonial periods. This has been partly because of the restrictions imposed on African participants in any form of

business by the colonial administration and partly because of lack of capital and entrepreneurial skills . . . of the total nominal company capital registered between 1946 and 1963, 68 per cent was European, 21 per cent Asian, 11 per cent combined Asian and European, and less than 1 per cent African. This small figure of African entrepreneurship in the formal manufacturing industry, apparently does not take into account the large number of African businessmen in the blacksmith, carpentry, motor vehicle and tailoring activities that had emerged. . . . This new breed of African semi-skilled technicians had begun to establish the informal manufacturing of *Jua Kali* industries throughout the country and was fast replacing Asian producers in certain lines of production.

(pp. 302–3)

It would therefore appear that many indigenous African entrepreneurs have tended to stay within the informal sector because of a lack of capital and opportunity. The corollary of this might be that those indigenous Africans who have had the opportunity since independence have taken up careers in the public sector, whereas those of Indian descent have not had the opportunity to enter the public sector, and have made careers and opportunities in the small and medium enterprise (SME) sector. Western multinational have tended to dominate in the large enterprise sector. The lack of African entrepreneurs, owners and top managers in the formal SME and large enterprise sectors may explain the lack of African influence in management generally in Kenya. As in other sub-Saharan countries this may account for the disparaging of African culture in relation to the successful operation of organizations. We have discussed at some length the influence of Western management principles on organizations and management in Africa. Little or nothing has been published that provides insight into the influence of Indian principles in Africa, yet this appears to be important in Kenya, at least in a significant part of the economy.

Kamoche's (1992) study of HRM practices in five organizations in Kenya focuses on Western multinational organizations. It is not surprising therefore that he concludes that practices resemble the Western HRM model to a lesser or greater extent. He therefore provides little or no information on indigenous or Indian influences. Again, in the book that develops his thesis (Kamoche, 2000) he makes reference to some of the literature on management in Africa, yet we learn very little about indigenous Kenyan approaches.

Kuada (1994) takes a different approach through undertaking management surveys in Ghana and Kenya. He draws out the commonalities of African cultural influences in the two countries. In particular, he concludes that in both Ghana and Kenya managers are influenced by 'culturally established values and rules of behaviour found in society' (p. 223). In particular, these influences are:

1   age and the culturally defined relationships between elderly and younger people of the society;
2   status arrangements and power differences defined by such social attributes as position, wealth and levels of education;

3    familism, clanism and ethnicity as well as their practical manifestations in collective obligations and the disproportionate family burden on few relatively well-off family members;

4    metaphysical considerations, particularly ideas and philosophies of organized religions and traditional belief systems.

(pp. 223–4)

He suggests that the first two influences are particularly noticeable in superior–subordinate relations in organizations, as well as the social relations among organizational members and their attitudes and expectations towards each other. Leadership styles, he contends, are shaped by these influences such that managers exhibit styles of 'authoritarian benevolence' and 'selective treatment' of subordinates. The third factor tends to influence recruitment of staff lower down the organization, and in the extreme caution of junior managers in avoiding any actions that could displease their senior managers and put their careers or jobs in jeopardy.

From our own management surveys (Table 5.1 and Figures 5.2 and 5.3) the similarities between Ghana and Kenya are palpable, and confirm Kuada's (1994) findings. This may be a result of similarities in their economic and social development that have influenced management and organizational attributes. As with other countries in our study, Kenyan managers indicate that their organizations are only moderately results oriented, and would wish to see their organizations far more results oriented as well as far more people oriented, getting away from the current control orientation (Figure 5.2 and 5.3). In comparison with the other African countries in the study Kenyan managers see their organizations as less controlling than managers from others countries apart from Rwanda and Mozambique (Table 5.1). The score for people focus is around the average for all country managers, albeit with a negative standard score (indicating a score lower than managers' mean score for all items on the questionnaire). Others countries that score higher on people focus are Mozambique, Namibia, Rwanda, South Africa and Côte d'Ivoire. Countries that score lower include Botswana, Burkina Faso and DRC. Similar patterns emerge if we examine scores for consultation. Diversity management compares favourably against South Africa, Nigeria and DRC, and Kenya had one of the higher scores for this aspect. This may be the case because diversity and cross-cultural management has not been raised as much as an issue as it has in South Africa, for example. Certainly it appears not to be part of the overt management agenda in education programmes, for example in offerings from the Kenya Institute of Management (although the management faculty of the United States International University have an active programme in cross-cultural management). Yet companies such as Davis and Shirtliff, a medium size water pump fabrication and distribution company, owned by a white Kenyan family, but whose senior management has been predominantly Kikuyu, are aware of the issues arising from the predominance of one ethnic group, and are attempting to address these issues.

Kenyan managers do not see their organizations as going through rapid change. Certainly change is seen less than in South Africa and Namibia; but more than Burkina Faso, DRC, Côte d'Ivoire, Mozambique and Rwanda. The gap between the way they see change now and what they would wish indicates that ideally Kenyan managers would like far more change (Table 5.2). With many of the other countries, trade unions appear to be weak, with a wish that ideally they should be stronger. Family influences are not prominent. Ideally managers would wish for even less family influence. Government influence appears to be more, but of less prominence than in Botswana, Burkina Faso, DRC, Malawi, and Namibia. With other countries in the study, risk taking is moderately low. Kenyan managers indicate that ideally their organizations should be prepared to take more risks.

Generally, the picture of management in Kenyan painted by managers in this survey appears to be fairly middle of the road, and, reflecting a country that has undergone some degree of liberalizations, is influenced by Western management principles (perhaps in seeing the need to be more results oriented and more risk taking), but also by a higher ideal people orientation. As with other African countries in our study, managers may be seeing the post-colonial influence of high control systems as increasingly inappropriate.

## African and Asian cultural influences

In our original management surveys in Kenya, we focused only on African Kenyan managers. However, because of the influence of Asian Africans on management practice, particularly in SMEs, it became more important to obtain comparisons, not only among ethnic groups, but also with Asian Kenyans, and as an added dimension with a sample of managers from India in order to investigate similarities and differences among Kenyan managers from different cultural backgrounds, and to assess the hypothesis that Kenya could be acting as a bridge between Asia and Africa.

From a total of 330 Kenyan managers in our study we could identify the following cultural groupings: Kenyan Asian (n = 35), Kenyan Kikuyu (94), Kenyan Meru (28) Kenyan Akamba (30), Kenyan Luyia (22), Kenyan Luo (20), Kenyan Nilotic (other than Luo, including Kalenjin, Iteso, Kipsigi, Nandi, Marakwet). Others respondents either did not identify their ethnic group, or were too small a sample size. For example only three identified themselves as Masai (we did not group these with the other Nilotic group). With such groups as Turkana and Somali, which were absent from our survey, although a significant proportion of the general population, the Masai people do not figure prominently in the management population in the formal economy. Our samples were obtained by mail, through the database of the Kenya Institute of Management. Despite the prominence of members from the Asian Kenyan population, we only obtained three Asian Kenyan responses. We therefore obtained a further sample of Asian Kenyans through a collaborator from USIU who personally approached managers. Our sample of 141 managers from India were obtained mainly in the north east and predominantly in Punjab, Jammu, Gujarat and Delhi, reflecting in part the origins of Asian Kenyans and where there might still be family and professional contacts.

Our results reflected the similarities among the Bantu groups (particularly Kikuyu, Meru and Kamba) identified by Berg-Schlosser (1994), and significant differences that did exist were mainly between the Indian group and Bantu groups or between

Asian Kenyans and African Kenyan groups. However, these differences were few. The managers from India (standardized score = –0.079) indicated that their organizations were less results focused than were Kikuyu managers (0.290; F = 3.24, significance = 0.002). The Kikuyu managers (0.667) expressed a stronger desire for their organizations to be more consultative than did their counterparts in India (0.383; F = 3.13, significance = 0.003). The Asian Kenyans (–0.234) indicated more family influence in their organizations than did the Meru (–1.154) and other Nilotic group (–1.266; F = 3.18, significance = 0.003). The only significant differences among the African groups were between the Luo (0.762) who indicated that their organizations were more influenced by government relations than did the Meru (–0.272) group (F = 2.35, significance = 0.023). In terms of the ideal for government influences, the Kamba managers (–0.727) indicated that they wanted less than did the Luo (0.285) and Asian Kenyans (0.231; F = 2.76, significance = 0.008).

These results may provide an indication of the similarities between Indian and Asian Kenyan managers, and between these two groups and the African Kenyan groups. It may be the case that organizations in India may be less consultative and less results oriented than organizations in Kenya. The main indication of cultural attitudinal differences is in the expressions of ideal management systems. In this case there is a stronger desire of Kikuyu managers (the biggest African group in our samples of Kenyan managers and prominent in management generally in Kenya) to have more consultative management compared with Indian managers. This may provide some insights into relative management systems in that there are no significant differences between Indian and Asian Kenyan managers. However, the main differences among the cultural groups within the Kenyan study can be seen when we focus on motivation.

## Motivation and cultural differences

In Chapter 6 (see Table 6.1) we looked at differences among managers from different sub-Saharan countries. Compared with the overall mean score, Kenyan managers appeared to be motivated more by the security of a steady job, opportunities to learn, being part of a team, and freedom to adopt their own approach in their jobs. Work was not central in their lives. They had a higher internal locus of control and a lower external locus of control than the average for all managers across the fifteen countries.

In our study of Kenyan and Indian managers, the main African groups (Kikuyu: score 0.6,568; Meru: 0.740; Luo: 0.953; and other Nilotic: 0.932) all score significantly higher on the motivation for security in the job than did their counterparts from India (score = 0.144; F = 6.23, significance = 0.000). The Indians are also less negative about unpredictability in their work (–0.293) than are the other Nilotic managers (–1.07; F = 2.85, significance = 0.007), and less negative about working alone (Indian score = –0.551) than are the Asian Kenyans (–1.136), Kikuyus (–0.964) and Meru (–1.305; F = 4.22, significance = 0.000). The Asian Kenyans (–0.265) appear to be significantly more motivated to direct people than do the Luo (–0.738; F = 2.13, significance = 0.040), although still indicating a negative standardized score).

Work centrality appears to be higher among the Indian group (0.601) than amongst the Kikuyu (–0.392), the Akamba (0.019), the Meru (–0.140) and the Luo (–0.581). When looked at within Kenya alone, the Asian Kenyans (0.250) appear to have a higher work centrality than do Kikuyus and Luo managers (F = 13.04, significance = 0.000). The Indian group (–0.238) also appear to have a higher external locus of control than do the other Nilotic group (–0.770), and the Akamba (–0.003) have a higher external locus than do the other Nilotic group (F = 3.21, significance = 0.003).

It would therefore appear that there are many similarities among the indigenous groups of managers, differences between managers in India and indigenous groups in Kenya, and some similarities between Indian managers and those of Indian descent in Kenya. As might be expected, Asian Kenyans are more similar to African Kenyans than Indians are to Kenyan Africans. Most differences appear to be in the areas of individual motivation, with few and smaller differences in the perceptions of aspects that relate to management systems.

## Implications for managers

There appears to be in India, a much clearer articulation of how crossvergence of cultures and organizational hybridization may be managed through the concept of HRD and how it may successfully combine Western and indigenous influences while overcoming some of the negatives of post-colonial systems of management. It is not the purpose of this present text to be prescriptive, but rather to explore some of the approaches towards more adaptive and appropriate management systems in sub-Saharan Africa. In Kenya, as in Nigeria (Chapter 9) there appears to be little articulation of a Kenyan or African approach to management. Asian Kenyans appear to be learning from a number of different influences, including Indian influences. India is going through similar processes of liberalization of the economy and changing systems of management as Kenya. It may be possible to learn from Indian management responses to these processes. The work of T.V. Rao (1996) is particularly important in understanding the human factor in management in developing countries. He outlines the key assumptions that we paraphrase as follows:

- HRD requires sensitivity to changing needs in order to set appropriate priorities.
- It is both a means and an end, and a balance should be kept between the two.
- Developing people is central and should be an important goal in ultimately serving people in terms of improving their happiness through better quality and standards of life.
- HRD holds the key for economic development through enabling people to become more productive.
- HRD strategies have made a difference in reducing poverty in some developing countries while others have done well economically in terms of their GNP, yet the distribution of economic benefits have been unequal with benefits limited to the rich. HRD strategies should focus therefore on poverty alleviation and investment at the national level on education, health and creation of employment.

- Opportunities should be made for people to take advantage of the results of increased globalization and the use of, for example, information technology.
- There is an increasing recognition also at the national level to involve people through participation, empowerment, better access and opportunity, and also by applying principles of democracy and just and honest government.
- There is an increased recognition of the strategic role of women in human resource and economic development.
- Attention should be focused on the ineffective use of human resources in the growing unemployment of youth.
- Some countries undergoing structural adjustment have ignored the social dimension. This has lead to a decline in the quality of human resources and social development, and also makes the poor more vulnerable.
- Privatization schemes that are without a socially responsible private sector, have led to exploitation of the poor.
- There is an erroneous expectation that external aid will solve all human resource development problems.
- Development is becoming more people focused, and NGOs may help in this process.
- There is becoming a better understanding of the linkages between social, health and educational programmes, the role of women, unemployment, quality of human resources and the composition of existing capabilities such as knowledge, attitudes and skill base.
- There is increased criticism of inefficient and wasteful public services.

This is a far more embracing concept than that of Western HRM, and looks at the wider stakeholder base. It sees the development of people both as a means to an end (instrumental) and an end in itself (humanistic). It therefore attempts to marry many of the concepts discussed in the current text. It is aligned with the UNDP concept of Human Development, and was reflected in the United Nations Programme of Action for African Economic Recovery and Development 1989–90. At the national level this included the creation of new ministries responsible for HRD, establishing entities to coordinate the inclusion of vulnerable groups in development and the implantation of measures aimed at the disadvantaged, and actions for more effective participation of people and communities in development including support for indigenous entrepreneurial capabilities. This approach is in part reflected in the Human Factor Approach that has gained some currency in Africa (Chivaura and Mararike, 1998) and reflects, as in Indian HRD the bringing together of instrumental and humanistic concepts of people inside organizations, while bringing in the wider stakeholder community including those disadvantaged groups that would normally be ignored by purely instrumental approaches to management.

Indian HRD approaches are suggestive of what might be appropriate in the African context. From some of the empirical research presented above, although there may be some differences between Indian and indigenous African cultures such as higher vertical collectivism in the Indian context and higher horizontal collectivism in the African context, there may well be more similarities than dissimilarities. It may be pertinent for managers in Africa to include such approaches among their repertoire of resources to draw upon, including Western, Japanese, and African influences in order to develop effective hybrid management systems that are adaptive to the African context.

We now turn towards approaches developed more specifically on the African continent, in South Africa, in order to ask the question: is this the future of sub-Saharan Africa?

# Chapter 12

# South Africa

## The future of management in Africa?

With *Lynette Louw*

---

South Africa has a government, political and other social formations and masses of the people who see themselves as part of the motive forces for the victory of the African renaissance. Our first task, therefore, is to transform our society consistent with this vision. Our second task is to join hands with all other like-minded forces on our continent, convinced that the peoples of Africa share a common destiny.

(Thabo Mbeki, Prologue, to Makgoba, 1991: xiii–xxi)

### Introduction: South Africa and sub-Saharan Africa

The perspectives presented here is that South Africa is important to developments in sub-Saharan Africa as a whole. Events since the ending of apartheid and lifting of sanctions has meant a renewed investment interest in South Africa from multinational companies, and possibly decreasing interest from the international donor and development community with a perspective that the job is now done. Yet the development of effective managers and organizations in South Africa is just beginning. Metropolitan, one of the leading insurance groups in South Africa has an advanced empowerment policy encouraging multicultural teambuilding and positive discrimination towards previously disadvantaged groups. Yet looking around the staff restaurant one can still see groups of black Africans, Asians, and whites all sitting on separate tables. Major social problems and inequities still exist. Major problems of illiteracy and a lack of basic skills, let alone management skills, are just beginning to be addressed. Eskom, for example, is the biggest provider of electricity in southern Africa. As a state-own company it has been a major player in the new South Africa's Reconstruction and Development Programme: providing basic amenities to the majority of the population, and assisting in the uplifting of previously disadvantaged communities. A main thrust of this programme has been to positively discriminate towards the previously disadvantaged in terms of job and development opportunities within companies such as Eskom, and to develop basic literacy programmes to ensure that all employees can read and write (Jackson, 1999).

Yet South Africa, for many different peoples and stakeholders in sub-Saharan Africa, is seen as a beacon of hope. Multinational organizations are seeing the country as a springboard to the rest of the sub-continent. Bodies of management thought are developing, such as the *ubuntu* movement, and starting to be applied in other sub-

Saharan African countries. Management principles and practices are being adapted and hybrid systems are being developed. For example, Koopman (1991), presents one such successful case, Cashbuild, a chain of building materials wholesalers which, as managing director, he guided through the process of democratizing the workplace and building multicultural teams. Thought and effort are therefore being given to addressing basic problems in organizations like illiteracy, and more complex management problems such as developing multi-ethnic teams out of the ravages of blatant race discrimination. Equity programmes, including positive discrimination towards previously disadvantaged groups, are being initiated, some successfully, some not so successful. Yet no other country is like South Africa.

However, its depths of problems and possible solutions, plus its huge potential means that in many ways South Africa is seen as pointing the way forward. Yet South Africa has for many years been an influence on events in southern Africa and beyond, often negatively so. With South Africa's comparative economic advantages over the rest of the continent, its growing business and management influence could be seen as another form of imperialism. Indeed, although some of the companies whose managers we interviewed in South Africa saw that increasingly their markets lay north of their borders, they also did not think they had very had very much to learn from managers in other African countries. For example, managers in Metropolitan spoke about 'An aggressive move to go north – Botswana, Namibia and Lesotho' and that 'This reinforces the future vision for Africa, and embraces the African renaissance'. Another senior manager stated that, 'We do not know enough about African influences to implement such principles. Predominantly we operate Western policies, and they are adapted to suit the South African environment. We work in Botswana and Namibia: they look at us – we don't look at them'. Yet South African managers have developed a wealth of knowledge and experience. This particularly applies to the cross-cultural management of people and change.

Jackson (1999: 306–7) wrote

> Western and non-Western cultures have for many years existed side by side (perhaps not too happily) in South Africa, although the enforced policy of separate ethnic development has warped the relationship. With the ending of apartheid, the situation has been left, perhaps as it always was, with a multicultural, polyglot society (with eleven official languages) of overwhelming complexity, deep historical antagonisms, profound differences between rich and poor, but now with unlimited potential to achieve centre stage in the global community.

This complexity is perhaps both a challenge and an opportunity. Almost without exception, sub-Saharan African countries are multicultural, have deep post-colonial legacies and similar acute problems of poverty, under-education and under-skilling, as well as under-investment in the fabric of organizational and community life. South Africa may be in a unique position to take a lead in developing appropriate solutions to the problems it and other sub-Saharan African countries are facing, by developing highly adaptive hybrid management systems capable of managing change through utilizing the strengths and synergies of a multicultural workforce. We return to these issues, and the potential of the South African model as a possible way forward for sub-Saharan Africa after we first discuss the literature, and our findings in our present study in connection with: the operating constraints and opportunities of organizations in South Africa, and how managers deal with these; strategy, governance and stakeholders management; decision-making; leadership and management principles; commitment and motivation; the management of multiculturalism; and training and development.

## Operating constraints and opportunities

Although South Africa today has far lower export concentration ratios, its original economic development was based on extraction and agriculture aimed at an export rather than a domestic market. According to the African Development Report (2000: 136) Africa's share in global exports fell from 4.5 per cent in 1977 to 2 per cent in 1997 (in US dollar terms 2000). This focus on export-led production had the effects of negating the need to develop a consumer-based economy, leading to the under-development of processing and service industries, and skills associated with the secondary and tertiary sectors. In South Africa the distinction between labour predominantly for the mining and other heavy industry and a much smaller base for consumer products was formalized by apartheid along racial lines. Thus the movement of labour was heavily controlled through a system of migratory labour. Homelands were created and black Africans excluded from white urban city areas. Separate educational systems were established with an under-resourcing of education for over 80 per cent of the population who were black (Jackson, 1999).

This has ensured the under-education and under-skilling of vast numbers of people who are ill equipped for jobs in a highly competitive global marketplace. This of course reflects the situation in many African countries. Yet while these countries could simply be described as 'poor', the situation in South Africa is more complex than this, and full of contradictions. Its economy's gross national product per capita (GNP) of US$3,170 in 1999 places it in the upper-middle income group of semi-industrialized economies, yet it performs more in line with the typical lower-middle income countries if one considers its social indicators (African Development Indicators, 2001: 5). Its health performance is worse than some low-income countries like Sri Lanka and China. It has the lowest life expectancy (62 years) of the upper-middle income countries, and a quality of life index of only 66 (Luiz, 1996).

The population exceeded 40.58 million at the 1996 census (76.7 per cent black, 10.9 per cent white, 8.9 per cent coloured and 2.6 per cent Indian/Asian), while the expanded unemployment rate was 37.6 per cent (South Africa Yearbook, 2000/2001; Statistics South Africa, 1998: 8). An estimated 15 per cent of population 15 years and older are illiterate (African Development Indicators, 2001: 320).

With high levels of unemployment, a large division between rich and poor, a recent history of violence and weapons proliferation, and lower than European average numbers of police officers per head of population, violent crime is high (Mills *et al.*, 1995). This has had a negative effect on foreign investment and tourism. But South

Africa has shown a steadily expanding economy. Following a decade of limited growth averaging 0.5 per cent per annum, the GDP growth averaged 2.3 per cent a year between 1995 and 1999 and 1.3 per cent annually over the decade (African Development Report, 2000: 79–80).

Inflation was 7.4 per cent in 1996, the lowest since 1972 (Budget Speech 1997–8). However, Mills *et al.* (1995) estimates that a growth rate anything below 4.0 per cent per annum will not create sufficient jobs given projected population increases, with around 400,000 people (80 per cent black) entering the job market annually. Only 31,000 jobs were created annually between 1985 and 1989. Yet by 2005 there is expected to be a shortage of 920,000 skilled workers and a surplus of 11.5 million unskilled or semi-skilled workers (Mills *et al.*, 1995).

Demographic constraints include not only a growing population but contained within this a high dependency ratio, a youthful age structure and a continuing high rate of urbanization (Luiz, 1996). The high incidents of AIDS in South Africa, as in many other African countries, could be a contributing factor to the high dependency ratio of the population. For example, although the figures for incidents of HIV and AIDS is hotly contested in South Africa, the Stellenbosch University Bureau for Economic Research projects that the labour force will shrink 21 per cent by 2015 because of AIDS, and that real gross domestic product will be 1.5 per cent lower by 2010 than it would without AIDS, and may be 5.7 per cent lower by 2015 (*Sunday Times Business Times*, 7 October 2001: 6).

In manufacturing industry, which now accounts for 23.5 per cent of GDP, productivity (a function of skills, technology, capital and labour) has been slow to grow (0.4 per cent in the 1970s and 0.5 per cent in the 1980s). This reflects the poor education provision under apartheid for the large majority of the (black) population. The 1994 World Competitive Report covering 42 country economies, ranked South Africa 35 out of 42. The 'people' dimension of this assessment covered: public expenditure on education; pupil–teacher ratios; company investment in training; economic and computer literacy; and the availability and quality of human resources. For this part of the assessment South Africa was ranked number 42 (Watson, 1996).

Exacerbating this issue may also be the factor of employment equity, which may initially contribute to an under-skilling of the workforce (e.g. Bowmaker-Falconer *et al.*, 1998). Approximately 11,300 affirmative action posts have been allocated in the public sector since April 1994 (Horwitz *et al.*, 1996). The Employment Equity and Skills Development Bills of 1997 are aimed at redressing racial and gender based employment inequalities. The Employment Equity Bill requires companies with more than 50 staff to formulate plans to develop a workforce whose racial composition reflects that of the country. Organizations are not compelled to dismiss existing staff and mitigating circumstances include the unavailability of skills. However, the legislation provides for fines for companies who are deemed not to have tried hard enough after five years (*Financial Times*, 24 March 1998).

Yet private sector organizations in South Africa spend only an estimated 2 per cent of payroll per year on education and training, compared with 6–8 per cent in the leading industrial nations (Horwitz *et al.*, 1996). There are also lower levels of tertiary education in technical and scientific subjects than in other (developing) countries. This is likely to affect the skills pool.

It may therefore be easy for managers to provide a list of constraints and threats to operating in South Africa and indeed in Africa as a whole. Foremost may be the socio-economic threats to stability, employment and profitability. These may also include the problems of successfully completing the transition away from authoritarian rule towards a robust democracy with inherited economic problems as well as high inequalities of wealth, ethnic rivalry and levels of violence. Ethnic constraints are inherent within South Africa's highly fragmented society and moves towards redistribution through affirmative action, and the implication of discrimination against those not covered by affirmative action may harbour further threats (Luiz, 1996). Long lists of constraints, as we have seen in previous chapters, could also be drawn up for other African countries, yet it is an organization's ability to be able to turn these around into opportunities that may make the difference between a mal-adaptive management system and a highly adaptive system. Organizations do thrive and prosper under adverse conditions.

## Constraints and opportunities for Metropolitan

Metropolitan is an example of a South African company whose managers are articulating their approach to addressing constraints and assessing opportunities (Table 12.1). One of the key issues is seen as reaching out to the community in order both to develop products, such as 'AIDS products', and also to help local authorities in these issues, by providing education, and not merely by donating to good causes. Part of effective management within Africa, we have previously argued, is to be able to include within strategic objectives the multiple interests of a wider stakeholder base.

## Strategy, governance and stakeholder management

Like many sub-Saharan African countries, following the adoption of World Bank and IMF-led structural adjustment programmes, South Africa (following the end of apartheid and sanctions) has been launched into a competitive global marketplace at a time when the overriding trend for organizations in industrial (mainly Western) countries is to radically change by downsizing and delayering in order to make the organization more competitively meaner and leaner (Cameron, 1994; Freeman, 1994). As a result of this, companies in South Africa may be becoming increasingly results-focused, and along with that have a primacy of shareholder value as their main strategic driver.

## Colgate-Palmolive

Colgate-Palmolive South Africa, a subsidiary of the American company, is described in a published case (Beaty, 1998). Many American companies have developed social responsibility programmes in South Africa under the guidelines of the Sullivan Code. Colgate-Palmolive has achieved 'an outstanding Category 1 rating' under this code. Its contributions have been to fund various educational projects at schools and universities (equipment, electricity, burglar-proofing of premises, supplements for teacher upgrades, outreach programmes, student bursaries, provision of career advice); and community projects (water purification and sanitation, funds for centres for the elderly, drug rehabilitation, mental illness, AIDS). The list is very long, and includes a number of health and dental projects. The code requires that the company directs 12 per cent of its salary budget to such projects.

With an annual turnover of $100 million and a workforce of 600 employees, the company had set up a $3 million Colgate Palmolive Foundation. The management and allocation of funding to projects was a responsibility of the company-appointed management rather than being representatives of the various stakeholder communities that stood to benefit from these projects. The trade union has criticized the company for not involving them. Sometimes projects were funded, for example in the area of dental care, it was said out of enlightened self-interest (as part of marketing its own products) rather than altruism or a sense of what is required to contribute to the development of people within the community.

Many companies like Colgate-Palmolive have been radically downsizing, and operating with a minimum of staff. While Eskom, for example, has also been downsizing, it has attempted to balance the needs of developing people and therefore contributing to the community, rather than simply donating to worthy causes.

### Balancing stakeholder interests

One participant in our present study, is a subsidiary of an American multinational that operates in over 50 countries and employs nearly 100,000 people worldwide. Although the multinational company could be said to replicate subsidiaries in its own image through its published company philosophy, the company has a policy of decentralized management whereby each subsidiary is 'focused on a specific product franchise and/or geographical area, and whereby 'our individual managements are responsible for their business' (1999 Annual Report). Their philosophy sets out the first responsibility to be to meet the needs of all those who use their products, and

Table 12.1 Constraints and opportunities identified by twelve managers interviewed in Metropolitan

| Constraints | Addressed by (strategies) | Opportunities |
|---|---|---|
| Restructuring of legislation that affects business and lack of transparency of government | | The country has a sound infrastructure and has the opportunity to catch up |
| Low value of the Rand | Interact more with communities and clients | Market positioning and credentials, particularly in the black market |
| Stiff competition | Attract customers by advancing empowerment | A growing market in Africa becoming friendlier and more legitimate |
| | Aggressively move north into Africa | Seeing ourselves as an African-based organization |
| | Focus on becoming more client-oriented | Capitalizing on new markets, and sourcing business from the government |
| | Broader product range | |
| | Leveraging empowerment credentials with the government | |
| | Set up business as entrepreneurial units | |
| Lack of incentives for long-term savings, and financial over-extension of a growing black middle class | Shift towards health type benefits and short term investments | |
| HIV/AIDS | Develop AIDS models for products | |
| Poverty | Help local authorities with issues such as AIDS, without attaching conditions like using the name of Metropolitan, to avoid benefiting from people's misfortunes | |
| Lack of research on risk management in South Africa | | |
| Technology is expensive in South Africa, behind on technical skills as well as technology | | |
| Skilled people are leaving country | | |
| Labour market is overstretched and too legalized | | A lot of people available, just needing to be up-skilled; but a higher number of people could be given jobs in the company |

| | | |
|---|---|---|
| A tendency to separate business from the communities and to be too business-like | Participate in education processes rather than just donate money to causes | Bringing in other race groups into management |
| As much as business tries, it is there to make money rather than alleviate poverty: foreign companies are not helping as they do not do much to bring jobs | Employ and develop local people in African countries in which they are operating | Capitalizing on diversity and recognition of cultural differences |
| A situation of flux and changing boundaries in the company, with a changing organization culture | Develop a workplace of enabled and accountable individuals, with everyone with 'soulful' work, to sustain individuals and the organization | Opportunities are limitless for black women especially, and other disadvantaged groups |
| Baggage of the past (apartheid) from some white males in the company inhibiting progress | Change mindsets, and create new culture in company | Massive opportunities to develop and put your ideas forward |
| Resistance to empowerment and employment equity in some areas | | Skills level problem is a misnomer as whites were given jobs because of colour of skins. Now blacks are bringing new skills into the organization. |
| Managers, who have to implement strategy, are not involved in strategic decision-making | Encourage staff to become more entrepreneurial and empowered | |
| Lack of information sharing | Implement a two-year fast-track graduate programme, aimed at black empowerment | |
| Lack of skilled people | | |

to ensure high quality at reasonable prices, to service customers' orders promptly and accurately, and allow their distributors to make a fair profit.

It refers to their responsibilities to employees to be considered as individuals, respecting their dignity and recognizing their merit, giving them a sense of security in their jobs and compensating them fairly and adequately, providing them with clean orderly and safe working conditions, and allowing employees the freedom to make suggestions and complaints. This also includes equal opportunities for employment, development and advancement for those qualified. It also requires the provision of competent management whose actions are just and ethical.

The philosophy states that they are responsible to the communities in which they live and work, and to the world community as well, and for being good citizens through supporting good works and charities and bearing their fair share of taxes, encouraging civic improvement and better health and education, maintaining in good order the property they use, and protecting the environment and natural resources.

The philosophy lastly states that the responsibility is to their stockholders (shareholders), in that the business must make a sound profit. They must experiment with new ideas, carry out research, innovate programmes and pay for mistakes. New equipment must be purchased, new facilities must be provided and new products launched. Reserves must be created to provide for adverse times. By 'operating according to these principles, the stockholders should realise a fair return' (Company Philosophy).

The company's international competitors are all in South Africa, and they compete aggressively in all the product categories the company has. The strategy that the company has employed to address this competition, is to have local manufacturing left in key competency areas. They know they can compete in these areas as they have benchmarked themselves internationally against the other subsidiaries. In any other areas outside these key competencies they will import, or source from a local supplier. In order to be able to make a profit in those particular markets, they source raw material at the best cost-availability. Yet they also spend a lot of money on consumer and trade advertising to build up the visibility of the brands.

To meet the threat from competition, both domestic and international, and to cope with the economic situation within the country, the company has for a long time been a downsizing organization. The 'mean and lean' structure is however a double edged sword, as it has had an impact on people in the company. It impacts negatively on the potential for human resource planning for the future, and this becomes a constraint on the business. In 1982 the company employed about 1,600 people. This is now down to 300.

One of the values emanating from the company's philosophy is social responsibility within the community in which the company operates. When a company downsizes so much that it creates few employment and development opportunities within the community, this value may be difficult to reconcile with the exigencies of a free market economy where companies need to be efficient and competitive. It is often difficult to assess what a company is giving back to the local community in these circumstances. We asked one manager who told us:

The company has contributed to the country's efforts for a long time. They didn't pull out during sanctions. They saw themselves as if they did that they would be helping to perpetuate apartheid. As a business, our contribution worldwide is very small. They could have shut it down. They had concern for the people who worked here. When Mandela was released, they gave employees a free day on full pay. This gave the company a very good name. The company does a lot of work in the community, for example, with the Department of Health and disadvantaged schools, and have made a lot of donations. There is a strong linkage, for example, with the local university, where they are funding a professorship.

It is therefore in this way that the company is contributing to the community, and are trying to reconcile their responsibilities outlined in their published philosophy to the many stakeholders involved: principally addressing the needs to be 'mean and lean' and deliver a return to their shareholders, and at the same time contributing to the local community as stakeholders in the face of employing fewer people from this community.

As with the case of Colgate-Palmolive, this may represent a lack of inclusion of community stakeholders into the decision processes of the organization.

### Relative importance of stakeholders

Jackson (1999) found during his previous study that managers saw their organizations as having a low priority towards employees, managers and local community as stakeholders. They saw their organizations as viewing quality and growth as important key success factors but job satisfaction and success of affirmative action being viewed as of low importance as success factors. Perhaps one of the biggest challenges today in South Africa, as in so many other African countries, is how to reconcile both the need to grow people within the wider society, and for corporations to contribute to that by employment equity and providing development opportunities within the organization, and the need to be globally competitive, to be 'mean and lean' and to develop a profit focus. It may be that the latter position is untenable in Africa and that the logic of downsizing and delayering does not hold true, with such an underdeveloped skills base. There is a need for organizations to be a means to developing people for the future (Jackson, 1999). Organizations, to be effective in South Africa (as well as other African countries) by all other measures apart from profit and financial efficiency, may have to reflect the multiple interests of a broader base of stakeholders, and incorporate these within the strategic objectives of the organization. It may also be in this way that managers can interpret wider the way in which constraints may be turned into opportunities.

Certainly Jackson's (1999) study concluded that companies were driven by the two imperatives of downsizing to respond to financial constraints and commercial imperatives, and responding to the social and developmental needs for affirmative action: hence, a managing of interests from different types of stakeholders. But the study also warned that despite indications of 'best practice' from the three organizations described in the study, the current nature of managers and organizations in South Africa might militate against reconciling such differences. The study (Jackson, 1999) set out to test the proposition in South Africa that organizational culture and management styles reflect a predominantly instrumental orientation, where people as stakeholders within the organization are relatively less important than the corporate (executive) objectives of the organization. Hence developmental and humanistic aspects of people management can be expected to be downplayed, and task concerns to be more prominent.

Managers were asked to indicate the level of importance given by their organization to its various stakeholders (defined as 'those who have an interest in the organization'). In order of importance, managers indicated: customers first, shareholders second, and government third. Of least importance as stakeholder at the bottom of the pile were: suppliers, employees, managers and the local community (Jackson, 1999). This would seem to indicate that managers see their organizations as being focused more towards their business, rather than to their internal stakeholders (employees and managers) and the local community. It also supports a view of the strong influence of government on the different types of organization within South Africa.

We have previously argued that in order to incorporate the interests of multiple stakeholders, organizations must have effective means to give voice to those interests, and incorporate them within the dialogue of the organization, its strategy, objectives, policies and practices, through its decision processes.

## Decision-making

Previous studies of South African organizations suggest that management is conservative and traditional. Based on a legacy of racial discrimination, organizations often have employment practices that are discriminatory, and have adversarial employee relations (Roodt, 1997; Bowmaker-Falconer et al., 1998). Viljoen (1987) found in a sample of 199 companies, that dominant management styles were autocratic in 46 per cent, collaborative in 33 per cent, and participative in 12 per cent of the companies.

In a further study Hofmeyer (1998) found that South African organizations were generally over-managed and under-led: management styles were often seen as rigid, bureaucratic, directive and task-oriented, and sometimes decision-making was over-centralized; and leadership aspects such as direction, vision and effectiveness were often seen as lacking. Hofmeyr (1998) further concluded that his sample was less positive in 1997 than in 1974 regarding South African organizations, and less positive than managers in comparable studies in the United States, although 50 per cent of his sample believed their organizations would change for the better.

With the influence of democratic processes, Western approaches to management, and perhaps even African approaches, organizations may well be looking towards more involvement of its people in the decision process. Hence Jackson (1999) found elements of consultative management, but not participative management. He found that organizations were seen as hierarchical, centralized, fairly rule-bound yet having an element of consultative management.

Only lip service may be being paid to participative management in South African organizations. Often downsizing and delayering leads to 'empowerment' of managers and staff at lower levels of the organization than was previously required (for a review in the Western literature see Cameron, 1994, and Freeman, 1994; see also Chapters 4 and 5 of the current text). This may well lead to the impression of participative management. Yet because of the diversity of interests in South African organizations as in many African countries, participative management may only arise through the active empowerment of all such interest groups. With more than 79 per cent of the management population white, and over 78 per cent of all managers being male (Breakwater Monitor, 2000) full participation in decision-making of all members of the stakeholder populations of organizations may be some way off.

## Decision-making in a Japanese organization

One company that participated in our study is part of a large Japanese manufacturer. It began as a family business with a concession from the Japanese to buy and assemble parts in South Africa. Now the Japanese multinational has acquired nearly 30 per cent of the share capital in the South African organization, after buying out minority shareholders and is set to increase their shareholding to over 35 per cent after de-listing from the Johannesburg Stock Exchange.

We built up a picture of decision-making processes through interviews with six key managers. Overall the culture is seen as conservative with decisions being made top-down, but there is an attempt to be more open and involve people in decision-making. There is a lot of participation in teams. But the teams are not centralized. There is consultation, but only after the decisions are made at the top level. Yet managers do have their own degree of autonomy within their area, although reacting to strategic decisions from high level managers. Tactical decisions about implementation are taken below. It is an example of a flat organization, with most of the decisions taken at the top level, based on information given by employees. Feedback to employees is said to be missing. Employees would like to take part we were told, but this is not always possible. Yet there is a drive to involve people more.

There is an attempt therefore to make the organization more democratic. This appears to be consultative rather than participative. The company started as a family culture, with it being a family-owned company. It still continues with this culture. Hence there is an open door policy right up to the managing director. Decisions are taken through discussion in groups. Nobody takes a decision without it being discussed.

From being a family-owned business with a culture akin to a 'family', the Japanization of the company is having an effect. Hence decision-making is sometimes a long process, and there is also a tendency to have to get decisions from the Japanese top management. Decision-making therefore reflects a combination of influences from the family-owned origins of the company, including both autocratic and open-door principles, and influences from the Japanese multinational where decisions involve a slow process, from the centre, yet involving information flows through such media as groupware communications. A move towards consultation may be partly driven by Japanization, but more likely to stem from the open door family policy together with a desire to make the process more democratic. Yet this is far removed from participation of different interest groups, let alone employees and managers. Decisions from the top are strategic, and implementation involves tactical decision-making by managers up to senior levels. Even some of the general managers feel that they lack input at strategic levels.

The levels of control in an organization also have implications for the nature of decision-making. Again, this appears to reflect the top-down decision-making process where regional offices are provided with decisions from the centre. Although not overly constrained by rules and procedures, staff throughout have to be accountable for their decisions and actions. They have highly visible controls including a lot of regulations and written down procedures in operations facilities.

Generally controls are seen positively, although there may be mixed feelings with a perception that these still work better for previously advantaged white groups than for black groups. They have taken out a lot of the authority levels of the organization and combined grades, so that they no longer have supervisors. Yet this has implications for opportunities and movement up the organization. Equal opportunities and access to decision-making is all part of encompassing decision processes which take account of multiple interests and aspirations within the organization. Certainly the company used to be white (Afrikaans) dominated. Yet this is slowly changing. There is now no reason why anyone should not be developed into any position. But still white males dominate the Board. We were told that they are not in a position merely to window dress to put someone in a position, because business is too tough for that.

In sum, decision-making within the company presents a number of issues, including access to it by the various stakeholders groups, in order to make it more encompassing of these diverse interests at both strategic as well as tactical levels. Although the company is focusing some attention on this, the greater influence of the Japanese corporation does not at this stage seem to be making a difference. Rather it is adding an additional decision-making stratum and process, at the head-office corporate level.

### A split between strategic and tactical decision levels

Certainly the definite split between strategic and tactical decision-making levels is repeated in other organizations in South Africa that participated in our study. All are addressing the old-style autocracy and developing more democratic processes, yet participation in decisions mostly involves interpreting and implementing a brief from the top, rather than managers (let alone staff) participating in and contributing to strategic decisions. Similarly, as we discussed in connection with Colgate-Palmolive, community stakeholders are less likely to participate in strategic or tactical decision-making, even in areas that affect the local community.

We have previously argued that in African societies, as in other communalistic societies, the barriers between community life and organizational life must be reconciled in order to provide a context for commitment and motivation of the workforce (as Dia, 1996, notes, during colonial times institutions alien to African communities were tacked on to African societies, and the legacy of this remains today). This may go hand in hand with bringing in a form of participation that involves stakeholder interests from the community as well as within the corporation.

## Commitment and motivation

As we have previously seen (Chapter 7), Blunt and Jones (1992) suggest that African employees (in sub-Saharan African countries) have an instrumental view of their work organization: that is, they work in order to earn money to pay for what they need in life. There is an indication of a lack of commitment to the organization by employees therefore. Jackson (2002a) proposes that of collectivistic societies, corporations in Japan have been successful in harnessing the wider societal collectivism to corporate life, in order to foster commitment by employees in a reciprocal relationship with the corporation, although they may not operate like this in other countries, and this may not be directly applicable in South Africa (as the Japanese organization discussed above attests). Corporations in most other collectivistic societies have failed to do this, and this is mostly due to the legacies of colonial institutions and their failure to integrate with their host societies. Jackson (1999) partially investigated this aspect within the context of managers' and employees' motivation in South African corporations.

Managers (from a predominantly black sample) were asked to rank in order of importance to them various aspects of life both within and outside of work. Giving plenty of time to my family was ranked number one. Making work central in my life was number two. Being actively involved in the community was ranked third. Pursuing my religion was ranked fourth, and pursuing my leisure activities was ranked last. This seems to indicate, not an alienation from the workplace, but a primacy of family life in one's total life. The fact that work life and community life were ranked second and third indicates the importance of these aspects as well, without indicating how well integrated these aspects are (Jackson, 1999).

Jackson's (1999) study also included an organizational climate survey of 200 employees in three organizations. This indicated that there was generally higher satisfaction with working conditions, content of job and job security, yet lower satisfaction with appraisal systems, recognition of employee worth, union-management relations among other factors and the extent to which employees felt involved in matters that affected them. This may well be indicative of the extent to which employees in South Africa feel separated from decision-making (discussed above, p. 260), although there was no indication of a low level of disengagement from the corporation.

The same study seems to indicate differences among cultural groups, as managers from other cultural groups were more negative than white managers regarding equal opportunities and the implementation of affirmative action. Respondents at higher management levels were generally more positive than those at lower levels regarding their perceptions of organizational culture (see also our current results for South Africa in Chapters 5 and 7).

### Commitment and motivation in the Japanese organization

The Japanese company included in our study appears to be grappling with conflicting pressures, as well as different management principles when it comes to addressing staff motivation and commitment. One of the most senior managers we interviewed explained:

> We are going through major changes at the moment and people don't always grasp the importance of those as they are not aware of the outcomes. Those that know where they are going are more comfortable with the change. But we do have very loyal employees. . . . We don't pay above average increases. I believe we should give bonuses but we don't. We have a low staff turnover. We give internal people a chance of upcoming jobs first, and then we go outside.

Another manager reinforced this:

> When you talk motivation everyone is looking for an extra pay cheque. But this doesn't happen in this company. We are not very creative about motivation. All get the same, if one doesn't do a good job – you get the same. It is difficult to motivate people.

If money is not used as a motivator, what is? One manager told us: 'we motivate people by communication. This has been undertaken by the staff development and communication programme'. The General Manager, Human Resources explains.

> We deliberately involve people. This is what we want it to be like. We aim at employees who are fully trained, motivated and are passionate about their work. We put everybody through a two-day management session, getting people to take full responsibility as if they are running their own business. Also to make sure people are marketable: so that the company itself could employ you. Practising Kaisen, and '13 work habits' are part of this programme. We can't motivate people by money – so we try to create a climate where people can fulfil their dreams. This is part of the targets set for managers: to ensure people are motivated. We also have a family day occasionally on a Saturday. We have an annual feedback day where people are told what we are achieving. We have staff awards, where people are identified and recognized.

The programme is customer driven, and is said to be 'a total business philosophy based on customer satisfaction' and 'way of life'. This is undertaken in the company by a number of training sessions where employees and managers are encouraged to adopt '13 new work habits':

> become quick-change agents; commit fully to our jobs; be as responsive as possible; accept ambiguity and uncertainty; behave as though we are in business for ourselves; constantly improve our levels of knowledge; hold ourselves

accountable for outcomes; add value; see ourselves as individual service centres; take control of our own morale; practise Kaisen; be fixers, not finger-pointers; and positively alter our expectations.

Despite these efforts, company surveys still reflect a perception of the company as authoritarian, with top-down decision-making, although successive surveys have shown an improvement. Yet staff turnover is low. However, this may also have a down side because movement through the organization may be slow with limited promotion opportunities. There are lots of people who have been doing the same jobs for several years. The need for a mean and lean organization may further reduce opportunities through downsizing and may well affect motivation levels. Yet expansion into new markets may provide the key to the lack of promotion opportunities.

The nature of opportunities may also be seen to be changing where 'employment is stronger for the previously disadvantaged', as one manager told us. The Employment Equity General Manager expanded on this: 'Rewarding and fulfilling assignments were only given to white people with unequal distribution of resources. . . . You find pockets of good managers who keep employees motivated. Many do not and there are a lot of problems involving pay and equal opportunities.'

These conflicting pressures are not unique to this company: a need to be competitive and lean, a need to be customer focused, a need to motivate employees through greater involvement and through creating opportunities, and a need to respond to Employment Equity Legislation. In this case the company's programme may provide an appropriate means to integrate customer needs and employee satisfaction. However, the extent to which motivation and staff commitment strategies make a link between staff's cultural values within the community and their home life, and life at work may still be an issue that is largely not addressed in South African corporations.

The way a corporation pays attention to employee commitment and motivation through integrating the links between corporation and community, the bringing in of different stakeholder interests and the regard for its people, is driven by its management systems: that is its principles, policies and practices. In South Africa, as in other African countries, these systems are culturally influenced through an admixture of post-colonial, Western (and perhaps Eastern) and African inputs. The management of these inputs in hybrid systems of management that are likely to be adaptive, rather than mal-adaptive, to their African context may depend to a large extent on managers' abilities to recognize and articulate these cultural influences.

## Leadership and management principles

One of the concerns of the study by Jackson (1999) was the apparent antithesis between Western and non-Western ideas of organization and management: between an idea of people as a resource (human resource management) and people with a value in themselves (as encapsulated in the word *ubuntu*, from the aforementioned Xhosa proverb 'Ubuntu ungamntu ngabanye abantu' – people are people through other people). It may be possible to reconcile this antithesis, but it would seem logical that before this can happen, managers should be aware of these different perspectives. Within this study (Jackson, 1999), and the predominantly black management sample, managers saw themselves as generally oriented towards the view of an intrinsic value of people for themselves rather than as a means to an end of the organization. The consensus was that people should be valued in their own right, they should be consulted, and they should be treated fairly and ethically in an organization that is not merely concerned with short-term results and making profits or gaining results above all else. However, they more favoured the view of the organization regarding people as a valuable resource rather than the well-being of people being the objective of the organization.

Whilst the study indicated that organizations are making strides to address the developmental aspects of people, there still seems to be a gap between humanistic and developmental intentions of organizations and their somewhat instrumental orientation. The fact that organizations were often seen as hierarchical, authoritarian and rule bound, and that they were trying to move towards a results focused operation

## Management principles in Western District Municipality

Western District Municipality is a local government organization, operating in an area of approximately 60,000 km within the western part of the Eastern Cape province. It is responsible for such functions as the supply of water, refuse schemes, health services, roads and local councils, and functions involved in the establishment, improvement and maintenance of infrastructural services and facilities.

There does not seem to be an articulation of a particular South African management approach here. However, given the diversity of both the top and middle level management, such an approach seems to be more implicit than explicitly expressed. Top management included four who were black, one who was coloured and two who were white, while middle management consisted of nine who were black, two who were coloured, nine who were white and one Indian. Even though no specific reference was made to the South African *ubuntu* approach to management, some of its principles were implicitly evident. But because cultural diversity was not addressed, the organizational culture was laced with misunderstanding and a lack of trust amongst management as well as between management and staff members. Against this background, the type of organizational culture, management practices and principles at the municipality may well be a product of the legacies of the past. Table 12.2 provides examples of responses from four managers on the management attributes currently in the organization, the way they would like it, and the way they think it is going.

Table 12.2 Management responses for nature of management principles in Western District Municipality

| Respondent | The way my organization is at the moment | The way I would like my organization to be | The way my organization is going |
|---|---|---|---|
| White female | My organization does not manage change<br>Its leaders are not willing to take decisions and implement them<br>We are reactive and not proactive<br>Scared of taking risks and lead<br>Management does not recognize achievements and work in a team<br>They feel threatened | Dynamic, proactive, achievement is recognized<br>Employees are made responsible and accountable<br>Team work is encouraged<br>People are supported and encouraged to reach their full potential<br>Vision, willing to take risks | From bad to worse. |
| White female | In a state of uncertainty regarding its future due to legislation, financial constraints and there appears to be no common goal at top management level | Goal orientated with clear plans of action in how to achieve its goals.<br>More focused towards the communities served by the organization | It seems to be falling apart! |
| Black female | Has set objectives, but does not have the organizational structure as a mechanism to implement them | An organization that manages by objectives; with managers that have both management and leadership skills. This will ensure that the organization achieves its objectives, utilizing its employees as human beings and effectively | It is trying to restructure itself to implement the goals of the national government:<br>if they are doing it the right way I am not sure!<br>I do not think there is team-work in the whole process.<br>If implementing mechanisms are not good, I fear that there will be a strategic drift in future |
| Black male | High level management in certain departments, do not delegate functions | To understand and respect each other's mandates and achievements<br>To encourage and motivate all employees | Has high mistrust attitude towards other level of management<br>Centralized decision-taking, even minor issues |

as well as encouraging more employee participation, indicates a move from post-colonial influences towards Western influences (Jackson, 1999). This is reflected in a number of other studies (although Hofmeyr's, 1998, findings indicated a lack of optimism about the change from the one to the other).

To a large extent, creating a greater awareness among key managers of the influences of different management principles and how this can be integrated into appropriate practices, involves a more comprehensive understanding of the different cultures unique to South Africa. This involves more than simply the management of diversity. In addition, a recognition and thorough understanding of different cultures by both management and staff is required. If done successfully, it can set an example to the rest of local authority institutions in South Africa, and indeed to the rest of Africa.

Yet it may also be that there is still a low articulation of an 'African' approach (even within a largely black managed organization such as the municipality), and very little evidence that, for example, *ubuntu* principles are being applied. This may be in part due to a lack of articulation about these different influences, as a result of a lack of conscious management of multiculturalism not only at the macro-level of management systems, but also at the level of managing a culturally diverse workforce with different expectations about the way people should be managed.

## The management of multiculturalism

The management of multiculturalism can be undertaken from a number of perspectives. In South Africa, as in most African countries, this would involve not only managing differences in culture and gender from the point of view of understanding different cultures, it would also involve managing the power relations that are bound up with the relationships among people of different cultures (see, for example, Human, 1996b). A huge distortion in the relative power of different cultural groups exists as a result of apartheid in South Africa. In other countries with large white settler populations, such as Zimbabwe, such distortions also still exist, as they do in most other African countries between dominant and subordinate cultural groups, either at country or corporate level. In South Africa, managing such relationships involves compliance to employment equity legislation on the one hand in order to redress the imbalances between dominant and disadvantaged groups both at corporate and country level, and consciously managing the process of multicultural working on the other hand.

### The Breakwater Monitor

Figures from the Breakwater Monitor (2000) which monitors employment equity in South Africa through some 200 voluntarily participating organizations, indicates that in 2000 9.52 per cent of managers were African, 5.53 per cent were Indian, 5.31 per cent were coloured and 79.64 per cent were white. Of the total 78.66 per cent were male and 21.34 per cent were female. The relative power balance of ethnic groups within these sample companies may be deduced if the managerial populations are

## Managing multiculturalism in Metropolitan

Empowerment is a large part of the identity and image of Metropolitan. Empowerment is also a large part of how intercultural relations are managed. It raises the question not only of how these relations are managed, but also of the access to decision-making processes and resources, such as promotion opportunities, that are available to different groups of people. The preamble to New Africa Capital's (the holding company) Empowerment Code states:

> NAC will implement corrective processes aimed at rectifying the inequalities and inequities of the past and ensuring that historically disadvantaged people have an equal opportunity and the ability to maximize their participation in and ownership of the business and the benefits they derive from it. These processes will focus on the deracialisation, transformation and normalisation of the business.

Implicit within the impetus to deracialize, transform and normalize the business is the addressing of inter-ethnic relationships, including the distribution of power and access to resources among different groups. Of the twelve managers we interviewed five were white, four were black, and three were coloured or Asian. There were some difference among these groups as to the perception of intercultural relations and how they are managed within the company.

One white manager remarked that relations are

> fairly good. If not good, then there are processes to let off steam, to deal with issues. People have learnt more about their fellow South Africans. We were at the forefront as an empowerment company. However, many people don't mix outside work. They go to different areas and houses.

Another echoed the positive aspect of this: 'Three years ago we didn't have so much diversity. Now we have. In my division it works well. We do a regular cultural audit, and there are no problems.' However, another white manager has reservations:

> There is mutual respect because people are in a position and living up to expectations. People are polite, but it is difficult to know how much is natural or what is forced, because we are trying to be politically correct. I mean them as well as us. Coloured people are stuck in the middle. So we say, if you are not white you are black – and therefore previously disadvantaged. In workshops blacks here said that white women should not be included in empowerment.

Another white manager is somewhat more critical of the general situation: 'Things are far from where we would like to be. There is still suspicion and distrust. There is a lot of resentment from white males [throughout the country], which is impacting negatively.'

As one manager suggests above, coloured people are struck in the middle. This may also apply to the Asian managers. One Asian manager stated that intercultural relations are

> fairly good. We don't have any hang-ups in my division. There is a debate opening up. The company is giving people the opportunity to talk. We have workshops to talk about these things. It was predominantly an Afrikaans organization. I have seen the changes over the years. There is a lot of tolerance.

Another manager suggested that relations are 'fairly good, but not brilliant. But there is caution among certain ethnic groups. In the cafeteria ethnic groups stick together.'

There is therefore an indication that attention is being paid to these issues, through, for example, empowerment workshops. However, one black manager indicated one of the outcomes of tension, which is not being addressed:

> There is a lot of guilt that my white counterparts carry. So they treat me carefully. You sometimes look for the warmth of [professional] relationships and think, how long are they going to carry on this guilt? This creates a problem on evaluating performance. People are careful. I have warned that managers should be careful of bending over backwards for their black staff. People don't know how to behave in this situation.

compared with the total representation of these four racial groupings within these organizations. These are 49.20 per cent for Africans, 5.63 per cent for Indians, 14.42 per cent for coloured and 30.76 per cent for whites. Of these, 72.07 per cent are male and 27.93 per cent are female (Breakwater Monitor, 2000). There still appears to be considerable room for further redressing the power balances in corporations among the racial groupings.

Although training courses in intercultural management and awareness sessions address issues of interaction, they may add very little directly to addressing issues arising from power imbalances within corporations that are culturally related. Nor do they address imbalances within the total stakeholder population. Just looking at this statistically, the racial split in the population of the Breakwater Monitor is fairly representative of the Economically Active Population according to the 1999

Household Survey (although it over-represents whites, and under-represents African females), yet this does not reflect the total population as indicated above (75.5 per cent African, 2.5 per cent Asian, 8.6 per cent coloured and 13.1 per cent white in the 1991 census). Simply the number of Africans outside the economically active populations indicates a disparity in power relations among the racial groups in the total stakeholder community.

With these imbalances, which are historically derived and still prevalent, it is difficult for corporations to argue that simply complying with the legislation is sufficient. Proactively managing across cultures would seem necessary in order to redress some of the power imbalances by building awareness, but also developing general cross-cultural competencies. Because of the multicultural nature of South African society and corporations, South African management seems highly placed to take a lead in developing innovative ways to manage multiculturalism. By the very nature of the ethnic composition of African countries generally, the growing stress on regional cooperation among African countries, for example within SADC, and the intercultural influences of post-colonial, Western (and Eastern) and African influences, effective managing in Africa is premised on effectively managing cross-culturally.

Approaches to this seem to fall into two camps: maximalist and minimalist (Human, 1996a). Maximalist approaches are content-focused and involve providing descriptions of different cultures. Much of this work is typically built on Hofstede's (1980a) work of distinguishing country cultural groups by reference to broad value orientations. For example Boysen's (2001) research in South Africa concludes that: black managers are more collectivist than white managers who are more individualistic; white managers show a higher intolerance for uncertainty than black managers; white and black managers show no significant differences in power distance; black managers measure higher than white managers on humane orientation (that is the degree to which a society encourages and rewards fairness, altruism, generosity and kindness as opposed to aggressiveness and hostile actions); white managers measure higher than black managers on assertiveness and gender egalitarianism (masculinity as opposed to femininity); white managers score higher on performance orientation than black managers (the extent to which society encourages and rewards achievement and excellence). McFarlin *et al.* (1999) generally supports this type of model, and concludes that one of the main purposes of management development in South Africa should be to enable management to be more sensitive to an African and Africanized workforce, and to move towards Afrocentric approaches to training and development, that is, moving corporations towards a more African-based value system.

Human (1996a and 1996b) is critical of the maximalist approach which, she claims, creates stereotypes. As these stereotypes are value-laden they have serious implications for both how individuals and groups perceive themselves and how they are perceived by others. They therefore acquire a self-fulfilling nature. Previously these led to perceptions about the inferiority of black cultures from both blacks and whites. She contends that more recently there have been perceptions created, for example through the *ubuntu* movement, that African approaches are 'nice' and that managers should be aiming to acquire more Africanized approaches. She argues for a 'minimalist' position which 'takes an interactional approach to culture and argues that culture constitutes a subconscious part of a person's identity as a communicator and is therefore constructed to a large extent by the perception of the other party in the interaction' (Human, 1996b: 51).

One conclusion that may be drawn from this discussion is that in order to effectively manage across cultures, it is necessary to have an awareness of the types of stereotypes with which one is working, in order to overcome some of the negatives, and focus on the positive aspects of cross-cultural working: to see multiculturalism as a positive aspect whereby different stakeholders from different cultural perspectives can make a variety of contributions, and where this input is not simply desirable, it is necessary to economic and social prosperity. A starting point in this is for individuals to have a high awareness of their own cultural background, its values, and the contribution that their values, perceptions and expectations can make.

Perhaps one of the major problems with the maximalist approach described above, is that concepts such as those developed by Hofstede (1980a) may describe national culture in a very general way, but they do not provide enough detail and sensitivity to describe the many different cultures represented in South African society, and indeed the numerous cultures within sub-Saharan Africa. They also do not provide the means for describing the manifestations of those cultures in corporate life. For example, there has been much debate around the concept of collectivism: that it is target specific and that its influence on corporate life may vary considerably among countries (Hui, 1990), let alone within culturally heterogeneous countries such as South Africa. More specific information is needed about the way people feel about their own culture, and about the way they feel about others' cultures.

Also relevant here is Human's (1996b) charge of the maximalist approach that it gives rise to self-fulfilling stereotypes that colour a person's perceptions of themselves. For example, this may give rise to negative views of the value of one's culture among black Africans who have acquired such views through the legacy of apartheid, or (in common with the educated elite in other African countries) through receiving a Western or Westernized education that has had the effect of downgrading African culture in relation to Western culture.

It is only very recently that there has been an articulation of the relation of African culture to management through the work of such authors as Mbigi (1997; Mbigi and Maree, 1995) in South Africa. Other African countries may be lagging behind in this articulation. White managers in South Africa may yet be lacking in confidence to clearly articulate the relation of their culture to management in the wake of apartheid, or simply from an assumption of the universality of management principles (see, for example, Hofstede, 1980b) through an education heavily influenced by American/Western traditions.

In a multicultural context, the lack of understanding and articulation of the nature and influence of one's culture may be a serious stumbling block to building synergies from cultural diversity. Yet Human (1996b) argues that this is not enough. A clear understanding of the way power relations impact on stereotyping of groups and on the perceptions of individuals and the expectation one has of such individuals is necessary. She goes on to describe the managing diversity skills training programme in which she has been involved with companies in South Africa. This is designed first to make managers aware of the negative impact of the maintenance of inaccurate stereotypes and resulting expectations based on power relations that are transmitted through ideas relating to culture. Second it attempts to make managers understand themselves. Third it attempts to provide the communication skills that are needed to minimize the impact of negative stereotypes and expectations, and to reinforce the process by which more accurate (and presumably more positive) stereotypes may occur. This is all dependent on a high level of awareness of one's self and other's culture, and the perceptions and expectations that have occurred as a result of the legacies of the past. Applied to other parts of Africa, this may involve grappling with many of the legacies of colonialism, and its impact on cultural perceptions and stereotypes.

## Training and development

McFarlin *et al.* (1999) argue that management development in South Africa still reflects strategies used by the European colonial powers, and have been dominated by rationalism, individualism and autocracy. They further argue that Western approaches have a high degree of legitimacy, while African co-operative and communal philosophies are ignored. This has an effect of predominantly white managers pushing a largely 'Third World' workforce to accept 'First World' productivity standards and value systems. They suggest that this is why efforts at 'modernization', which include merit pay systems and formal grievance procedures, have largely failed as they ignore local cultural values. After arguing that the first stage to more appropriate management development and training is an aggressive affirmative action process, they urge that South Africa needs to develop its own unique approach that builds in both the context and the indigenous philosophies and values. This, they suggest, should include values of: personal trust as a moral base rather than 'cold' approaches to eliminating unfairness; interdependence, emphasizing cooperative relations and wealth being best achieved through a pragmatic but humanistic approach to business; and spiritualism, combining celebration and ceremonies with leadership that provides moral guidance.

A number of organizations in South Africa have taken up management development processes that incorporate the values of *ubuntu* (Swartz and Davies, 1997), yet this may be far from widespread. The hegemony of Western management principles, bound up with the type of power relations discussed above, may take time to supersede. The development of adaptive hybrid management systems in South Africa, through concerted efforts of employment equity and appropriate cross-cultural training that reflects the propositions here discussed, may be the way forward, not only for management in South Africa, but in sub-Saharan Africa as a whole.

## Implications for managers

In this chapter we have tried to provide an account of the way management has been developed and adapted in South Africa. We have not tried to show that all is perfect, as it clearly is not. Yet managers in South Africa have developed a whole repertoire of skills and expertise that may not be available elsewhere. Such competencies as the ability to manage in a complex multicultural situation may be in demand anywhere in the world. However, complacency and even arrogance that closes off learning from other parts of Africa may be problematic. Other African countries may have much to learn from managers in South Africa, but the converse is also true. Successfully managing across cultures in Nigeria, managing power relations and the informal organization in Cameroon, and marrying different management philosophies and developing successful hybrid forms in Kenya may all have something to teach South African managers, and indeed managers anywhere in the world.

Although this chapter effectively brings us to the end of this book, we are not necessarily giving South African managers the last word. Yet we do feel that the best self-articulation of the issues and possibly some solutions have emanated from South Africa. This is not to say that the rest of Africa has nothing to offer. However, it is to say that there is an under-articulation of what sub-Saharan African countries have to offer global management generally. One of the purposes of this book has been to begin the process of that articulation, and to begin to make clearer, by cutting through some of the fog, what Africa can offer both itself and the rest of the world.

# References

Abdulai, A.I. (2000) Human resource management in Ghana: prescriptions and issues raised by the Fourth Republican Constitution, *The International Journal of Public Sector Management*, 13(5), 447–66.

Abudu, F. (1986) Work attitudes of Africans, with special reference to Nigeria, *International Studies of Management and Organization*, 16(2), 17–36.

Achebe, C. (1983) *The Trouble with Nigeria*, Oxford: Heinemann.

Adedeji, A. (1999) Comparative strategies of economic decolonization in Africa, in A.A. Mazrui (ed.) *Africa Since 1935, Vol. VIII of UNESCO General History of Africa*, Berkeley, CA: James Currey, pp. 393–431.

Adigun, I.O. (1995) Effects of domestic multiculturalism on job attitudes in Nigeria: a research note, *The International Journal of Human Resource Management*, 6(4), 910–29.

Adler, N.J. (1991) *International Dimensions of Organizational Behaviour*, second edition, Boston: PWS-Kent.

African Development Report (2000) *Regional Integration in Africa*, African Development Bank, Oxford: Oxford University Press.

African Development Indicators (2001) *African Development Indicators 2001*, Washington: The World Bank.

Ahluwalia, P. (2001) *Politics and Post-Colonial Theory: African Inflections*, London: Routledge.

Akinnusi, D.M. (1991) Personnel management in Africa: a comparative analysis of Ghana, Kenya and Nigeria, in C. Brewster and S. Tyson (eds) *International Comparisons in Human Resource Management*, London: Pitman, pp.159–72.

Allinson, C.W. and Hayes, J. (1988) The learning styles questionnaire: an alternative to Kolb's inventory, *Journal of Management Studies*, 25(3), 269–81.

Allinson, R. (1993) *Global Disasters: Inquiries into Management Ethics*, New York: Prentice Hall.

Allport, G.W. (1939) Attitudes, in C. Murchison (ed.) *Handbook of Social Psychology*, Worcester, MA: Clark University Press.

Ankomah, K. (1985) African culture and social structures and development of effective public administration and management systems, *Indian Journal of Public Administration*, 30, 393–413.

Anyanwu, S.O. (1998) The human factor and economic development in Africa, in V.G. Chivaura and C.G. Mararike (eds) *The Human Factor Approach to Development in Africa*, Harare: University of Zimbabwe Publications, pp. 66–75.

Argyris, C. (1992) *On Organizational Learning*, Oxford and Cambridge, MA: Blackwell.

Armstrong, M. (1999) *A Handbook of Human Resource Management*, London: Kogan Page.

Arthur, W. Jr., Woehr, D.J., Akande, A. and Strong, M.H. (1995) Human resource management in West Africa: practices and perceptions, *The International Journal of Human Resource Management*, 6(2), 347–67.

Aycan, Z., Kanungo, R.N. and Sinha, J.B.P (1999) Organizational culture and human resource management practices: the model of cultural fit, *Journal of Cross-Cultural Psychology*, 30(4), 501–26.

Ayittey, G.B.N. (1991) *Indigenous African Institutions*, New York: Transnational Publishers.

Ayittey, G.B.N. (1999) How the multilateral institutions compounded Africa's economic crisis, *Law and Policy in International Business*, Summer 1999, sourced at http://global. umi.com, to which version page numbers refer.

Bae, K. and Chung, C. (1997), Cultural values and work attitudes of Korean industrial workers in comparison with those of the United States and Japan, *Work and Occupations*, 24(1), 80–96.

Balogun, M.J. (1989) The African culture and social structure: lessons from contemporary public administration, in *AAPAM, The Ecology of Public Administration in Africa*, Vikas.

Banai, M. (2002) A test of Etzioni's control–compliance model: in Israeli Kibbutzim, *International Journal of Cross Cultural Management*, 2(2), 155–70.

Barr, A. and Oduro, A. (2001) *Ethnic Fractionalization in an African Labour Market*, Oxford: Centre for the Study of African Economics, University of Oxford.

Barratt-Brown, M. (1995) *Africa's Choices: After Thirty Years of the World Bank*, London: Penguin.

Baruch, Y. and Clancy, P. (2000) Managing AIDS in Africa: HRM Challenges in Tanzania, *International Journal of Human Resource Management*, 11(4): 789–806.

Bazemore, G. and Thai, K.V. (1995) Institutional and management building in sub-Saharan Africa: the role of training, *International Journal of Public Administration*, 18(9), 1447–83.

Beals, R. (1953), Acculturation, in A.L. Kroebner (ed.) (1953) *Anthropology Today*, Chicago: University of Chicago Press.

Beaty, D.T. (1998) Colgate Palmolive in Post-Apartheid South Africa, reprinted in G. Oddou and M. Mendenhall (eds) *Cases in International Organizational Behavior*, Malden, MA: Blackwell, pp. 136–42.

Beer, M. and Spector, B. (1985) Corporate wide transformations in human resource management, in R.E. Walton and P.R. Lawrence (eds) *Human Resource Management: Trends and Challenges*, Boston, MA: Harvard Business School Press, pp. 219–253.

Bentham, J. (1789/1970) *An Introduction to the Principles of Morals and Legislation*, J.H. Burns and H.L.A. Harts (eds), London: University of London Press.

Berg-Schlosser, D. (1994) Ethnicity, social classes and the political process in Kenya, in W.O. Oyugi, *Politics and Administration in East Africa*, Nairobi: East African Educational Publishers, 1994.

Berry, J.W., Poortinga, Y.H., Segall, M.H. and Dasen, P.R. (1992) *Cross-cultural Psychology: Research and Application*, Cambridge: Cambridge University Press.

Beugré, C.D. and Offodile, O.F. (2001) Managing for organizational effectiveness in sub-Saharan Africa: a culture-fit model, *International Journal of Human Resource Management*, 12(4), 535–50.

Biko, S. (1984) Some African cultural concepts, *Frank Talk*, 1(4: September/October) 29–31, and reprinted in P.H. Coetzee and A.P.J. Roux (eds) (1998) *Philosophy from Africa: A Text with Readings*, Johannesburg: International Thomson Publishing, p. 26.

Binet, J. (1970) *Psychologie Economique Africaine*, Paris: Payot.

Blunt, P. and Jones, M.L. (1992) *Managing Organizations in Africa*, Berlin: Walter de Gruyter.

Blunt, P. and Jones, M.L. (1997) Exploring the limits of Western leadership theory in East Asia and Africa, *Personnel Review*, 26(1/2), 6–23.

Blunt, P. (1976) Management motivation in Kenya : some initial impressions, *Journal of Eastern African Research and Development*, 6(1), 11–21.

Boahen, A.A. and Webster, J.B. (1970) *History of Africa*, New York: Praeger.

Boon, M. (1996) *The African Way: The Power of Interactive Leadership*, Johannesburg: Zebra Press.

Boysen, L. (2001) Cultural influences among white and black managers in South Africa, *Management Today*, Yearbook 2001, 32–35.

Bovin, O. (1998) Towards a learning organization, in *Management Development*, Geneva: International Labour Office, 1998, pp. 357–77.

Bowmaker-Falconer, A., Horwitz, F., Jain, H., and Tagger, S. (1998) Employment equality programmes in South Africa, *Industrial Relations Journal*, 29(3), 222–33.

Boyacigiller, N.A. and Adler, N.J. (1991) The parochial dinosaur: organizational science in a global context, *Academy of Management Review*, 16(2), 262–90.

Brady, F.N. (1990) *Ethical Managing: Rules and Results*, London: Macmillan.

Breakwater Monitor (2000) *Breakwater Monitor Report 2000/1*, University of Cape Town Graduate School of Management: Cape Town, South Africa.

Breytenbach, W. (1999) The history and destiny of national minorities in the African renaissance: the case for better boundaries, in M.W. Makgoba (ed.) *African Renaissance: The New Struggle*, Sandton, SA: Mafube/Cape Town: Tafelberg, pp. 91–100.

Brown, D. (1989) Bureaucracy as an issue in Third World Management: an African case study, *Public Administration and Development*, 9, 369–80.

Burawoy, M. (1972) Another look at the mineworker, *African Social Research*, 14, 239–87.

Busia, K.A. (1951) *The Position of the Chief in the Modern Political System of Ashanti*, Oxford: Oxford University Press.

Cameron, K.S. (1994) Strategies for successful downsizing, *Human Resource Management*, 33(2), 189–211.

Carlsson, J. (1998) Organization and leadership in Africa, in L. Wohlgemuth, J. Carlsson and H. Kifle (eds) *Institution Building and Leadership in Africa*, Uppsala, Sweden: Nordiska Afrikainstitutet, pp. 13–32.

Chen, M. (1995) *Asian Management Systems*, New York: Routledge.

Child, J. (1994) *Management in China During the Age of Reform*, Cambridge: Cambridge University Press.

Chinese Cultural Connection (1987) Chinese values and the search for culture-free dimensions of culture, *Journal of Cross-Cultural Psychology*, 18, 143–64.

Chivaura, V.G. (1998) European culture in Africa and human factor development, in V.G. Chivaura and C.G. Mararike (eds) *The Human Factor Approach to Development in Africa*, Harare: University of Zimbabwe Publications, pp. 97–110.

Chivaura, V.G. and Mararike, C.G. (eds) (1998) *The Human Factor Approach to Development in Africa*, Harare: University of Zimbabwe Publications.

Chombo, Ignatius (1998) The human factor and education content in Zimbabwe, in V.G. Chivaura and C.G. Mararike (eds) *The Human Factor Approach to Development in Africa*, Harare: University of Zimbabwe Publications, pp. 44–57.

Choudury, A.M. (1986) The community concept of business: a critique, *International Studies in Management and Organization*, 16(2), 79–95.

CIA World Factbook (2003) Cameroon, http//www.cia.gov/cia/publications/factbook/geos/cm.html, 07/10/03.

Cole, R.E. (1979) *Work, Mobility and Participation*, Berkeley: University of California Press.

Collier, P. (1997) Africa: problems and prospects, *Economic Review*, November, 4–6.

Cooke, B. and Kothari, U. (eds) (2002) *Participation: The New Tyranny?*, London: Zed Books.

Courade, G. (2000) *Le Désarroi Camerounais. L'Epreuve de l'Economie-Monde*, Paris: Editions Karthala.

Cray, D. and Mallory, G.R. (1998) *Making Sense of Managing Culture*, London: Thomson.

Crowder, M. (1999) Africa under British and Belgian domination, 1935–45, in Mazrui, A.A. (ed.) *General History of Africa: VIII Africa Since 1935*, Paris: UNESCO, pp. 76–101.

Dahl, R.A. (1957) The concept of power, *Behavioural Science*, 2, 201–18.

Davidson, B. (1992) *The Black Man's Burden: Africa and the Curse of the Nation-State*, Oxford: James Currey.

de Boer, C. (1978) The polls: attitudes towards work, *Public Opinion Quarterly*, 42, 414–23.

de Heusch, L. (1995) Rwanda: responsibilities for a genocide, *Anthropology Today*, 11(4), 3–7.

de Sardan, J.P.O. (1999) A moral economy of corruption in Africa? *The Journal of Modern African Studies*, 37(1), 25–52.

de Waal, A. (1994) Genocide in Rwanda, *Anthropology Today*, 10(3), 1–2.

Derr, C.B., Roussillon, S. and Bournois, F. (eds) (2002) *Cross-cultural Approaches to Leadership Development*, Westport, CT: Quorum.

Dia, A.L. (1990) Le management Africain: mythe ou réalité? *African Development*, 15(1), 61–78.

Dia, M. (1996) *Africa's Management in the 1990s and Beyond*, Washington, DC: World Bank.

Dondo, A. and Ngumo, M. (1998) Africa: Kenya in A. Morrison (ed.) *Entrepreneurship: An International Perspective*, Oxford: Butterworth-Heinemann, pp. 15–26.

Doz, Y., Prahalad, C.K. and Hamal, G. (1990) Control, change and flexibility: the dilemma of transnational collaboration, in C.A. Bartlet, Y. Doz and G. Hedlund (eds) *Managing the Global Firm*, London: Routledge, pp. 117–143.

Dumont, R. (1960) *False Start in Africa*, London: Andre Deutsch.

Durkheim, E. (1915/1971) *The Elementary Forms of the Religious Life*, London: George Allen and Unwin.

Earley, P.C. and Mosakowski, P.M. (1998) Creating hybrid team cultures: an empirical test of transnational team functioning, Working paper. Indiana University.

Elron, E., Shamir, B. and Ben-Ari, E. (1999), Why don't they fight each other? Cultural diversity and operational unity in multinational peacekeeping forces, *Armed Forces and Society*, 26, 73–98.

England, G.W. (1975) *The Manager and His Values: An International Perspective*, Cambridge, MA: Ballinger.

Etzioni, A. (1975) *A Comparative Analysis of Complex Organizations*, New York, NY: The Free Press, 1975.

Eze, N. (1989) Developing successful management in Africa through psychological strategies, *Management in Nigeria*, March/April: 40–55 and May/June: 46–8.

Fashoyin, T. and Matanmi, S. (1996) Democracy, labour and development: transforming industrial relations in Africa, *Industrial Relations Journal*, 27(1), 38–49.

Fiedler, F. (1967) *A Theory of Leadership Effectiveness*, New York: McGraw-Hill.

Flyvbjerg, B. (2001) *Making Social Science Matter*, Cambridge: Cambridge Uniersity Press.

Freeman, S.J. (1994) Oranizational downsizing as convergence or reorientation: implications for human resource management, *Human Resource Management*, 33(2), 213–38.

Freund, J. (1972) *The Sociology of Max Weber*, Harmondsworth: Penguin.

Gannon, M.J. (1994) The Nigerian marketplace, in M.J. Gannon, *Understanding Global Cultures: Metaphoric Journeys Through 17 Countries*, Thousand Oaks, CA: Sage, pp. 233–52.

Gannon, M.J. and Karen L. Newman (2002) *The Blackwell Handbook of Cross-cultural Management*, Oxford: Blackwell.

Gelfand, M. (1973) *The Genuine Shona*, Harare: Mambo Press.

Gethaiga, W. (1998), Language, culture and human factor development, in V.G. Chivaura and C.G. Mararike (eds) *The Human Factor Approach to Development in Africa*, Harare: University of Zimbabwe Publications, pp. 111–120.

Gibbs, J.L. Jr (ed.) (1965) *Peoples of Africa*, New York: Holt Rinehart and Winston.

Gluckman, M. (1956) *Custom and Conflict in Africa*, Oxford: Basil Blackwell.

Griffeth, R.W. and Hom, P.W. (1987) Some multivariate comparisons of multinational managers, *Multivariate Behavioral Research*, 22, 173–91.

Grzeda, M.M. and Assogbavi, T. (1999) Management development programs in francophone sub-Saharan Africa, *Management Learning*, 30(4), 413–29.

Haire, M., Ghiselli, E. and Porter, L. (1966) *Managerial Thinking: An International Study*, New York: John Wiley.

Hall, E.T. (1959) *The Silent Language*, New York: Anchor Press/Doubleday.

Hambrick, D.C., Davison, S.C., Snell, S.A. and Snow, C.C. (1998) When groups consist of multiple nationalities: towards a new understanding of the implications, *Organization Studies*, 19, 181–205.

Harré, R., Clarke, D. and de Carlo, N. (1985) *Motives and Mechanism: An Introduction to the Psychology of Action*, London: Methuen.

Harris, R.P. and Moran, R.T. (1989) *Managing Cultural Differences*, Houston: Gulf Publishing.

Hayes, J. and Allinson, C.W. (1989) Cultural differences in learning styles of managers, *Management International Review*, 28(3), 75–80.

Hendry, C. and Pettigrew, A. (1990) Human resource management: an agenda for the 1990s, *International Journal of Human Resource Management*, 1(1), 17–44.

Hendry, J. (2000) *Shell in Nigeria*, (University of Cambridge), Cranfield: European Case Clearing House, No. 300–070–1.

Herzberg, F. (1966) *Work and the Nature of Man*, Cleveland: World Publishing Co.

Herzberg, F., Mausner, B. and Snyderman, B. (1959) *The Motivation to Work*, New York: Wiley.

Hickson, D.J. and Pugh, D.S. (1995) *Management Worldwide*, London: Penguin.

Hochschild, A. (1998) *King Leopold's Ghost*, London: Macmillan.

Hofmeyer, K. (1998) South African managers need to be more positive, *People Dynamic*, 16(10), 16–20.

Hofmeyer, K., Templar, A. and Beaty, D. (1994), South Africa: researching contrasts and contradictions in a context of change, *International Studies of Management and Organization*, 24(1–2), 190–208.

Hofstede, G. (1980a) *Culture's Consequences: International Differences in Work Related Values*, Beverly Hills, CA: Sage.

Hofstede, G. (1980b) Motivation, leadership and organization: do American theories apply abroad?, *Organizational Dynamics*, Summer, pp. 42–63.

Hofstede, G. (1991) *Cultures and Organizations: Software of the Mind*, London: McGraw-Hill.

Hofstede, G. (1994) The business of international business is culture, *International Business Review*, 3(1), 1–14.

Hofstede, G., Neuijen, B., Ohayv, D.D. and Sanders, G. (1990) Measuring organizational cultures: a qualitative and quantitative study across twenty cases, *Administrative Science Quarterly*, 35, 286–316.

Honey, P. and Mumford, A. (1982) *The Manual of Learning Styles*, Maidenhead: Peter Honey.

Horwitz, F.M., Bowmaker-Falconer, A. and Searll, P. (1996) Human resources development and managing diversity in South Africa, *International Journal of Manpower*, 17(4/5), 134–51.

Howell, P., Strauss, J. and Sorensen, P.F. (1975) Cultural and situational determinants of job satisfaction among management in Liberia, *Journal of Management Studies*, 12, 225–7.

Hughes-Weiner, G. (1986), 'The "learn-how-to-learn" approach to cross-cultural orientation', in *International Journal of Intercultural Relations*, 10, 485–505.

Hui, C. H. (1990) Work attitudes, leadership styles and managerial behaviors in different cultures, in R.W. Brislin (ed.) *Applied Cross-cultural Psychology*, Newbury Park, CA: Sage, pp. 186–208.

Human, L. (1996a) *Contemporary Conversations*, Dakar, Senegal: The Goree Institute.

Human, L. (1996b) Managing workforce diversity: a critique and example from Southern Africa, *International Journal of Manpower*, 17(4/5) 46–64.

Ibru, O.M. (1997) The development of international business in Africa (1947–1997), *The International Executive*, 39(2), 117–33.

Iguisi, O. (1994) Appropriate management in an African culture, *Management in Nigeria*, January–February, 16–24.

Iguisi, O. (1997) The role of culture in appropriate management and indigenous development, *Proceedings of the First African Seminar on Culture Dimensions to Appropriate Management in Africa*, Makerere University, Kampala, Uganda, December 1995, Paris: UNESCO, pp. 18–46.

IMF (2002) International Monetary Fund Country Report No. 02/32, Cameroon, Washington: IMF.

Jackson, S.E. (1992) *Diversity in the Workplace*, New York: Guilford Press.

Jackson, T. (1993) *Organizational Behaviour in International Management*, Oxford: Butterworth-Heinemann.

Jackson, T. (1995) European management learning: a cross-cultural interpretation of Kolb's learning cycle, *Journal of Management Development*, 14(6), 42–50.

Jackson, T. (1996) Understanding management learning across cultures: some East–West comparison, paper presented at *Academy of International Business Annual Meeting*, Banff, Alberta, Canada, September.

Jackson, T. (1999) Managing change in South Africa: developing people and organizations, *International Journal of Human Resource Management*, 10(2), 306–26.

Jackson, T. (2000) Making ethical judgements: a cross-cultural management study, *Asia Pacific Journal of Management*, 17(3), 443–72.

Jackson, T. (2001) Cultural values and management ethics: a 10-nation study, *Human Relations*, 54(10), 1267–1302.

Jackson, T. (2002a) *International HRM: A Cross-cultural Approach*, London: Sage.

Jackson, T. (2002b) The management of people across cultures: valuing people differently, *Human Resource Management*, 41(4), 455–75.

Jackson, T. (2002c) Reframing human resource management in Africa: a cross-cultural perspective, *International Journal of Human Resource Management*, 13(7), 998–1018.

Jackson, T. and Bak, M. (1998) Foreign companies and Chinese workers: employee motivation in the People's Republic of China, *Journal of Organizational Change Management*, 11(4), 282–300.

Jackson, T. and Kotze, E. (in press) Management and change in the South Africa National Defence Force, *Administration and Society.*

Jaeger, A.M. and Kanungo, R.N. (1990) *Management in Developing Countries*, London: Routledge.

Joergensen, J.J. (1990) Organizational life-cycle and effectiveness criteria in state-owned enterprises: the case of East Africa, in A.M. Jaeger and R.N. Kanungo *Management in Developing Countries*, London: Routledge, pp. 62–82.

Jones, M.L. (1986) Management development: an African focus, *Management Education and Development*, 17(3), 302–16 (and reproduced in *International Studies of Management and Organization*, 1989, 19(1), 74–90).

Jones, M.L. (1988) Managerial thinking: an African perspective, *Journal of Management Studies*, 25(5), 481–505.

Kamoche, K. (1992) Human resource management: an assessment of the Kenyan case, *The International Journal of Human Resource Management*, 3(3), 497–521.

Kamoche, K. (1997) Competence creation in the African public sector, *International Journal of Public Sector Management*, 10(4), 268–78.

Kamoche, K.N. (2000) *Sociological Paradigms and Human Resources: An African Context*, Aldershot: Ashgate.

Kanungo, R. (1990) Work alienation in developing countries: Western models and eastern realities, in A.M. Jaeger and R.N. Kanungo (eds) *Management in Developing Countries*, London: Routledge, pp. 193–208.

Kanungo, R.N. and Jaeger, A.M. (1990) Introduction: The need for indigenous management in developing countries, in A.M. Jaeger and R.N. Kanungo (eds) *Management in Developing Countries*, London: Routledge, pp. 1–23.

Kaphagawani, D.N. (1998) Themes in a Chewa Epistemology, in P.H. Coetzee and A.P.J. Roux (eds) (1998) *Philosophy from Africa*, Johannesburg: Thomson, p. 242.

Katz, D. and Kahn, R.L. (1978) *The Social Psychology of Organizations*, second edition, New York: Wiley.

Kedia, B.L. and Bhagat, R.S. (1988) Cultural constraints on transfer of technology across nations: implications for research in international and comparative management, *Academy of Management Review*, 13(4), 559–71.

Kerr, C., Dunlop, J.T., Harbison, F.H. and Myers, C.A. (1960) *Industrialism and Industrial Man*, Cambridge, MA: Harvard University Press.

Kifle, H. (1998) Capacity building in Africa: the role of multilateral financial institutions, in L. Wohlgemuth, J. Carlsson and H. Kifle (eds) *Institution Building and Leadership in Africa*, Uppsala, Sweden: Nordiska Afrikainstitutet, pp. 79–90.

Kiggundu, M.N. (1988) Africa, in R. Nath (ed.) *Comparative Management: A Regional View*, Cambridge, MA: Ballinger.

Kiggundu, M.N. (1989) *Managing Organizations in Developing Countries*, West Hartford, CT: Kumarian Press.

Kiggundu, M.N. (1991) The challenges of management development in sub-Saharan Africa, *Journal of Management Development*, 10(6), 32–47.

Kluckholm, F. and Strodtbeck, F. (1961) *Variations in Value Orientation*, Westport, CT: Greenwood Press.

Kolb, D.A. (1984) *Experiential Learning*, Englewood Cliffs, New Jersey: Prentice-Hall.

Kolb, D.A., Rubin, I.M. and Osland, J.S. (1991) *Organizational Behaviour: An Experiential Approach*, fifth edition, Englewood Cliffs, NJ: Prentice-Hall.

Koopman, A. (1991) *Transcultural Management*, Oxford: Basil Blackwell.

Kuada, J.E. (1994) *Managerial Behaviour in Ghana and Kenya: A Cultural Perspective*, Aalborg, Denmark: Aalborg University Press.

Lane, H.W., DiStefano, J.J. and Maznevski, M.L. (1997) *International Management Behaviour*, third edition, Malden, MA: Blackwell.

Larrain, J. (1979) *The Concept of Ideology*, London: Hutchinson.

Lau, D.C. and Murnighan, K.J.K. (1998) Demographic diversity and faultlines: the compositional dynamics of organizational groups, *Academy of Management Review*, 23, 325–340.

Laurent, A. (1989), A cultural view of change, in P. Evans, Y. Doz and A. Laurent (eds) *Human Resources Management in International Firms: Change Globalization, Innovation*, London: Macmillan.

Legge, K. (1989) Human resource management: a critical analysis, in J. Storey (ed.) *New Perspectives on Human Resource Management*, London: Routledge.

*Le Messager* (1998) Où et comment s'exerce le pouvoir? *Un Rapport Diplomatique*, no. 784 du 6 juillet, et no. 785 du 8 juillet.

Leonard, D.K. (1987) The political realities of African management, *World Development*, 15(7), 899–910.

Lessem, R. (1989) *Global Management Principles*, London: Prentice-Hall.

Leys, C. (1975) *Underdevelopment in Kenya: The Political Economy of Neo-colonialism*, Nairobi: East Africa Educational Publishers. Republished 1994.

Lincoln, J.R. and Kalleberg, A.L. (1990) *Culture, Control and Commitment: A Study of Work Organization and Work Attitudes in the United States and Japan*, Cambridge, UK: Cambridge University Press.

Lorenzen, C. (2000) *Danish Firms Working in Sub-Saharan Africa*, unpublished Masters dissertation, Roskilde University, Denmark.

Luiz, J.M. (1996) The socio-economic restructuring of a post-apartheid South Africa, *International Journal of Social Economics*, 23(10/11), 137–49.

McClelland, D.C. (1987) *Human Motivation*, Cambridge: Cambridge University Press.

McClelland, D.C. and Winter, D.G. (1969) *Motivating Economic Achievement*, New York: Free Press.

McFarlin, D., Coster, E.A. and Mogale-Pretorius, C. (1999) South African management development in the twenty-first century: moving towards an Africanized model, *Journal of Management Development*, 18(1), 63–78.

McGregor, D. (1960) *The Human Side of Enterprise*, New York: McGraw-Hill.

Maier, K. (2000) *This House Has Fallen: Nigeria in Crisis*, London: Penguin.

Makgoba, M.W. (ed.) (1999) *African Renaissance*, Sandton: Mafube and Cape Town: Tafelberg.

Makoba, J.W. (1983) Public control and public enterprise performance in sub-Saharan Africa: the case of Tanzania and Zambia, *Africa Development*, 15, 911–29.

Maphosa, F. (1998) The human factor and corporate social responsibility in Zimbabwean business organizations, in V.G. Chivaura and C.G. Mararike (eds) *The Human Factor Approach to Development in Africa*, Harare: University of Zimbabwe Publications, pp. 148–70.

Marsden, D. (1991) Indigenous management and the management of indigenous knowledge, paper presented at *GAPP Conference on The Anthropology of Organizations*, Centre for Development Studies, University College of Swansea, January 4–6.

Maslow, A. (1958/1970) *Motivation and Personality*, second edition, New York, Harper and Row.

Mbaku, J.M. (1998) Improving African participation in the global economy: the role of economic freedom, *Business and the Contemporary World*, 10(2), 297–338.

Mbeki, T. (1998) Prologue, *African Renaissance*, Sandton: Mafube and Cape Town: Tafelberg.

Mbigi, L. (1997) *Ubuntu: The African Dream in Management*, Randburg, S. Africa: Knowledge Resources.

Mbigi, L. and Maree, J. (1995) *Ubuntu: The Spirit of African Transformational Management*, Randburg, S. Africa: Knowledge Resources.

Merrill-Sands, D. and Holvino, E. (2000) *Working with Diversity: a Framework for Action*, Working Paper 24, CGIAR (Consultative Group on International Agricultural Research) Gender and Diversity Program, Nairobi.

Mills, G., Beeg, A. and Van Nieuwkerk, A. (1995) *South Africa in the Global Economy*, Johannesburg: South African Institute of International Affairs.

Montgomery, J.D. (1987) Probing managerial behaviour: image and reality in Southern Africa, *World Development*, 15(7), 911–29.

Morais, R.C. (1997) Africa: the untold story, *Forbes*, 17 November, 85–9.

MOW (Meaning of Working) International Research Team (1987), *The Meaning of Working*, London: Academic Press.

Mulat, T. (1998) Multilateralism and Africa's regional economic communities, *Journal of World Trade*, 32(4), 115–38.

Mule, H. (2001) Kenya's globalisation in the new millennium: changes and opportunities, 29th Tom Mboya lecture of 3 November 1999, *Management: A Journal of the Kenya Institute of Management*, May–July, 6–9.

Munene, J.C., Schwartz, S.H. and Smith, P.B. (2000) Development in sub-Saharan Africa: cultural influences and managers' decision behaviour, *Public Administration and Development*, 20.

Mutabazi, E. (2002) Preparing African leaders, in C.B. Derr, S. Roussillon and F. Bournois (eds) *Cross-cultural Approaches to Leadership Development*, Westport, CT: Quorum Books, pp. 202–23.

Mutizwa-Mangiza, D. (1991) An evaluation of workers' participation in decision-making at enterprise level, *Zambezia*, 8, 35–48.

Mwai, R.G. (2001) The private sector and poverty reduction strategies, in *Management: A Journal of the Kenya Institute of Management*, May–July, p. 12.

Nana Nzepa, O. (in press) Bonne governance et politisation des administrations publiques en Afrique.

Närman, A. (1998) The human factor and structural adjustment programmes, in V.G. Chivaura and C.G. Mararike (eds) *The Human Factor Approach to Development in Africa*, Harare: University of Zimbabwe Publications, pp. 171–81.

Ndongko, T. (1999) Motivating the workforce in Africa, in J.M. Waiguchu, E. Tiagha and M. Mwaura (eds), *Management of Organizations in Africa: A Handbook and Reference*, Westport, Connecticut, pp. 125–49.

Negandhi, A.R. (1987) *International Management*, Boston: Allyn and Bacon.

Nevis, E. (1983) Cultural assumptions and productivity: the United States and China, *Sloan Management Review*, 24, 17–29.

Niles, F.S. (1995) Cultural differences in learning motivation and learning strategies: a comparison of overseas and Australian students at an Australian University, *International Journal of Intercultural Relations*, 19(3), 369–85.

Noorderhaven, N.G. and Tidjani, B. (2001) Culture, governance, and economic performance: an exploratory study with a special focus on Africa. *International Journal of Cross Cultural Management*, 1(1), 31–52.

Noorderhaven, N.G., Vunderink, M. and Lincoln, P. (1996) African values and management: a research agenda, *Ife PsychologIA*, 4(1), 13–50.

North, D. (1990) *Institutions, Institutional Change and Economic Performance*, Cambridge: Cambridge University Press.

Nyambegera, S.M. (2002) Ethnicity and human resource management practice in sub-Saharan Africa: the relevance of the managing diversity discourse, *The International Journal of Human Resource Management*, 13(7), 1077–90.

Nzomo, M. (1994) External influence on the political economy of Kenya: the case of the MNCs, in Walter O. Oyugi (ed.) *Politics and Administration in East Africa*, Nairobi: East African Educational Publishers, pp. 429–67.

Nzongola-Ntalaja, G. (1999) The crisis in the Great Lakes region, in M.W. Makgoba (ed.), *African Renaissance: The New Struggle*, Sandton, SA: Mafube and Cape Town: Tafelberg, pp. 62–76.

ODA (Overseas Development Agency: UK) (undated) Management cultures and practices in developing countries, *ODA Background Papers*, London.

Odubogun, K.P. (1992) *Management Theory: Relevance for management practice in Nigeria*, Maastricht: The Netherlands Institute for Management.

Ogonda, R.T. (1992) Kenya's industrial progress in the post-independence era: an overview of Kenya's industrial performance up to 1980, in W.R. Ochieng' and R.M. Maxon (eds) *An Economic History of Kenya*, Nairobi: East African Educational Publishers, pp. 297–311.

Oha, O. (1999) Cross-cultural conversations and the semiotics of ethocultural domination in Nigeria, *Anthropology of Africa and the Challenges of the Third Millennium – Ethnicity and Ethnic Conflicts*, UNESCO, www.ethnobet-Africa.org/pubs/p95oha.htm, 14/08/2002.

Olivier, N.J.J. (1969) The governmental institutions of the Bantu peoples of southern Africa, in *Recueils de la Societies Jean Bodin XII*, Brussels: Fondation Universitaire de Belgique.

O'Reilly, C.A. and Roberts, K.H. (1973) Job satisfaction among Whites and non-Whites: a cross-cultural approach, *Journal of Applied Psychology*, 57, 295–9.

Pakenham, T. (1991) *The Scramble for Africa*, London: Phoenix Press.

Pareek, U. and Rao, T.V. (1992) *Designing and Managing Human Resources Systems*, New Delhi: Oxford and IBH.

Parsons, T. and Shils, E.A. (1951) *Toward a General Theory of Action*, Cambridge, MA: Harvard University Press.

Perry, C. (1997) Total quality management and reconceptualizing management in Africa, *International Business Review*, 6(3), 233–43.

Peterson, M.F. and Pike, K.L. (2002) Emic and etics for Organizational Studies: a lesson in contrasts from Linguistics, *International Journal of Cross Cultural Management*, 2(1), 5–20.

Picard, L.A. and Garrity, M. (1995) Development management in Africa, in P. Fitzgerald, A. McLennan and B. Munslow (eds) *Managing Sustainable Development in South Africa*, Cape Town: Oxford University Press, pp. 63–85.

Porter, L.W. and Lawler, E.E. (1968) *Managerial Attitudes and Performance*, Illinois: Dorsey Press.

Price, R.M. (1975) *Society and Bureaucracy in Contemporary Ghana*, Berkeley, CA: University of California Press.

Priem, R.L., Love, L.G. and Shaffer, M. (2000) Industrialization and values evolution: the case of Hong Kong and Guangzhou, China, *Asia Pacific Journal of Management*, 17(3), 473–92.

Project Globe (1999) Cultural influences on leadership and organization, *Advances in Global Leadership*, 1: 171–233.

Putnam, R.D. (1973) *The Beliefs of Politicians*, New Haven, CT: Yale University Press.

Ralston, D.A., Holt, D.H., Terpstra, R.H. and Kai-Cheng, Y. (1997) The impact of national culture and economic ideology on managerial work values: a study of the United States, Russia, Japan and China, *Journal of International Business Studies*, 28(1), 177–207.

Rao, T.V. (1996) *Human Resource Development: Experiences, Intervention, Strategies*, New Delhi: Sage.

Reader, J. (1998) *Africa: A Biography of the Continent*, London: Penguin.

Revans, R. (1965) *Science and the Manager*, London: MacDonald.

Reynolds, P.D. (1986) Organizational culture as related to industry, position and performance: a preliminary report, *Journal of Management Studies*, 23(3), 333–45.

Rimmer, D. (1991) Thirty years of independent Africa, *Africa Insights*, 21(2), 90–6, reprinted in P. Blunt, M.L. Jones and D. Richards (eds) (1993) *Managing Organizations in Africa: Readings, Cases and Exercises*, Berlin: Walter de Gruyter.

Roeder, P.G. (2001) Ethnolinguistic Fractionalization (ELF) Indices 1961 and 1985, http//:weber.ucsd.edu\~proeder\elf.htm, 19/08/2002.

Rohmetra, N. (1998) *Human Resource Development in Commercial Banks in India*, London: Ashgate.

Roodt, A. (1997) In search of a South African corporate culture, *Management Today*, 13(2), 14–16.

Rotter, J.B. (1966) Generalized expectancies for internal versus external control of reinforcement, *Psychological Monographs*, 80(609), whole issue.

Rust, J. and Golombok, S. (1989) *Modern Psychometrics*, London: Routledge.

Sawadogo, G. (1995) Training for the African mind, *International Journal of Intercultural Relations*, 19(2), 281–93.

Schapera, I. (1955) *A Handbook of Tswana Law and Custom*, Oxford: Oxford University Press.

Schermerhorn, J.R. and Nyaw, M.-K. (1990) Managerial leadership in Chinese industrial enterprises, *International Studies of Management and Organization*, 20(1–2), 9–21.

Schwartz, S.H. (1994) Beyond individualism/collectivism: new cultural dimensions of values, in U. Kim, H.C. Triandis, C. Kâğitçibaşi, S.C. Choi and G. Yoon (eds) *Individualism and Collectivism: Theory, Method and Application*, Beverly Hills, CA: Sage, pp. 85–119.

Schwartz, S.H. (1999) Cultural value differences: some implications for work, *Applied Psychology: An International Review*, 48, 23–47.

Senge, P. (1990) *The Fifth Discipline: The Art and Practice of the Learning Organization*, London: Century Business.

Senghor, L.S. (1965) *On African Socialism*, Stanford: Pall Mall.

Shin, Y.K. and Kim, H.G. (1994) Individualism and collectivism in Korean industry, in G. Yoon and S.C. Choi (eds) *Psychology of the Korean People: Collectivism and Individualism*, pp. 189–208.

Silvera, D.M. (1988) *Human Resource Development: The Indian Experience*, New Delhi: New Delhi Publications.

Silverman, D. (1970) *The Theory of Organizations*, Aldershot: Gower.

Singh, R. (1981) Prediction of performance from motivation and ability: an appraisal of the cultural difference hypothesis, in J. Pandey (ed.) *Perspectives on Experimental Social Psychology in India*, New Delhi: Concept, pp. 21–53.

Smith, B.E. and Thomas, J.M. (1972) Cross-cultural attitudes among managers: a case study, *Sloan Management Review*, 13(3), 35–50.

Smith, P.B. and Peterson, M.F. (1988) *Leadership, Organizations and Culture*, London: Sage.

Smith, P.B., Misumi, J., Tayeb, M.H., Peterson, M. and Bond, M. (1989) On the generality of leadership styles across cultures, *Journal of Occupational Psychology*, 62, 97–109.

Smith, P.B., Trompenaars, F. and Dugan, S. (1995) The Rotter locus of control scale in 43 countries: a test of cultural relativity, *International Journal of Psychology*, 30, 377–400.

Smith, P.B., Dugan, S. and Trompenaars, F. (1996) National cultures and values of organizational employees: a dimensional analysis across 43 nations, *Journal of Cross-cultural Psychology*, 27(2), 231–64.

Sogolo, G.S. (1993) Logic and rationality, in *Foundations of African Philosophy*, Ibadan: Ibadan University Press, pp. 68–88, and reprinted in P.H. Coetzee and A.P.J. Roux (eds) (1998), *Philosophy from Africa: A Text with Readings*, Johannesburg: International Thomson Publishing, pp. 217–33.

South African Yearbook (2000/2001) *South African Yearbook 2000/2001*, Pretoria: Government Communication and Information System.

Sow, A.I and Abdulaziz, M.H. (1999) Language and social change, in A.A. Mazrui (ed.) *Africa Since 1935, Vol. VIII of UNESCO General History of Africa*, Berkeley, CA: James Currey, pp. 522–52.

Sparrow, P. and Budhwar, P. (1995) Developments in Indian HRM in the new economic environment, European Institute for Advance Studies in Management conference *Cross-cultural Perspectives: Comparative Management and Organizations*, Henley Management College, UK, 10–12 November 1995.

Statistics South Africa (1998) *Unemployment and Employment in South Africa*, Pretoria.

Steers, R.M. and Sanchez-Runde, C. (2002) Culture, motivation, and work behavior, in M.J. Gannon, and K.L. Newman, *Handbook of Cross-cultural Management*, Oxford: Blackwell, pp. 190–216.

Storey, J. (1992) *Developments in Management of Human Resources*, Oxford: Blackwell.

Suzman, M. (1996) Africa's lion cub learns to roar, *Asian Business*, June 1996.

Swartz, E. and Davies, R. (1997) *Ubuntu*: the spirit of African transformational management – a review, *Leadership and Organization Development Journal*, 18(6), 260–94.

Tannenbaum, A.S. (1974) *Hierarchy in Organizations*, San Francisco: Jossey-Bass.

Tatah Mentan, E. (undated) Colonial legacies, democratization and the ethnic question in *Cameroon, in Democratization and Ethnic Rivalries in Cameroon*, Ethno-Net, http://www.ethnonet-Africa.org/pubs/p95cir2.htm, 14/08/2002.

Tayeb, M.H. (2000) The internationalisation of HRM policies and practices: the case of Japanese and French companies in Scotland, 11th Congrés de l'AGRH, 16–17 November 2000, ESCP-EAP, Paris.

Taylor, H. (1992) Public sector personnel management in three African countries: current problems and possibilities, *Public Administration and Development*, 12, 193–207.

Taylor, H. (2002) Insights into participation from critical management and labour process perspectives, in B. Cooke and U. Kothari (eds) *Participation: The New Tyranny?*, London: Zed Books, pp. 122–38.

Thomas, A. and Bendixen, M. (2000) The management implications of ethnicity in South Africa, *Journal of International Business Studies*, 31(3), 507–19.

Thomas, D.C. (2002) *Essentials of International Management: A Cross Cultural Perspective*, Thousand Oaks, CA: Sage.

Thomson, A. (2000) *An Introduction to African Politics*, London: Routledge.

Thurley, K. and Wirdenius, H. (1989) *Towards European Management*, London: Pitman.

Townley, B. (1994) *Reframing Human Resource Management: Power, Ethics and the Subject at Work*, London: Sage.

Triandis, H.C. (2002) Generic individualism and collectivism, in M.J. Gannon and K.L. Newman (eds) *The Blackwell Handbook of Cross-cultural Management*, Oxford: Blackwell, pp. 16–45.

Triandis, H.C., Brislin, R. and Hui, C.H. (1988) Cross-cultural training across the individualism-collectivism divide, *International Journal of Intercultural Relations*, 12, 269–89.

Trompenaars, F. (1993) *Riding the Waves of Culture*, London: Brealey.

Tsui, A.S., Egan, T.D. and O'Reilly, C.A. (1992) Being different: relational demography and organizational attachment, *Administrative Science Quarterly*, 39, 412–38.

Tung, R.L. (1991) Motivation in Chinese industrial enterprises, in R.M. Steers and L.W. Porter (eds) *Innovation and Work Behaviour*, fifth edition, New York: McGraw-Hill.

Tyson, S. and Fell, A. (1986) *Evaluating the Personnel Function*, London: Hutchinson.

Ugwuegbu, D.C.E. (2001) *The Psychology of Management in African Organizations*, Westport, CT: Quorum.

UNCTAD (2000) *World Investment Report*, Geneva: United Nations Conference on Trade and Development.

UNDP (2002) *Human Development Report 2001*, Human Development Index.

UNESCO (1997) *A Cultural Approach To Development – Planning Manual: Concepts and Tools*, Paris: UNESCO.

UNIDO (1999) *African Industry, 2000: The Challenge of Going Global*, Vienna: United Nations Industrial Development Organization.

Utomi, P. (1998) *Managing Uncertainty: Competition and Strategy in Emerging Economies*, Ibadan, Nigeria: Spectrum Books.

Vaughan, E. (1994) The trial between sense and sentiment: a reflection on the language of HRM, *Journal of General Management*, 19, 20–32.

Vengroff, R., Belhaj, M. and Momar, N. (1991) The nature of managerial work in the public sector: an African perspective, *Public Administration and Development*, 11, 95–110.

Vertinsky, I., Tse, D.K., Wehrung, D.A. and Lee, K.-H. (1990) Organizational design and management norms: a comparative study of managers' perceptions in the People's Republic of China, Hong Kong and Canada, *Journal of Management*, 16(4), 853–67.

Viljoen, J. (1987) Corporate culture: the perceptions of personnel managers in South Africa, *South African Journal of Business Management*, 18(4), 235–42.

Vroom, V. (1973) A new look at managerial decision-making, *Organizational Dynamics*, Spring.

Waiguchu, J.M., Tiagha, E. and Mwaura, M. (eds) (1999) *Management of Organizations in Africa: A Handbook and Reference*, Westport, CT: Quorum Books.

Wallis, M. (1994) Central–local relations, in W.O. Oyugi, (ed.) *Politics and Administration in East Africa*, Nairobi: East African Educational Publishers, pp. 107–28.

Watson, C. (1996) Directions for HR directors, *People Dynamics* (South Africa), 14(1), 19–25.

Wentzel, L.A. (1999) *A Survey of South African National Values and the Implications for Human Resource Management*, unpublished MBA Dissertation, Graduate School of Business of the University of Stellenbosch, South Africa.

Wescott, C. (1999) Guiding principles on civil service reform in Africa: an empirical review, *The International Journal of Public Sector Management*, 12(2), 145–70.

Wild, V. (1997) *Profit Not for Profit Sake: History and Business Culture of African Entrepreneurs in Zimbabwe*, Harare: Baobab Books.

Williams, C. (1987) *The Destruction of Black Civilization*, Chicago: Third World Press.

Wiredu, K. (1992) The moral foundations of an African culture, Person and Community (CIPSH/UNESCO), pp. 193–206, and reprinted in Coetzee and Roux (eds) (1998), pp. 306–16.

Wiredu, K. (1995) Are there cultural universals? *The Monist*, 78 (January), 52–31, and reprinted in P.H. Coetzee and A.P.J. Roux (eds) (1998), *Philosophy from Africa: A Text with Readings*, Johannesburg: International Thomson Publishing, pp. 31–40.

Wohlgemuth, L., Carlsson, J. and Kifle, H. (1998) introduction in L. Wohlgemuth, J. Carlsson and H. Kifle (eds) *Institution Building and Leadership in Africa*, Uppsala, Sweden: Nordiska Afrikainstitutet, pp. 5–11.

Woodford-Berger, P. (1998) Gender, organizational cultures and institutional development, in L. Wohlgemuth, J. Carlsson and H. Kifle (eds) *Institution Building and Leadership in Africa*, Uppsala, Sweden: Nordiska Afrikainstitutet, pp. 33–42.

World Bank (1991) *Vocational and Technical Education and Training*, Washington DC: World Bank.

World Bank (1996) *Structural Aspects of Manufacturing in Sub-Saharan Africa: Findings from a Seven Country Enterprise Survey*, World Bank Discussion Paper No. 346.

World Investment News (2002) www.winne.com/cameroon/report/history.htm,05/06/2002.

Yakan, M.Z. (1999) *Almanac of African Peoples and Nations*, New Brunswick: Transaction Publishers.

# Index